Collins

The Shanghai Maths Project

For the English National Curriculum

Teacher's Guide 4B

Teacher's Guide Series Editor: Amanda Simpson

Practice Books Series Editor: Professor Lianghuo Fan

Authors: Laura Clarke, Caroline Clissold, Linda Glithro, Steph King and Paul Wrangles

Collins

William Collins' dream of knowledge for all began with the publication of his first book in 1819.

A self-educated mill worker, he not only enriched millions of lives, but also founded a flourishing publishing house. Today, staying true to this spirit, Collins books are packed with inspiration, innovation and practical expertise. They place you at the centre of a world of possibility and give you exactly what you need to explore it.

Collins. Freedom to teach.

Published by Collins
An imprint of HarperCollins*Publishers*
The News Building
1 London Bridge Street
London
SE1 9GF

Browse the complete Collins catalogue at
www.collins.co.uk

978-0-00-822604-6

Teacher's Guide Series Editor: Amanda Simpson

Practice Books Series Editor: Professor Lianghuo Fan

Authors: Laura Clarke, Caroline Clissold, Linda Glithro, Steph King and Paul Wrangles

British Library Cataloguing in Publication Data

A catalogue record for this publication is available from the British Library.

Publishing Manager: Fiona McGlade
In-house Editor: Mike Appleton
In-house Editorial Assistant: August Stevens
Project Manager: Emily Hooton
Copy Editors: Tracy Thomas, Tanya Solomons and Karen Williams
Proofreader: Gerard Delaney
Cover design: Kevin Robbins and East China Normal University Press Ltd
Internal design: 2Hoots Publishing Services Ltd
Typesetting: 2Hoots Publishing Services Ltd
Illustrations: QBS
Production: Sarah Burke
Printed and bound by CPI Group (UK) Ltd, Croydon, CR0 4YY

Photo acknowledgements

The publishers wish to thank the following for permission to reproduce photographs. Every effort has been made to trace copyright holders and to obtain their permission for the use of copyright materials. The publishers will gladly receive any information enabling them to rectify any error or omission at the first opportunity.

(t = top, c = centre, b = bottom, r = right, l = left)

p. 38 tr Trompinex/Shutterstock, p. 38 br Lawrence Wee/Shutterstock, p. 38 cl monkey1974/Shutterstock, p. 38 cr Zoart Studio/Shutterstock, p. 38 tl Roman Sigaev/Shutterstock, p. 38 bl Andrey Demkin/ Shutterstock, p. 49 cl Sari ONeal/Shutterstock, p. 49 tl Alexey Kljatov/Shutterstock, p. 49 tr Peteri/ Shutterstock, p. 49 br Mark Christopher Cooper/ Shutterstock, p. 49 tc onair/Shutterstock, p. 49 cr Annette Shaff/Shutterstock, p. 49 bl Scandphoto/ Shutterstock, p. 51 bl Mikadun/Shutterstock, p. 99 br giedre vaitekune/Shutterstock, p. 99 bc WDG Photo/ Shutterstock, p. 99 bl Glass frog/Shutterstock, p. 103 tr grandnat/Shutterstock, p. 103 c Stocklifemax/ Shutterstock, p. 103 bl EgudinKa/Shutterstock, p. 231 b valeo5/Shutterstock, p. 231 t Lorelyn Medina/ Shutterstock, p. 253 b ssguy/Shutterstock, p. 253 t Andrey Demkin/Shutterstock, p. 254 t Lawrence Wee/ Shutterstock, p. 254 b Zoart Studio/Shutterstock, p. 255 b Dariusz Jarzabek/Shutterstock, p. 255 cl santon1982/Shutterstock, p. 255 cr charnsitr/ Shutterstock, p. 255 t monkey1974/Shutterstock, p. 257 Trompinex/Shutterstock, p. 258 Trompinex/ Shutterstock, p. 259 Bobkov Evgeniy/Shutterstock, p. 260 Bildagentur Zoonar GmbH/Shutterstock, p. 261 Ekachai Sathittaweechai/Shutterstock, p. 262 Peyker/ Shutterstock, p. 280 tl Stockforlife/Shutterstock, p. 280 cbr John Konrad/Shutterstock, p. 280 cbl John Panella/Shutterstock, p. 280 tr dade72/Shutterstock, p. 280 ctr Andrjuss/Shutterstock, p. 280 b WitR/ Shutterstock, p. 280 ctl milezaway/Shutterstock, p. 283 Maxx-Studio/Shutterstock, p. 291 Shpadaruk Aleksei/Shutterstock, p. 296 bl EgudinKa/ Shutterstock, p. 296 c Stocklifemax/Shutterstock, p. 296 tr grandnat/Shutterstock

Contents

The Shanghai Maths Project: an overview

The Shanghai Maths Project is a collaboration between Collins and East China Normal University Press Ltd, adapting their bestselling maths programme, *One Lesson, One Exercise*, for England, using an expert team of authors and reviewers. This carefully crafted programme has been continually reviewed in China over the last 24 years, meaning that the materials have been tried and tested by teachers and children alike. Some new material has been written for The Shanghai Maths Project, but the structure of the original resource has been preserved and as much original material as possible has been retained.

The Shanghai Maths Project is a programme from Shanghai for Years 1–11. Teaching for mastery is at the heart of the entire programme, which, through the guidance and support found in the Teacher's Guides and Practice Books, provides complete coverage of the curriculum objectives for England. Teachers are well supported to deliver a high-quality curriculum using the best teaching methods; pupils are enabled to learn mathematics with understanding and the ability to apply knowledge fluently and flexibly in order to solve problems.

The programme consists of five components: Teacher's Guides (two per year), Practice Books (two per year), Shanghai Learning Book, Homework Guide and Collins Connect digital package.

In this guide, information and support for all teachers of primary maths is set out, unit by unit, so they are able to teach The Shanghai Maths Project coherently and confidently, and with appropriate progression through the whole mathematics curriculum.

Practice Books

The Practice Books are designed to serve as both teaching and learning resources. With graded arithmetic exercises, plus varied practice of key concepts and summative assessments for each year, each Practice Book offers intelligent practice and consolidation to promote deep learning and develop higher-order thinking.

There are two Practice Books for each year group: A and B. Pupils should have ownership of their copies of the Practice Books so they can engage with relevant exercises every day, integrated with preparatory whole-class and small-group teaching, recording their answers in the books.

The Practice Books contain:

- chapters made up of units, containing small steps of progression, with practice at each stage
- a test at the end of each chapter
- an end-of-year test in Practice Book B.

Each unit in the Practice Books consists of two sections: 'Basic questions' and 'Challenge and extension questions'.

We suggest that the 'Basic questions' be used for all pupils. Many of them, directly or sometimes with a little modification, can be used as starting questions, for motivation or introduction or as examples for clear explanation. They can also be used as in-class exercise questions – most likely for reinforcement and formative assessment, but also for pupils' further exploration. Almost all questions can be given for individual or peer work, especially when used as in-class exercise questions. Some are also suitable for group work or whole-class discussion.

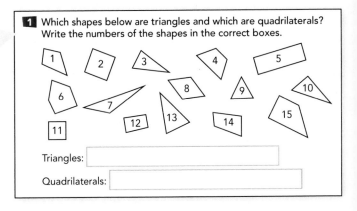

All pupils should be given the opportunity to solve some of the 'Challenge and extension questions', which are good for building confidence, but they should not always be required to solve all of them. A general suggestion is that most pupils try about 40–60 per cent of the 'Challenge and extension questions'.

Unit tests sometimes include questions that relate to content in the 'Challenge and extension questions'. This is clearly shown in the diagnostic assessment grids provided in the Teacher's Guides. Teachers should make their own judgments about how to use this information since not all pupils will have attempted the 'Challenge and extension questions'.

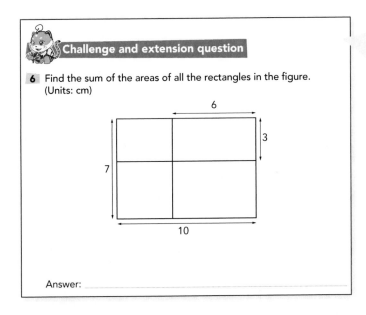

Teacher's Guides

Theory underpinning the Teacher's Guides

The Teacher's Guides contain everything teachers need in order to provide the highest quality teaching in all areas of mathematics, in line with the English National Curriculum. Core mathematics topics are developed with deep understanding in every year group. Some areas are not visited every year, though curriculum coverage is in line with Key Stage statutory requirements, as set out in the National curriculum in England: mathematics programmes of study (updated 2014).

There are two Teacher's Guides for each year group: one for the first part of the year (Teacher's Guide 4A) and the other for the second (Teacher's Guide 4B).

The Shanghai Maths Project is different from other maths schemes that are available, in that there is no book called a 'textbook'. Lessons are a mixture of teacher-led, peer and independent work. The Teacher's Guides set out subject knowledge that teachers might need, as well as guidance on pedagogical issues – the best ways to organise activities, to ask questions and to increase difficulty in small steps. Most importantly, the Teacher's Guides contain, threaded throughout the whole book, a strong element of professional development for teachers, focusing on the way mathematics concepts can be enabled to develop and connect with each other.

The Shanghai Maths Project Teacher's Guides are a complete reference for teachers working with the Practice Books. Each unit in the Practice Book for each year group is set out in the corresponding Teacher's Guide over a number of pages.

Most units will need to be taught over more than one lesson – some might need three lessons. In the Practice Books, units contain a great deal of learning, densely packed into a few questions. If pupils are to be able to tackle and succeed with the Practice Book questions, they need to have been guided to learn new mathematics and to connect it to their existing knowledge.

This can only be achieved when teachers are able to break down the conceptual learning that is needed and to provide relevant and high-quality teaching. The Teacher's Guides show teachers how to build up pupils' knowledge and experience so they learn with understanding in small steps. This way, learning is secure, robust and not reliant on memorisation.

The small steps that are necessary must be in line with what international research tells us about conceptual growth and development. The Shanghai Maths Project embodies that knowledge about conceptual development and about teaching for mastery of mathematics concepts and skills. The way that difficulty is varied, and the same ideas are presented in different contexts, is based on the notion of 'teaching with variation'. 'Variation' in Chinese mathematics carries particular meaning as it has emerged from a great deal of research in the area of 'variation theory'. Variation theory is based on the view that, 'When a particular aspect varies whilst all other aspects of the phenomenon are kept invariant, the learner will experience variation in the varying aspect and will discern that aspect. For example, when a child is shown three balls of the same size, shape, and material, but each of a different color: red, green and yellow, then it is very likely that the child's attention will be drawn to the color of the balls because it is the only aspect that varies.' (Bowden and Marton 1998, cited in Pang and Ling 2012)

In summary, two types of variation are necessary, each with a different function; both are necessary for the development of conceptual understanding.

Variation

Conceptual

Function – this variation provides pupils with multiple experiences from different perspectives.

'multi-dimensional variation'

Procedural

Function – this variation helps learners:
- aquire knowledge step by step
- develop pupils' experience in problem solving progressively
- form well-structured knowledge.

'developmental variation'

Teachers who are aiming to provide conceptual variation should vary the way the problem is presented without varying the structure of the problem itself.

The problem itself doesn't change but the way it is presented (or represented) does. Incorporation of a Concrete–Pictorial–Abstract (CPA) approach to teaching activities provides conceptual variation since pupils experience the same mathematical situations in parallel concrete, pictorial and abstract ways.

CPA is integrated in the Teacher's Guides so teachers are providing questions and experiences that incorporate appropriate conceptual variation.

Procedural variation is the process of:

- forming concepts logically and/or chronologically (i.e. scaffolding, transforming)
- arriving at solutions to problems
- forming knowledge structures (generalising across contexts).

In the Practice Book there are numerous examples of procedural variation in which pupils gradually build up knowledge, step by step; often they are exposed to patterns that teachers should guide them to perceive and explore.

It is this embedded variation that means that when The Shanghai Maths Project is at the heart of mathematics teaching throughout the school, teachers can be confident that the curriculum is of the highest order and it will be delivered by teachers who are informed and confident about how to support pupils to develop strong, connected concepts.

Teaching for mastery

There is no single definition of mathematics mastery. The term 'mastery' is used in conjunction with various aspects of education – to describe goals, attainment levels or a type of teaching. In teaching in Shanghai, mastery of concepts is characterised as 'thorough understanding' and is one of the aims of maths teaching in Shanghai.

Thorough understanding is evident in what pupils do and say. A concept can be seen to have been mastered when a pupil:

- is able to interpret and construct multiple representations of aspects of that concept
- can communicate relevant ideas and reason clearly about that concept using appropriate mathematical language
- can solve problems using the knowledge learned in familiar and new situations, collaboratively and independently.

Within The Shanghai Maths Project, mastery is a goal, achievable through high-quality teaching and learning experiences that include opportunities to explore, articulate thinking, conjecture, practise, clarify, apply and integrate new understandings piece by piece. Learning is carefully structured throughout and across the programme, with Teacher's Guides and Practice Books interwoven – chapter by chapter, unit by unit, question by question.

Since so much conceptual learning is to be achieved with each of the questions in any Practice Book unit, teachers are provided with guidance for each question, breaking down the development that will occur and how they should facilitate this – suggestions for teachers' questions, problems for pupils, activities and resources are clearly set out in an appropriate sequence.

In this way, teaching and learning are unified and consolidated. Coherence within and across components of the programme is an important aspect of The Shanghai Maths Project, in which Practice Books and Teacher's Guides, when used together, form a strong, effective teaching programme.

Promoting pupil engagement

The digital package on Collins Connect contains a variety of resources for concept development, problem solving and practice, provided in different ways. Images can be projected and shared with the class from the Image Bank. Other resources, for pupils to work with directly, are provided as photocopiable resource sheets at the back of the Teacher's Guides, and on Collins Connect. These might be practical activities, games, puzzles or investigations, or are sometimes more straightforward practice exercises. Teachers are signposted to these as 'Resources' in the Unit guidance.

Coverage of the curriculum is comprehensive, coherent and consolidated. Ideas are developed meaningfully, through intelligent practice, incorporating skilful questioning that exposes mathematical structures and connections.

Shanghai Year 4 Learning Book

Shanghai Year 4 Learning Books are for pupils to use. They are concise, colourful references that set out all the key ideas taught in the year, using images and explanations pupils will be familiar with from their lessons. Ideally, the books will be available to pupils during their maths lessons and at other times during the school day so they can access them easily if they need support for thinking about maths. The books are set out to correspond to each chapter* as it is taught and provide all the key images and vocabulary pupils will need in order to think things through independently or with a partner, resolving issues for themselves as much as possible. The Year 4 Learning Book might sometimes be taken home and shared with parents: this enables pupils, parents and teachers to form positive relationships around maths teaching that is of great benefit to children's learning.

---

* Note that because Chapter 5 in Year 4 is a Consolidation and enhancement Chapter, there is no Chapter 5 in the Year 4 Learning Book.

How to use the Teacher's Guides

Teaching

Units taught in the first half of Year 4:

Contents

Teacher's Guide 4A sets out, for each chapter and unit in Practice Book 4A, a number of things that teachers will need to know if their teaching is to be effective and their pupils are to achieve mastery of the mathematics contained in the Practice Book.

Each chapter begins with a chapter overview that summarises, in a table, how Practice Book questions and classroom activities suggested in the Teacher's Guide relate to National Curriculum statutory requirements.

Chapter overview

Area of mathematics	National Curriculum statutory requirements for Key Stage 1	Shanghai Maths Project reference
Statistics	Year 4 Programme of study: Pupils should be taught to: ■ interpret and present discrete and continuous data using appropriate graphical methods, including bar charts and time graphs.	Year 4, Units 7.1, 7.2, 7.3, 7.4
	■ solve comparison, sum and difference problems using information presented in bar charts, pictograms, tables and other graphs.	Year 4, Units 7.1, 7.2, 7.3, 7.4
	Year 5 Programme of study: Pupils should be taught to: ■ solve comparison, sum and difference problems using information presented in a line graph.	Year 5, Units 7.1, 7.2, 7.3, 7.4

It is important to note that the National Curriculum requirements are statutory at the end of each Key Stage and that The Shanghai Maths Project does fulfil (at least) those end of Key Stage requirements. However, some aspects are not covered in the same year group as they are in the National Curriculum Programme of Study – for example, end of Key Stage 1 requirements for 'Money' are achieved in Year 2 and 'Money' is not taught again in Year 2.

All units will need to be taught over 1–3 lessons. Teachers must use their judgment as to when pupils are ready to move on to new learning within each unit – it is a principle of teaching for mastery that pupils are given opportunities to grasp the learning that is intended before moving to the next variation of the concept or to the next unit.

All units begin with a unit overview, which has four sections:

Conceptual context – a short section summarising the conceptual learning that will be brought about through Practice Book questions and related activities. Links with previous learning and future learning will be noted in this section.

Conceptual context

This is the final unit of three in which pupils read and interpret line graphs. Pupils should have begun to appreciate when it is appropriate to use line graphs and their usefulness for representing data clearly.

Line graphs are used for two main purposes:

- To plot **continuous** data, such as temperature, because sensible intermediate values can be read from the graph of plotted points.
- To illustrate a trend over a period of time. In these graphs, although the data is **discrete**, it is connected by time, for example monthly sales figures.

(i) Discrete data is counted, for example the number of people at a football match, the number of cars passing a checkpoint. Bar charts are often used to display discrete data.

Continuous data is measured, for example temperature, height, weight. Continuous data is best represented by line graphs.

Learning pupils will have achieved at the end of the unit

- Pupils will have described the properties of line graphs using appropriate mathematical vocabulary and recognise when their use is appropriate (Q1)
- Pupils will have practised interpreting information presented in line graphs/time graphs using appropriate mathematical vocabulary (Q2)
- Pupils will have solved comparison, sum and difference problems using data in line graphs/time graphs (Q2)

This list indicates how skills and concepts will have formed and developed during work on particular questions within this unit.

These are resources useful for the lesson, including photocopiable resources supplied in the Teacher's Guide. (Those listed are the ones needed for 'Basic questions' – not for 'Challenge and extension questions'.)

This is a list of vocabulary necessary for teachers and pupils to use in the lesson.

Resources

mini whiteboards; **Resource 4.7.3a** Visitors to Black Castle; **Resource 4.7.3b** Matching graphs; **Resource 4.7.3c** Snowfall in New York and Chicago; **Resource 4.7.3d** Ice cream sales; **Resource 4.7.3e** Temperatures in London and Sydney

Vocabulary

data, horizontal axis, vertical axis, interval, unit, line graph, time graph, trend, gradient

The Shanghai Maths Project: an overview

After the unit overview, the Teacher's Guide goes on to describe how teachers might introduce and develop necessary, relevant ideas and how to integrate them with questions in the Practice Book unit. For each question in the Practice Book, teaching is set out under the following headings:

What learning will pupils have achieved at the conclusion of Question X?

This list responds to the following questions: Why is this question here? How does this question help pupils' existing concepts to grow? What is happening in this unit to help pupils prepare for a new concept about ...? This list of bullet points will give teachers insight into the rationale for the activities and exercises and will help them to hone their pedagogy and questioning.

> **What learning will pupils have achieved at the conclusion of Question 2?**
> - Pupils will have practised interpreting information presented in line graphs/time graphs using appropriate mathematical vocabulary.
> - Pupils will have solved comparison, sum and difference problems using data in line graphs/time graphs.

Activities for whole-class instruction

- Display these two height graphs:

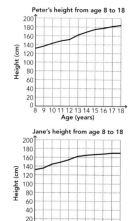

- Explain to pupils that Jane and Peter are twins, now aged 18. They have measured their heights each year on their birthday starting when they were eight.
- Look at the line graphs and answer the following questions together. Ask:
  - What do the graphs show?
  - What is plotted on each axis?
  - Who is taller aged 18, Jane or Peter? Is this what you would expect? What is the difference in their heights?
  - On which birthdays were the twins the same height?
  - Was Jane ever taller than Peter?
  - How old was each twin when their height was 168 cm?
  - What is the difference in height of the twins now they are 18?

Activities for whole-class instruction

This is the largest section within each unit. For each question in the Practice Book, suggestions are set out for questions and activities that support pupils to form and develop concepts and deepen understanding. Suggestions are described in some detail and activities are carefully sequenced to enable coherent progression. Procedural fluency and conceptual learning are both valued and developed in tandem and in line with the Practice Book questions. Teachers are prompted to draw pupils' attention to connections and to guide them to perceive links for themselves so mathematical relationships and richly connected concepts are understood and can be applied.

The Concrete–Pictorial–Abstract (CPA) approach underpins suggestions for activities, particularly those intended to provide conceptual variation (varying the way the problem is presented without varying the structure of the problem itself). This contributes to conceptual variation by giving pupils opportunities to experience concepts in multiple representations – the concrete, the pictorial and the abstract. Pupils learn well when they are able to engage with ideas in a practical, concrete way and then go on to represent those ideas as pictures or diagrams, and ultimately as symbols. It is important, however, that a CPA approach is not understood as a one-way journey from concrete to abstract and that pupils do not need to work with concrete materials in practical ways if they can cope with abstract representations – this is a fallacy. Pupils of all ages do need to work with all kinds of representations since it is 'translating' between the concrete, pictorial and abstract that will deepen understanding, by rehearsing the links between them and strengthening conceptual connections. It is these connections that provide pupils with the capacity to solve problems, even in unfamiliar contexts.

In this section, the reasons underlying certain questions and activities are explained, so teachers learn the ways in which pupils' concepts need to develop and how to improve and refine their questioning and provision.

Usually, for each question, the focus will at first be on whole-class and partner work to introduce and develop ideas and understanding relevant to the question. Once the necessary learning has been achieved and practised, pupils will complete the Practice Book question, when it will be further reinforced and developed.

Same-day intervention

Pupils who have not been able to achieve the learning that was intended must be identified straight away so teachers can try to identify the barriers to their learning and help pupils to build their understanding in another way. (This is a principle of teaching for mastery.) In the Teacher's Guide, suggestions for teaching this group are included for each unit. Ideally, this intervention will take place on the same day as the original teaching. The intervention activity always provides a different experience from that of the main lesson – often the activity itself is different; sometimes the changes are to the approach and the explanations that enable pupils to access a similar activity.

> ### Same-day intervention
> - Some pupils lose track of the number of sides while counting them, and this can lead to them naming shapes incorrectly.
> - Using the shapes created from straws and string, pupils should first count the number of vertices by touching each one in turn. Pupils should identify a vertex from which they will start counting and use a felt pen to mark it. Touching each side in turn, pupils should then count each side, taking care to notice when they have returned to their starting point.
> - Ask: *What do you notice about the number of vertices in each shape and the number of sides? Can pupils explain that there is the same number of vertices as sides?*

> ### Same-day enrichment
> - Pupils have created a number of shapes in this session. To deepen their understanding of the properties of 2-D shapes, pupils should investigate their properties.
> - Ask: *Is it always, sometimes or never true that there is at least one right angle in each type of shape?*
> - Working in small groups, pupils should investigate.

Same-day enrichment

For pupils who do manage to achieve all the planned learning, additional activities are described. These are intended to enrich and extend the learning of the unit. This activity is often carried out by most of the class while others are engaged with the intervention activity.

Lessons might also have some of the following elements:

Information point

Inserted at points where it feels important to point something out along the way.

> (i) The angle IS NOT the space between the lines. The angle is the amount of turn that is needed to move one of the lines so that it sits exactly on top of the other when the point where they meet is the turning point. It is important that pupils experience this physically. This can be done using their bodies and turning on the spot, using two metre rulers to demonstrate how one can be rotated from a fixed point to form an angle or looking at the measure of turn created when a door is opened and closed. They need to learn that the angle is the measure of the turn and that angles can range from very small to a whole turn. Pupils should explore making small angles and large angles.

All say ...

Phrases and sentences to be spoken aloud by pupils in unison and repeated on multiple occasions whenever opportunities present themselves during, within and outside of the maths lesson.

> All say ... *A right angle is 90°, and one line is perpendicular to the other.*

> Look out for ... pupils whose knowledge of shapes is limited to the visual recognition of a limited number of examples rather than based on the number of sides and vertices. Limited experience with shapes may result in some pupils thinking that as all squares are quadrilaterals, all quadrilaterals are squares.

Look out for ...

Common errors that pupils make and misconceptions that are often evident in a particular aspect of maths. Do not try to prevent these but recognise them where they occur and take opportunities to raise them in discussion in sensitive ways so pupils can align their conceptual understanding in more appropriate ways.

Within the guidance there are many prompts for teachers to ask pupils to explain their thinking or their answers. The language that pupils use when responding to questions in class is an important aspect of teaching with The Shanghai Maths Project. Pupils should be expected to use full sentences, including correct mathematical terms and language, to clarify the reasoning underpinning their solutions. This articulation of pupils' thinking is a valuable step in developing concepts, and opportunities should be taken wherever possible to encourage pupils to use full sentences when talking about their maths.

Ideas for resources and activities are for guidance; teachers might have better ideas and resources available. The principle guiding elements for each question should be 'What learning will pupils have achieved at the conclusion of Question X?' and the 'Information points'. If teachers can substitute their own questions and tasks and still achieve these learning objectives they should not feel concerned about diverging from the suggestions here.

Planning

The Teacher's Guides and Practice Books for Year 4 are split into two volumes, 4A and 4B, one for each part of the year.

- Teacher's Guide 4A and Practice Book 4A cover Chapters 1–6.
- Teacher's Guide 4B and Practice Book 4B cover Chapters 7–10.

Each unit in the Practice Book will need 1–3 lessons for effective teaching and learning of the conceptual content in that unit. Teachers will judge precisely how to plan the teaching year, but, as a general guide, they should aim to complete Chapters 1–5 in the autumn term, Chapters 5–8 in the spring term and Chapters 8–10 in the summer term.

The recommended teaching sequence is as set out in the Practice Books.

Statutory requirements of the National Curriculum in England 2013 (updated 2014) are fully met, and often exceeded, by the programme contained in The Shanghai Maths Project. It should be noted that some curriculum objectives are not covered in the same year group as they are in the National Curriculum Programme of Study – however, since it is end of Key Stage requirements that are statutory, schools following The Shanghai Maths Project are meeting legal curriculum requirements.

A chapter overview at the beginning of each chapter shows, in a table, how Practice Book questions and classroom activities suggested in the Teacher's Guide relate to National Curriculum statutory requirements.

Level of detail

Within each unit, a series of whole-class activities is listed, linked to each question. Within these are questions for pupils that will:

- structure and support pupils' learning, and
- aid teachers' assessments during the lesson.

Questions and questioning

Within the guidance for each question are sequences of questions that teachers should ask pupils. Embedded within these is the procedural variation that will help pupils to make connections across their knowledge and experience and support them to 'bridge' to the next level of complexity in the concept being learned.

In preparing for each lesson, teachers will find that, by reading the guidance thoroughly, they will learn for themselves how these sequences of questions very gradually expose more of the maths to be learned, how small those steps of progression need to be, and how carefully crafted

the sequence must be. With experience, teachers will find they need to refer to the pupils' questions in the guidance less, as they learn more about how maths concepts need to be nurtured and as they become skilled at 'designing' their own series of questions.

Is it necessary to do everything suggested in the Teacher's Guide?

Activities are described in some detail so teachers understand how to build up the level of challenge and how to vary the contexts and representations used appropriately. These two aspects of teaching mathematics are often called 'intelligent practice'. If pupils are to learn concepts so they are long-lasting and provide learners with the capacity to apply their learning fluently and flexibly in order to solve problems, it is these two aspects of maths teaching that must be achieved to a high standard. The guidance contained in this Teacher's Guide is sufficiently detailed to support teachers to do this.

Teachers who are already expert practitioners in teaching for mastery might use the Teacher's Guide in a different way from those who feel they need more support. The unit overview provides a summary of the concepts and skills learned when pupils work through the activities set out in the guidance and integrated with the Practice Book. Expert mastery teachers might, therefore, select from the activities described and supplement with others from their own resources, confident in their own 'intelligent practice'.

Assessing

Ongoing assessment, during lessons, will need to inform judgments about which pupils need further support. Of course, prompt marking will also inform these decisions, but this should not be the only basis for daily assessments – teachers will learn a lot about what pupils understand through skilful questioning and observation during lessons.

At the end of each chapter, a chapter test will revisit the content of the units within that chapter. Attainment in the text can be mapped to particular questions and units so teachers can diagnose particular needs for individuals and groups. Analysis of results from chapter tests will also reveal questions or units that caused difficulties for a large proportion of the class, indicating that more time is needed on that question/unit when it is next taught.

Shanghai Year 4 Learning Book

As referenced on page vii, The Shanghai Maths Project Year 4 Learning Book is a pupil textbook containing the Year 4 maths facts and full pictorial glossary to enable children to master the Year 4 maths programmes of study for England. It sits alongside the Practice Books to be used as a reference book in class or at home.

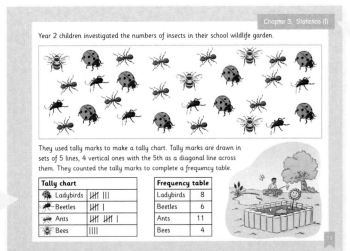

Maths facts correspond to the chapters in the Practice Books for ease of use.

Key models and images are provided for each mathematical concept.

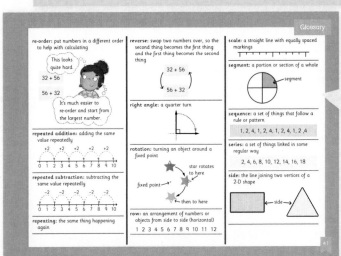

A visual glossary defines the key mathematical vocabulary children need to master.

Homework Guides

The Shanghai Maths Project Homework Guide 4 is a photocopiable master book for the teacher. There is one book per year, containing a homework sheet for every unit, directly related to the maths being covered in the Practice Book unit. There is a 'Learning Together' activity on each page that includes an idea for practical maths the parent or guardian can do with the child.

Homework is directly related to the maths being covered in class.

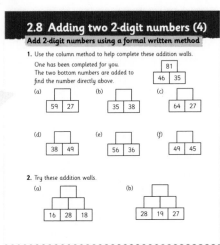

An idea for practical maths the parent or guardian can do with the child

Collins Connect

Collins Connect is the home for all the digital teaching resources provided by The Shanghai Maths Project.

The Collins Connect pack for The Shanghai Maths Project consists of four sections: Teach, Resources, Record, Support.

Teach

The Teach section contains all the content from the Teacher's Guides and Homework Guides, organised by chapter and unit.

- The entire book can be accessed at the top level so teachers can search and find objectives or key words easily.
- Chapters and units can be re-ordered and customised to match individual teachers' planning.
- Chapters and units can be marked as complete by the teacher.
- All the teaching resources for a chapter are grouped together and easy to locate.
- Each unit has its own page from which the contents of the Teacher's Guide, Homework Guide and any accompanying resources can be accessed.
- Teachers can record teacher judgments against National Curriculum attainment targets for individual pupils or the whole class with the record-keeping tool.
- Units from the Teacher's Guide and Homework Guide are provided in PDF and Microsoft Word versions so teachers can edit and customise the contents.
- Any accompanying resources can be displayed or downloaded from the same page.

Resources

The Resources section contains 35 interactive whiteboard tools and an image bank for front-of-class display.

- The 35 maths tools cover all topics, and can be customised and used flexibly by teachers as part of their lessons.
- The image bank contains the images from the Teacher's Guide, which can support pupils' learning. They can be enlarged and shown on the whiteboard.

Record

The Record section is the home of the record-keeping tool for The Shanghai Maths Project. Each unit is linked to attainment targets in the National Curriculum for England, and teachers can easily make records and judgments for individual pupils, groups of pupils or whole classes using the tool from the 'Teach' section. Records and comments can also be added from the 'Record' section, and reports generated by class, by pupil, by domain or by National Curriculum attainment target.

- View and print reports in different formats for sharing with teachers, senior leaders and parents.
- Delve deeper into the records to check on the progress of individual pupils.
- Instantly check on the progress of the class in each domain.

Support

The Support section contains the Teacher's Guide introduction in PDF and Word formats, along with CPD advice and guidance.

Chapter 7
Statistics (III)

Chapter overview

Area of mathematics	National Curriculum statutory requirements for Key Stage 1	Shanghai Maths Project reference
Statistics	Year 4 Programme of study: Pupils should be taught to: ■ interpret and present discrete and continuous data using appropriate graphical methods, including bar charts and time graphs.	Year 4, Units 7.1, 7.2, 7.3, 7.4
	■ solve comparison, sum and difference problems using information presented in bar charts, pictograms, tables and other graphs.	Year 4, Units 7.1, 7.2, 7.3, 7.4
	Year 5 Programme of study: Pupils should be taught to: ■ solve comparison, sum and difference problems using information presented in a line graph.	Year 4, Units 7.1, 7.2, 7.3, 7.4

Unit 7.1
Knowing line graphs (1)

Conceptual context

In Book 2, pupils were introduced to tallying data to make statistical tables. They learned to interpret and construct block diagrams and pictograms using data. In Book 3, new learning in statistics covered interpreting and representing data using bar charts.

This chapter has three units that will develop pupils' ability to interpret information presented in line graphs. A line graph is used to display connected numerical information that changes over time. Sometimes these graphs are called time graphs. Time is always recorded on the horizontal axis. Data is plotted as a series of points that are joined with straight lines. The line allows values between the plotted points to be estimated.

Pupils need lots of experience 'reading' line graphs. They should form the habit of reading the main title that answers the question, 'What does this graph show?' They should look at the label for each axis in turn and check the scale to see what each unit or interval represents. The units for time on the horizontal axis may range from seconds to years, depending on what is being measured.

(i) The shape of the plotted line is the key to interpreting the graph. Is the line going up/ coming down/remaining unchanged? What does this mean? A line in an upward direction tells us that the value is increasing and vice versa. The slope of the line is described as the gradient. The steeper the slope, the greater the rate of change. Series of measurements that remain unchanged are shown by a horizontal line.

Learning pupils will have achieved at the end of the unit

- Pupils will have been introduced to line graphs/time graphs (Q1)
- The habit of reading the title of the graph to determine what it shows will have been developed (Q1)
- Pupils will have practised looking at the label on each axis and checking its scale to see what each interval and unit represents (Q1)
- Pupils will have interpreted information presented in line graphs/time graphs using appropriate mathematical vocabulary (Q1, Q3)

Resources

Resource 4.7.1a Growth of a sunflower graph; **Resource 4.7.1b** Growth of sunflowers in light and shade graphs

Vocabulary

data, horizontal axis, vertical axis, interval, unit, line graph, time graph, trend, upward/downward tendency, gradient

Questions 1 and 2

1 Jo was ill and in hospital. The line graph below shows her body temperature recorded by the nurse at different times of the day. Graphs like this are also called time graphs.

Read the graph and answer the questions below.

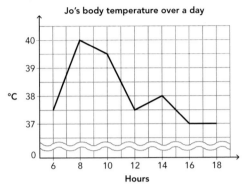

Jo's body temperature over a day

(a) What does the horizontal axis represent?

_____

What does the vertical axis represent?

_____

What does a single unit on the vertical axis stand for (in Celsius)?

_____

(b) At what time did Jo have the highest body temperature? What was her temperature at that time?

_____

(c) The nurse checked Jo's temperature every _____ hours.

(d) When did Jo's temperature go up the fastest?

_____

(e) When did her temperature go down the fastest?

_____

(f) When was there no change in her temperature?

_____

(g) Did Jo get better or worse? How can you tell?

_____

2 Use the information given in the line graph above to complete the table below.

Time	06:00	08:00	10:00	12:00	14:00	16:00	18:00
Temperature (°C)							

What learning will pupils have achieved at the conclusion of Questions 1 and 2?

- Pupils will have been introduced to line graphs/ time graphs.
- The habit of reading the title of the graph to determine what it shows will have been developed.
- Pupils will have practised looking at the label on each axis and checking its scale to see what each interval and unit represents.
- Pupils will have interpreted information presented in line graphs/time graphs using appropriate mathematical vocabulary.

Activities for whole-class instruction

- Display the diagram of the line graph showing the temperature of a school classroom over a whole day.

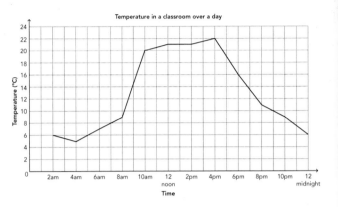

Temperature in a classroom over a day

- Tell pupils to study the line graph for about 30 seconds without speaking and then to talk to their partner about what the graph shows. Depending on pupils' experience with line graphs in other subjects, this session introduces or revises their properties.
- Ask the following questions and answer them together.
- *What does the graph show? How do you know?* (temperature of a classroom over a day)
- Explain that the title of any graph is vital for data to be useful.

 All say ... *Any graph must always have a title describing what is being measured.*

- *What is being recorded on the horizontal axis?* (time in hours)
- *What numbers are written on the horizontal axis?* (time every two hours)
- *Are they evenly spaced?* (Yes) *Why?* (Because each space represents the same length of time.)
- *What is each unit/interval worth?* (Each unit is one hour, labelled every two hours.)
- *Does the scale start at zero?* (Yes)
- Explain that it is usually good practice to start scales at zero, or the data can look misleading. Sometimes this is not appropriate, and it is possible to start from points other than zero.
- *What is being measured on the vertical axis?* (Temperature in degrees Celsius)
- *What numbers are written on the vertical axis?* (2, 4, 6, 8, …)
- *Are they evenly spaced?* (Yes)
- *Does the scale start at zero?* (Yes)

- *What is each unit/interval worth?* (Each unit is one degree, labelled every two degrees.)
- *How often is the temperature being measured?* (Every two hours)
- *What is the highest temperature? At what time did that occur? How do you measure it? Does it seem reasonable that the highest temperature occurs at this time?* (Highest temperature is 22 °C. Look for the highest value, track horizontally along to the vertical axis and read the number. Yes, the classroom is usually warm at the end of the day.)
- *What is the lowest temperature in the classroom? What time did this occur? How do you measure it? Does it seem reasonable that the lowest temperature occurs at this time? Are you in school at this time?* (Lowest temperature is 5 °C. Look for the lowest value, track horizontally along to the vertical axis and read the number. Yes, this is very early morning when it is very cold. No, we are not in school but fast asleep in bed.)
- *What is the difference between the highest and lowest temperatures?* (22° − 5° = 17°. The difference is 17°.)
- *Where is the gradient steepest? What does this mean?* (The steepest gradient is from 8–10 a.m. It means that the temperature is increasing more rapidly over that period than at any other time of the day.)

- Tell pupils that the central heating is programmed to switch on and switch off automatically. About what times do they think it comes on and turns off? Explain how you decided on those times. (The programmer is probably turned on at 8 a.m. and turned off at 4 p.m. This means that the school is at a comfortable temperature for them to learn mathematics – and other things.)

- Discuss with pupils how they have used the data presented in the graph to explain what is happening to the temperature during the day and how this fits in with their general knowledge.

(i) Remember, when time is measured, it is **always** plotted on the horizontal axis.

- Pupils should complete Questions 1 and 2 in the Practice Book. Before they begin, look at the wiggly lines on the graph and discuss what they mean and why they are there. (They show that some of the vertical scale has been omitted because there are no results for values below 37.)

Same-day intervention

- Give pupils **Resource 4.7.1a** Growth of a sunflower graph. Ask them to look at the graph and answer the questions, individually or in pairs.

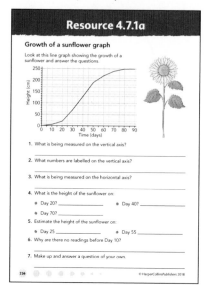

(Answers: 1. Height in cms; 2. 50 cm, 100 cm, 150 cm and so on. A unit is worth 10 cm; 3. Time in days. A unit is worth 5 days; 4. Day 20 20 cm, Day 40 130 cm, Day 70 240 cm; 5. Day 25 approx. 45 cm, Day 55 approx. 205 cm; 6. The seed was germinating and not visible above ground; 7. Answers may vary.)

Same-day enrichment

● Give pupils **Resource 4.7.1b** Growth of sunflowers in light and shade graphs. Ask them to look at the graphs answer the questions, individually or in pairs.

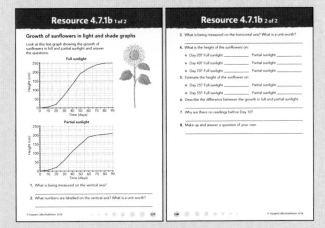

(Answers: 1. Height in cms; 2. 50 cm, 100 cm, 150 cm and so on. A unit is worth 10 cm; 3. Time in days. A unit is worth 5 days; 4. Day 20 FS 20 cm PS 20 cm, Day 40 FS 130 cm PS 110 cm, Day 70 FS 240 cm PS 200 cm; 5. Day 25 FS approx. 45 cm PS approx. 40 cm, Day 55 FS approx. 205 cm PS approx. 170 cm; 6. Until day 20 the two plants are the same height, then full sunlight grows faster and by 90 days it is 40 cm taller; 7. The seed was germinating and not visible above ground; 8. Answers may vary.)

Challenge and extension question

Question 3

3 Read the graph below and answer the questions.

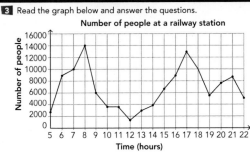

Number of people at a railway station

(a) At what times did the number of people reach a peak at the station? Why did it reach a peak at those times?

(b) At what time was the number of people the least at the station? Why do you think this is?

(c) What other questions can you pose? Discuss the questions with your friends.

This question asks questions about a line graph showing the number of people at a railway station during the course of a day. The challenge lies in explaining the 'story' of the data and in posing further appropriate questions.

Unit 7.2
Knowing line graphs (2)

Conceptual context

This second unit in the series about line graphs builds on the previous one. The shape of each graph is examined, focusing on the highest and lowest values and the gradient of the lines joining the points. Pupils identify the places on the graph that show an upward tendency and vice versa, indicating trends. They apply general knowledge to give reasons for the shape of the graph. Pupils' knowledge of how to interpret graphical representations of statistical information that changes over time is becoming more secure.

Learning pupils will have achieved at the end of the unit

- Pupils will have practised interpreting information presented in line graphs/time graphs using appropriate mathematical vocabulary (Q1, Q2)
- Pupils will have solved comparison, sum and difference problems using data in line graphs/time graphs (Q1, Q2)

Resources

Resource 4.7.2 Reading and interpreting line graphs

Vocabulary

data, horizontal axis, vertical axis, interval, unit, line graph, time graph, trend, upward/downward tendency, gradient

Question 1

1 The line graphs below show the sales of duvets and picnic blankets in a shop in 2018. Read the graphs carefully and answer the questions below.

Monthly sales of duvets

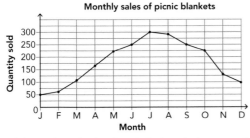

Monthly sales of picnic blankets

(a) In each graph, what does the horizontal axis represent?

What does the vertical axis represent?

(b) Which month has the highest sales volume of duvets?

Which month has the lowest?

What is the difference in sales volume between these two months?

What is the sum?

(c) From which month to which month does the sales volume of duvets show an upward tendency?

From which month to which month does it show a downward tendency?

(d) Which month has the highest sales volume of picnic blankets?

Which month has the lowest?

What is the difference in sales volume between these two months?

What is the sum?

(e) From which month to which month does the sales volume of picnic blankets show an upward tendency?

From which month to which month does it show a downward tendency?

(f) If the above two line graphs showed the monthly sales of picnic blankets and duvets but without the titles, could you use your knowledge from daily life to tell which one is a sales graph for picnic blankets and which one is for duvets? Give your reasons.

What learning will pupils have achieved at the conclusion of Question 1?

- Pupils will have practised interpreting information presented in line graphs/time graphs using appropriate mathematical vocabulary.
- Pupils will have solved comparison, sum and difference problems using data in line graphs/time graphs.

Activities for whole-class instruction

- Display these two height graphs:

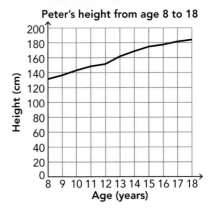

Peter's height from age 8 to 18

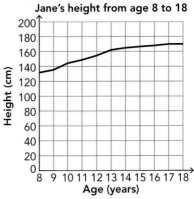

Jane's height from age 8 to 18

- Explain to pupils that Jane and Peter are twins, now aged 18. They have measured their heights each year on their birthday starting when they were eight.
- Look at the line graphs and answer the following questions together. Ask:
  - *What do the graphs show?*
  - *What is plotted on each axis?*
  - *Who is taller aged 18, Jane or Peter? Is this what you would expect? What is the difference in their heights?*
  - *On which birthdays were the twins the same height?*
  - *Was Jane ever taller than Peter?*
  - *How old was each twin when their height was 168 cm?*
  - *What is the difference in height of the twins now they are 18?*

– *Where does the gradient become less steep on each graph? What does this mean?*

– *Do you think they have stopped growing?*

● Pupils are ready to complete Question 1 in the Practice Book.

Same-day intervention

● Give pairs of pupils a copy of **Resource 4.7.2** Reading and interpreting line graphs. Ask them to look at the graphs and answer the questions.

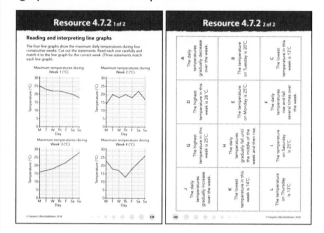

Answers: Graph 1: A, E, G; Graph 2: B, F, K;
Graph 3: D, J, I; Graph 4: C, H, L

Same-day enrichment

● Ask pupil pairs to complete the Same-day intervention task, using **Resource 4.7.2** Reading and interpreting line graphs.

● Challenge them to write another fact for each graph.

Challenge and extension question

Question 2

2 Two statistical graphs are shown below. Observe the graphs carefully and answer the questions.

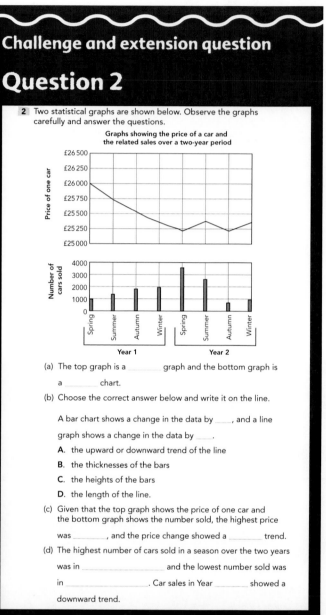

(a) The top graph is a _____ graph and the bottom graph is a _____ chart.

(b) Choose the correct answer below and write it on the line.

A bar chart shows a change in the data by _____, and a line graph shows a change in the data by _____.

A. the upward or downward trend of the line

B. the thicknesses of the bars

C. the heights of the bars

D. the length of the line.

(c) Given that the top graph shows the price of one car and the bottom graph shows the number sold, the highest price was _____, and the price change showed a _____ trend.

(d) The highest number of cars sold in a season over the two years was in _____ and the lowest number sold was in _____. Car sales in Year _____ showed a downward trend.

This question requires pupils to interpret information from a line graph and a bar chart using their knowledge and understanding of both statistical forms.

Unit 7.3
Knowing line graphs (3)

Conceptual context

This is the final unit of three in which pupils read and interpret line graphs. Pupils should have begun to appreciate when it is appropriate to use line graphs and their usefulness for representing data clearly.

Line graphs are used for two main purposes:

● To plot **continuous** data, such as temperature, because sensible intermediate values can be read from the graph of plotted points.

● To illustrate a trend over a period of time. In these graphs, although the data is **discrete**, it is connected by time, for example monthly sales figures.

(i) Discrete data is counted, for example the number of people at a football match, the number of cars passing a checkpoint. Bar charts are often used to display discrete data.

Continuous data is measured, for example temperature, height, weight. Continuous data is best represented by line graphs.

Learning pupils will have achieved at the end of the unit

● Pupils will have described the properties of line graphs using appropriate mathematical vocabulary and recognise when their use is appropriate (Q1)

● Pupils will have practised interpreting information presented in line graphs/time graphs using appropriate mathematical vocabulary (Q2)

● Pupils will have solved comparison, sum and difference problems using data in line graphs/time graphs (Q2)

Resources

mini whiteboards; **Resource 4.7.3a** Visitors to Black Castle; **Resource 4.7.3b** Matching graphs; **Resource 4.7.3c** Snowfall in New York and Chicago; **Resource 4.7.3d** Ice cream sales; **Resource 4.7.3e** Temperatures in London and Sydney

Vocabulary

data, horizontal axis, vertical axis, interval, unit, line graph, time graph, trend, gradient

Question 1

1 Think carefully and then fill in each box with the most suitable answer given below.

   A. line   **B.** trend   **C.** change   **D.** magnitude

   (a) A line graph can show clearly not only the ⬚ of the quantity, but also the ⬚ of the quantity.

   (b) A line graph is often used to show a ⬚ over a period of time.

   (c) It is often more appropriate to present statistical data such as monthly sales in a year, which emphasises the change of the data over a period of time, by using a ⬚ graph.

What learning will pupils have achieved at the conclusion of Question 1?

- Pupils will have described the properties of line graphs using appropriate mathematical vocabulary and recognise when their use is appropriate.

Activities for whole-class instruction

- Give pupils **Resource 4.7.3a** Visitors to Black Castle and ask them to answer the questions or work though them orally together, dealing with any difficulties.

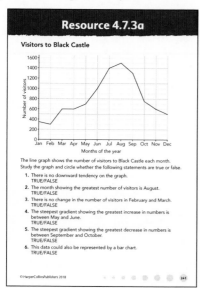

Answers: 1. F; 2. T; 3. F; 4. F; 5. T; 6. T

- Pupils should complete Question 1 in the Practice Book.

Same-day intervention

- Give pairs of pupils **Resource 4.7.3b** Matching graphs, and ask them to complete the questions.

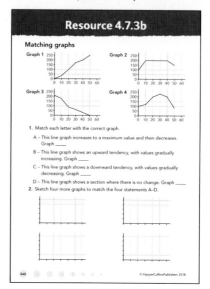

Answers: 1. A – Graph 4, B – Graph 1, C – Graph 3, D Graph – 2; 2. Answers may vary.

Same-day enrichment

- Give pairs of pupils a copy of **Resource 4.7.3c** Snowfall in New York and Chicago. Ask them to compose their questions and then swap to answer each other's questions.

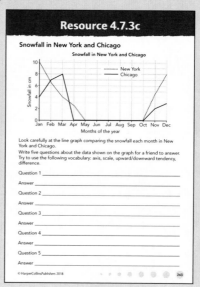

Question 2

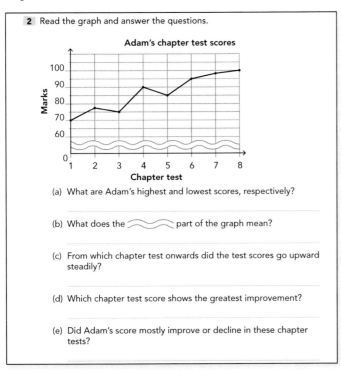

2 Read the graph and answer the questions.

Adam's chapter test scores

(a) What are Adam's highest and lowest scores, respectively?

(b) What does the ～～～ part of the graph mean?

(c) From which chapter test onwards did the test scores go upward steadily?

(d) Which chapter test score shows the greatest improvement?

(e) Did Adam's score mostly improve or decline in these chapter tests?

What learning will pupils have achieved at the conclusion of Question 2?

- Pupils will have practised interpreting information presented in line graphs/time graphs using appropriate mathematical vocabulary.
- Pupils will have solved comparison, sum and difference problems using data in line graphs/time graphs.

Activities for whole-class instruction

- Give pupils mini whiteboards. Display the graph of monthly sales of bikes. Ask the following questions and invite pupils to write answers on their whiteboards or to answer orally.

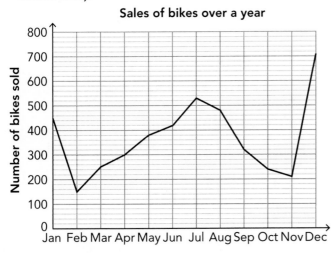

Sales of bikes over a year

- Ask:
  - *Which month has the highest sales, and why might that be?* (November; being bought as Christmas presents)
  - *Which month has the next highest sales, and why might that be?* (July; because it is summer)
  - *Between which months does the line graph show an upward trend? What does this mean?* (February to July and November to December; sales are increasing)
  - *Which period shows a downward trend? What does this mean? Why does this tend to happen?* (January to February and July to November; sales are decreasing)
  - *Between which two months is the greatest increase in sales? How do you know?* (November to December; the upward slope of the line is the steepest)
  - *Between which two months is the greatest decrease in sales? How do you know?* (January to February; the downward slope of the line is the steepest)

- Many further questions are possible, for example the number of bikes sold in particular months, the difference between sales in particular months, calculation of the total sales over the year.

- Pupils should now complete Question 2 in the Practice Book.

Same-day intervention

- Give pupils **Resource 4.7.3d** Ice cream sales. Ask them to look at the graph and answer the questions.

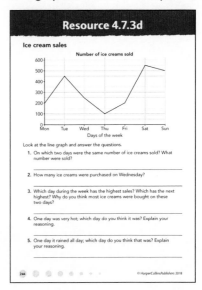

Resource 4.7.3d

Ice cream sales

Number of ice creams sold

Look at the line graph and answer the questions.

1. On which two days were the same number of ice creams sold? What number were sold?

2. How many ice creams were purchased on Wednesday?

3. Which day during the week has the highest sales? Which has the next highest? Why do you think most ice creams were bought on these two days?

4. One day was very hot; which day do you think it was? Explain your reasoning.

5. One day it rained all day; which day do you think that was? Explain your reasoning.

© HarperCollinsPublishers 2018

Answers: 1. Monday and Friday, 200; 2. 250; 3. Saturday, Sunday, explanations may vary; 4. For example, Tuesday because the most weekday sales occured, or Saturday because the most ice creams were sold; 5. For example, Thursday, because the least ice creams were sold.

Same-day enrichment

• Ask pupils to complete **Resource 4.7.3e** Temperatures in London and Sydney.

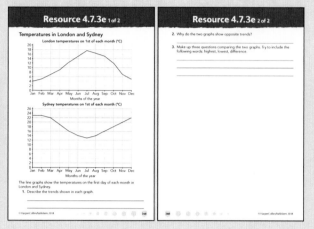

Answers: 1. London: temperatures increasing from January to July, then decreasing to December; Sydney: temperatures decreasing from January to July, then increasing to December. 2. They are in opposite hemispheres of the earth, so have opposite seasons. 3. Answers may vary.

Challenge and extension question

Question 3

3 Use the line graph above to answer the questions below.

(a) Fill in the table based on the line graph and work out the answers.

Chapter	One	Two	Three	Four	Five	Six	Seven	Eight
Scores	77						98	

(b) Can you briefly comment on Adam's study?

(c) Can you use your own maths test scores over a recent period of time to make a table, and then construct a statistical graph? Please also try to give comments on your own study.

Pupils are challenged to make a table of their own test scores and to construct a statistical graph from the results, commenting on any trend in their scores.

Unit 7.4
Constructing line graphs

Conceptual context

In this unit, having learned how to interpret or 'read' line graphs, pupils now begin to construct line graphs. At this stage in their learning, they should be given plenty of opportunities, provided with structured support (for example pre-drawn axes or suggested scales), and they should be closely monitored to ensure that they establish good habits. Always ensure that pupils use a sharp pencil, a transparent ruler and suitable squared or graph paper.

 To draw a graph from a data table requires a number of stages.
Good practice includes:

- First decide on the scope and title of the graph by asking the question 'What is it about?'
- Choose appropriate graph paper and decide whether the best graph is portrait or landscape.
- Draw the horizontal and vertical axes (leaving room for the numbers and labels).
- Select suitable scales for each axis so that the graph is a good size. Sensible scale intervals that are easy to manage are 1, 2, 5, 10, 20, 50, 100.
- Scales should always start from zero. (Wiggly lines can be used to indicate that part of a graph has been omitted; see, for example Unit 7.3, Question 2 in the Practice Book.
- Remember, time is always shown on the horizontal axis. Mark the scale points on this axis so that the largest value fits on the scale. Ensure that the marks are equally spaced.
- Add the scale points on the vertical axis, again making sure that the marks are evenly spaced and that the largest value of the data will fit. For example if the vertical axis is measuring height in centimetres and the largest value is 95 cm, the scale should be drawn to 100 cm. If the vertical axis is measuring mass in kilograms and the largest value is 21 kg, the scale should be drawn to 25 or 30 kg. Show pupils a variety of squared and graph paper and discuss the scales that could be used with them. Think about what each unit is worth for different scales.
- Carefully plot the points. To plot a point, find the value on both axes and use your pencil, finger or eyes to trace along from these values to the point where the lines intersect. Mark this point with a very small dot.
- Join the points with a ruler. (Later, particularly in Science, pupils will learn about drawing a line of 'best fit' for a line graph.) Pupils should also be introduced to using appropriate computer programs to construct graphs.

Learning pupils will have achieved at the end of the unit

- Pupils will have considered the steps required to construct a line graph and be able to articulate them (Q1, Q2)
- Pupils will have practised interpreting information presented in line graphs/time graphs using appropriate mathematical vocabulary (Q1, Q2)
- With support, pupils will have constructed line graphs (Q2, Q4)
- Pupils will have solved trend, sum and difference problems using data in line graphs/time graphs (Q2)
- Construction of bar charts will have been revisited (Q3)
- Pupils will have explored which graphical method is most appropriate (Q2, Q3)

Resources

various types of graph paper; squared paper; sharp pencils; transparent ruler; **Resource 4.7.4a** Graphs; **Resource 4.7.4b** Line graph or bar chart?; **Resource 4.7.4c** Length of a baby; **Resource 4.7.4d** Heating water

Vocabulary

data, horizontal axis, vertical axis, scale, interval, line graph, trend, gradient, continuous data, discrete data

Question 1

> **1** Steps for constructing a line graph.
>   (a) Decide the scope and structure of the line graph.
>   (b) Decide the content of the graph, such as the title and
>
>   ....
>
>   (c) Draw and mark the scale points on the .... so that the maximum scale points on both the horizontal axis and the vertical axis can show the time (order) and the greatest value of the data.

What learning will pupils have achieved at the conclusion of Question 1?

- Pupils will have considered the steps required to construct a line graph and be able to articulate them.

Activities for whole-class instruction

- Display the six line graphs. Each of the line graphs has an error. Challenge pupils to identify and discuss each one in turn.

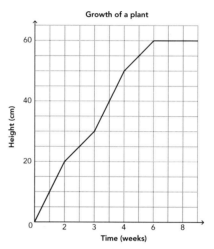

Growth of a plant

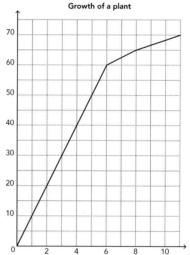

Growth of a plant

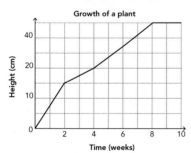

Growth of a plant

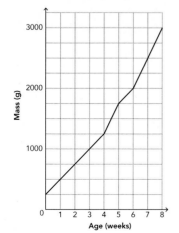

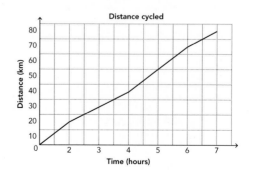

Distance cycled

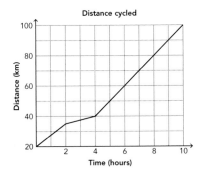

(Answers: Graph 1 – inconsistent scale on vertical scale; Graph 2 – No title; Graph 3 – inconsistent scale on horizontal scale; Graph 4 – axes not labelled; Graph 5 – the spaces on the vertical axis have been labelled not the lines; Graph 6 – vertical scale does not start at zero.)

- Now that pupils have explored common errors, discuss with them the stages involved in constructing their own line graph. Display a blank line graph.

- Establish the following steps:

  - Start by checking equipment, a sharp pencil, transparent ruler and appropriate graph paper.

  - Decide on the scope and title of the graph – what is it about?

  - Draw the horizontal and vertical axes (leaving room for the numbers and labels).

  - Time is always shown on the horizontal axis. The scale points should be marked so that the largest value fits on the scale and the graph covers most of the page.

  - Discuss sensible scales. Intervals that are easy to manage are 1, 2, 5, 10, 20, 50, 100 because they are easy to multiply mentally and it will be necessary to skip-count square by square.

  - Add the scale points on the vertical axis, again making sure that the largest value of the data can be plotted. For example if the vertical axis is measuring height in centimetres and the largest value is 95 cm, the scale should be drawn to 100 cm. If the vertical axis is measuring mass in kilograms and the largest value is 21 kg, the scale should be drawn to 25 or 30 kg.

  - Carefully plot the points with a very small dot.

  - Join the points with a ruler. (Later, particularly in Science, pupils will learn about drawing a line of 'best fit' for a line graph.)

- Pupils should now complete Question 1 in the Practice Book.

Same-day intervention

- Give pupils **Resource 4.7.4a** Graphs, to complete.

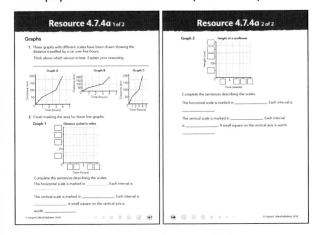

- Question 1 is designed to show pupils the importance of choosing a scale that is not too cramped in either direction.

- Question 2 gives pupils practice in completing scales and describing intervals.

- If there is an adult with this group, these graphs can be used to explore other aspects of line graphs, for example reading the distance travelled after a certain time, explaining what the horizontal portion means, looking for the parts of the graph with the steepest gradient and explaining what that means.

  Answers: 1. Graph A is best. The other two each have a compressed scale which is more difficult to read; 2. Graph 1: vertical axis 10, 30, 40, 50; horizontal axis 1, 2, 4, 5; hours, 1 hour; miles, 10 miles; 5 miles; Graph 2: vertical axis 50, 150, 200, 250; horizontal axis 2, 6, 8, 10; weeks, 2 weeks; centimetres, 50 cm, 25 cm.

Same-day enrichment

- Give pupils **Resource 4.7.4b** Line graph or bar chart? to complete.

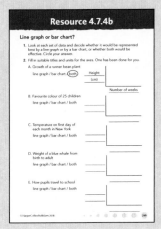

Answers: 2. A. Both, but line graph allows intermediate values to be estimated more accurately. Horizontal axis days or weeks, vertical axis height (cm); B. Bar chart – data is discrete and unconnected; Horizontal axis favourite colour, vertical axis number of children; C. Both. Line graph shows trend(s) more clearly, horizontal axis month, vertical axis temperature (°C); D. Line graph because data is continuous, horizontal axis days or weeks, vertical axis mass (kg); E. Bar chart – data is discrete and unconnected. Horizontal axis mode of transport, vertical axis number of pupils.

Questions 2 and 3

2 The table below shows the number of pedestrians crossing at a busy road junction recorded by a traffic officer in a week. Construct a line graph using the data and work out the answers.

Time	Monday	Tuesday	Wednesday	Thursday	Friday	Saturday	Sunday
Number of people	40	44	46	38	30	28	18

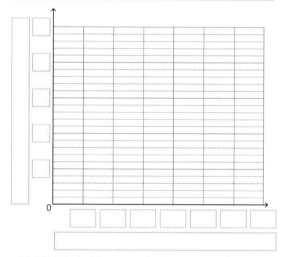

(a) Which day had the most pedestrians crossing in the week? What was the number of pedestrians crossing?

(b) Between which two days was there the greatest decrease in the number of pedestrians crossing the junction?

(c) From the statistics of that week, what is the tendency of people crossing the junction?

(d) What is the total number of pedestrians crossing recorded over the whole week?

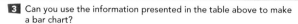
3 Can you use the information presented in the table above to make a bar chart?

(a) Show your results below.

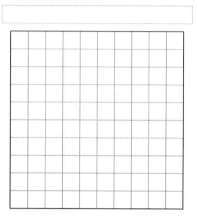

(b) Which graphical method, a line graph or a bar chart, do you think is more appropriate to present the data for pedestrians crossing, in the above question? Briefly give your reason.

What learning will pupils have achieved at the conclusion of Questions 2 and 3?

- Pupils will have considered the steps required to construct a line graph and be able to express them.
- With support, pupils will have constructed line graphs.
- Pupils will have practised interpreting information presented in line graphs/time graphs using appropriate mathematical vocabulary.
- Pupils will have solved trend, sum and difference problems using data in line graphs/time graphs.
- Construction of bar charts will have been revisited.
- Pupils will have explored which graphical method is most appropriate.

Activities for whole-class instruction

- Display the image of the table and graph.

A team of children take part in a long-distance walk. The table shows how long it took each child to complete each stage.

Time (hours)	0	1	2	3	4	5	6	7	8	9
Distance walked (km)	0	5	10	15	15	20	25	25	27.5	30

- Look at the table and ask individual pupils to say what is being measured and how often.
- Ask: *What does this graph show? What is a suitable title?* Establish that it is 'Distance walked' – write this on the graph.
- Ask: *What is always recorded on the horizontal axis?* Confirm that it is time and agree that the label is 'Time (hours)'. Remind pupils that the units, here hours, should always be shown.
- Ask: *What scale is required on the horizontal axis?* Establish that the marks should be hours, beginning at zero and going up each hour. Add the marks, 0, 1, 2, 3, 4, 5, 6, 7, 8, 9.
- Ask: *What do we need to record on the vertical axis?* Confirm that it is distance and agree that the label is 'Distance (km)'. Remind pupils that the units, here km, should always be shown or else the graph does not convey the information.
- Ask: *What is the total distance walked?* Agree that it is 30 km.
- Say: *We need to decide on a good scale for the vertical axis. Is it possible to use ones as on the horizontal axis?* Agree that this is not possible because we would need 30 intervals.
- Ask: *What is a good interval to use?* Establish that the main intervals should be marked in fives, from 0 to 35. Add these marks and labels.
- Ask: *What is the first point to plot?* Agree that it is (0, 0). Plot this point.
- Demonstrate how to plot the next point, find the 1 hour vertical line. Locate the 5 km mark and move along horizontally until it intersects with the 1 hour vertical line. This is the point to plot.
- Ask individual pupils to plot subsequent points, building the whole graph, explaining what they are doing as they do it.
- Look at the finished graph and tell pupils to discuss the shape of the graph and to explain what each part means with a partner.
- Ask: *How far did the team walk in the first three hours?* Agree that they walked 15 km. Ask a pupil to explain how they found this out.
- Ask: *What do the horizontal lines in the graph mean?* Confirm that these are rest (perhaps meal) times when the team did not walk, so the distance does not increase.
- Ask: *How many rests did the team have?* Agree that they had two because there are two horizontal segments on the graph.

- Ask: *What do you notice about the gradient of the section from 7–9 hours? Can you explain what this means?* Agree that the gradient in this section is less steep, which means that the team is not walking as fast as they did in the rest of the walk. Possible explanations are that the team were tired or that the course was uphill over this stretch.
- Ask: *If the team started walking at 9:00 a.m., what time did they finish?* Agree that they finished at 6:00 p.m.
- Pupils will build up this line graph.

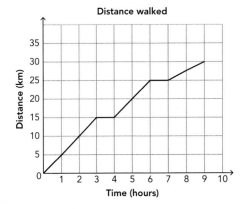

- Pupils should now complete Questions 2 and 3 in the Practice Book.

Same-day intervention

- Give pupils **Resource 4.7.4c** Length of a baby, to complete.

Answers: 1. Age (months); 2. Length (cm); 3. 30 cm; 4. Scales may vary, for example: vertical scale 0, 10, 20, 30; horizontal scale 0, 3, 6, 9, 12; 5. 25 cm.

Same-day enrichment

● Give pupils **Resource 4.7.4d** Heating water, to complete. Check they have a sharp pencil!

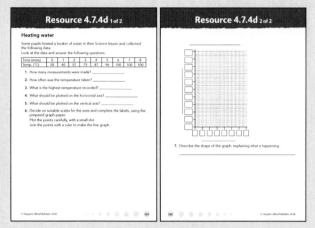

Answers: 1. 8; 2. Every 1 minute; 3. 100˚C; 4. Time (minutes); 5. Temperature (˚C); 6. Suitable scales could be: vertical axis 0, 10, 20, 30, 40, 50, 60, 70, 80, 90, 100; horizontal axis 0, 1, 2, 3, 4, 5, 6, 7; temperature increasing steadily at first, then more slowly until boiling point of 100˚C is reached.

Challenge and extension question

Question 4

4   Use your height measurements from the age of 6 to the present to complete the table below. Then construct a line graph and predict your height after three more years.

Age					
Height (cm)					

My prediction: _____

This question requires pupils to know their height from age 6 to the present, to plot this as a line graph, and then to predict their height in three years' time by

extrapolating the line. Pupils need to think carefully about the maximum scale points on both axes. The question helpfully provides support in the form of a table and a blank graph with spaces for labels.

Chapter 7 test (Practice Book 4B, pages 14–20)

Test question number	Relevant unit	Relevant questions within unit
1	Not specific to unit	
2	Not specific to unit	
3	Not specific to unit	
4	7.1	1
	7.2	1
	7.3	1, 2
5	7.1	1
	7.2	1
	7.3	1, 2
6	7.1	1
	7.2	1
	7.3	2
7	7.4	2, 3

Chapter 8
Geometry and measurement (1)

Chapter overview

Area of mathematics	National Curriculum Statutory requirements for Key Stage 2	Shanghai Maths Project reference
Geometry – properties of shapes	Year 4 Programme of study: Pupils should be taught to: ■ compare and classify geometric shapes, including quadrilaterals and triangles, based on their properties and sizes	Year 4, Units 8.2, 8.3, 8.4, 8.5, 8.7
	■ identify acute and obtuse angles and compare and order angles up to two right angles by size	Year 4, Units 8.1, 8.4, 8.5, 8.7
	■ identify lines of symmetry in 2-D shapes presented in different orientations	Year 4, Unit 8.6
	■ complete a simple symmetric figure with respect to a specific line of symmetry.	Year 4, Unit 8.6
Measurement	Year 4 Programme of study: Pupils should be taught to: ■ find the area of rectilinear shapes by counting squares.	Year 4, Units 8.8, 8.9
Measurement	Year 5 Programme of study: Pupils should be taught to: ■ calculate and compare the area of rectangles (including squares), and including using standard units, square centimetres (cm^2) and square metres (m^2) and estimate the area of irregular shapes.	Year 4, Units 8.9, 8.10, 9.11:

Unit 8.1
Acute and obtuse angles

Conceptual context

This unit provides pupils with the opportunity to revise aspects of geometry learned in Book 3 and develop their understanding of the properties of right, acute and obtuse angles. Images of angles are presented in a range of contexts and orientations so pupils develop their understanding that the properties of angles are constant and unchanging, irrespective of orientation. They will recognise the relative sizes of angles (greater or less than 90°) and associate the angles' properties with their names.

Learning pupils will have achieved at the end of the unit

- Pupils will have developed and applied their understanding of right, acute and obtuse angles through recognising angles in a variety of contexts (Q1, Q2, Q3, Q4, Q5)
- Pupils will be able to recognise an angle irrespective of its orientation and understand that the orientation of an angle does not affect its properties (Q1, Q2, Q3, Q4, Q5)
- Pupils will have developed fluency in using appropriate mathematical terms to support their mathematical reasoning (Q1, Q2, Q3, Q4, Q5)

Resources

photos of buildings (those familiar to the pupils and those that are not); clock faces (photos and pupil clocks); selection of 3-D shapes and packaging; sticky notes; card strips and paper fasteners; pipe cleaners; polygon side strips; **Resource 4.8.1a** Identifying angles in buildings; **Resource 4.8.1b** Angles all around us; **Resource 4.8.1c** Identifying angles

Vocabulary

angle, acute, obtuse, degrees, orientation, 2-D shape, 3-D shape, parallel, perpendicular, right-angle

Question 1

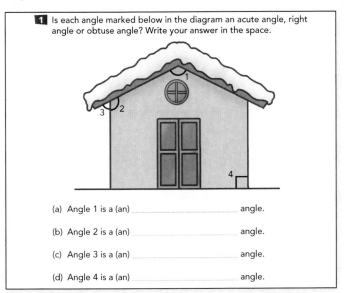

1 Is each angle marked below in the diagram an acute angle, right angle or obtuse angle? Write your answer in the space.

(a) Angle 1 is a (an) _____ angle.

(b) Angle 2 is a (an) _____ angle.

(c) Angle 3 is a (an) _____ angle.

(d) Angle 4 is a (an) _____ angle.

What learning will pupils have achieved at the conclusion of Question 1?

- Pupils will have developed and applied their understanding of right, acute and obtuse angles through recognising angles in a variety of contexts.
- Pupils will be able to recognise an angle irrespective of its orientation and understand that the orientation of an angle does not affect its properties.
- Pupils will have developed fluency in using appropriate mathematical terms to support their mathematical reasoning.

Activities for whole-class instruction

- In each of these tasks, pupils will create multiple examples of each angle. This will enable pupils to generalise about their properties and not rely upon one or two particular representations of each angle type.
- **Making acute angles.** Use two straight strips of card joined together with a split pin to help demonstrate to pupils that an angle is a measure of turn that is created when two straight lines are moved apart around a fixed point. Start with the two lines overlapping, then rotate one line to form an acute angle. Ask pupils to make an acute angle, and another, and another in order to demonstrate that every angle less than 90° is an acute angle.

 An acute angle is less than 90°.

(i) The angle IS NOT the space between the lines. The angle is the amount of turn that is needed to move one of the lines so that it sits exactly on top of the other when the point where they meet is the turning point. It is important that pupils experience this physically. This can be done using their bodies and turning on the spot, using two metre rulers to demonstrate how one can be rotated from a fixed point to form an angle or looking at the measure of turn created when a door is opened and closed. They need to learn that the angle is the measure of the turn and that angles can range from very small to a whole turn. Pupils should explore making small angles and large angles.

- **Making right angles.** Rotate one line further to form a right angle. Repeat the demonstration emphasising that the term right angle refers only to a 90° angle, unlike an acute angle, which is any angle up to 90°, so acute angles can be many different sizes. Ask pupils to make a right angle and rotate it. Emphasise that the term right angle refers to any 90° angle and does not refer to its position or orientation.

 A right angle is 90°, and one line is perpendicular to the other.

- **Making obtuse angles.** Continue to rotate one line beyond a right angle to make an obtuse angle. Emphasise that an obtuse angle is any measure of turn that is greater than 90° and less than 180°. Ask pupils to use their pairs of lines to make an obtuse angle, and another, and another. Each time check that the angles created are between 90° and 180°.

 An obtuse angle is greater than 90° and less than 180°.

- **Making angles.** Pupils take it in turns to use their cardboard strips to make angles. The teacher should ask questions such as: *Make me an angle less than 90°. Show me an obtuse angle. What is the name of an angle that is 90°?*
- For reference, the angles made using the cardboard strips should look like those shown below.

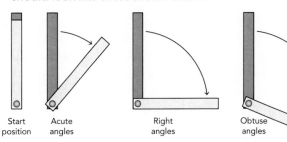

Start position | Acute angles | Right angles | Obtuse angles

- Display the images shown below and give pupils a copy of **Resource 4.8.1a** Identifying angles in buildings (which is a duplicate of the slide images).

- Referring to the pictures of the buildings, explain that the pupils will identify angles in each image.

- Ask: *How many degrees are in a right angle? Which is larger, a right angle or an acute angle? What is the name for an angle that is greater than 90° and less than 180°.*

- Give pupils sticky notes and ask them to write 'acute', 'right' and 'obtuse' on separate labels and stick each label on one of the pictures. Each time a label is positioned, pupils should use the relevant 'All say …' statement to explain how they knew that they had labelled the angle correctly. Ensure that pupils identify angles in a range of orientations, for example all four right angles in a rectangular window.

> **All say …** *An acute angle is less than 90°. A right angle is 90° and one line is perpendicular to the other. An obtuse angle is greater than 90° and less than 180°.*

> **Look out for** *… pupils who do not identify angles in non-typical orientations.*

- Once the angles on the images have been correctly identified and named, ask pupils to complete Question 1 in the Practice Book.

Same-day intervention

- Use an image of a square. Ask pupils to name the angles and identify each right angle. Clarify that a right angle is 90° and is formed when two lines that join or cross each other are perpendicular to each other. Rotate the square through 45° and ask pupils to identify the right angles. Agree that they are the same as before, except that they have simply been rotated. Emphasise that the size of the angle does not change as the shape is rotated. Repeat with other images.

- Use the image of the right-angled apex roof and identify the right angle.

- Rotate the image if pupils cannot initially spot the right angle. Rotate the image again and ensure that pupils can identify the right angle in a new orientation. Continue to identify other angles within the image.

- Use the right angles of a square to identify right angles, angles that are smaller than a right angle (acute angles) and greater than a right angle, but less than 180° (obtuse angle), and name each of these angles correctly.

Same-day enrichment

- Using a variety of images of angles in a range of everyday contexts (**Resource 4.8.1b** Angles all around us), pupils should identify and label every angle that they can.

- Working with a partner, a pupil scores a point for every angle that is identified correctly, and their partner scores a point for every angle missed or incorrectly named.

Question 2

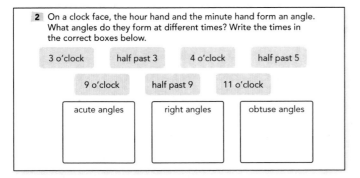

> **2** On a clock face, the hour hand and the minute hand form an angle. What angles do they form at different times? Write the times in the correct boxes below.
>
> 3 o'clock   half past 3   4 o'clock   half past 5
>
> 9 o'clock   half past 9   11 o'clock
>
> acute angles   right angles   obtuse angles

What learning will pupils have achieved at the conclusion of Question 2?

- Pupils will have developed and applied their understanding of right, acute and obtuse angles through recognising angles in a variety of contexts.
- Pupils will be able to recognise an angle irrespective of its orientation and understand that the orientation of an angle does not affect its properties.
- Pupils will have developed fluency in using appropriate mathematical terms to support their mathematical reasoning.

Activities for whole-class instruction

- Use a clock and its hands to demonstrate that as the hands move, angles are formed, and this shows the dynamic aspect of angles. Discuss the different angles made. The static aspect of angle is developed through images of angles that are presented in different orientations.
- Ask: *How many different orientations can I have for a right angle on a clock face?* It is likely that pupils will suggest four, as shown below.

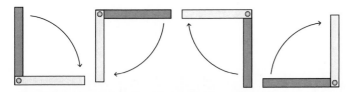

- Remind pupils that as long as the two lines are perpendicular to each other, the angle will be a 90° right angle, regardless of their orientation.
- Ask pupils to work in pairs to find all the right angles they can when one of the lines is on 12 or 6. Pupils should then create as many acute and obtuse angles as they can with one line on the 12 or 6 and the other on a different number. As each angle is formed, the pupils should use

the 'All say ...' (above) to explain what type of angle it is and whether or not it is equal to, greater than or less than 90°.

 Look out for ... pupils who are confused by the names of right angles and call some 90° angles 'left' angles.

- Ask pupils to complete Question 2 in the Practice Book.

Same-day intervention

- Use a book corner to make a 'right angle checker'. Explain that any 90° angle is called a right angle, regardless of its orientation. Use the 'right angle checker' to find examples of 90° angles around the classroom in different orientations.

Same-day enrichment

- Pupils should answer the following questions:
  - *How many minutes apart must the hands be to make a right angle?*
  - *How many right angles do you think can be made using the hands on a clock face? Convince someone else that you have found them all.*

Question 3

> **3** Count and find out the number of right angles in each digit below. Write the answers in the boxes.
>
> 9 4 5 8

What learning will pupils have achieved at the conclusion of Question 3?

- Pupils will have developed and applied their understanding of right, acute and obtuse angles through recognising angles in a variety of contexts.
- Pupils will be able to recognise an angle irrespective of its orientation and understand that the orientation of an angle does not affect its properties.
- Pupils will have developed fluency in using appropriate mathematical terms to support their mathematical reasoning.

Activities for whole-class instruction

- Every pupil should have a right angle checker; this could be made out of a book corner, folded cardboard strips joined together or other resource that has a right angle such as a slim 3-D cuboid.

- Use a selection of images incorporating right angles (**Resource 4.8.1a** Identifying angles in buildings and **Resource 4.8.1b** Angles all around us).

- In pairs, pupils should identify a right angle and write their initials on it, and use the 'All say …' to reinforce that a right angle has 90°. Once it has been checked by their partner they will score a point; if they identify an angle incorrectly the point goes to their partner. They take turns to find all of the right angles in the image.

- Once completed, the teacher should project a similar image so that all pupils can see them. Ask pupils to come out and identify all of the right angles, ensuring that they can recognise right angles regardless of orientation.

- Once this has been completed, display the image of a zero (0) as it would appear when presented on a calculator and identify all of the right angles in any orientation correctly.

 A right angle has 90°.

… pupils who think that the size of an angle may change if the lengths of the lines making it are longer or shorter.

- Pupils should now complete Question 3 in the Practice Book.

Same-day intervention

- Use **Resource 4.8.1b** Angles all around us. Pupils should use their right angle checker to identify right angles. Ensure that pupils can identify right angles in any orientation.

- Identify right angles in situations in which they may think the angle is larger, such as doors, windows and floor tiles. Let pupils use their right angle checker to reinforce that the size of the angle is not affected by the length of the sides that create it.

Same-day enrichment

- Considering all of the digits from 0 to 9 written in calculator format, ask pupils to order the digits by the number of right angles they each have. Then ask them to predict the number of right angles in letters, using the same format. They should then sketch and check.

- Reason mathematically about whether it is possible to make a letter or number with more than eight right angles.

Question 4

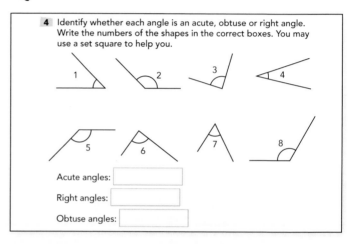

What learning will pupils have achieved at the conclusion of Question 4?

- Pupils will have developed and applied their understanding of right, acute and obtuse angles through recognising angles in a variety of contexts.

- Pupils will be able to recognise an angle irrespective of its orientation and understand that the orientation of an angle does not affect its properties.

- Pupils will have developed fluency in using appropriate mathematical terms to support their mathematical reasoning.

Activities for whole-class instruction

- Working in pairs, pupils should use their right angle checkers to identify acute angles and obtuse angles in a range of familiar 2-D shapes on **Resource 4.8.1c** Identifying angles.

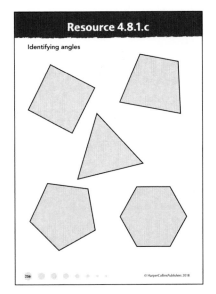

- In pairs, pupils should identify an acute or obtuse angle and write their initials on it, and use the 'All say …' to reinforce that an acute angle is less than 90° and obtuse angles are greater than 90° and less than 180°. Once it has been checked by their partner they will score a point. If they identify an angle incorrectly the point goes to their partner. They take turns to find all of the acute and obtuse angles in the images.

- Once completed, the teacher should project a similar image so that all pupils can see it. Ask pupils to come out and identify the acute and obtuse angles, ensuring that they can recognise these angles regardless of orientation.

 An acute angle is less than 90° and obtuse angles are greater than 90° and less than 180°.

 … pupils who do not recognise angles in atypical orientations.

- Once pupils can confidently identify the angles correctly, they should complete Practice Book Question 4.

Same-day intervention

- Pupils use their right angle checker to identify acute and obtuse angles around the classroom and in pictures in books. Pupils should be supported to identify angles when in atypical orientations and be able to explain that any angle less than a right angle is an acute angle, and all angles between 90° and 180° are obtuse angles.

Same-day enrichment

- Reason mathematically to answer the question:

  - *Is it always, sometimes or never true that you can draw a shape with at least one acute, one obtuse and one right angle?*

Question 5

> **5** True or false? (Put a ✓ for true and a ✗ for false in each box.)
>
> (a) Right angles are smaller than acute angles. . . . . ☐
>
> (b) All the acute angles are smaller than a right angle. . . . . ☐
>
> (c) When half past 9 shows on the clock face, the hour hand and the minute hand form a right angle. . . . . . ☐
>
> (d) If you use a magnifier to read an acute angle, the angle will become greater. ☐

What learning will pupils have achieved at the conclusion of Question 5?

- Pupils will have developed and applied their understanding of right, acute and obtuse angles through recognising angles in a variety of contexts.

- Pupils will be able to recognise an angle irrespective of its orientation and understand that the orientation of an angle does not affect its properties.

- Pupils will have developed fluency in using appropriate mathematical terms to support their mathematical reasoning.

Activities for whole-class instruction

- In small groups, pupils discuss whether each of the following statements is true or false:

  - *A right angle is the opposite of a left angle.*

  - *Two acute angles will be equal to a right angle.*

  - *Longer lines make larger angles.*

- Each group of pupils should take one statement. For each statement, pupils should decide if the statement is true or false. They should develop their explanation using appropriate terms correctly and provide their explanations in full sentences and provide images to support their explanations.

- Groups who have worked on the same statement should discuss their explanations and ensure that each pupil can explain their response fluently. Responses should then be discussed as a class.

... pupils who think that as an acute angle is less than a right angle, two will be equal to a right angle; this is a common misconception.

- Ask pupils to complete Question 5 in the Practice Book.

Same-day intervention

- Pupils will use a selection of acute angles and their right angle checker. Ask pupils to say if they think it is true or false that two acute angles will be equal to a right angle. Use polygon side strips, pipe cleaners or card strips to create two acute angles of approximately 35°. Compare these two angles combined against the right angle checker. Ask pupils if this shows that the statement is true.

- Then, use an angle of approximately 70° and one of 35°. Compare these two angles combined against the right angle checker. Ask pupils if this shows that the statement is false. Use further examples to generalise that only if the two acute angles equal 90° will they make a right angle.

Same-day enrichment

- Develop reasoning about geometry to answer the following:

  - *Is it always, sometimes or never true that if two lines intersect, four right angles are formed?*

- Pupils should use diagrams and correct mathematical language to support their answers.

Challenge and extension questions

Questions 6 and 7

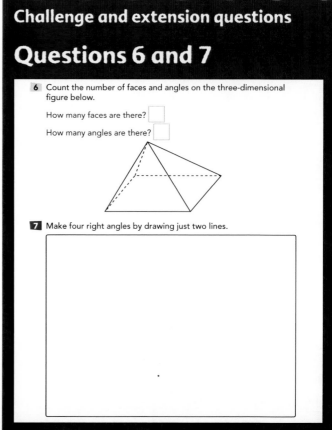

6 Count the number of faces and angles on the three-dimensional figure below.

How many faces are there? ☐

How many angles are there? ☐

7 Make four right angles by drawing just two lines.

Pupils have deepened their understanding of the properties of acute, right and obtuse angles in images and classroom objects. This knowledge is developed and applied through relating it to a square-based pyramid and recognising angles in a 2-D representation of a 3-D shape. Doing so will help to identify pupils' ability to identify angles in different orientations and begin to use angle to help establish the characteristics of shapes.

Unit 8.2
Triangles and quadrilaterals (1)

Conceptual context

In this unit, pupils will be introduced to the properties of triangles and quadrilaterals through examining the shapes in a range of contexts. Through these experiences, pupils will develop their understanding of the similarities and differences between these shapes and recognise that the general properties of quadrilaterals and triangles are constant and do not alter with any change of orientation. This helps to provide pupils with knowledge essential to support their ability to generalise and reason mathematically about shapes.

Learning pupils will have achieved at the end of the unit

- Pupils will have investigated properties of triangles and quadrilaterals (Q1, Q2, Q3, Q4, Q5)
- Pupils will have used mathematical language fluently to describe triangles and quadrilaterals (Q1, Q2, Q3, Q4, Q5)
- Pupils will be able to generalise about the properties of triangles and quadrilaterals (Q1, Q2, Q3, Q4, Q5)
- Pupils' ability to visualise shapes and recognise their properties will have been enhanced by creating tangram shapes (Q5)

Resources

scissors; squared paper; coloured drinking straws cut into four different lengths; string; geoboards; rulers; pencils; images or 2-D classroom shapes of squares and rectangles; **Resource 4.8.2a** Floor tiles; **Resource 4.8.2b** Isometric paper; **Resource 4.8.2c** Tangram; **Resource 4.8.2d** Tangram animals

Vocabulary

angle, side, equal, triangle, quadrilateral, pentagon, hexagon

Question 1

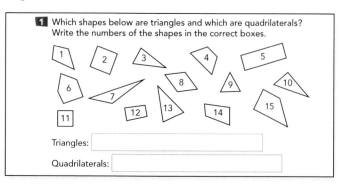

> **1** Which shapes below are triangles and which are quadrilaterals?
> Write the numbers of the shapes in the correct boxes.
>
> Triangles: _____
>
> Quadrilaterals: _____

What learning will pupils have achieved at the conclusion of Question 1?

- Pupils will have investigated the properties of triangles and quadrilaterals.

- Pupils will have used mathematical language fluently to describe triangles and quadrilaterals.

- Pupils will be able to generalise about the properties of triangles and quadrilaterals.

Activities for whole-class instruction

- Using the images on **Resource 4.8.2a** Floor tiles, pupils should work in pairs and identify the floor tiles in each picture as quadrilaterals, triangles or 'other shapes'. (Display each floor tile image on the board at the same time for the class to see.)

- Pupils should identify each part and assert their decision saying either 'I know this is a triangle because it has three straight sides and three angles' or 'I know this is a quadrilateral because it has four sides and four angles.' Any other shapes should be identified simply as 'other shape'.

- Ask pupils to complete Question 1 in the Practice Book.

Same-day intervention

- Cut up each of the images of the floor tiles from **Resource 4.8.2a** into their individual shape parts. For each part, pupils should name the shape (triangle, quadrilateral or other shape) and identify as many of its properties as possible (they may use their existing knowledge of types of angles to enhance their explanations).

- Rotate the shape and align it with those on the floor tile image.

- Ask: *What do you notice about the part we cut out and the one in the floor tile?*

- Emphasise that the properties of the shapes remain unchanged as its orientation changes. Repeat and check with other shapes and floor tiles to demonstrate that the properties of shapes remain unchanged even if their orientation (and size) change.

Same-day enrichment

- Pupils should work in pairs to draw triangles and quadrilaterals that enable them to answer the following questions.

  - *Is it always, sometimes or never true that a triangle must have at least one right angle?*

  - *Is it always, sometimes or never true that a quadrilateral must have at least one right angle?*

Question 2

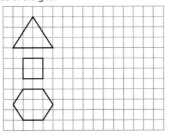

2 Look at each figure below and draw the same figure on the right-hand side of the grid.

What learning will pupils have achieved at the conclusion of Question 2?

- Pupils will have investigated the properties of triangles and quadrilaterals.
- Pupils will have developed fluency in their use of appropriate mathematical language to describe shapes.
- Pupils will be able to generalise about the properties of triangles and quadrilaterals.

Activities for whole-class instruction

- Ask pupils to sort the parts of the images from **Resource 4.8.2a** into triangles, quadrilaterals and other shapes. Then the set of triangles should be sorted and classified by side length; pupils should identify any with three equal sides, two equal sides and no equal sides.
- Pupils should use the shapes they have sorted and draw them as accurately as possible on squared paper.
- Once pupils have drawn each triangle they should use a ruler to check that the side lengths that should be equal are the same length, and use this information to correctly identify triangles with three equal sides, two equal sides and no equal sides.
- Ask pupils to complete Question 2 in the Practice Book.

Same-day intervention

- Squared paper can be helpful when drawing shapes with right angles, but when drawing other shapes isometric dotty paper can be more helpful (**Resource 4.8.2b** Isometric paper).
- Pupils should create an equilateral triangle, a right-angled isosceles triangle, a right-angled scalene triangle, an isosceles triangle and a scalene triangle using elastic bands and geoboards.
- Pupils take it in turns to trace the outline of each triangle with their finger. As they do so pupils should try and describe the shape as accurately as they can. They may say 'These two lines meet at an acute angle; when I follow this side I get to a right angle. At the end of this side is another acute angle.' Once they have described the shapes, pupils should draw them. They should notice which have right angles and which do not and use this to help decide whether squared paper or isometric paper is appropriate. Pupils should then use a pencil and a ruler to draw each triangle as accurately as they can.
- Pupils should use **Resource 4.8.2b** Isometric paper to help draw triangles without right angles.

Resource 4.8.2b

Isometric paper

© HarperCollins Publishers 2018   363

Same-day enrichment

- Pupils will extend their knowledge of the properties of triangles and quadrilaterals by investigating how many different examples of each type of triangle they can draw.

- Using **Resource 4.8.2b** Isometric paper, pupils should draw as many triangles as possible. In pairs, pupils should sort the triangles by the lengths of their sides and name them.

- Using **Resource 4.8.2b** Isometric paper, pupils should draw as many quadrilaterals as possible. In pairs, pupils should sort the quadrilaterals by the lengths of their sides and name as many as possible.

Questions 3 and 4

3 Fill in the boxes.

(a) A triangle can be formed using [ ] sticks.

Four sticks of the same size are needed to form a _____ .

(b) A triangle has [ ] sides and [ ] angles.

A quadrilateral has [ ] sides and [ ] angles.

(c) Both rectangles and squares are _____ .

The _____ sides of a rectangle are equal.

A square has [ ] equal sides.

(d) A _____ is a special rectangle.

(e) Make a count. In the figure on the right, there are [ ] triangles and [ ] quadrilateral(s).

4 True or false? (Put a ✓ for true and a ✗ for false in each box.)

(a) A diagram with four lines is a quadrilateral. .... [ ]

(b) A rectangle is a special square. .... [ ]

(c) A quadrilateral with four right angles is a rectangle. .... [ ]

(d) A triangle is a special quadrilateral. .... [ ]

What learning will pupils have achieved at the conclusion of Questions 3 and 4?

- Pupils will have investigated the properties of triangles and quadrilaterals.

- Pupils will have used mathematical language fluently to describe triangles and quadrilaterals.

- Pupils will be able to generalise about the properties of triangles and quadrilaterals.

Activities for whole-class instruction

- Pupils should work in pairs using some string and coloured straws cut into four different lengths to make:

  - a triangle with three equal sides

  - a triangle with two equal sides

  - a triangle with no equal sides.

- Once the triangles have been constructed, discuss and agree general properties that should then be used to generate the 'All say ...' statement:

 Triangles always have three straight sides and three angles.

- Pupils should then make quadrilaterals:

  - one with four equal sides

  - one with two pairs of equal sides (opposite sides)

  - one with two pairs of equal sides (adjacent)

  - one with four different sides.

- Once the quadrilaterals have been constructed they should be described as fully as possible to develop the 'All say ...' statement:

 Rectangles always have four straight sides and four right angles. The opposite sides are equal.

- Ask: *What can you tell me about squares?* Pupils must understand that they are rectangles because they have four straight sides and four right angles and the opposite sides are equal. This fact should be emphasised.

- Explain that squares are 'special rectangles' since all four sides are equal.

- Pupils should then try and make a range of quadrilaterals that are not regular. In pairs, pupils should try and see how many quadrilaterals they can create with:

  - no right angles

  - only one right angle

  - two right angles, and

  - with all sides a different length.

- Ask pupils to complete Questions 3 and 4 in the Practice Book.

Same-day intervention

- Pupils should be provided with images or 2-D classroom shapes of squares and rectangles to act as a guide when making them.

- Looking at a shape, ask: *Are the opposite sides equal? Are all of the sides equal?* Pupils should select straws to make a rectangle or a square using straws of the same length to show either that opposite sides are equal or that all sides are equal.

- Before threading the pieces of straw onto string, pupils should lay out each side to create the shape, checking that they have positioned the equal-length sides correctly.

- Once the straws have been threaded onto the string, pupils should practise naming the shape and identifying the equal-length sides.

Same-day enrichment

- Building upon the earlier task involving making quadrilaterals with different numbers of right angles, pupils can explore creating quadrilaterals with sides that are different lengths.

- Pupils should create and then record the variety of quadrilaterals they can create when they vary the order of the lengths that they thread onto the string. Pupils should look carefully to identify shapes that are rotations of previously made shapes.

- For each completed shape they should identify what combination of right, acute and obtuse angles have created each triangle.

What learning will pupils have achieved at the conclusion of Question 5?

- Pupils will have investigated the properties of triangles and quadrilaterals.

- Pupils will have used mathematical language fluently to describe triangles and quadrilaterals.

- Pupils will be able to generalise about the properties of triangles and quadrilaterals.

- Pupils' ability to visualise shapes and recognise their properties will have been enhanced by creating tangram shapes.

Activities for whole-class instruction

- Pupils' ability to visualise shapes and recognise their properties can be enhanced by creating familiar shapes through combining shapes. Using tangrams provides pupils with opportunities to experiment with combining shapes and identifying the shapes created through doing so. Pupils should work in pairs with a set of tans for each pair. Pupils should cut out pieces from **Resource 4.8.2c** Tangram and create:

  - a square using two pieces

  - a square using three pieces

  - squares using four or five pieces.

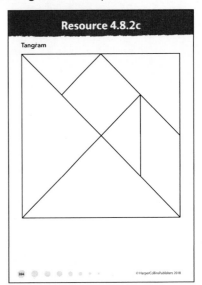

Question 5

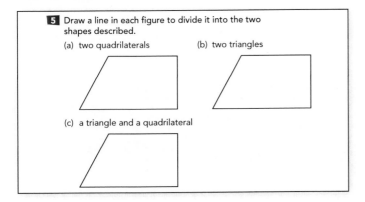

5 Draw a line in each figure to divide it into the two shapes described.

(a) two quadrilaterals

(b) two triangles

(c) a triangle and a quadrilateral

● The solutions are:

Tangram solutions

A square with two pieces

A square with three pieces

A square with four or five pieces

● Ask pupils to complete Question 5 in the Practice Book.

Same-day intervention

● Provide pupils with **Resource 4.8.2d** Tangram animals to help develop their skills in recognising shapes in different orientations and how the pieces can be combined to create new shapes.

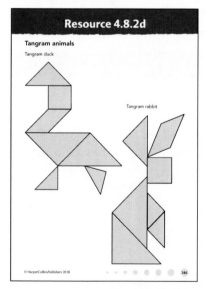

● When each triangle has been drawn, ask pupils questions such as: *Where can you see right angles? Where is the right-angled isosceles triangle?*

Same-day enrichment

● Continuing to use **Resource 4.8.2c** Tangram, challenge pupils to find two ways of arranging all seven tangram pieces to re-create a square. (Keep supplies of the original resource sheet out of sight as this provides a solution!)

Challenge and extension question

Question 6

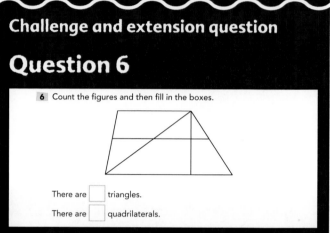

6   Count the figures and then fill in the boxes.

There are ☐ triangles.

There are ☐ quadrilaterals.

The challenge question provides pupils with a further opportunity to both consolidate their ability to recognise shapes and to visualise how shapes can be combined to make new shapes.

Unit 8.3
Triangles and quadrilaterals (2)

Conceptual context

In this unit, pupils are provided with further opportunities to deepen their understanding of the properties of triangles and quadrilaterals and other 2-D shapes. Pupils will continue to use their knowledge of correct mathematical terms to describe shapes and identify similarities and differences between shapes and describe these accurately.

Learning pupils will have achieved at the end of the unit

- Pupils will have developed their understanding of the properties of triangles, quadrilaterals and other 2-D shapes (Q1, Q2, Q3, Q4)
- Pupils will have developed their use of mathematical terms when describing triangles, quadrilaterals and other 2-D shapes (Q1, Q2, Q3, Q4)
- Pupils will be able to reason mathematically about the properties of 2-D shapes (Q1, Q2, Q3, Q4)

Resources

straws and string; a range of 2-D shapes; squared paper

Vocabulary

acute angle, obtuse angle, right angle, equal, sides, vertices, equilateral triangle, isosceles triangle, scalene triangle, quadrilaterals, square, rectangle, pentagon

Questions 1 and 2

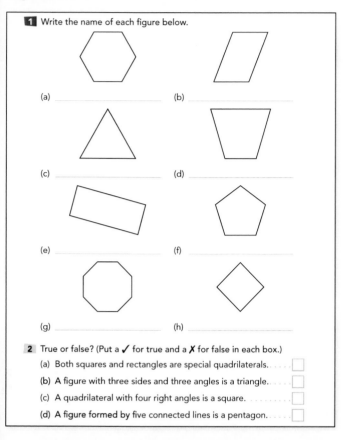

1 Write the name of each figure below.

(a) _____   (b) _____

(c) _____   (d) _____

(e) _____   (f) _____

(g) _____   (h) _____

2 True or false? (Put a ✓ for true and a ✗ for false in each box.)

(a) Both squares and rectangles are special quadrilaterals. . . . . . ☐

(b) A figure with three sides and three angles is a triangle. . . . . ☐

(c) A quadrilateral with four right angles is a square. . . . . ☐

(d) A figure formed by five connected lines is a pentagon. . . . . ☐

What learning will pupils have achieved at the conclusion of Questions 1 and 2?

- Pupils will have developed their understanding of the properties of triangles, quadrilaterals and other 2-D shapes.
- Pupils will have developed their use of mathematical terms when describing triangles, quadrilaterals and other 2-D shapes.
- Pupils will be able to reason mathematically about the properties of 2-D shapes.

Activities for whole-class instruction

- Working in pairs, pupils focus on one type of shape: triangles, quadrilaterals, shapes with five sides. Using straws and string (see Unit 8.2), each pupil should make as many variations of each shape as they can and sketch them as accurately as they can.

- Once they have made all the shapes they think they can, each pair should talk to another pair and compare the shapes they have made. Pupils should describe each shape using their knowledge of types of angles and lengths of sides. For example 'My shape has five equal-length sides

and five obtuse angles' (pentagon) or 'My shape has four sides of different lengths. It has two right angles, one acute angle and one obtuse angle' (quadrilateral).

- After the shapes have been compared, ask: *Is it possible to make a triangle with more than one right angle? What is the same about squares and rectangles? What is the difference between squares and rectangles?*

- Emphasise that a square is a special type of rectangle, as all of its sides are equal in length.

- Ask pupils to complete Questions 1 and 2 in the Practice Book.

Same-day intervention

- Some pupils lose track of the number of sides while counting them, and this can lead to them naming shapes incorrectly.

- Using the shapes created from straws and string, pupils should first count the number of vertices by touching each one in turn. Pupils should identify a vertex from which they will start counting and use a felt pen to mark it. Touching each side in turn, pupils should then count each side, taking care to notice when they have returned to their starting point.

- Ask: *What do you notice about the number of vertices in each shape and the number of sides?* Can pupils explain that there is the same number of vertices as sides?

Same-day enrichment

- Pupils have created a number of shapes in this session. To deepen their understanding of the properties of 2-D shapes, pupils should investigate their properties.

- Ask: *Is it always, sometimes or never true that there is at least one right angle in each type of shape?*

- Working in small groups, pupils should investigate.

Questions 3 and 4

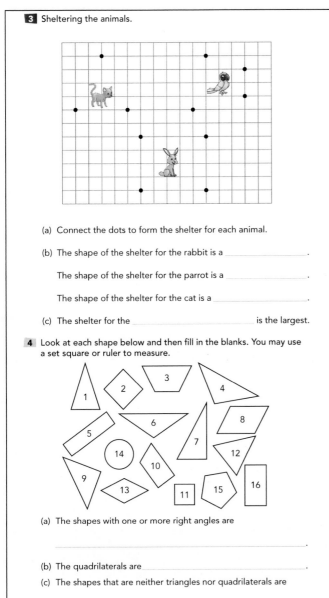

3 Sheltering the animals.

(a) Connect the dots to form the shelter for each animal.

(b) The shape of the shelter for the rabbit is a _____ .

The shape of the shelter for the parrot is a _____ .

The shape of the shelter for the cat is a _____ .

(c) The shelter for the _____ is the largest.

4 Look at each shape below and then fill in the blanks. You may use a set square or ruler to measure.

(a) The shapes with one or more right angles are

_____

(b) The quadrilaterals are _____ .

(c) The shapes that are neither triangles nor quadrilaterals are

_____

What learning will pupils have achieved at the conclusion of Questions 3 and 4?

- Pupils will have developed their understanding of the properties of triangles, quadrilaterals and other 2-D shapes.
- Pupils will have developed their use of mathematical terms when describing 2-D shapes.
- Pupils will be able to reason mathematically about the properties of 2-D shapes.

Activities for whole-class instruction

- Pupils often focus on the number and lengths of sides when categorising shapes. In order to focus their attention on vertices, ask:
  - *What shape would you make if you drew three dots to mark vertices?*
  - *Where would you position the vertices to make a triangle with three sides the same length?* (equilateral)
  - *Where would you position the vertices to make a triangle with two sides the same length?* (isosceles)
  - *Where would you position the vertices to make a triangle with three sides of different length?* (scalene)
- Pupils should then investigate the range of quadrilaterals they can make with one, two or four right-angled vertices. As each shape is drawn, pupils should use the 'All say ...' to describe it.

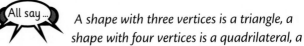 All say ...　*A shape with three vertices is a triangle, a shape with four vertices is a quadrilateral, a shape with five vertices is a pentagon, a shape with six vertices is a hexagon, a shape with seven vertices is a heptagon, a shape with eight vertices is an octagon.*

Look out for　... pupils whose knowledge of shapes is limited to the visual recognition of a limited number of examples rather than based on the number of sides and vertices. Limited experience with shapes may result in some pupils thinking that as all squares are quadrilaterals, all quadrilaterals are squares.

- Ask pupils to complete Questions 3 and 4 in the Practice Book.

Same-day intervention

- Shape-sorting task: pupils should be given a range of 2-D shapes to sort by number of vertices.
- Once the shapes have been sorted, pupils should use the 'All say ...' statement to define the properties of each shape.
- Pupils should be able to respond to questions such as: *Show me a shape with four vertices. What do we call a shape with three vertices? Show me an example of a quadrilateral, and another, and another, and another. What is the same about them all?*

Same-day enrichment

- Pupils should be provided with opportunities to develop their understanding of the properties of shapes and the language used to describe them.

- Visualisation task 'Imagine a white square'. Read the following to pupils, slowly, giving them time to focus and visualise.

  - *Imagine a white square. Imagine that a black, right-angled triangle has been laid over the square so that the right angle of the triangle is on top of one of the right angles in the square. Imagine a second black, right-angled triangle has been laid over the square so that the right angle of the triangle is on top of one of the right angles in the square. Draw the white shape that you see once the two black triangles have been positioned.*

- Pupils should describe the shape they have made as fully as possible and compare these to shapes formed by other pupils. Possible solutions include:

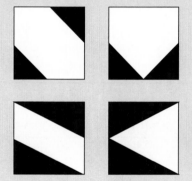

Challenge and extension questions

Questions 5 and 6

5 Make one cut in a square to get two figures of the same shape and size. How many ways can you think of? Draw to show your methods in the squares below.

☐ ☐ ☐ ☐ ☐

6 There are 5 sheep in a square field. Draw another square in this square field so that all 5 sheep are separated.

Question 5 further develops pupils' ability to visualise shapes and to recognise how shapes can be formed from other shapes. Pupils can be further challenged in Question 6 by being asked to consider how the shapes can be split into two parts of the same shape and size but with more than one cut.

Unit 8.4
Classification of triangles (1)

Conceptual context

This unit develops what pupils have already learned in this chapter about angles and the properties of triangles. Explicitly combining their knowledge of 2-D shapes and angles is important as it enables pupils to deepen their understanding, strengthening related concepts, as they recognise relationships and connections between them. Within this unit, pupils will consider not only the lengths of sides but also the sizes of angles when classifying triangles.

Learning pupils will have achieved at the end of the unit

- Pupils will have applied their understanding of angles to identify acute-angled, obtuse-angled and right-angled triangles (Q1, Q2, Q3, Q4, Q5)
- Pupils will have developed fluency in reasoning mathematically about the properties of triangles (Q1, Q2, Q3, Q4, Q5)
- Pupils will have developed skills in drawing triangles accurately (Q4)

Resources

rulers; coloured pens; scissors; geoboards and elastic bands; coloured straws; string; **Resource 4.8.2b** Isometric paper (from Unit 8.2); **Resource 4.8.4a** Triangles; **Resource 4.8.4b** Triangles to sort; **Resource 4.8.4c** Venn diagram; **Resource 4.8.4d** How many triangles?; **Resource 4.8.4e** Quadrilaterals to split into triangles

Vocabulary

acute-angled triangle, obtuse-angled triangle, right-angled triangle

Questions 1 and 2

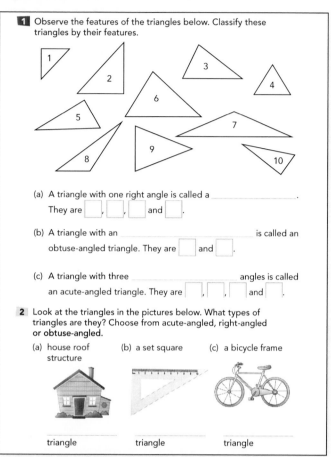

1 Observe the features of the triangles below. Classify these triangles by their features.

(a) A triangle with one right angle is called a ....
They are ☐ , ☐ , ☐ and ☐ .

(b) A triangle with an .... is called an obtuse-angled triangle. They are ☐ and ☐ .

(c) A triangle with three .... angles is called an acute-angled triangle. They are ☐ , ☐ , ☐ and ☐ .

2 Look at the triangles in the pictures below. What types of triangles are they? Choose from acute-angled, right-angled or obtuse-angled.

(a) house roof structure

(b) a set square

(c) a bicycle frame

.... triangle   .... triangle   .... triangle

What learning will pupils have achieved at the conclusion of Question 1?

- Pupils will have applied their understanding of angles to identify acute-angled, obtuse-angled and right-angled triangles.

- Pupils will have developed fluency in reasoning mathematically about the properties of triangles.

Activities for whole-class instruction

- To help pupils to deepen and extend their understanding of the properties of triangles they need to continue to experience triangles presented in a range of contexts and orientations. Display the following image and ask pupils questions such as: *How many acute angles can you see? Are there any triangles with a right angle in the gate? What is the name of the triangle in the road sign? What types of angles is it made from? There is an angle less than 60°, what is it called?* Using the 'all say' statements above pupils should name and describe the different triangles they can see in the images.

- Using **Resource 4.8.4a** Triangles, pupils should work with a partner to cut out each of the triangles, name them and describe them in terms of their angles.

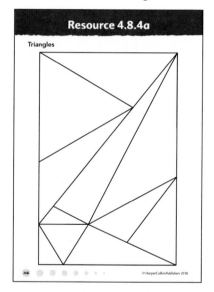

Resource 4.8.4a

Triangles

- Pupils should then create a decision tree (see below) to help identify in more detail the similarities and differences between them. Pupils could include questions such as, 'Does it have three sides the same length?' 'Does it have only two acute angles?' Subsequent questions help to sort each type of triangle.

- In the example below the first question is, 'Does it have equal sides?' There are only two possible answers: Yes or No. The next question on the 'Yes' branch is, 'Does it have three equal angles?' to include two properties of an equilateral triangle. On the 'No' branch the second question is, 'Does it have two equal sides?' This will help to distinguish between isosceles and scalene triangles.

Decision tree

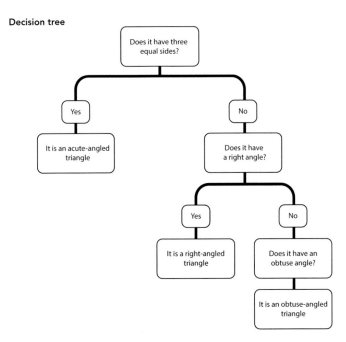

- Pupils should complete Questions 1 and 2 in the Practice Book.

- Pupils should then choose two triangles. They should take it in turns to say something that is the same about both triangles and something that is different about each triangle.

- Each pupil will score a point every time they correctly identify a similarity or a difference and use appropriate mathematical terms to do so. For example, 'This triangle has an obtuse angle, the other does not' or 'Both triangles have at least one acute angle.'

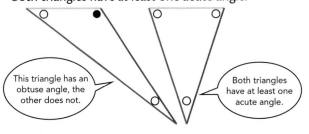

Same-day intervention

- Using the images of triangles on **Resource 4.8.4b** Triangles to sort, establish that pupils can describe the properties of each triangle accurately.

- Ask pupils to identify acute angles, obtuse angles and right angles in triangles and sort the triangles into acute-angled, obtuse-angled and right-angled.

- Working in pairs, pupils should use coloured pens to indicate whether an angle is acute, obtuse or a right angle. This will help pupils to recognise which types of angle have formed each triangle.

Same-day enrichment

- Using the triangles on **Resource 4.8.4b** Triangles to sort, pupils work in pairs using **Resource 4.8.4c** Venn diagram, to sort the triangles according to their angles ('acute angles', 'obtuse angles' and 'right angles').

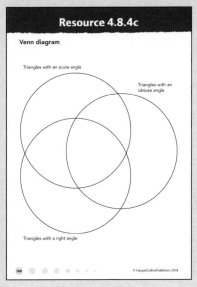

Questions 3 and 4

> **3** True or false? (Put a ✓ for true and a ✗ for false in each box.)
> (a) Triangles can be classified as acute-angled, right-angled or obtuse-angled. . . . . ☐
> (b) A triangle may have two right angles. . . . . ☐
> (c) All right-angled triangles are the same size. . . . . ☐
>
> **4** Draw an acute-angled triangle, a right-angled triangle or an obtuse-angled triangle on the grid below.

What learning will pupils have achieved at the conclusion of Questions 3 and 4?

- Pupils will have applied their understanding of angles to identify acute-angled, obtuse-angled and right-angled triangles.
- Pupils will have developed fluency in reasoning mathematically about the properties of triangles.
- Pupils will have developed skills in drawing triangles accurately.

Activities for whole-class instruction

- Pupils have had opportunities to define triangles that they have been given. In order to deepen their understanding of the properties of triangles they must be able to generalise about the properties of triangles in general as well as the properties of each particular type of triangle.
- Pupils should use a ruler and pencil on isometric paper (**Resource 4.8.2b** Isometric paper) to draw triangles to explore the questions and describe the triangles they have drawn. As they draw more and more examples, pupils should begin to apply their knowledge of the properties of each triangle type and recognise how these may appear in less common examples of each shape.
- Say: *Draw me an example of a right-angled triangle … and another … and another … and another. What type(s) of triangles have you drawn?* If pupils have drawn only one type of triangle they should draw the other type before proceeding.
- Ask pupils to draw an example of an obtuse-angled triangle … and another … and another … and another.

Say: *Draw me an example of an obtuse-angled triangle that no one else will think of.* (This will encourage pupils to draw triangles in non-typical orientations).

- Say: *Draw an example of an acute-angled triangle … and another … and another … and another.*
- Pupils should complete Questions 3 and 4 in the Practice Book.

Same-day intervention

- Some pupils' experience and memory of shapes is only of prototypical examples, and consequently they might find it hard to draw other variations of a shape. To provide additional experience of triangles, pupils should work in groups of four using the straws and string (used in previous units) to create: a right-angled triangle, an acute-angled triangle and an obtuse-angled triangle.
- Pupils should take it in turns to name and describe their triangles.
- As each triangle is named and described, pupils should use **Resource 4.8.2b** Isometric paper to draw them.
- Pupils should be asked to identify examples of acute-angled triangles, right-angled triangles and obtuse-angled triangles from the triangles that have been created.

Same-day enrichment

- Pupils should work together in groups of four to solve the puzzle on **Resource 4.8.4d** How many triangles?

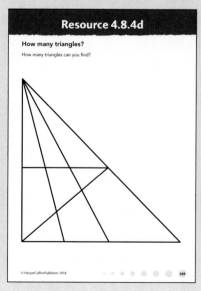

- Initially, each pupil should work out how many triangles they think there are in the image and then convince the others in the group that they have found them all, and can identify the different types of triangles and the angles that have created them.

- Once the four pupils have compared the triangles they have found, they should share their solution with another group of four to ensure that all the triangles have been successfully identified and their properties described.

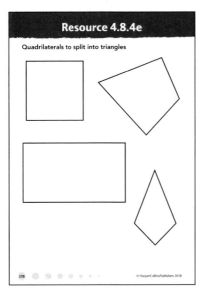

Resource 4.8.4e

Quadrilaterals to split into triangles

270   © HarperCollins Publishers 2018

- Pupils should complete Question 5 in the Practice Book.

Question 5

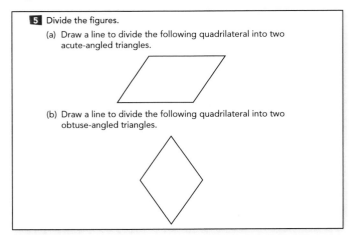

5 Divide the figures.

(a) Draw a line to divide the following quadrilateral into two acute-angled triangles.

(b) Draw a line to divide the following quadrilateral into two obtuse-angled triangles.

Same-day intervention

- If pupils have been unable to complete the whole-class tasks successfully they should use a geoboard and elastic bands to create quadrilaterals. Pupils can then use a piece of string or a second band to try and create triangles. For example:

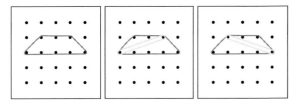

What learning will pupils have achieved at the conclusion of Question 5?

- Pupils will have applied their understanding of angles to identify acute-angled, obtuse-angled and right-angled triangles.

- Pupils will have continued to use correct mathematical language to describe the properties of triangles.

- Pupils will have developed fluency in reasoning mathematically about the properties of triangles.

Activities for whole-class instruction

- Pupils' ability to draw and describe the triangles they have drawn is developed further through providing them with conditions that may restrict the triangles they may choose to draw and prompt them to think more creatively and deeply about what they draw.

- Using **Resource 4.8.4e** Quadrilaterals to split into triangles, pupils should investigate how many different ways they can split each one into triangles.

Same-day enrichment

- Pupils' knowledge of different types of triangles will develop as their experience of them increases. Using the quadrilaterals from **Resource 4.8.4e**, pupils should overlap them to create triangles (and other polygons). Once the new shapes have been created, pupils should name them and their angles and identify any sides of the same length. For example:

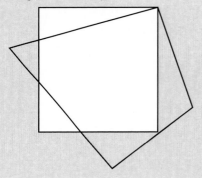

Challenge and extension question

Question 6

6 In the figure below there are five angles in a pentagon. If one of the five corners is cut off, how many angles are there in the remaining part of the figure?

Within this question, pupils are provided with further opportunities to visualise and investigate which shapes can be formed when a shape is manipulated. In this case, the focus is on the number of angles that can be created when the corners of a familiar shape are cut off. Some pupils may benefit initially from having multiple copies of the pentagon and scissors to help them identify what changes occur.

Unit 8.5
Classification of triangles (2)

Conceptual context

This chapter has provided pupils with a deepening understanding of triangles, presented in a range of contexts. This has focused on the size of angles; the length of sides is not yet a focus but will become more of a consideration later in the chapter. Pupils have a good knowledge about what is common to all triangles (the number of sides and types of angles) and might be different (size of angles). This unit develops pupils' mathematical reasoning and deepens pupils' understanding of the properties of triangles.

Learning pupils will have achieved at the end of the unit

- Pupils will have investigated the size of angles in triangles (Q1, Q2)
- Pupils will have reasoned about which properties of triangles are common to all and which only to some triangles (Q1, Q2)
- Pupils will have developed their mathematical reasoning skills through supporting their points with examples (Q1, Q2, Q3)
- Pupils will have learned how to develop generalisations (Q2, Q3)
- Pupils will have developed their ability to work systematically and to find all the possibilities (Q3)
- Pupils will have considered further how combining shapes or splitting up shapes can create new ones (Q3, Q4)

Resources

coloured felt-tipped pens or pencils; rulers; set square or other right angle checker; square-shaped sheets of paper; scissors; **Resource 4.8.2b** Isometric paper (from Unit 8.2); **Resource 4.8.5a** Always, sometimes or never; **Resource 4.8.5b** Triangle diagram; **Resource 4.8.5c** Combining triangles and exploring angles; **Resource 4.8.5d** How many triangles?

Vocabulary

acute-angled triangle, obtuse-angled triangle, right-angled triangle, hexagon, quadrilateral, rectangle

Questions 1 and 2

---

1 Classify the triangles as indicated. Write the answers in the boxes.

The acute-angled triangles are [   ].

The right-angled triangles are [   ].

The obtuse-angled triangles are [   ].

2 Multiple choice questions. (For each question, choose the correct answer and write the letter in the box.)

(a) A triangle has at least [ ] acute angles.

    A. 1   B. 2

    C. 3   D. cannot be determined

(b) In a triangle, if the greatest angle is an acute angle, it is [ ].

    A. a right-angled triangle   B. an acute-angled triangle

    C. an obtuse-angled triangle   D. cannot be determined

(c) Two right-angled triangles of the same size and shape can be combined into [ ].

    A. a right-angled triangle   B. an acute-angled triangle

    C. an obtuse-angled triangle   D. all of the above are possible

(d) The part of the figure covered by the paper as shown in the diagram is [ ].

    A. a right-angled triangle

    B. a rectangle

    C. a square

    D. all of the above are possible

(e) In the following shapes, [ ] does not have any acute angles.

    A. an acute-angled triangle   B. a rectangle

    C. a right-angled triangle   D. an obtuse-angled triangle

(f) Fold a piece of paper in half from top to bottom and then fold it again in half from left to right. Now unfold the paper; there are [ ] right angles made by the two creases.

    A. 1   B. 2   C. 3   D. 4

What learning will pupils have achieved at the conclusion of Questions 1 and 2?

- Pupils will have investigated the size of angles in triangles.

- Pupils will have considered which properties of triangles are common to all and which only to some triangles.

- Pupils will have developed their mathematical reasoning skills through supporting their points with examples.

- Pupils will learn how to develop generalisations.

Activities for whole-class instruction

- Provide pupils with copies of **Resource 4.8.2b** Isometric paper (from Unit 8.2).

- Working in pairs, pupils should use different coloured felt-tipped pens or pencils to mark whether angles are acute, obtuse or right. Triangles should be labelled acute-angled, obtuse-angled or right-angled.

- Give pairs of pupils one of the statements from **Resource 4.8.5a** Always, sometimes or never.

- Ask pupils to spend 3 minutes working individually at first, to decide what they think the answer is and why. Then they should discuss their thoughts with their partner and agree their answers.

- They should work together to provide examples to prove their answer. Once they have convinced themselves of their solution they should convince another pair of pupils.

- Discuss ideas. Explain that, by finding 'rules' about what is always or never true, pupils are generalising.

- Ask pupils to complete Questions 1 and 2 in the Practice Book. Discourage pupils from rotating the book so that they develop the ability to recognise different types of triangles and angles in any orientations.

Same-day intervention

- Some pupils may need support in recognising that some characteristics may apply to more than one type of triangle.

● Provide pupils with **Resource 4.8.5b** Triangle diagram.

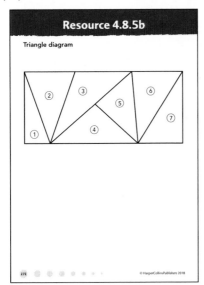

● Ask pupils to cut out the triangles. In pairs, they should find examples (if possible) to match the following statements to help reach their conclusions.

Find examples of	Always true, sometimes true, never true? Or cannot be determined?
A triangle with 1 acute angle	
A triangle with 2 acute angles	
A triangle with 3 acute angles	
A triangle with a right angle	
A triangle with no right angles	
An obtuse-angled triangle with an acute angle	
An obtuse-angled triangle without no acute angles	

● As they gather their examples, ask questions such as: *Since you have found triangles with and without right angles, can it be true that triangles ALWAYS have a right angle?*

Same-day enrichment

● Even though pupils have not learned to use a protractor to measure angles, the image in Question 1 can be used to develop their mathematical reasoning about the size of angles that can be created through combining triangles.

● Ask pupils what they know about the angles in an acute-angled and a right-angled triangle.

● Ask: *We know that a right-angled triangle has a right angle, what might the other two angles be? Could one of them be obtuse?* Pupils should justify their answers.

● Give pupils **Resource 4.8.5c** Combining triangles and exploring angles, and ask them to identify which type of triangles have been used in each image.

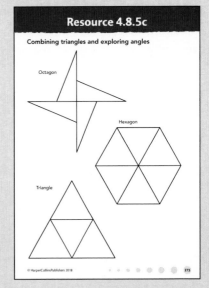

● Check that pupils can correctly identify the angles in each of the triangles and then ask: *What do you notice about the angles in the hexagon?* Ask pupils about the triangle and the octagon too.

● Having discussed the angles of the three shapes, ask pupils to use the triangle to investigate whether it is possible to create a shape using triangles that has only acute angles.

Question 3

3 Count the triangles in the diagram shown.

There are ☐ triangles in total. There are ☐ acute-angled triangles, ☐ right-angled triangles and ☐ obtuse-angled triangles in it.

What learning will pupils have achieved at the conclusion of Question 3?

● Pupils will have developed their mathematical reasoning skills through supporting their points with examples.

● Pupils will have developed generalisations.

- Pupils will have developed their ability to work systematically and to find all the possibilities.
- Pupils will have considered further how combining shapes or splitting up shapes can create new ones.

Activities for whole-class instruction

- Display the following image. Ask: *What type of triangle is used in this diagram?*

How many triangles?

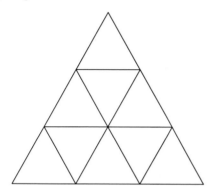

- Ask pupils to discuss with a partner how many triangles they think are included in the image.
- Once pupils think they have found all of the triangles, pupils should try to convince another pair of pupils that they have found all of them.
- Demonstrate an approach to identifying all of the triangles systematically.

How many triangles? Answers

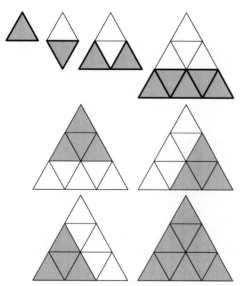

- Ask pupils to complete Question 3 in the Practice Book.

Same-day enrichment

- Using **Resource 4.8.5d** How many triangles?, ask pupils to estimate and check how many triangles would be formed if another row of triangles were added to the bottom of the diagram.

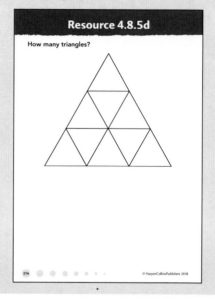

Question 4

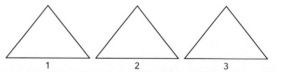

4 Divide a triangle.
  (a) Draw a line in the figure 1 to divide it into two acute-angled triangles.
  (b) Draw a line in the figure 2 to divide it into two right-angled triangles.
  (c) Draw a line in the figure 3 to divide it into one triangle and one quadrilateral.

What learning will pupils have achieved at the conclusion of Question 4?

- Pupils will have considered further how combining shapes or splitting up shapes can create new ones.

Activities for whole-class instruction

- Pupils should each have a square piece of paper that they fold diagonally to create four triangles. Pupils should name the small triangles they have made and describe their properties as accurately as possible.

- Can pupils reason that the angles in the centre are right angles without using a set square or right angle checker, using knowledge that two right angles make a straight line?

- Can pupils reason that, because the two sides are the same length and the vertex between them is a right angle, the other angles must be equal?

- Pupils should then cut the square into four triangles and investigate how many shapes they can make by joining two, three or four of the triangles back together.

- For each shape that they create and name they earn one point. They can earn bonus points by correctly identifying the type of angle within that shape and an extra point if they can describe the size of the angle.

- Pupils should convince a friend that they can describe the shapes that they have made and work together to identify shapes that are rotations of those already made. For example:

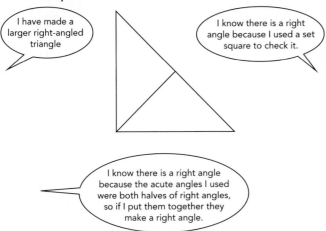

I have made a larger right-angled triangle

I know there is a right angle because I used a set square to check it.

I know there is a right angle because the acute angles I used were both halves of right angles, so if I put them together they make a right angle.

Look out for … pupils who include the internal sides when working out the shapes they have created – they may state that this is a four-sided shape △.

- Ask pupils to complete Question 4 in the Practice Book.

Same-day intervention

- Once pupils have created a shape they should use a coloured felt-tipped pen and a ruler to draw around the outside sides of the shape. Once this has been done they may continue to use the pens to mark the different angles so that their descriptions are as accurate as possible.

- Pupils should investigate further how the triangle can be split up. Is it possible to split the triangle up to make:

  - only acute-angled triangles?
  - two obtuse-angled triangles?
  - more than five triangles?
  - more than two triangles with right angles?

- For each question, pupils should use diagrams to support their justifications.

Challenge and extension question

Question 5

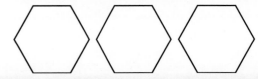

5 Use diagonals to divide a hexagon into four separate triangles that do not overlap. How many different ways can you find? Rotating or flipping the hexagon does not count. Work it out on your own.

The challenge question introduces the idea of diagonals as a way of splitting up shapes so that the shape is split from vertex to vertex, not from vertex to side or from side to side. This question builds on what pupils have already experienced when splitting up triangles and provides them with opportunities to apply what they have learned to splitting up hexagons.

Unit 8.6
Line symmetry

Conceptual context

Exploring line symmetry introduces pupils to a new aspect of geometry. Pupils' understanding of line symmetry is developed through experiencing examples of it in a variety of contexts and begin to recognise line symmetry as a property of shapes. This helps them develop their understanding of what line symmetry is and reveals any misconceptions. Learning about line symmetry within a series of lessons on triangles and 2-D shapes helps pupils to contextualise this new concept and connect it to their existing understanding of the properties of 2-D shapes.

Learning pupils will have achieved at the end of the unit

● Pupils will be able to explain what line symmetry is (Q1, Q2, Q3, Q4)
● Pupils will be able to identify examples of line symmetry and non-examples of line symmetry (Q3, Q4)
● Pupils will have broadened their understanding of line symmetry through applying their knowledge to a variety of images in a range of contexts (Q1, Q2, Q3, Q4)
● Pupils will be able to generalise about what changes and what stays the same when a shape is reflected in a line of symmetry (Q1, Q2, Q3, Q4)

Resources

mirrors; squared paper; mini whiteboards; **Resource 4.8.6a**
Shapes to demonstrate line symmetry; **Resource 4.8.6b**
More shapes to demonstrate line symmetry; **Resource 4.8.6c** Grids to shade; **Resource 4.8.2a** Floor tiles (from Unit 8.2); **Resource 4.8.6d** Line symmetry in different fonts

Vocabulary

symmetry, reflection, congruent, line, mirror line

Questions 1 and 2

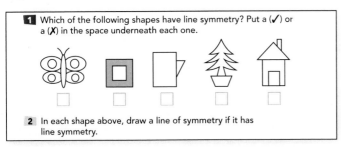

1 Which of the following shapes have line symmetry? Put a (✓) or a (✗) in the space underneath each one.

2 In each shape above, draw a line of symmetry if it has line symmetry.

What learning will pupils have achieved at the conclusion of Questions 1 and 2?

- Pupils will be able to explain what line symmetry is.

- Pupils will have broadened their understanding of line symmetry through applying their knowledge to a variety of images in a range of contexts.

- Pupils will be able to generalise about what changes and what stays the same when a shape is reflected in a line of symmetry.

Activities for whole-class instruction

- So that pupils understand that symmetry appears in nature and influences how we build and design things, display the following images and ask what they notice about the butterfly and the birds.

- Demonstrate where the line of symmetry would be and explain that the part on each side of the line of symmetry is a mirror image of the other.

- Ask pupils to suggest where else they might see lines of symmetry.

- Display the following images to demonstrate further examples of symmetry in nature and highlight that sometimes there may be more than one line of symmetry.

- Ask pupils to discuss and use mirrors to find out 'Is your face symmetrical?' Explain that although both sides of our faces are usually similar, they are not usually identical. There is only line symmetry in a shape if both sides are exactly symmetrical.

- Working in pairs, pupils should take each of the images on **Resource 4.8.6a** Shapes to demonstrate line symmetry and fold them in half as carefully as possible.

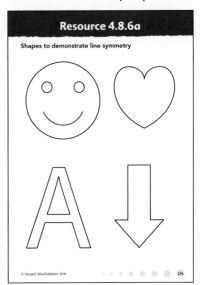

- Ask pupils to unfold each image and ask: *What do you notice about the image?*

- Pupils should notice that one part of the image mirrors the other. Explain that when a shape is folded exactly in the middle the fold line is a line of symmetry, sometimes called a mirror line, and it makes the parts of the image look the same. Pupils should place a mirror on the fold and check that both sides of the image look the same.

- Continue to ask pupils what they have noticed about the two sides of the image until they say that each part is the same size and a reflection of the other. Explain that when two shapes are identical to each other, as is the case with the shapes either side of a line of symmetry, these shapes are said to be congruent.

- Display the images from **Resource 4.8.6a** and ask pupils to show where the line of symmetry in each image would be.

 An image has line symmetry if each part of the shape mirrors the other.

- Encourage pupils to use this 'All say …' statement to explain what they notice about images in which they identify lines of symmetry, in the lesson and outside it.

- Pupils' understanding of line symmetry is developed through looking at less-typical examples and non-examples using **Resource 4.8.6b** More shapes to demonstrate line symmetry. This will help them to recognise that a shape has a line of symmetry if it creates two images that mirror each other, regardless of the orientation of the shape.

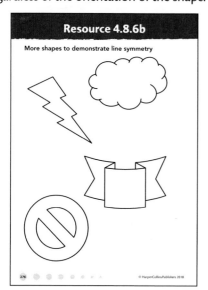

- Ask pupils to complete Questions 1 and 2 in the Practice Book.

Same-day intervention

- Some pupils can confuse folding a shape in half with finding a line of symmetry. To help pupils to recognise the difference between these two ideas, pupils should fold shapes in half and use the mirror line to check that both sides of the image mirror each other. Give pupils a rectangle and ask them to find any lines of symmetry and to use a mirror to check whether or not both parts mirror each other.

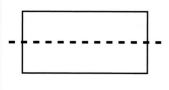 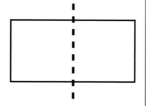

- Ask: *Can this rectangle have a line of symmetry that is diagonal?* Pupils should use a mirror to help them realise that although a diagonal fold splits the rectangle into two halves, it is not a line of symmetry as the two parts do not mirror each other.

- To help demonstrate this further, pupils should fold the shape along the diagonal line. If the line is a line of symmetry then one part of the shape will fit exactly on to the other, but this does not happen with rectangles.

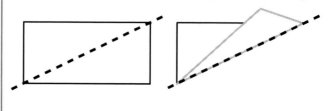

Same-day enrichment

- It is important that pupils understand that lines of symmetry can be horizontal, vertical or diagonal, depending on the shape.

- Pupils should work in pairs to shade the grids on **Resource 4.8.6c** Grids to shade, in as many ways as possible so that when a line of symmetry is added each part is congruent. One pupil should use a mirror and folding to check that the lines of symmetry have been correctly positioned. (Pupils do not have to colour in whole squares to create their symmetrical images.)

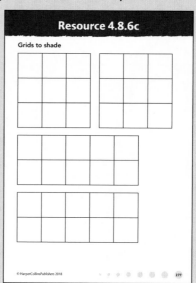

Question 3

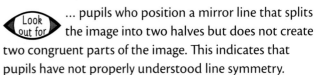

3 Which of the ten digits from 0 to 9 have line symmetry?
Write them down and draw their lines of symmetry.

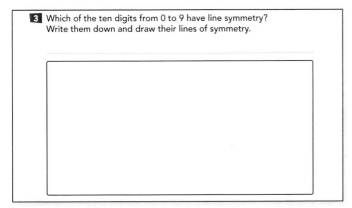

What learning will pupils have achieved at the conclusion of Question 3?

- Pupils will have identified examples of line symmetry and non-examples of line symmetry.

- Pupils will have broadened their understanding of line symmetry through applying their knowledge to a variety of images in a range of contexts.

- Pupils will be able to generalise about what changes and what stays the same when a shape is reflected in a line of symmetry.

Activities for whole-class instruction

- Explain to pupils that symmetry is used extensively in design.

- Display the images below to provide some examples of symmetry in buildings. Ask pupils to volunteer to come to the front and correctly position the line of symmetry.

- Ask: *Can you see or think of any examples of line symmetry in our classroom or around our school?* They may notice the design of the classroom door, the arrangements of

windows either side of a door, or perhaps a design on the school playground. Pupil's own belongings or clothing might have symmetrical logos.

- Ask pupils to investigate with a partner whether or not they think that some numbers have line symmetry, using whiteboards to draw them. Use the 'All say …' to explain how they know which digits have line symmetry.

- Ask pupils to complete Question 3 in the Practice Book.

Same-day intervention

Look out for … pupils who position a mirror line that splits the image into two halves but does not create two congruent parts of the image. This indicates that pupils have not properly understood line symmetry.

- Working in pairs, pupils should use the images on **Resource 4.8.2a** Floor tiles (from Unit 8.2) and a mirror to identify lines of symmetry. Each time a pupil thinks a line of symmetry has been found their partner must check that the other part mirrors the other. Pupils can experiment and position the mirror horizontally, vertically and diagonally to identify if there is more than one line of symmetry.

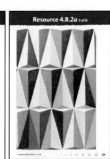

Same-day enrichment

- Whether or not a number has line symmetry depends on the style or font in which it is written.
- Using **Resource 4.8.6d** Line symmetry in different fonts, pupils should identify which of the numbers have line symmetry.
- Pupils should investigate whether it is possible to draw each of the numbers so that they all have line symmetry.

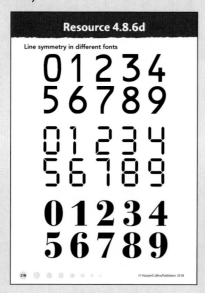

- Pupils' understanding of line symmetry will be deepened in Question 4 as pupils have to visualise and draw the other part of the image rather than identify the position of a line of symmetry.

Activities for whole-class instruction

- Ask: *If a shape has line symmetry, what will you notice about the two parts of the shape?* Ensure that pupils know that an image has line symmetry if each part of the shape mirrors the other.
- Display the images shown below. Ask pupils to sketch the other half of the shape on their whiteboards. The teacher tries to finish the first two shapes. Ask: *How will I know if what I have drawn is correct?* Pupils should use the 'All say …' statement (If a shape has a line of symmetry the parts on either side of the line mirror each other.) to justify their answers.

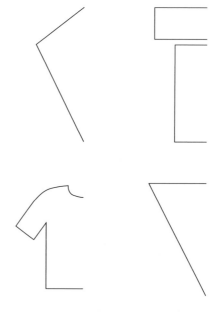

- Pupils should complete Question 4 in the Practice Book.

Question 4

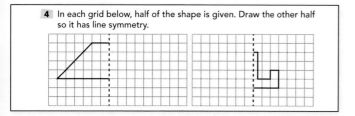

4 In each grid below, half of the shape is given. Draw the other half so it has line symmetry.

What learning will pupils have achieved at the conclusion of Question 4?

- Pupils will be able to explain what line symmetry is.
- Pupils will have identified examples of line symmetry and non-examples of line symmetry.
- Pupils will have broadened their understanding of line symmetry through applying their knowledge to a variety of images in a range of contexts.
- Pupils will be able to generalise about what changes and what stays the same when a shape is reflected in a line of symmetry.

Same-day enrichment

- Pupils should work with a partner and take it in turns to draw one half of an image while their partner draws the congruent image on the other side of the mirror line. Difficulty can be added by positioning the mirror line diagonally across the squared paper. Pupils should use the mirror to check that what they have drawn is correct.

Challenge and extension questions

Questions 5 and 6

5 In the 26 capital letters of the English alphabet, how many of them have line symmetry? Write down those letters that do and draw their lines of symmetry.

6 In each grid below, half of the shape is given. Draw the other half so it has line symmetry.

(a)

(b)

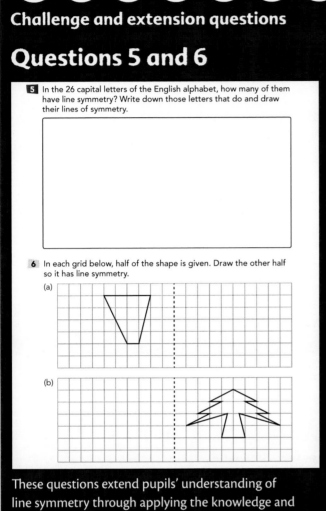

These questions extend pupils' understanding of line symmetry through applying the knowledge and strategies developed in Questions 1–4 to more difficult contexts. Pupils will apply what they have learned about finding line symmetry in numbers and apply this to letters.

Pupils' ability to draw the other half of a shape mirrored in a line of symmetry is extended by positioning the mirror line alongside the shape rather than bisecting the shape itself. This deepens pupils' understanding of symmetry so that they understand that the two parts are congruent even if they form two shapes rather than two halves of one shape.

Unit 8.7
Classification of triangles (3)

Conceptual context

So far, when classifying triangles, pupils have focused on the size of angles at the vertices of the triangles. This unit develops pupils' knowledge about triangles by also considering the length of the sides of the triangle in each case in order to be able to name it as equilateral, isosceles or scalene. Pupils will also connect knowledge about triangles with another aspect of mathematics; lines of symmetry. Revisiting aspects of mathematics that pupils have explored through extensive first-hand experience of them provides opportunities to develop fluency in describing shapes and automaticity in discriminating different types of triangles, according to their properties.

Learning pupils will have achieved at the end of the unit

- Pupils will have deepened their understanding of triangles to recognise how different types of angles and lengths of sides are combined to form equilateral, isosceles and scalene triangles (Q1, Q2, Q3, Q4)
- Pupils will be able to talk fluently about triangles, using appropriate vocabulary (Q1, Q2, Q3)
- Pupils will have extended their knowledge of the properties of triangles to include lines of symmetry (Q1, Q2, Q3)
- Pupils will have begun to recognise triangles in a range of contexts and orientations (Q2, Q3)

Resources

geoboards and elastic bands; mirrors; squared paper; straws cut to different lengths; string; **Resource 4.8.7a** Descriptions of triangles to create; **Resource 4.8.4b** Triangles to sort (from Unit 8.4); **Resource 4.8.7b** Triangles in the real world; mini whiteboards; **Resource 4.8.7c** Identifying triangles within another shape

Vocabulary

equilateral, isosceles, scalene, symmetry, triangle

Questions 1 and 2

1 Fill in the answers.

(a) A triangle with two equal sides is called

an _____ triangle.

(b) A triangle with three equal sides is called

an _____ triangle.

(c) An isosceles triangle has line _____ .

It has [ ] line(s) of symmetry.

(d) An equilateral triangle has line _____ .

It has [ ] line(s) of symmetry.

(e) An equilateral triangle is a _____ isosceles
triangle.

(f) When classified according to its angles, an equilateral triangle

is an _____ triangle.

2 Look at the triangles below and fill in the boxes with the numbers
of the triangles.

(a) The equilateral triangles are [_____] .

(b) The isosceles triangles are [_____] .

(c) The scalene triangles are [_____] .

What learning will pupils have achieved at the conclusion of Questions 1 and 2?

- Pupils will have deepened their understanding of triangles to recognise how different types of angles and lengths of sides combined to form equilateral, isosceles and scalene triangles.

- Pupils will be able to talk fluently about triangles, using appropriate vocabulary.

- Pupils will have extended their knowledge of the properties of triangles to include lines of symmetry.

Activities for whole-class instruction

- To revisit their knowledge of triangles, pupils should work in pairs to take it in turns to use elastic bands to create triangles on pegboards to match the instructions in **Resource 4.8.7a** Descriptions of triangles to create, and check that each triangle has been created correctly.

Resource 4.8.7a

Descriptions of triangles to create

Create a triangle with 3 sides of equal length.	Create a triangle with 2 equal angles but no right angles.
Create a triangle with 1 right angle and 2 equal acute angles.	Create a triangle with sides of different lengths.
Create a triangle with 3 equal angles.	Create a triangle with angles of different sizes.

© HarperCollinsPublishers 2018   179

- Ask: *What do you notice about the length of the sides of the acute-angled triangle?* Pupils should know that the sides are the same length. tell them this is called an equilateral triangle – 'equi' meaning same and 'lateral' meaning sides.

- Tell pupils that in mathematics, we divide triangles into three main groups:
  - equilateral triangles
  - isosceles triangles
  - scalene triangles.

- Point out that they already know what equilateral triangles are – they have three equal sides and three equal angles.

- Ask pupils to consider the triangles they made that had two equal sides. Tell them these are called isosceles triangles. Ask: *What can you tell me about the angles in isosceles triangles?* For each statement that pupils make, they should give you an example where possible. They should found that:
  - two angles are equal
  - there may or may not be a right angle – therefore, some isosceles triangles are right-angled triangles
  - the two equal angles can never be obtuse
  - the two equal angles might be acute
  - there may or may not be one obtuse angle – therefore, some isosceles triangles are obtuse-angled triangles.

- Ask: *What do you think scalene triangles are?* Discuss ideas. Guide pupils to agree that these are triangles that have three different length sides and three different angles.

- Returning to the pegboards, pupils should use another elastic band and a mirror to identify how many lines of symmetry each triangle has.

- Pupils should then be able to complete the following statements:
  - An equilateral triangle has ... lines of symmetry.
  - An isosceles triangle has ... lines of symmetry.
  - A scalene triangle has ... lines of symmetry.
- Ask pupils to complete Questions 1 and 2 in the Practice Book.

Same-day intervention

- Use the triangles from **Resource 4.8.4b** Triangles to sort (from Unit 8.4).

- Pupils should first name each triangle and describe its properties. Using a mirror, pupils should find out whether each triangle has a line of symmetry. They should draw the line of symmetry on the shape and ask a friend to use a mirror to check whether or not their lines are correctly positioned.

Same-day enrichment

- Pupils can expand their experience of triangles as 2-D shapes and identify them in the real world. Using the images of triangular prisms in **Resource 4.8.7b** Triangles in the real world, pupils should identify and name any triangles that form part of the prism and name the other 2-D shapes that form the other faces of the shape.

- Pupils should list and sketch any triangles that can be found in the classroom.

Question 3

> **3** Draw an isosceles triangle and an equilateral triangle and their lines of symmetry on the grid below.

What learning will pupils have achieved at the conclusion of Question 3?

- Pupils will be able to talk fluently about triangles, using appropriate vocabulary.
- Pupils will have extended their knowledge of the properties of triangles to include lines of symmetry.
- Pupils will have begun to recognise triangles in a range of contexts and orientations.

Activities for whole-class instruction

- Display the images of the triangles as shown below. Ask the pupils: *What type of triangle could be behind the wall? Are there any types of triangles that it cannot be?*

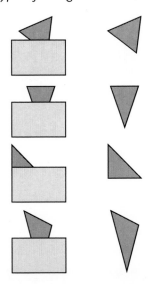

- Once students have justified their suggestions about the type of triangle each one is, they should use their whiteboards and pens to sketch the triangle and suggest how many lines of symmetry it has. Their sketches should be compared to the images of the triangles that have been hidden and pupils be encouraged to use what they know about triangles to explain how many lines of symmetry each triangle has.
- Ask pupils to complete Question 3 in the Practice Book.

Same-day intervention

- Pupils should revisit making triangles out of cut length of straws to reinforce their understanding of the structure of equilateral, isosceles and scalene triangles. Once they have made one of each type of triangle pupils should use a mirror to identify any lines of symmetry. They should draw the triangles they have made and the lines of symmetry they have found onto squared or dotty paper.

Same-day enrichment

- Using **Resource 4.8.7c** Identifying triangles within another shape, pupils should identify as many triangles as they can within the shape. Multiple copies of the shape are provided so that pupils can shade different combinations of small triangles to make larger triangles on each shape. These can be formed through combining triangles to form new ones as well as through counting the separate triangles they can see.

- Once all of the triangles have been identified and named pupils should draw on their lines of symmetry using the facts they know about triangles to explain why some triangles have three, one or no lines of symmetry.

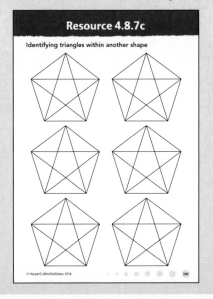

Challenge and extension questions

Questions 4 and 5

4 (a) Divide an equilateral triangle into three triangles of the same shape and the same size.
(b) Divide an equilateral triangle into four triangles of the same shape and the same size.

(a)   (b)

5 Fill in the boxes.
(a) In the figure below, there are ☐ isosceles triangles, and there are ☐ equilateral triangles.

(b) In the figure below, there are ☐ isosceles triangles.

The challenge and extension questions apply and extend pupils' understanding of how triangles can be combined to create shapes and how shapes can be split into triangles. The questions also require pupils to draw accurately and to persevere with the problem until a solution is found.

Unit 8.8
Areas

Conceptual context

Pupils learned about perimeter in Book 3. Here they will learn about area. Although it has not yet been formally taught, pupils will have some informal understanding of area from their real-life experience. Pupils will learn that area is the amount of space covered by a two-dimensional object. In this first unit, pupils will be finding areas by counting squares and half squares and embed the concept that area is measured in square units

Pupils' sound knowledge of arrays will support them to perceive the connection between arrays and area and prepare them to calculate the area of rectilinear shapes that is introduced in the next unit.

Learning pupils will have achieved at the end of the unit

- The concept of area will be understood as the amount of space covered by a two-dimensional object (Q1)
- Pupils will know that area is measured in square units (as a number of squares) and be able to count squares on squared paper to respond to 'How many squares are occupied?' (Q1, Q2)
- Pupils will have found the area of 2-D objects by counting squares and half squares (Q3)

Resources

squared paper; counters; 2-D shapes

Vocabulary

area, perimeter, array, fraction, polyhedra (such as cubes, pyramids), compound shape

Question 1

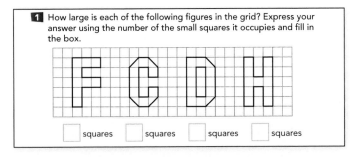

1 How large is each of the following figures in the grid? Express your answer using the number of the small squares it occupies and fill in the box.

☐ squares   ☐ squares   ☐ squares   ☐ squares

What learning will pupils have achieved at the conclusion of Question 1?

- Pupils will have been introduced to area as the amount of space covered by a two-dimensional object.
- Pupils will have found the area of shapes by counting squares.

Activities for whole-class instruction

- Ask pupils what they think the word 'area' means. Agree that area is the size of a surface or the amount of space covered by a two-dimensional object, such as a square, floor or table top. It can also be a vertical surface, like a wall. Ensure pupils understand that the greater the surface, the greater the area. Can they remember that the boundary of an area is called the perimeter? They learned about this in Book 3.

 The area is the amount of space covered by a two-dimensional object.

- Ask pupils to run their hand over the cover of their Practice Book.

 This is the area of the cover of my Practice Book.

- Pupils repeat this for other surfaces, such as the surface of the seat of their chair or their table.
- Link this to the faces of different polyhedra. Give pupils different shapes and ask them to run their fingers over the faces of these. They then draw around them and write inside the 2-D shape. For example 'This is the area of the square face of my cube.'
- Next, make the link to fractions. Display or draw this shape on the board:

- Shade one square. Ask pupils what area of the rectangle has been shaded. Expect them to use their knowledge of fractions and tell you that one half of the area is shaded. Explain that fractions of shapes are parts or areas of a whole shape.

 One half of the area of this shape is shaded.

- Give pupils a sheet of squared paper. Ask them to draw a 4 × 4 square. Ask them to suggest how they could find the area of the square. Agree that they could count the squares.
- Some pupils might link this grid to array work from multiplication and division from previous years and multiply. Agree that the area is 16 squares. Repeat this for other rectangles. Next, ask them to draw a triangle that covers whole and half squares, for example:

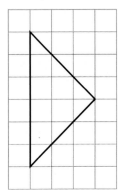

- Discuss how they could find the area of the triangle. Agree that they could count the whole squares and then add the half squares. In this example the area would be 9 squares. Repeat this for other shapes. If they choose shapes that cover parts of a square other than half, encourage them to make a sensible estimate. For example display the following:

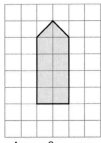   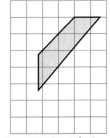

Area = 9 squares   Area is approximately 6 squares

9 squares > 6 squares, so shape 1 has greater area than shape 2.

Look out for ... pupils who do not recognise that squares can be halved in different ways: [figure]. This unit is about area not fractions, but it is worth making the link between the two. Pupils sometimes develop the misconception that fractions are to do with shape. They might think that if the fractions of the whole are not the same shape then they cannot possibly be the same fraction. It is important that they link fractions to area. For example the four shapes above cannot be quarters because they are different shapes. They are quarters because the areas are the same.

- Ask pupils to complete Question 1 in the Practice Book.

Same-day intervention

- Give pupils different objects and ask them to run their fingers over the areas of their surfaces. They should draw them and write inside the faces, for example 'This is the area of this part of my pencil case.'

Same-day enrichment

- Ask pupils to draw the other letters of the alphabet in a similar way to those in the question and to find the areas of them in squares. Which has the greatest area? Which has the least area?

Question 2

2 The figure below shows the floor plan of Tom's new house.

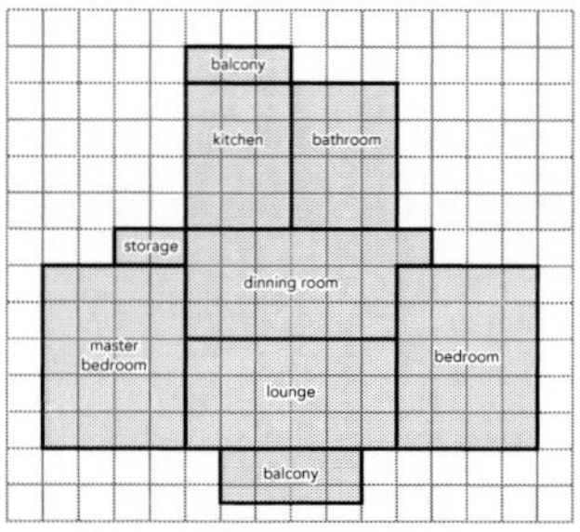

[floor plan diagram with labels: balcony, kitchen, bathroom, storage, dinning room, master bedroom, bedroom, lounge, balcony]

Answer the following questions based on the floor plan.

The master bedroom occupies ☐ squares.

The bedroom occupies ☐ squares.

The lounge occupies ☐ squares.

The dining room occupies ☐ squares.

The kitchen occupies ☐ squares.

The bathroom occupies ☐ squares.

The storage room occupies ☐ squares.

The house occupies ☐ squares in total.

What learning will pupils have achieved at the conclusion of Question 2?

- Pupils will have explored the concept of area.
- Pupils will have found the area of shapes by counting squares.

Activities for whole-class instruction

- Recap the meaning of the word area. Agree that area is the size of a surface or the amount of space covered by a two-dimensional object.

- Draw or display this shape on the board:

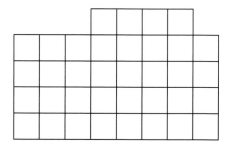

- Explain that your shape represents the floor plan of a flat. What do pupils think a floor plan is? Establish that it shows the layout of, in this case, the floor of a flat. The first four squares at the top represent a balcony and the other squares represent the rest of the flat. Tell pupils that eight squares represent the bedroom. Invite a pupil to shade eight possible squares to show the bedroom. Tell pupils that another eight squares represent the kitchen. Invite another pupil to shade another eight squares to show the kitchen. Inform them that four squares represent the bathroom. Invite a third pupil to shade four squares to show the bathroom. Tell pupils that the rest of the space represents the rest of the living area. Ask the class to look at the way that the plan has been divided up.

- Ask: Is this a good layout for a flat? Ask pupils to tell you the areas of all the rooms in the flat by counting the squares. So, for example, the living area is 12 squares.

- Give pairs of pupils a piece of squared paper and ask them to draw a floor plan for a flat. They can choose the number of squares for each of the rooms in their flat. They shade the bedroom, kitchen and bathroom and then write down the area of each room and the remaining living space. What is the total floor area of their flat?

- Ask pupils to complete Question 2 in the Practice Book.

Same-day intervention

- Pupils should work in groups of 2–4. Give each group 40 square pieces of paper, around 2 cm by 2 cm. They arrange these to make a floor plan of a flat. They identify the different rooms and write down their areas as a number of squares.

Same-day enrichment

- Tell pupils that the total floor area of a flat is 80 squares. Challenge them to draw three different layouts:
  - one with a large kitchen and one bedroom
  - one with two bedrooms
  - one with three bedrooms.
- Pupils should list the area of each room for each layout.

Question 3

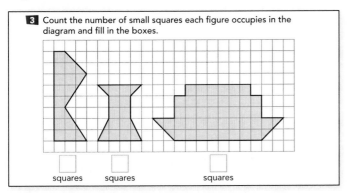

3 Count the number of small squares each figure occupies in the diagram and fill in the boxes.

squares   squares   squares

What learning will pupils have achieved at the conclusion of Question 3?

- Pupils will have consolidated their understanding of finding areas of shapes by counting squares.

Activities for whole-class instruction

- Recap the meaning of 'area'. Ensure that pupils know that an area is the amount of space covered by a two-dimensional object. Draw a circle on the board and invite a pupil to shade its area.

Area is the amount of space covered by a two-dimensional object.

- Give each pupil a piece of squared paper. Ask them to draw a 10 × 10 square onto it.

- Ask: *How could you find the area of the square?* Agree that they could count the squares.
- Do they recognise that the small squares are arranged as an array? Ask them to remind you how multiplication and division can be seen in arrays. They could use the same idea for areas of squares and rectangles and multiply the number in each row by the number of rows.
- Ask pupils to draw their own squares and rectangles and find their areas. Give them an area, for example 24, and one length, for example 8. Can they work out the other length using division? Making connections and reasoning about concepts is important.
- Give each pupil a piece of squared paper and ask them to draw a rectilinear compound shape. Explain that a rectilinear compound shape is a shape made up of two or more rectangles. Pupils should then find its area by counting the squares. Encourage them to count the squares in the quickest way that they can using multiplication, if appropriate. For example:

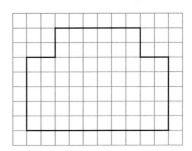

- After practising this, ask pupils to draw rectilinear compound shapes to give to a partner who must find the area by counting the squares in an efficient way.
- Ask pupils to complete Question 3 in the Practice Book.

Same-day intervention

- Give pupils squared paper. Ask them to draw small squares and other rectangles, using the squares on the paper. They find the areas of these shapes by multiplying the number of rows by the number of columns.

Same-day enrichment

- Ask pupils to make up different floor plans similar to the one in Question 3 of the Practice Book and give these to a partner who then finds the area of the different rooms.

Challenge and extension questions

Question 4

4   Draw three 2-D shapes that occupy 7 squares, 9 squares and 12 squares, respectively, on the grid below.

This question asks pupils to draw any 2-D shapes in the grid to show particular areas in squares. These shapes could be made of whole squares and half squares. Encourage pupils to be creative.

Question 5

5   Count and then write the number of squares that each figure occupies in the following grids.

      squares   squares

This question asks pupils to find the areas in squares of two shapes that include parts of squares that are not halves. Encourage them to reason about how to put the parts together to make whole squares.

Unit 8.9
Areas of rectangles and squares (1)

Conceptual context

Pupils' new concept of area is varied incrementally so that they learn the formula for finding area with deep understanding that enables them to solve problems. Having learned that area is measured in square units, pupils now learn that the squares that are used to measure area can be of any size. They will focus on squares that measure 1 cm along each side and understand that each of these is called 1 square centimetre.

Multiplicative knowledge used to calculate products using arrays is used and linked with finding areas of squares and rectangles as pupils explore how length × width = area, and solve word problems.

Learning pupils will have achieved at the end of the unit

- Pupils will be able to count and calculate the area of a given square or rectangle in cm² (Q1)
- Pupils will know how to refer to square centimetres – as 'square centimetres' or 'cm²' – and will understand why they are so-called (Q1)
- Pupils will know that, to find the area of a square or rectangle, they should multiply length × width (Q2)
- Pupils will have solved problems involving finding areas of rectangles, including squares (Q3, Q4, Q5)

Resources

squares and rectangles cut from centimetre squared paper; envelopes; squared paper; plain paper; cuboids and cubes; rulers; scissors

Vocabulary

square centimetres, cm²

Question 1

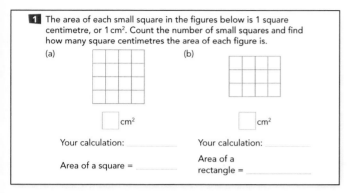

1 The area of each small square in the figures below is 1 square centimetre, or 1 cm². Count the number of small squares and find how many square centimetres the area of each figure is.

(a)

(b)

☐ cm²

☐ cm²

Your calculation: _____

Your calculation: _____

Area of a square = _____

Area of a rectangle = _____

What learning will pupils have achieved at the conclusion of Question 1?

- Pupils will be able to count and calculate the area of a given square or rectangle in cm².

- Pupils will know how to refer to square centimetres – as square centimetres or cm² – and will understand why they are so-called.

Activities for whole-class instruction

- Cut out a variety of rectangles and squares from 1 cm squared paper, put them in envelopes and give them to pairs of pupils. They take each one at a time and count the squares to find the area and write the area onto the appropriate shapes.

- Ask them to measure the sides of each small square. Agree that each one has sides 1 cm long. Ask pupils what they think these are called. Establish that they are 'square centimetres'. Explain that we abbreviate square centimetre to cm² and this is one of the units used to measure area.

- Ask pupils to write cm² beside the area measurements that they wrote on their shapes (so each number now has cm² next to it). Ask them to sort the shapes in whatever way they wish.

- Encourage them to do this in two or three different ways. How did they sort them? Did any sort into squares and irregular rectangles? They might have chosen to sort them according to their size, for example greater than 20 cm², less than 20 cm² or into those with the same areas or lengths.

- Discuss whether they needed to count to find the total number of squares. Expect some pupils to realise that they can use their knowledge of multiplication and arrays. They should be able to tell you that they can multiply the number of squares in each row by the number of rows. Discuss the generalisation that can be made for finding

the area of rectangles: agree that area can be found by multiplying length by width.

- Give pupils an area, for example 24 cm². Ask them to work out what the lengths of the sides could be using their multiplication facts and knowledge of factors, for example 2 cm and 12 cm, 3 cm and 8 cm.

- They then draw a rectangle on squared paper. They can count the sides of the squares for the lengths and widths. They label the sides and the area. How many different rectangles can they draw with the same area? What do they notice? Expect them to be able to tell you that shapes can have the same area but different perimeters.

Look out for ... pupils who continue to count squares individually. Encourage them to use repeated addition if they are not confident enough to multiply.

- Ask pupils to complete Question 1 in the Practice Book.

Same-day intervention

- Give pupils a list of measurements, for example 3 cm by 4 cm, 5 cm by 2 cm. They draw rectangles by counting the sides of the squares, for example 3 squares by 4 squares. They then multiply 3 × 4 or 4 × 3 and label the area inside their rectangle (with units).

Same-day enrichment

- Give pupils squared paper. Ask them to draw their own squares and rectangles and to find their areas using the generalisation. Encourage them to write, for example $w \times l = a$ as well as in numbers so that they can consolidate the generalisation.

Question 2

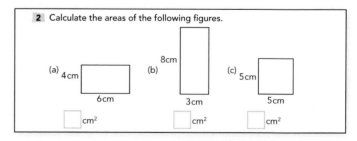

2 Calculate the areas of the following figures.

(a) 4 cm ... 6 cm ... ☐ cm²

(b) 8 cm ... 3 cm ... ☐ cm²

(c) 5 cm ... 5 cm ... ☐ cm²

What learning will pupils have achieved at the conclusion of Question 2?

- Pupils will have begun to develop the generalisation for finding the areas of rectangles, by multiplying their lengths by their widths.

Activities for whole-class instruction

- The aim at the end of these activities is for all pupils to be able to confidently find the areas of rectangles, including squares, using the formula without having squares drawn. To prepare pupils for this, they might need further opportunities to find areas on centimetre squared paper before carrying out the first activity below. If so, ask pupils to draw their own rectangles, label their lengths and widths and then find areas in the most efficient way that they can (multiplying the number of squares in each row by the number of rows).

- Give pupils a cube, a cuboid and plain paper. Ask them to draw around one of the faces of the cube. They measure the length to the nearest centimetre. They label the length and width with the measurement. Ask: *How can you find the area of the square?* Agree that they could multiply the length by the width. They do this and write the area inside the square. Ask: *What must we write to show this is area?* Ensure they write cm² after the number.

- Ask pupils to draw around a rectangular face (that is not a square) of their cuboid. They measure the length and width of the rectangle to the nearest centimetre and label them. Ask: *Can you multiply the length by the width to find the area?* Agree that they can. They do this and label the area. If there are any pupils that need to use centimetre squared paper to support them, provide this.

- Ask pupils to use a ruler and to carefully draw their own rectangles. These should be whole centimetre lengths and widths. They give these to a partner who measures and labels the lengths and widths and works out the areas.

- Discuss the generalisation for finding the area of rectangles, including squares. Ensure that pupils understand that they can multiply the length by the width, so the formula would be *l* × *w*. Give pupils different lengths and widths of rectangles and ask them to find the areas, for example length is 10 cm, width is 15 cm, area equals 10 × 15, which is 150 cm².

- Ask pupils to complete Question 2 in the Practice Book.

Same-day intervention

- Give pupils rectangles, including squares that have been pre-drawn to whole centimetres. They measure the length and width and then find the area. They could repeatedly add the lengths or widths the appropriate number of times if they are not confident with multiplying so that they consolidate the conceptual connection.

Same-day enrichment

- Ask pupils to draw rectangles with lengths of a whole number of centimetres and widths in centimetres and millimetres. Encourage them to multiply the width by the length to find the area.

Questions 3, 4 and 5

> **3** The length of a rectangle is 45 cm. It is 5 times the width. What is its area?
>
> Answer: ....
>
> **4** The length of a rectangle is 40 cm. It is 10 cm longer than the width. What is its area?
>
> Answer: ....
>
> **5** One side of the screen of a tablet computer measures 20 cm and the other side is 15 cm. What is the area of the screen?
>
> Answer: ....

What learning will pupils have achieved at the conclusion of Questions 3, 4 and 5?

- Pupils will have solved problems involving finding areas of rectangles, including squares.

Activities for whole-class instruction

- Recap how to find the area of rectangles, including squares. Can pupils tell you that they multiply the length by the width or vice versa? Ask them to tell you the formula for finding area. Expect them to tell you *w* × *l* or *l* × *w*.

- Give the pupils problems such as:
  - The length of one side of a square is 9 cm. What is the area?
  - The width of one side of a rectangle is 3 m. The length is twice the width. What is the area?
  - The length of one side of a rectangle is 8 cm. It is four times the width. What is the area?

- For each problem, discuss the information given and what needs to be done with it to find the unknown information in order to solve the problem. Draw attention to the link with factor × factor = product. For example:
  - The length of one side of a square is 9 cm. What is the area?

  The pupils need to know that a square has sides of equal length, so to find the area they need to calculate 9 × 9 = 81. Because it is area, we are looking at centimetres multiplied by centimetres, so the area is 81 cm².

– The width of one side of a rectangle is 3 cm. The length is twice the width. What is the area?

The pupils need to know that they double the width to give the length of 6 cm. They then multiply 3 cm by 6 cm to give an area of 18 cm².

– The length of one side of a rectangle is 8 cm. It is four times the width. What is the area?

The pupils need to find the width, so they should find a quarter of 8 cm or divide 8 by 4 to give 2 cm. They then multiply 8 cm by 2 cm to give an area of 16 cm².

● Ask similar problems but use increasingly larger numbers.

● Ask pupils to complete Questions 3, 4 and 5 in the Practice Book.

Same-day intervention

● Give pupils squared paper and ask them to solve this problem:

– Sophie drew a square; one side of the square was 3 cm. Draw Sophie's square and find its area.

● Vary the problem by changing the side of Sophie's square to 4 cm, 5 cm and so on.

Same-day enrichment

● Ask pupils to make up their own problems similar to those above for rectangles in centimetres for a partner to solve.

Challenge and extension questions

Question 6

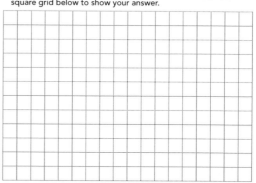

6 Put 12 small squares of 1 cm² together to form a rectangle. How many different rectangles can be formed? Draw them on the square grid below to show your answer.

This question asks pupils to make rectangles that have an area of 12 square centimetres. Ensure they make all the possible whole number rectangles. There are three, but each can be presented in two different ways, for example 1 square by 12 horizontally and 1 square by 12 vertically.

Question 7

7 Yasmin cut out the largest square possible from a rectangular piece of coloured paper. The rectangular piece of paper was 17 cm long and 12 cm wide. What is the area of Yasmin's quare?

Answer: _____

This question asks pupils to find the area of the largest square that can be cut out from a rectangle that is 17 cm by 12 cm. Watch out for the method they use for this calculation. They may partition 17 cm into 10 cm and 7 cm and multiply each by 12 and recombine to give 204 cm². They may multiply 17 cm by 6 using a written method and double. You could find out the pupils' methods and agree on which is the most efficient.

Unit 8.10

Areas of rectangles and squares (2)

Conceptual context

This unit is a continuation of Unit 8.9. Pupils should, by now, have understood and used the generalisation for finding the area of rectangles: length multiplied by width or $l \times w = area$. They continue to work with square centimetres, deepening their understanding. Pupils need to apply their knowledge about area to solving more challenging word problems, including two-step problems.

Learning pupils will have achieved at the end of the unit

- Pupils will have consolidated their understanding that the area of a rectangle is calculated by multiplying its length by its width (Q1)
- Pupils will be able to find an unknown dimension from a given area (Q1, Q4)
- Reasoning is developed, using knowledge about area to solve multi-step problems (Q3, Q4, Q5)

Resources

squared paper; plain paper

Vocabulary

area, square centimetres, cm^2

Question 1

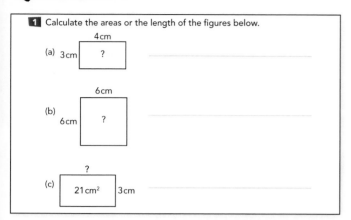

1 Calculate the areas or the length of the figures below.

(a) 3cm [4cm, ?]

(b) 6cm [6cm, ?]

(c) [21cm², ?] 3cm

What learning will pupils have achieved at the conclusion of Question 1?

- Pupils will have consolidated their understanding that the area of a rectangle is calculated by multiplying the length by the width.
- Pupils will be able to find an unknown dimension from a given area.

Activities for whole-class instruction

- Give dimensions of rectangles to pupils, for example length = 21 cm and width = 12 cm. Ask them to draw the rectangles and work out the area. Discuss ways to multiply the two-digit numbers, for example:
  - Partition 21 cm into 20 cm and 1 cm. Then multiply 20 cm by 12 using knowledge that 2 × 12 = 24, therefore 20 cm multiplied by 12 must be 240 cm. Then add 12 cm to give an area of 252 cm².
  - Multiply 21 cm by 6 and then double the result.
- Discuss suggestions from pupils. When they have found the area they should label the length, width and area for each rectangle.
- Ask: *If the area of a rectangle is 16 cm², what is the length of each side? Is there only one possible answer?* Pupils should draw the rectangles and label the length, width and area.
- Ask: *If the area of a rectangle is 21 cm² and the width of the rectangle is 3 cm, what is its length?* Pupils should draw the rectangle and label the length, width and area.
- Ask: *If the area of a rectangle is 36 cm² and the length of the rectangle is 9 cm, what is its width?* Pupils should draw the rectangle and label the length, width and area.
- Ask pupils to complete Question 1 in the Practice Book.

Same-day intervention

- Give pupils the area and length of small rectangles. They work out the width and then draw them. Give pupils squared paper on which to draw them.

Same-day enrichment

- In Chapter 3, pupils learned how to multiply a two-digit number by a two-digit number. Apply this skill to finding areas of larger rectangles. Give each pupil a set of digit cards; they pick pairs and make two two-digit numbers. One number represents the length and the other the width. They draw a rectangular representation, label the length and width, then give to their partner to find the area.

Questions 2 and 3

2 The width of a rectangular table is measured as 90 cm. It is 15 cm shorter than the length. What is the area of the rectangular table?

Answer: _____

3 A rectangular piece of iron sheet is 60 cm long and 50 cm wide. Mr Lee cut off its length by 15 cm and its width by 10 cm. By how many square centimetres has the area of iron sheet decreased? Draw a diagram to help work out the answer.

What learning will pupils have achieved at the conclusion of Questions 2 and 3?

- Pupils will have solved word problems involving finding area in cm².

Activities for whole-class instruction

- Set a variety of problems for the pupils to solve. For example:
  - The width of a large piece of paper is 60 cm. The length is 24 cm greater. What is its area?
- Ask pupils to talk to a partner about how they would solve this problem. Expect them to know that to find the length they add 24 cm to 60 cm. How would they multiply 84 cm by 60 cm? They could multiply 84 cm by 6

and then 10 (or by 10 and then 6, though this would be less efficient). They could use the written column method to do this or they may prefer to use an informal method, such as partition 84 cm into 80 cm and 4 cm, multiply each part and then recombine. Encourage them to try different methods.

- Ask: *What is the area?* Agree that it is 5040 cm². Ask further questions, varying the width of the paper.
  - *The length of the cover of Sophie's book is 30 cm and its width is 20 cm. What is the area of the cover?*
- Ask pupils how they would find the area of Sophie's book. Agree this would be found by multiplying the width by the length. Discuss ways to do this. The most efficient way would be to use multiplication facts. If pupils know that 30 cm multiplied by 2 cm is 60 cm² they should know that 30 cm multiplied by 20 cm is 10 times greater, so 600 cm². Ask further questions, varying either the width or length (not both) of the cover.
- Ask pupils to complete Questions 2 and 3 in the Practice Book.

Same-day intervention

- Collect different objects from around the classroom. Choose one face of each object. Pre-label them with their lengths and widths in centimetres. Ask pupils to calculate their areas.

Same-day enrichment

- Pupils should work in pairs to make up similar problems to those you have asked that involve multiplying multiples of 10, for example 'The television screen measures 90 cm by 60 cm. What is the area of the screen?' They can use diagrams or pictures with their questions. They give these to another pair to solve.

Questions 4 and 5

4 The length of a rectangle is 18 cm. If the length is increased by 5 cm while the width is kept unchanged, the area is increased by 40 cm². Find the area of the original rectangle. Clue: draw a diagram to help.

5 Ellie's father made a photo frame for her. The length of the frame is 22 cm and the width is 16 cm. The width of the inner wooden frame is 3 cm. Find the area of the glass within the wooden frame.

What learning will pupils have achieved at the conclusion of Questions 4 and 5?

- Reasoning is developed, using knowledge about area to solved multi-step problems.

Activities for whole-class instruction

- Ask pupils to tell you all that they now know about area. Expect them to be able to tell you that area is the amount of space covered by a two-dimensional object. Area is measured using squares. So far, the squares used have been square centimetres, which are shown using the abbreviation cm².
- Tell pupils that they will be solving more complex problems. Ask pupils to draw a rectangle on plain paper, measuring 10 cm by 6 cm. They work out the area. (60 cm²) Tell them that the width of the rectangle has been increased by two centimetres. They draw the increased width and work out the new area. (80 cm²) Ask: *How much greater is the area now that the width has been enlarged?* (20 cm²) Repeat the problem with different lengths, for example 12 cm, 15 cm, 25 cm, keeping the width and the increase the same.
- Set a similar problem, but this time with a width decrease. Ask pupils to draw a square with sides of 12 cm. Ask them to calculate the area. (144 cm²) Tell them that two opposite lengths have been decreased by 2 cm. Pupils must show the new shape on their drawing and calculate the new area. (120 cm²) Ask: *How much has the area decreased by?* (24 cm²)
- Draw or display the following image on the board:

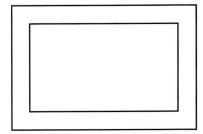

- Tell pupils that it is a postcard made from two rectangles, a smaller one stuck onto a larger one.
- Label the outside rectangle to show length 20 cm and width 15 cm. Pupils should draw and label the postcard showing all dimensions – tell them that the inner rectangle is 15 cm long and 10 cm wide.

- Ask: *What is the area of the border on the card?* Allow time for pupils to discuss strategies with partners. Do they realise they need to find the area of both rectangles and subtract the smaller one from the larger?

- Repeat the problem, varying the lengths and widths of the rectangles. Give them the dimensions of the smaller rectangle, for example 12 cm by 9 cm, and the area of the border, for example 48 cm². Pupils work out the area of the large rectangle ($108\,cm^2 + 48\,cm^2 = 156\,cm^2$) and then its length and width (13 cm and 12 cm).

- Ask pupils to complete Questions 4 and 5 in the Practice Book.

Same-day intervention

- If pupils have difficulty solving multi-step problems, give them problems involving two-steps. For example:

  - Sophie drew a rectangle; its length was 12 cm and its width was 5 cm. Ben drew a rectangle half the area of Sophie's. What was the area of Ben's rectangle?

- Once they have found the solution to this, vary the problem by changing the length of Sophie's rectangle.

Same-day enrichment

- Ask pupils to make up their own multi-step problems based on Question 5 in the Practice Book (Mary's father and the photo frame). They should work out the solutions to test that their problems can be solved and then give them to a partner.

Challenge and extension question

Question 6

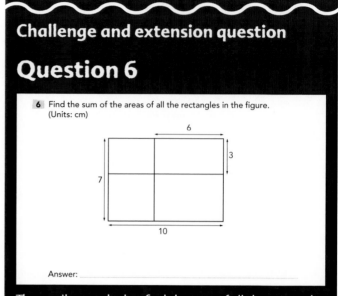

6 Find the sum of the areas of all the rectangles in the figure. (Units: cm)

Answer: _____

The pupils are asked to find the sum of all the rectangles in the figure drawn. There are four obvious rectangles, but several less obvious. They need to find the areas of all the rectangles. The two rectangles at the top can be put together to make one rectangle and the two rectangles on the left can be put together to make another rectangle. When approaching this question, ensure pupils understand that they need to find all the possible rectangles. There are nine altogether.

Unit 8.11
Square metres

Conceptual context

Pupils have learned about measuring area in square centimetres. They know that the area of something is the amount of space covered by a two-dimensional object. In this unit, pupils learn that the squares that are used to measure area are not always squares with 1 cm sides – that they can be squares with sides of any length. They will experience measuring area using squares with one metre sides, that is, square metres (m^2). Pupils will learn that small areas are measured in square centimetres and larger areas can be measured in square metres.

Learning pupils will have achieved at the end of the unit

- Pupils will have consolidated their understanding that area is measured in square units (Q1)
- Pupils will have explored different-sized square units for measuring area, including square metres (Q2)
- Pupils will have calculated area using square metres (Q3)
- Pupils will have applied their understanding of area to solve single- and two-step problems (Q4, Q5, Q6)

Resources

metre sticks; tape measures; plain paper; squared paper; **Resource 4.8.11a** Apartment floor plan

Vocabulary

area, perimeter, square centimetre, cm^2, square metre, m^2

Questions 1 and 2

> **1** Fill in the spaces.
>
> (a) The area of a square with sides of length 1 m is _____,
>
> written as _____ .
>
> (b) The area of a square with sides of length 1 cm is _____,
>
> written as _____ .
>
> **2** Fill in the boxes with suitable units.
>
> (a) The area of a square table in Asif's home is about 1 ☐ .
>
> (b) The area of a stamp is about 12 ☐ .
>
> (c) The area of a classroom is about 48 ☐ .
>
> (d) The area of a pencil box is about 86 ☐ .
>
> (e) The length of the running track in the school sports field
>
> is about 200 ☐ .
>
> (f) The area of the little finger nail is about 1 ☐ .
>
> (g) The area of Poppy's new house is about 132 ☐ .
>
> (h) The area of a whiteboard in a classroom is about 3 ☐ .

What learning will pupils have achieved at the conclusion of Questions 1 and 2?

- Pupils will have explored different-sized square units for measuring area, including square metres.
- Pupils will have explored the appropriate units for measuring area.

Activities for whole-class instruction

- Ask: *What units do we use to measure area?* Agree square centimetres.
- Ask: *Are there any other units that we could use?* Expect pupils to tell you metres. Ask: *What would the abbreviations look like for this unit?* Agree m².
- Discuss the sizes of these areas with examples, for example the area of the classroom floor would be measured in square metres. Ask pupils to think of other examples. You could make a list on the board.

 All say ...   *We can measure area in square centimetres and square metres.*

- Ask pupils to work with a partner and to create a table headed with the two units. Pairs think of examples to put in each section, for example:

cm²	m²
seat of a chair	wall of the classroom
cover of a book	carpet

- Give them a few minutes to think of their ideas. They could look at books with pictures in for ideas or use items in the classroom.
- Ask pupils to help you to use four metre sticks to demonstrate what a square metre looks like. This will help them visualise just how big it is. Agree that each side of the square is one metre long. Discuss the fact that centimetres would not be an efficient way to measure something of this size and larger.
- You could ask pupils to work out the area of the metre square in square centimetres to illustrate this: sides of 100 cm would give an area of 10 000 cm. So, much larger areas would be many thousands of square centimetres.
- Show the pictures of the items that are measured in metres. Explain that the pictures have been scaled down and that in real life, for example the field would be many metres in length and width, and so measuring the areas of these in centimetres would be inefficient because the numbers being used would be huge and mistakes would be likely. For example if the field was 50 m by 40 m, the area would be 2000 m², which is equivalent to 20 000 000 cm².
- Explain to pupils that this is 20 million – a huge number that is far too big for us to work with so it makes sense to use larger units of measurement that mean we can work with more manageable numbers.
- Ask pupils to look at the square metres made by the metre sticks. Ask them to identify items that have a surface that covers less than a square metre and those surfaces that they think would be greater than a square metre. They could draw a table, for example:

< 1 m²	> 1 m²
surface of front cover of book	whiteboard surface
surface of side of pencil case	top surface of teacher's desk

- How many different items did the class find? Test some of their suggestions.
- Ask pupils to work in groups and, using metre sticks and tape measures, measure the surface of different items in the classroom, hall and playground that have dimensions that are greater than 1 m. They do this to the nearest whole metre and then find their areas. They draw these as representational rectangles on plain paper. Label their widths and lengths and write the area in the middle.
- Ask pupils to complete Questions 1 and 2 in the Practice Book.

Same-day intervention

- Make a list of items with areas that are measured in square centimetres and square metres. These can be a mixture of classroom items and everyday items found at home. Pupils work with a partner to discuss each one and together write cm² or m² as they think appropriate.

Same-day enrichment

- Give pupils a copy of **Resource 4.8.11a** Apartment floor plan

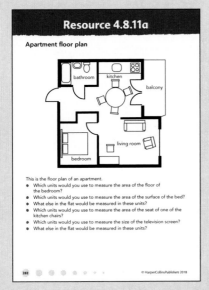

- Pupils should answer questions about appropriate units, cm² or m², for measuring areas in an apartment.

  Answers: m² for the bedroom floor area and the bed; other rooms or large items such as the table would be measured in m²; cm² for the seat of a kitchen chair or for the television; other smaller items such as a pillow or the bathroom basin would be measured in cm².

Question 3

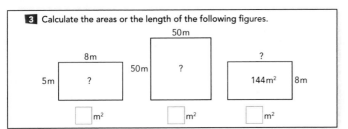

What learning will pupils have achieved at the conclusion of Question 3?

- Pupils will have extended what they know about cm² to be able to calculate area in m².

Activities for whole-class instruction

- Draw a rectangle on the board and label the length 12 m and the width 5 m. Ask pupils how they would work out the area of the rectangle. Establish that the process for finding the area of rectangles, including squares, is the same no matter what unit is used. If your rectangle was in centimetres the area would be $l \times w$, which is 12 cm × 5 cm, which equals 60 cm². The generalisation is the same when measuring in metres. So the area of the rectangle you drew would be 12 m × 5 m = 60 m².

- Give pupils a list of metre dimensions for rectangles, for example 6 m by 4 m, 15 m by 10 m. Tell them that these are too large to draw, so they can scale these down by using 1 cm to represent each metre. On the drawing, pupils should label the sides, using dimensions in metres and then work out their areas.

- Ask pupils to draw rectangles measured with whole centimetre lengths and widths. They give these to a partner who measures the sides, and labels the lengths and widths using metre units. They then work out their areas.

- Ask pupils to complete Question 3 in the Practice Book.

Same-day intervention

- Give pupils a list of lengths and widths in metres. Keep the numbers below 10. They choose one of each and draw a representation of the rectangle with those dimensions using centimetres. They then find the area of each.

Same-day enrichment

- Give pupils an area and one dimension as in Question 3 in the Practice Book, for example area 24 m² and width 4 m, area 36 m² and length 12 m. They work out the missing dimension and draw the appropriate rectangle using centimetre units, labelling the dimensions and the area.

Questions 4, 5 and 6

> **4** The village fishpond is 60 m long and 40 m wide. What is the area of the fishpond?
>
>
>
> **5** Ella bought a square mouse pad. Its side length is 20 cm. What is its area?
>
>
>
> **6** The length of a wheat field is 100 metres, which is four times the width. If 2 kilograms of wheat can be harvested from 1 square metre of the land, how many kilograms of wheat can be harvested from this piece of wheat field?

What learning will pupils have achieved at the conclusion of Questions 4, 5 and 6?

- Pupils will have applied their understanding of area to solve single- and two-step problems.

Activities for whole-class instruction

- Set this problem:
  - The lawn in Jake's garden has a width of 15 metres and a length of 25 metres. He wants to sow new grass seed and needs to know the area of the lawn. Can you work that out for him?
- Pupils should draw Jake's garden and label the dimensions. Agree that, to calculate the area, they should multiply length × width.
- Discuss strategies for multiplying 15 m by 25 m. Agree that an efficient method for multiplying by 15 is to partition 15 m into 10 m and 5 m, then multiply both by 25 and add

the products together. Remind pupils that multiplying by 10 is easy and multiplying by 5 is related (can they tell you how?), so this is an efficient method.

- 25 m × 10 = 250 m, then halve that to find 25 × 5 (125 m); add the two products together = 375 m²

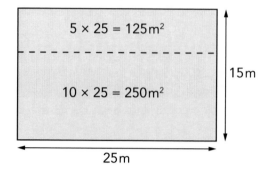

- Ask the problem several times, varying the length of the lawn.
- Set this problem:
  - Jenny's aunt has a small square rug. One side measures 60 cm. What is its area?
- Pupils should draw a representation, remembering that all sides must be the same length because it is a square, and find the area.
- Discuss strategies for multiplying 60 cm by 60 cm. Using multiplication facts would be an obvious one. If they know that 6 × 6 = 36, then they know that 60 × 6 = 360 and 60 × 60 = 3600, so the area of the rug is 3600 cm².
- Ask similar problems but vary the length of the rug.
- Set this problem:
  - The length of a field is 100 m. This is twice the width. What is the area of the field?
- Discuss how to find the width and the area. Establish that to find the width they halve 100 m. 100 m × 50 m = 5000 m².
- Ask similar problems, varying the length of the field.
- Ask pupils to complete Questions 4, 5 and 6 in the Practice Book.

Same-day intervention

- Give pupils problems that involve using multiplication facts to find areas. For example:
  - Sam's fishpond is 20 m in length and 9 m wide. What is its area?
- Pupils use 2 × 9 and then make 18 ten times bigger.
- Use the same problem but vary the length of the fishpond to other multiples of 10.

Same-day enrichment

- Ask pupils to make up problems similar to Question 6 in the Practice Book for a partner to solve. Initially, these could be a variation of the one in the book.

Challenge and extension questions

Questions 7 and 8

7 The side of a square flowerbed is 20 m long. Its four sides are surrounded with 2 m width of grass. Find the area of the grass.

Answer: _____

8 The length of the straight running track in a school sports field is 80 m, and the width of the track is evenly divided into five lanes, each of which is 80 cm wide. What is the total area of all five lanes?

Answer: _____

Questions 7 and 8 are more complex problems. Question 7 involves pupils finding the area of a flowerbed and then the area of the flowerbed and its grass surround. They then subtract the flowerbed from the whole to find the area of the grass surround. They were asked a question similar to this about a picture frame in Unit 8.10. Question 8 involves a mixture of metres and centimetres.

Chapter 8 test (Practice Book 4B, pages 56–62)

Test question number	Relevant unit	Relevant questions within unit
1	8.1	1, 2, 3, 4, 5
2	8.2	1
	8.3	1, 4
	8.4	1
3	8.4	1, 2
4	8.2	3
	8.4	5
5	8.5	1, 2
6	8.4	5
7a, b, c	8.11	1, 2, 8
7d	8.4	1, 2
8	8.4	1
9a	8.5	1, 2
9b	8.11	no relevant question for 9b
9c	8.9	2
	8.10	1
10a	8.5	1, 2
10b	8.11	5
10c	8.7	1
11	8.9	2
	8.10	1
12	8.7	3
13	8.8	1, 3, 5
14a	8.10	2
14b	8.11	6
14c	8.10	5
14d	8.10	4

Chapter 9
Geometry and measurement (II)

Chapter overview

Area of mathematics	National Curriculum Statutory requirements for Key Stage 2	Shanghai Maths Project reference
Geometry	Year 4 Programme of study: Pupils should be taught to: ■ describe positions on a 2-D grid as coordinates in the first quadrant.	Year 4, Unit 9.5
Measurement	Year 4 Programme of study: Pupils should be taught to: ■ Convert between different units of measure [for example, kilometre to metre; hour to minute]	Year 4, Units 9.1, 9.6:
	■ measure and calculate the perimeter of a rectilinear figure (including squares) in centimetres and metres	Year 4, Units 9.2, 9.3, 9.4
	■ find the area of rectilinear shapes by counting squares	Year 4, Units 9.2, 9.3, 9.4
	■ estimate, compare and calculate different measures, including money in pounds and pence	Year 4, Units 9.6, 9.7
	■ read, write and convert time between analogue and digital 12- and 24-hour clocks	Year 4, Unit 9.6
	■ solve problems involving converting from hours to minutes; minutes to seconds; years to months; weeks to days.	Year 4, Unit 9.6
	Year 5 Programme of study: Pupils should be taught to: ■ calculate and compare the area of rectangles (including squares), and including using standard units, square centimetres (cm^2) and square metres (m^2) and estimate the area of irregular shapes.	Year 4, Units 9.2, 9.3, 9.4

Unit 9.1
Converting between kilometres and metres

Conceptual context

In Book 3, pupils measured and compared lengths using metres, centimetres and millimetres. They converted between centimetres and millimetres and between metres and centimetres, so they should have mastered the fact that 10 millimetres is equivalent to 1 centimetre and 100 centimetres is equivalent to 1 metre. They looked at converting between measurements. In Book 4 the focus is on converting between kilometres and metres. Kilometres are used to measure distance. In the UK we use miles to measure distance, so pupils may not be familiar with this unit. To help them make sense of kilometres, it is helpful if pupils know that one kilometre is just over half a mile.

Learning pupils will have achieved at the end of the unit

- Pupils' concepts of length and distance will have expanded to include kilometres as they
  - convert kilometres to metres and vice versa (Q1), and
  - explore suitable units to measure the length of different objects and spaces (Q2)
- Pupils will have developed their understanding of fractions and decimal fractions in order to apply them to kilometre distances (Q1)
- Pupils will have applied their understanding of addition and subtraction to the measurement of distance (Q1)
- Pupils will have applied their understanding of addition and subtraction in the context of the measurement of distance (Q2)
- Pupils will have considered what distance can be covered in various ways in different periods of time (Q2)
- Pupils will have consolidated comparing and ordering different kilometre and metre lengths (Q3, Q4)
- Pupils will have solved word problems involving metres (Q5)

Resources

metre stick; trundle wheel; plain paper; **Resource 4.9.1a** Distance; **Resource 4.9.1b** Distance chart; **Resource 4.9.1c** Distance digit games

Vocabulary

kilometres, metres, length, width, height, distance, equivalence, greater than, less than, equal to

Question 1

> **1** Write suitable numbers in the boxes.
>
> (a) 8 km = ☐ m
>
> (b) 1.6 km = ☐ m
>
> (c) $\frac{1}{10}$ km = ☐ m
>
> (d) 700 m = ☐ km
>
> (e) 4000 m = ☐ km
>
> (f) 470 000 m = ☐ km
>
> (g) 5 km + $\frac{1}{4}$ km = ☐ m
>
> (h) 4 km + 26 m = ☐ m
>
> (i) 19 km − 10 000 m = ☐ km
>
> (j) 1 km + 780 m = ☐ m
>
> (k) 30 km − 14 000 m = ☐ m
>
> (l) 6 km + ☐ m = 6.5 km

What learning will pupils have achieved at the conclusion of Question 1?

- Pupils' concepts of length and distance will have expanded to include kilometres as they convert kilometres to metres and vice versa.

- Pupils will have developed their understanding of fractions and decimal fractions in order to apply them to kilometre distances.

- Pupils will have applied their understanding of addition and subtraction in the context of the measurement of distance.

Activities for whole-class instruction

- Ask pupils to tell you the units used to measure length. Expect them to be able to tell you millimetres, centimetres and metres. Ask: *Do you know which metric unit is used for long distances?* Establish kilometres. Ask: *What units are used to measure distance?* Agree miles, which is an imperial unit of measurement. Tell them that one kilometre is just over half a mile.

- Ask pupils how many metres they think is equivalent to one kilometre. Establish that 1000 metres is equivalent to one kilometre. Write the equivalence on the board. Ask pupils to use this fact to generate other facts, for example 2000 m = 2 km, 500 m = $\frac{1}{2}$ km, 2500 m = $2\frac{1}{2}$ km, 250 m = $\frac{1}{4}$ km, 2250 m = $2\frac{1}{4}$ km.

- Ask pupils to tell you how many metres they think would be equivalent to $\frac{1}{10}$ of a kilometre. Repeat for other tenths. Ask them to use these facts to find metre equivalences to fifths. Do they remember that $\frac{1}{10}$ is half of $\frac{1}{5}$, so they need to add two tenths to make $\frac{1}{5}$, four to make $\frac{2}{5}$ and so on?

- On the board, write: 4 km 300 m + $\frac{1}{2}$ km. Ask: *How could you work out the sum in kilometres and metres?*

(4 km 800 m). Then ask them to write the sum with the metres as a fraction of a kilometre ($4\frac{8}{10}$ km and $4\frac{4}{5}$ km) and then a decimal (4.8 km). Repeat for other amounts, such as $3\frac{1}{4}$ km + $2\frac{1}{2}$ km, $5\frac{1}{5}$ + $4\frac{3}{4}$. Repeat for subtraction calculations.

- On the board, write: 13 km + 20 000 m. Discuss the best way to find the sum. Establish that, because the units are different, it would be best to change one distance into the other unit. For example, they could add 13 km and 20 km or 13 000 m and 20 000 m. Which do they think is the most efficient conversion? Repeat for other mixed units and then for subtraction.

- Pupils can now complete Question 1 in the Practice Book.

 All say…

There are 1000 metres in one kilometre.

 One kilometre is approximately 0.6 miles. Pupils do not need to remember this in Year 4.

Same-day intervention

- Ask pupils to focus on making equivalences between whole kilometres and metres. Encourage them to use a doubling approach, for example metre equivalence for 1 km, 2 km, 4 km and 8 km. They can then use these and add, subtract and multiply to make other equivalences.

Same-day enrichment

- Ask pupils to complete **Resource 4.9.1a** Distance, which asks them to make the link between kilometres and metres and their work on decimals in Chapter 6, for example 1.5 km = 1 km 500 m = 1500 m, 3.25 km = 3 km 250 m = 3250 m.

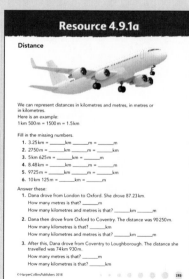

Answers: Missing numbers: 1. 3 km 250 m, 3250 m; 2. 2 km 750 m, 2.75 km; 3. 5.625 km, 5625 m; 4. 8 km 480 m, 8480 m; 5. 9 km 725 m, 9.725 km; 6. 10.125 km, 10 125 m.

Questions: 1. 87 230 m, 87 km 230 m; 2. 90.25 km, 90 km 250 m; 3. 74 930 m, 74.93 km.

Question 2

> 2 Write a suitable unit in each space.
>
> (a) A car can travel 110 _____ in one hour.
> (b) Meena can walk 70 _____ in one minute.
> (c) An aeroplane can fly about 800 _____ in one hour.
> (d) The length of the running track in a sports field is 200 _____ .
> (e) The distance between London and Edinburgh is about 600 _____ .

What learning will pupils have achieved at the conclusion of Question 2?

- Pupils' concepts of length and distance will have expanded to include kilometres as they explore suitable units to measure the length of different objects and spaces.
- Pupils will have considered what distance can be covered in various ways in different periods of time.

Activities for whole-class instruction

- Discuss the types of objects or lengths that the different metric units would measure, for example the width of a pencil nib in millimetres, the length of a pen in centimetres, the length of the playground in metres, the distance between London and Birmingham in kilometres. How many ideas can pairs of pupils think of? Collect ideas and write some on the board.
- Discuss the vocabulary to do with length and ask pupils to describe what is meant by 'length', 'width', 'height', 'distance'. Expect them to make up a sentence for each word, for example:
  - It is a long distance from my house to my gran's house.
  - The width of my book is about 20 cm.
  - The height of the door is approximately 2 m.

- With the class, create a table to show whether different lengths and distances are likely to be measured in metres or kilometres. For example:

Kilometres	Metres
Distance a car would travel	The length of a garden
Distance from Paris to New York	The width of the school hall
The length of the M25	The height of a tree
Distance a train would travel	A walk around the playground

- Give pairs or small groups of pupils a metre stick and ask them to measure a 10 metre length on the field or in the school hall. They could time each other running for 10 m and then work out the approximate time it would take them to run 100 m and then 1 km or 1000 m. Take feedback on their findings. Ask: *Which unit of time would you use to measure the length of time to run 1 km?* Agree minutes.
- Ask pupils to make up other distances that could be covered in minutes, for example running in a 200 m race, walking 70 m to a friend's house, walking $2\frac{1}{2}$ km to the local shop. Ask pupils to consider what might be measured in hours, for example running a marathon, a car travelling 245 km, a plane travelling 3570 km.
- Pupils can now complete Question 2 in the Practice Book.

Same-day intervention

- Give pairs of pupils 10 cm strips of paper and a stopwatch. Tell them that they will time each other to place 10 strips of paper side by side. Ask them whether this could be completed in minutes or seconds.
- Ask them to estimate how many seconds or minutes it will take. One pupil lays the strips and the other times them. They swap roles. Who was faster?
- They compare the number of seconds/minutes with their estimates. They repeat this for 20 strips of paper.
- Can they use the results for 10 strips to make a sensible estimate of the time for 20 strips?

Same-day enrichment

- Ask pupils to work in pairs or small groups. They each draw a table as shown below:

Hours	Minutes	Seconds

- For each unit of time they list examples of distances that could be covered in that time, for example, an ant walking 10 cm in seconds, a man walking 1 km in minutes, a lorry driving 150 km in hours. Encourage them to discuss with each other and share ideas. You could share what they do with the whole class. Do the other pupils agree?

Questions 3 and 4

3 Fill in the ◯ with >, < or =.

(a) 8 km ◯ 7900 m

(b) 3700 m ◯ 4 km

(c) 670 m ◯ 6 km

(d) 10 km ◯ 10 000 m

(e) 28 km ◯ 2800 m

(f) 1 km and 60 m ◯ 160 m

(g) 8900 m ◯ 9 km

(h) 5090 m ◯ 5 km and 100 m

4 Use < to put the measurements in order.

(a) 5 km, 4545 m, 5454 m, 4 km

(b) 9 km, 20 202 m, 20 220 m, 10 000 m

What learning will pupils have achieved at the conclusion of Questions 3 and 4?

- Pupils will have consolidated comparing and ordering different kilometre and metre lengths.

Activities for whole-class instruction

- Invite a pupil to write the 'greater than' (>) symbol on the board. Ask: *Is this the correct symbol?* Invite someone to put two metre lengths on either side of the symbol so that the sentence is true. Ask other pupils to write other similar sentences. Repeat for the 'less than' (<) symbol. This time pupils write kilometre lengths on either side.

- Next, write: 2 km = __. Ask: *What could you put on the other side?* Expect them to say 2000 m. Some may suggest an addition, for example 1 km + 1 km, or a subtraction, for example 5 km − 3 km. Explore using addition and subtraction with a mixture of kilometre distances and metre lengths with the class, for example 400 m + 1 km 500 m = 1 km 900 m. Ask pupils to work with a partner. One

pupil writes a calculation on one side of the equals symbol and the other writes a different calculation that is equal.

- Ask pupils to give you a variety of two- and three-digit kilometre distances. Write these on the board. Invite a pupil to write them in descending order. Ask them how they know they are correct. Expect them to say, for example, 'I looked for the largest digit in the hundreds position and knew that had to be the longest distance.'

- Ask them what they would need to look at if the hundreds numbers were the same. Agree the tens number and, if these are the same, the ones.

- Repeat for metre lengths, in ascending order. Then repeat for a mixture of kilometre distances and metre lengths, for example 4 km 125 m, 4250 m, 4.5 km. Discuss the fact that to order these they might find it easier to change the distances to the same unit.

- Display the distance chart shown below. Explain that it shows the distances from one city to another when travelling by plane. Ask pupils to tell you the cities shown and to tell you which countries they are in. Ask questions from the chart to ensure they can read it, for example *What is the distance from Paris to Cairo?*

	London	Paris	Cairo	New York	Sydney
London		344 km	3510 km	5585 km	16 983 km
Paris	344 km		3209 km	5834 km	16 950 km
Cairo	3510 km	3209 km		9016 km	14 407 km
New York	5585 km	5834 km	9016 km		15 979 km
Sydney	16 983 km	16 950 km	14 407 km	15 979 km	

- Ask pupils to identify the greatest and the shortest distances. Give pairs their own copy of the chart (**Resource 4.9.1b** Distance chart). In pairs, they pick four distances and order them from shortest to longest. They then pick pairs of different distances and compare them using the greater than and less than symbols.

Resource 4.9.1b

Distance chart

	London	Paris	Cairo	New York	Sydney
London		344 km	3510 km	5585 km	16 983 km
Paris	344 km		3209 km	5834 km	16 950 km
Cairo	3510 km	3209 km		9016 km	14 407 km
New York	5585 km	5834 km	9016 km		15 979 km
Sydney	16 983 km	16 950 km	14 407 km	15 979 km	

- Next, ask them to make the distances equal by adding the correct number of kilometres onto the shorter one. They repeat this, but instead of adding they subtract the correct number of kilometres from the longer one. What do they notice? They should be able to tell you that the same number of kilometres is either added or subtracted.

- Pupils can now complete Questions 3 and 4 in the Practice Book.

Same-day intervention

- Give pupils a set of digit cards. They take three and make all the possible two-digit numbers. Encourage them to do this systematically. They write their numbers, which represent kilometres, on paper and then put them in ascending order.

Same-day enrichment

- Give pupils **Resource 4.9.1c** Distance digit games.

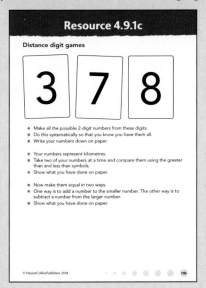

- The resource sheet asks them to make all the possible two-digit numbers from three given digits. Encourage them to do this systematically. They write the numbers, which represent kilometres, on paper. Then they take pairs and compare them using the greater than and less than symbols. They then make the pairs equal in two ways (by adding to one and subtracting from the other).

Question 5

5 Application problems.

(a) Theo walked from home to school and from school to the library. How many metres did he walk in total?

Theo's home — 1800 m → school — 1200 m → library

Answer: _____

(b) The total length of the Humber Bridge in East Yorkshire is 2220 m. The total length of the Forth Road Bridge in Edinburgh is 2512 m. The total length of the Severn Bridge connecting England and Wales is 1600 m.

(i) How many metres longer is the Forth Road Bridge than the Humber Bridge?

Answer: _____

(ii) What is the total length of the three bridges?

Answer: _____

What learning will pupils have achieved at the conclusion of Question 5?

- Pupils will have solved word problems involving metres.

Activities for whole-class instruction

- Call out some kilometre distances for pupils to turn into metres, for example 3.2 km, 5.75 km, 10 km.

- Call out some metre lengths for pupils to change into kilometres, for example 1200 m, 3275 m, 16 500 m.

- Draw this table on the board:

	Library	Hospital	School	Post office
Home	8000 m	12 000 m	5000 m	1500 m

- Ask questions such as:

  – *Sally walked from home to the hospital. How many kilometres did she walk?*

  – *Tom walked from home to school. How many kilometres did he walk?*

  – *Suzi walked from home to the post office and then back home again. How many kilometres did she walk?*

  – *Sam walked from home to the library and back again. How many kilometres did he walk?*

- Ask pupils to make up their own table with distances recorded in metres. They should make up questions to ask a partner.

- Use the table again. This time, ask pupils to work out how much further it is from home to the hospital than from home to the post office. Vary this by changing the post office to the school and then the library.

- Tell pupils:

  - *the length of Acorn Lane is 1500 m*

  - *the length of Hazelnut Road is 2400 m*

  - *Chestnut Road is 1750 m long.*

- Ask:

  - *How much longer is Hazelnut Road than the other two roads?*

  - *What is the sum of the lengths of Acorn Lane and Hazelnut Road?*

  - *If I walked all the way along Acorn Lane and Chestnut Road, how far would I walk?*

- Pupils can now complete Question 5 in the Practice Book.

Same-day intervention

- Write this information on a piece of paper:

  - The distance from London to Birmingham is about 193 km. The distance from Birmingham to Nottingham is about 82 km. The distance from Nottingham to Stoke on Trent is about 44 km.

- Together, draw a bar model to represent the problem. Ask pupils to work out the distance from London to Nottingham, from London to Stoke on Trent and then from Birmingham to Stoke on Trent.

Same-day enrichment

- Ask pupils to make up their own problems based around the fact that the length of a marathon is approximately 42.2 km, for example Fahmida ran a total of four marathons in 2016. How many kilometres did she run? They ask a partner to solve each problem and then check to make sure their partner is correct.

Challenge and extension question

Question 6

6 (a) An aeroplane travelled 420 km in half an hour. How many metres did it travel per minute? How many metres did it travel per second?

_____

_____

(b) Joe cycles to school. If he cycles 5 metres per second, how many kilometres per hour does he cycle?

_____

Question 6 is in two parts. Part (a) involves division to find the distances flown by an aeroplane in different units of time. Part (b) involves multiplication to find how many kilometres a boy cycles. For both, encourage pupils to use a mental calculation strategy to find their solutions.

Unit 9.2
Perimeters of rectangles and squares (1)

Conceptual context

In Book 3, pupils had their first introduction to perimeter. The perimeter is the distance around the outside of a shape or an area. Pupils were first introduced to area in Book 4, Chapter 8, so should be familiar with this concept. In Book 3, pupils began to measure perimeter using millimetres and centimetres. Pupils need to develop an understanding that perimeters of areas can be the same even if the areas are different. In this unit, pupils reinforce their understanding of finding perimeters and areas using centimetres and metres.

Learning pupils will have achieved at the end of the unit

- Pupils will have become fluent in calculating the perimeters of rectangles and squares, including using formulae (Q1)
- Pupils will have calculated the perimeter and area of rectangles for which dimensions are given but pictures are not provided (Q2)
- Flexible thinking and reasoning will have developed as pupils solve increasingly complex word problems involving perimeter (Q3, Q4, Q5)

Resources

rulers; squared paper; plain paper

Vocabulary

length, width, perimeter, area, centimetres, metres

Question 1

> **1** Calculate the perimeter of each of these shapes. The drawings are not to scale.
>
> (a) A square with a side length 10 cm
>
> (b) A rectangle with length 7 cm and width 4 cm
>
> 10 cm ___ cm
>
> 7 cm   4 cm   ___ cm

What learning will pupils have achieved at the conclusion of Question 1?

- Pupils will have become fluent in calculating the perimeters of rectangles and squares, including using formulae.

Activities for whole-class instruction

- Ask pupils to tell you what they remember about area and perimeter. Agree that area is the amount of space that a shape covers and the perimeter is the distance around the outside of it. Ask pupils to give you examples of areas and their perimeters in the classroom, for example a table: the surface is the area and the edge is the perimeter.

- Give pupils a piece of squared paper. Ask them to draw a 6 cm by 7 cm rectangle. Discuss how they could find the perimeter. Agree that they could add 6 cm, 7 cm, 6 cm and 7 cm.

- Can they remember a quicker way to do this? Expect them to tell you that they could add 6 cm and 7 cm and then double or they could double 6 cm, double 7 cm and add the two sums. Repeat this for other rectangles and also different-sized squares.

- Can they remember the formula for finding the perimeter of rectangles? Expect them to tell you $2l + 2w$ and also $2(l + w)$. Ask: *What could you do to find the perimeter of a square?* Expect them to tell you that they would multiply the length of one side by 4.

- Ask pairs of pupils to draw whole centimetre rectangles on plain paper. When they have drawn four, they swap papers and measure and label the length and width. They then find the perimeter. They swap papers and check their partner's work.

- Pupils can now complete Question 1 in the Practice Book.

Same-day intervention

- Give pupils squared paper to aid accuracy of drawing. They should draw their own whole centimetre rectangles and squares and label the lengths of the sides. They find the perimeters using one of the formulae. Encourage them to check their results using the other formula.

Same-day enrichment

- Give pupils squared paper. Ask them to draw all the rectangles that have a perimeter of 28 cm. How many can they find? Encourage them to be systematic. Remind them that they can use the formulae to work out the lengths and widths, for example $2(l + w) = 28$ cm so $l + w = 14$ cm. Which two numbers can they add to make 14 cm?

- As they work, do they notice a pattern, for example 1 cm by 13 cm, 2 cm by 12 cm, 3 cm by 11 cm? The width increases by 1 cm as the length decreases by 1 cm each time.

Question 2

> **2** (a) Complete the table with the perimeter and area of each rectangle.
>
> | Shape | Length | Width | Perimeter | Area |
> |---|---|---|---|---|
> | Rectangle A | 30 cm | 7 cm | | |
> | Rectangle B | 40 cm | 50 cm | | |
> | Rectangle C | 1 m | 600 cm | | |
>
> (b) Complete the table by writing the missing side length, or perimeter and the missing area for each square.
>
> | Shape | Side length | Perimeter | Area |
> |---|---|---|---|
> | Square A | 15 cm | | |
> | Square B | | 48 m | |

What learning will pupils have achieved at the conclusion of Question 2?

- Pupils will have calculated the perimeter and area of rectangles for which dimensions are given but pictures are not provided.

Activities for whole-class instruction

- Give each pupil a piece of squared paper. Ask them to draw a 4 cm by 8 cm rectangle. They should find the perimeter in the most efficient way they can. They then find the area of the rectangle. Can they remember the formula for finding area from Chapter 8? Agree that the perimeter is 24 cm and the area is length multiplied by width, which in this example is 32 cm². Repeat for other rectangles.

- On the board, write the side lengths of a variety of squares, for example 6 cm, 12 cm, 15 cm. Ask pupils to draw the squares and then find their perimeters and areas. Repeat for rectangles, this time writing the lengths and widths.

- Give pupils squared paper. Ask pairs of pupils to draw their own whole centimetre rectangles. When they have drawn four they swap with their partner who measures/counts and labels the sides of the rectangles. They then find the perimeters and areas by calculation, using a formula. Next, they return to their partner who checks to see if they are correct. Repeat this for squares by giving the side length.

- Ask pupils how they could find the perimeter and area of a rectangle that has a length of 5 m and a width of 200 cm. Establish that this would be easier if both measurements were in the same unit. They should tell you that they could change the 5 m to 500 cm or the 200 cm to 2 m. Adding and multiplying the single digit metre lengths would probably be simpler.

- Pupils can now complete Question 2 in the Practice Book.

Same-day intervention

- Give pupils pre-drawn rectangles, on squared paper, that have whole centimetre lengths and widths. Ask them to measure them accurately and then find the perimeter and area of each. Allow them to count the centimetre squares for the area. Expect them to be able to calculate the perimeters.

Same-day enrichment

- Ask pupils to draw rectangles (including squares) that are centimetre and millimetre lengths. They then find their perimeters and areas. Observe how they find the areas. Do they change the units to millimetres to multiply? Do they multiply the centimetres and millimetres separately and then add them?

Questions 3, 4 and 5

3　A rectangular vegetable patch is 40 m long and 5 m wide. Find the perimeter and area of the vegetable patch.

Answer: _____

4　The perimeter of a rectangular sports field is 300 m. If the width is 50 m, what is the length of the sports field?

Answer: _____

5　Kwame measured the swimming pool in paces. He walked the length of the pool in 100 paces and the width in 50 paces. Given that the length of Kwame's pace is 50 cm, find the perimeter of the swimming pool.

Answer: _____

What learning will pupils have achieved at the conclusion of Questions 3, 4 and 5?

- Flexible thinking and reasoning will have developed as pupils solve increasingly complex word problems involving perimeter.

Activities for whole-class instruction

- Present pupils with the following problem:
  - The length of a garden is 20 m. Its width is 12 m. What is the perimeter of the garden? What is the area?

- Repeat the problem but vary the length of the garden, for example 30 m, 15 m, 25 m. After asking a few with different lengths, repeat with the same length but vary the width, for example 8 m, 10 m, 14 m. Ask pupils to make up their own version of the problem for their partner to solve.

- Tell pupils: *The perimeter of a swimming pool is 40 m. It is a square-shaped pool. What is the length of its sides? What is the area of the surface of the water?*

- Repeat the problem but vary the perimeter of the pool, for example 44 m, 52 m, 64 m. Ask pupils to make up their own version of the problem for their partner to solve.

- Tell pupils: *Sam jogged around the outside edge of the school field. He jogged 500 m. The width of the field is 100 m. What is the length? What is the area of the field?*

- Again, repeat the problem but vary one piece of information, for example the distance Sam jogged. Repeat the problem for all distances that Sam jogged but vary the width of the field. Ask pupils to make up their own version of the problem for their partner to solve.

- Pupils can now complete Questions 3, 4 and 5 in the Practice Book.

Same-day intervention

- Give pupils squared paper. Give them this problem to solve:
  - Jodie's garden has a length of 10 m and a width of 5 m. What is the garden's perimeter and area? Vary the length. Then vary the width.

Same-day enrichment

- Ask pupils to make an information poster about perimeter and area. They should include definitions of both, an explanation of how to calculate them with examples and an explanation that the same perimeter can surround different areas.

Challenge and extension questions

Question 6

6 The figure shows a large rectangle with an area 2200 cm². What are the areas of Rectangle A and Rectangle B?

A	B

24 cm   76 cm

Rectangle A: _____

Rectangle B: _____

Questions 6 and 7 are more challenging problems. In Question 6, pupils are given the area of a large rectangle, which has been divided into two smaller rectangles. They have been given the width and length of the two smaller rectangles. Pupils need to add these and then divide the result into the whole area to find the width of the large rectangle. They then find the areas of the two smaller rectangles.

Question 7

7 A 24-centimetre-long wire is bent to form a rectangle. If the length and width of the rectangle are in whole centimetres, how many different rectangles can be formed? Complete the table with the length, width, perimeter and area of each possible rectangle.

Length (cm)					
Width (cm)					
Perimeter (cm)					
Area (cm²)					

Do all the rectangles have the same area? What patterns can you find?

_____

Question 7 gives the perimeter of a rectangle. Pupils need to work out the possible lengths and widths, then calculate the area. Encourage them to be systematic. Expect them to write down the pattern that they can see developing.

Unit 9.3
Perimeters of rectangles and squares (2)

Conceptual context

In this unit, pupils consolidate their understanding of perimeter and area. They will learn that shapes with the same area do not necessarily have the same perimeter and shapes with the same perimeter do not necessarily have the same area.

Learning pupils will have achieved at the end of the unit

- Pupils will know how to calculate the perimeter of rectangles (including squares) in metres using the formulae with understanding (Q1)
- Pupils will be able to calculate missing lengths, widths, perimeters and areas from given information with understanding (Q2)
- Pupils will have applied reasoning when solving a variety of problems involving perimeter and area (Q3, Q4, Q5)

Resources

rulers; squared paper; plain paper

Vocabulary

length, width, perimeter, area, centimetres, metres

Question 1

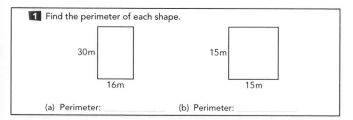

> **1** Find the perimeter of each shape.
>
> 30m   15m
>
> 16m   15m
>
> (a) Perimeter: _____   (b) Perimeter: _____

What learning will pupils have achieved at the conclusion of Question 1?

● Pupils will know how to calculate the perimeter of rectangles (including squares) in metres using the formulae with understanding.

Activities for whole-class instruction

● Ask pupils to tell a partner all they know about perimeter and area. Expect them to give a definition for both and also to say how both are calculated using the formulae $2l + 2w$ or $2(l + w)$ for perimeter and $l \times w$ for area. After a few minutes, take feedback. Expect them to be able to tell you that area is the amount of space covered by a shape or object and perimeter is the distance around an area. Tell pupils that there is no numerical relationship between perimeter and area – one is not a multiple of the other. Ask pupils to explore this by drawing the three possible rectangles, including a square, that have a perimeter of 12 cm. They should do this on squared paper and then calculate the area of each one. For example:

5cm
1cm

4cm
2cm

3cm
3cm

All say ... *These three rectangles have the same perimeter but the areas are all different. Same perimeter, different area.*

● Next, ask pupils to show that areas can be the same and perimeters different by drawing a rectangle and a square, each with an area of 9 cm². Again, they should do this on squared paper and calculate the perimeter. For example:

9cm
1cm

3cm
3cm

All say ... *These two rectangles have the same area but the perimeters are different. Same area, different perimeter.*

● Give pupils a piece of plain paper. Ask them to sketch four different rectangles, including squares. They label the sides to show that they have the same area, imagining that they are in metres and not centimetres. They should find the perimeters of their shapes. They then give their rectangles to a partner who checks that they are correct.

● Pupils can now complete Question 1 in the Practice Book.

Same-day intervention

● Give pupils squared paper to aid accuracy of drawing. They should draw their own whole centimetre rectangles and squares and label the sides using metres as the unit. They should find the perimeter and area of each one in whichever way they feel confident. Encourage them to use one of the formulae if they can.

● Then, pupils should identify any shapes that have the same area. Do they have the same perimeter? Are there any that have the same perimeter? Do they have the same area?

Same-day enrichment

● Give pupils squared paper. Ask them to draw all the rectangles that have an area of 36 cm². How many can they find? Encourage them to be systematic. As they work, do they notice that the length and width measurements are all factors of 36? In the same way, 36 is a multiple of all the length and width measurements.

● Next, challenge them to draw all the rectangles that have an area of 48 cm². Can they predict something interesting about the lengths of the sides?

Question 2

> **2** (a) Complete the table.
>
> | Shape | Length | Width | Perimeter | Area |
> |---|---|---|---|---|
> | Rectangle A | | 90 cm | 480 cm | |
> | Rectangle B | 19 cm | | | 437 cm² |
> | Rectangle C | 16 m | 900 cm | | |
>
> (b) Complete the table by writing the missing side length or perimeter and the missing area for each square.
>
> | Shape | Side length | Perimeter | Area |
> |---|---|---|---|
> | Square A | 24 cm | | |
> | Square B | | 1 m | |

What learning will pupils have achieved at the conclusion of Question 2?

- Pupils will be able to calculate missing lengths, widths, perimeters and areas from given information with understanding.

Activities for whole-class instruction

- Draw a table like this on the board:

Length	Width	Perimeter	Area
20 cm	10 cm		
50 cm	30 cm		
70 cm	40 cm		
90 cm	70 cm		

- Ask pupils to make a copy of it and sketch the rectangles. Ensure they consider the relative lengths and widths and aim to draw them in proportion. For example the first rectangle needs to be drawn with a width half of the length. Once they have done this, they calculate the perimeters and areas.

- Next ask pupils to draw another with their own measurements listed. They give this to a partner who sketches the rectangles and then works out their perimeters and areas.

- Ask pupils to discuss with a partner if it is possible to find the lengths and widths of a rectangle if given just the perimeter. Establish that it would be, but there would be several options. Ask: *Can you think of what else you need so that you can work out the size of a particular rectangle?* Agree that they would need to know either the length or the width, unless they knew it was a square. Make up a selection of perimeters and lengths, for example perimeter 24 cm, length 10 cm.

- Work through a few examples together. Ask: *What do you need to do to find the width?* Agree that they need to double the length to find the sum of two lengths. They then subtract this from the perimeter. This will give 4 cm, which is the sum of the two widths. They need to halve 4 cm to give two widths each measuring 2 cm. Ask: *If we know the length is 10 cm and the width is 2 cm, what is the area?*

- After working through a few examples, give some for the pupils to work through independently. Repeat this, giving perimeters and widths, for example perimeter 30 cm, width 5 cm. Pupils need to find the lengths and then the areas.

- Ask pupils to discuss with a partner if it is possible to find the length and width of a rectangle if given just the area. Establish that it would be but, again, there would be several options. They would need one of the dimensions to find the size of a particular rectangle. Work through a few examples together where area and length are known, for example area 36 cm², length 12 cm. Agree that the second dimension can be deduced and, once both dimensions are known, the perimeter can be calculated.

- Pupils work on some independently, including some where the given dimension is width, rather than length, and some where they are told the shape is a square.

- Ask pupils how they could find the side length and area of a square if simply given the perimeter. Agree that they could divide the perimeter by 4 (or halve and halve again). This would give the side length. They then multiply the side length and width for the area. Again, work through one example together and then ask pairs to work through other examples.

- Pupils can now complete Question 2 in the Practice Book.

Same-day intervention

- Give pupils squared paper to work on for accuracy. Write a table of perimeters for squares, for example:

Perimeter
20 cm
24 cm
28 cm
32 cm

- Pupils work out the sides by halving the perimeter twice. When they have the sides they draw the squares. Ask them to find the areas of the squares in whichever way they feel most confident. They could use the squares to help them.

Same-day enrichment

- Ask pupils to make up their own tables with a mixture of given and missing information. Their partner works out the missing information. Their table should include two given lengths, widths, perimeters and areas, as shown in this example:

Length	Width	Perimeter	Area
50 cm		140 cm	
12 cm			144 cm²
	25 cm	250 cm	
	9 cm		180 cm²

- Pupils should then add more rows, filling in only two pieces of information in each row. They must ensure they have a particular shape in mind, though, so that the two pieces of information they do insert actually make sense. Partners then fill in the blanks.

Questions 3, 4 and 5

3 Ava put together five identical squares with a side length 8 cm to form a rectangle. Find the perimeter and the area of the rectangle. Draw a diagram to help find the answer.

Perimeter: _____

Area: _____

4 A rectangular field is to be expanded. If only the length is increased by 8 m, the area increases by 160 m². If only the width is increased by 5 m, the area increases by 175 m². What is the perimeter of the original rectangular field?

Perimeter: _____

5 Mohan has a length of string that can form a square with sides of exactly 18 cm. He wants to use the string to form a rectangle with length 19 cm. What will the width be?

Width: _____

What learning will pupils have achieved at the conclusion of Questions 3, 4 and 5?

- Pupils will have applied reasoning when solving a variety of problems involving perimeter and area.

Activities for whole-class instruction

- Give pupils squared paper. Ask them to cut out six 4 cm by 4 cm squares. Once they have, they should position them to make the following two possible rectangles:

Ask them to work out the perimeter and area of each. Discuss strategies. Repeat this for seven and eight squares of the same size. Next, ask them to make 5 cm by 5 cm squares and repeat the exercise.

- Ask pupils this problem: *Samir drew a rectangle 10 cm long by 3 cm wide. Joe drew a rectangle 5 cm longer than Samir's. The width was the same. How much greater was the perimeter of Joe's rectangle? How much greater was its area?*

- Slowly work through the problem together step by step. First work out the length of Joe's rectangle. Ask pupils to draw and label the lengths of both rectangles. They could do this on 1 cm squared paper so they focus on the problem rather than the accuracy of the rectangles.

- Then ask other similar problems where you vary the size of Samir's rectangle and then the number of centimetres longer Joe's rectangle is.

- Tell pupils that Samir draws another rectangle, which is 5 cm longer than his first one. The width is the same. Ask them to draw a diagram to show this, for example:

- Next, ask them to find the perimeter and area of the new shape. As before, repeat the question but vary the number of centimetres longer Samir's new shape is.

- Tell pupils that they are going to find the perimeter and area of a rectangle that is made larger. There are two ways to make it larger – by making it longer or by making it wider.

- Explain that they don't know the dimensions of the rectangle at the start but, by drawing what happens to it, they will be able to work out what the starting measurements are. Ask: *What is a good way to help make sense of a complicated problem?* Pupils should suggest drawing a picture or diagram.

- Agree that drawing the rectangle is an excellent way to make things clear as you go along. Draw the starting rectangle with unknown dimensions.

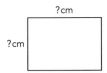

- Say: *We know that when the length is increased by 7 cm the area increases by 35 cm². Ask: How should we draw this? Agree on the following:*

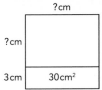

- Agree that the additional section on the diagram, representing the enlargement to the original rectangle, enables them to find the width of the original rectangle: ? × 7 = 35. The width was therefore 5 cm. However, the length is still not known.

- Say: *We know that, when the width of the original rectangle is increased by 3 cm, the area increases by 30 cm². Ask: How should we draw this? Agree on the following:*

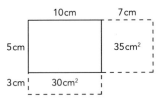

- Agree that the additional section on the diagram, representing the enlargement to the original rectangle, enables them to find the length of the original rectangle: ? × 3 = 30. The length was therefore 10 cm.

- So, now the length and width of the original rectangle are known.

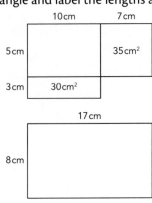

- Pupils can now work out the perimeter and area of the original rectangle very easily. Ask them to draw the new expanded rectangle and label the lengths and widths:

- Ask pupils to now work out the perimeter and area of the expanded rectangle.

- This is a complex problem. Repeat it, slightly varying the length and area and then the width and area. Pupils need to understand how they can break the problem up to find the unknowns, using diagrams and thinking clearly and methodically.

- Let pupils work with a partner so they can discuss what to do. Work with pupils who need support in a focus group.

- Ask pupils this problem: *Georgia had a piece of ribbon. She put it into the shape of a square with sides 10 cm. If she changed it to make a rectangle with a length of 12 cm, how long is the width?*

- Give each pupil a piece of 1 cm squared paper. Ask them to draw the square and label each side. They then investigate what they would need to do to change the square into a rectangle with a length of 12 cm. Can they tell you that they would need to take 2 cm from each width to 'give to' each length? This would give a rectangle of 12 cm by 8 cm.

- Ask them to work out the perimeter and area of both the square and the rectangle. What do they notice? They should be able to tell you that the perimeters are the same and the areas are different.

- Repeat the problem but vary the sides of the square to a length greater than 10 cm.

- Pupils can now complete Questions 3, 4 and 5 in the Practice Book.

Same-day intervention

- Give pupils four 5 cm by 5 cm squares. Ask them to put the squares together to make two different rectangles. Ask them to draw their rectangles and then label their sides. They then work out the perimeter and area of each rectangle. They record their results.

Same-day enrichment

- Ask pairs of pupils to make up their own problems that are similar to the rectangle problems you asked for Samir and Joe. They give their problems to another pair to solve and then check to make sure they are correct.

Challenge and extension questions

Question 6

6 Eight identical squares with side lengths 6 cm are put together to form a rectangle.

(a) How many different rectangles can be formed? ☐

(b) Find the perimeter of each possible rectangle.

Question 6 asks pupils to explore the different rectangles that can be made using eight identical 6 cm by 6 cm squares. They work out the perimeter for each one.

Question 7

7 The figure shows a rectangular piece of paper. If a square with maximum area is first cut from the paper, and then another square with maximum area is cut from the remaining rectangular piece, what are the area and perimeter of each of the squares? What are the area and perimeter of the remaining piece of paper? (Units: cm; drawing not to scale)

1st square – area: _____ perimeter: _____

2nd square – area: _____ perimeter: _____

Remaining piece – area: _____ perimeter: _____

Question 7 asks pupils to explore squares with the maximum areas from a rectangle. Encourage pupils to draw diagrams to help them visualise the square with the maximum area, the amount of the rectangle left and the next square with the maximum area.

Unit 9.4
Perimeters and areas of rectilinear shapes

Conceptual context

Pupils will now begin to use the term 'rectilinear' (if they have not already), understanding that rectilinear shapes are polygons in which all angles are right angles. For example:

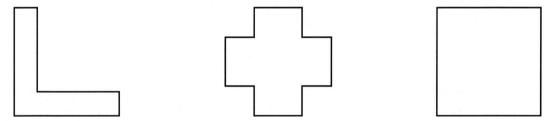

Pupils have already begun to form a concept of rectilinear shapes in previous units. In this unit, that is reinforced and developed and pupils' new knowledge about area and perimeter is applied and developed in the context of rectilinear shapes. Initially, they will explore perimeter and area by counting squares and then develop their understanding in order to explore rectilinear shapes without squares and find missing values.

Learning pupils will have achieved at the end of the unit

- Pupils will have calculated the perimeters and areas of compound rectilinear shapes by counting squares representing more than 1 cm side length (Q1)
- Pupils will be able to calculate perimeters and areas of rectilinear shapes without squares (Q2)
- Pupils will have solved word problems involving perimeter and area (Q3, Q4, Q5)

Resources

rulers; squared paper; plain paper; **Resource 4.9.4a** Perimeters and areas of rectilinear shapes 1; **Resource 4.9.4b** Perimeters and areas of rectilinear shapes 2

Vocabulary

rectilinear shapes, length, width, perimeter, area, centimetres, metres

Question 1

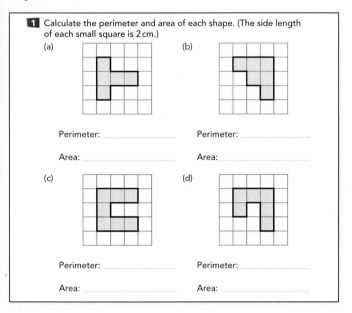

1 Calculate the perimeter and area of each shape. (The side length of each small square is 2 cm.)

(a)

(b)

Perimeter: ....

Perimeter: ....

Area: ....

Area: ....

(c)

(d)

Perimeter: ....

Perimeter: ....

Area: ....

Area: ....

What learning will pupils have achieved at the conclusion of Question 1?

- Pupils will have calculated the perimeters and areas of compound rectilinear shapes by counting squares representing more than 1 cm side length.

Activities for whole-class instruction

- Give pupils 1 cm squared paper. Ask them to draw the outline of this shape onto their paper and shade the squares:

- Ask pupils to tell you the rectangles that they can see in their shape. They should be able to see 10 small squares. In the horizontal rows there are four obvious rectangles. The diagrams below show the other possibilities:

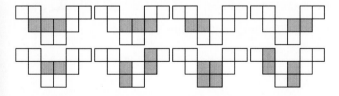

- Ask pupils to make up their own interesting rectilinear shapes and explore how many rectangles (including squares) they can spot. Take feedback, inviting pupils to share their rectilinear shapes with the class. Invite them to tell the class how many squares and rectangles they identified.

- Explain that the shapes they have drawn are rectilinear shapes because they have straight sides that join at right angles. Can pupils tell you that these are perpendicular lines?

- Ask pupils to discuss with a partner how they could find the perimeter of the rectilinear shapes they drew. Agree that they could count the lines that make up the outside edges of the small squares. Ask them to calculate the perimeters of all the shapes in the most efficient way they can, for example counting in twos rather than ones.

- Ask pupils to discuss how they could find the areas of the rectilinear shapes. Agree they could count the squares. Ask them to do this for all their shapes. Expect them to do this in an efficient way.

- Next tell them that the side of each square is 2 cm. Ask how they would find the new area. Discuss whether they can just double the first area they found. Elicit that a square with a side length of 2 cm has an area of 4 cm². Doubling the original area will not give the new one. Repeat this for other lengths, for example 3 cm, 5 cm, 6 cm.

- Pupils can now complete Question 1 in the Practice Book.

Same-day intervention

- Give pupils four square pieces of paper. Ask them to put them together so that they make a rectilinear shape, and another, and another. Pupils should make all the rectilinear shapes that they can with the four squares, drawing each one. Every square must be touching another along one side. The shapes should not be reflections or rotations. There are five:

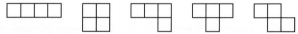

- Pupils should then find the perimeters of the five shapes. Ask: *What will the perimeters be if the length of the side of each square is 2 cm?*

Same-day enrichment

- Give pupils squared paper. Tell them that each square represents 4 cm² because the length of the side of each square is 2 cm. Working with a partner, they should draw all the rectilinear shapes that have an area of 20 cm². Every square must be touching another along one side and there can be no reflections or rotations.

- Once they have found them all, they work out their perimeters. They also name the different shapes they have drawn. There are 12 possibilities altogether.

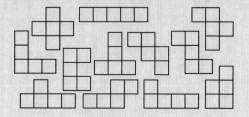

Question 2

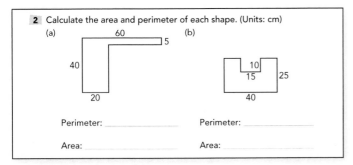

2 Calculate the area and perimeter of each shape. (Units: cm)

(a)

60

5

40

20

(b)

10

15

25

40

Perimeter: _____

Area: _____

Perimeter: _____

Area: _____

What learning will pupils have achieved at the conclusion of Question 2?

● Pupils will be able to calculate perimeters and areas of rectilinear shapes without squares.

Activities for whole-class instruction

● Ask pupils to tell a partner what a rectilinear shape is. Invite someone to share what they think with the class.

 A rectilinear shape is a shape with straight sides and all angles are right angles.

● Ask pupils to sketch some of their own rectilinear shapes on plain paper. Invite some pupils to draw one of their shapes on the board. Ask the class to say whether they agree that they are rectilinear. Ask: *Do they have straight sides? Are all angles right angles?*

● Draw this shape on the board – it has two of the dimensions omitted:

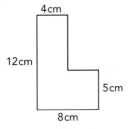

4 cm

12 cm

5 cm

8 cm

● Ask pupils how they could find the perimeter of this shape. Agree that they could add up the lengths of each side. Is there a problem? Ask them to talk to their partner about how to find the missing lengths. Take feedback.

● Agree that subtraction is needed to find missing dimensions, but enough information is provided to be able to do that. Ask pupils to find the perimeter of the shape. Agree that it is 40 cm. Did anyone spot that they could still use the formulae $2l + 2w$ or $2(l + w)$?

● Draw a few other rectilinear shapes on the board and repeat. Give pupils a copy of **Resource 4.9.4a** Perimeters

and areas of rectilinear shapes 1 and ask them to find the missing lengths and then the perimeters of all the rectilinear shapes.

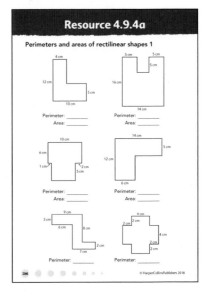

Resource 4.9.4a

Perimeters and areas of rectilinear shapes 1

Answers: 44, 78;   70, 204

42, 95;   52, 112;

46, 56;   32, 48.

● Return to the shape you have already drawn on the board:

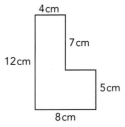

4 cm

7 cm

12 cm

5 cm

8 cm

● Ask pupils to tell you how they could find the area of the rectilinear shape. Encourage them to discuss ideas with a partner. Establish that they could make two rectangles, find the area of each and add them together. Invite a pupil to draw a line to make two rectangles and then invite someone else to draw an alternative way of making two rectangles, as shown in the two diagrams below:

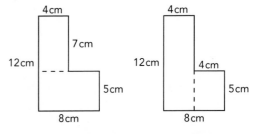

4 cm

7 cm

12 cm

5 cm

8 cm

4 cm

12 cm

4 cm

5 cm

8 cm

● Together, work out the area for the first diagram: $28 \text{ cm}^2 + 40 \text{ cm}^2 = 68 \text{ cm}^2$. Next, work out the area for the second diagram: $48 \text{ cm}^2 + 20 \text{ cm}^2 = 68 \text{ cm}^2$. Of course, the total area is the sum, regardless of how the compound shape is divided. Repeat with a few more examples and then ask pupils to find the areas of the rectilinear shapes on **Resource 4.9.4a** Perimeters and areas of rectilinear shapes 1.

● Pupils can now complete Question 2 in the Practice Book.

Same-day intervention

● Give pupils squared paper. Ask them to draw six of their own rectilinear shapes, each with more than four vertices, and to work out their perimeters and areas. Once they have done this they swap their work with a partner to check their results.

Same-day enrichment

● Ask pupils to complete **Resource 4.9.4b** Perimeters and areas of rectilinear shapes 2, which asks them to measure the sides of rectilinear shapes and then find their areas and perimeters.

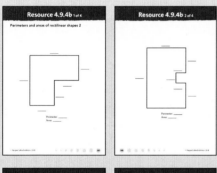
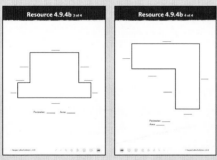

Answers: All the shape dimensions are cm: 1. 10, 5, 10, 5, 5, 5; Perimeter: 40 cm; Area: 75 cm²; 2. 8, 5, 2, 12, 2, 2, 5; Perimeter: 44 cm, Area: 92 cm²; 3. 10, 6, 6, 2.5, 2.5, 3, 3, 15; Perimeter: 48 cm, Area: 105 cm²; 4. 14, 5, 9, 13, 8, 5; Perimeter: 54 cm, Area: 110 cm²

Questions 3, 4 and 5

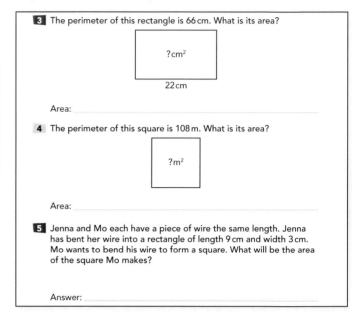

3 The perimeter of this rectangle is 66 cm. What is its area?

?cm²

22 cm

Area:

4 The perimeter of this square is 108 m. What is its area?

?m²

Area:

5 Jenna and Mo each have a piece of wire the same length. Jenna has bent her wire into a rectangle of length 9 cm and width 3 cm. Mo wants to bend his wire to form a square. What will be the area of the square Mo makes?

Answer:

What learning will pupils have achieved at the conclusion of Questions 3, 4 and 5?

● Pupils with have solved word problems involving finding perimeters and areas.

Activities for whole-class instruction

● Draw a rectangle on the board. Tell the pupils that the rectangle has not been drawn to scale. Its perimeter is 32 cm. Give them a piece of plain paper and ask them to sketch all the possible rectangles that it could be (1 cm × 15 cm, 2 cm × 14 cm, 3 cm × 13 cm, 4 cm × 12 cm, 5 cm × 11 cm, 6 cm × 10 cm, 7 cm × 9 cm, 8 cm × 8 cm).

● Next, tell them that one of the lengths is 10 cm. They use the information from their sketches to work out that the width must be 6 cm. Ask them to calculate the area of the rectangle. Repeat for other perimeters.

● Tell pupils that you are thinking of a square. It has a perimeter of 36 cm. Ask them to work out what the side lengths must be. They draw it accurately, label its sides and calculate the area. Repeat for other squares.

● Set this problem:

  – Paul drew a rectangle. It had a perimeter of 54 cm. Its length was 15 cm. Sarah drew a rectangle. It had a perimeter of 54 cm. Its length was 20 cm. Whose rectangle had the greater area?

● Ask pupils to tell you which rectangle they think had the greater area before calculating. What makes them think as they do? Ask them to work out the widths of the rectangles and then calculate the areas. Were their initial thoughts correct? Set similar problems, varying the length of the perimeter and then the length of Paul's rectangle. Ask pupils to make up and solve similar problems but varying the length of Sarah's rectangle.

- Ask pupils this problem:
  - Samira has a piece of string. She shapes it into a square. Each side measures 12 cm. What is the perimeter of Samira's square? What is its area? Ben has a piece of string the same length as Samira's. He shapes it into a rectangle. The length is 20 cm. What is the perimeter of Ben's rectangle? What is its area?
- Ask similar problems.
- Pupils can now complete Questions 3, 4 and 5 in the Practice Book.

Same-day intervention

- Give pupils a simple area for a rectangle, for example 12 cm². Ask them to work out the possible widths and lengths. They draw these on centimetre squared paper and then work out the perimeter. When they have done this, repeat for another area, for example 36 cm². What about 72 cm²?

Same-day enrichment

- Give pupils the area 72 cm². They draw all the possible rectangles and work out their perimeters. Ask them to make up a problem to go with each rectangle, for example 'The width of my notepad is 6 cm, the area is 72 cm². What is the perimeter of my notepad?'

Challenge and extension questions

Question 6

> **6** The shaded part in the figure below is the overlap of two identical rectangles. (Units: cm)
>
> ```
>              15
>         ┌──────────┐
>         │    6     │
>     ┌───┼──┐       │ 9
>     │ 6 │▓▓│       │
>   9 │   └──┼───────┘
>     │      │
>     └──────┘
>        15
> ```
>
> (a) Find the area of the unshaded part of the figure.
>
> _____
>
> (b) Find the perimeter of the whole figure.

Questions 6, 7 and 8 are similar to Questions 3, 4 and 5 but are more challenging problems. Question 6 asks

them to use their understanding of work in Unit 9.4 to work out missing measurements and then use what they have found out to find an area and a perimeter.

Question 7

> **7** The perimeter of a rectangle is 240 cm. It has a width of 30 cm. If both the length and the width are increased by 50 cm, by how many square centimetres will the area increase? Draw a diagram to help find the answer.
>
> Answer: _____

Question 7 asks the pupils to work out the new area of a rectangle with a given perimeter and one length. It is important that the pupils represent the problem pictorially and try out a few different rectangles to refine their ideas.

Question 8

> **8** The figure shows a rectangle inside a square. The side length of the square is 18 cm. The four vertices of the rectangle divide each side of the square into two parts. The longer part is twice the length of the shorter part. What is the area of this rectangle in square centimetres?
>
>
>
> Answer: _____

Question 8 involves the pupils reasoning that each side of the square has been divided by a vertex of the rectangle into $\frac{1}{3}$ and $\frac{2}{3}$. So the longer part is 12 cm and the shorter part is 6 cm. If they imagine that the two larger triangles are positioned together they will form a 12 × 12 square with an area of 144 cm². The two smaller triangles can be positioned together to give a 6 × 6 square with an area of 36 cm². They add these areas and subtract from the area of the 18 × 18 square (324 cm²) to find the area of the rectangle (144 cm²). Alternatively, they could find the solution by finding the areas of the four triangles, if they know that the area of a triangle is $\frac{1}{2}$base × height. The two larger triangles each have an area of 72 cm² and the two smaller ones have an area of 36 cm². When these areas are added, the total area of the triangles is also 180 cm². Subtract this from 324 cm² to give an area of 144 cm² for the rectangle.

Unit 9.5
Describing positions on a 2-D grid

Conceptual context

This unit introduces pupils to describing position in terms of its coordinates. In this unit, the terms 'horizontal' and 'vertical' are used to describe position on a grid to enable pupils to understand and remember the order of the coordinates. These terms will still be helpful later when coordinates are used in more than one quadrant and negative values are included. It is strongly recommended, therefore, that pupils securely understand horizontal and vertical at this stage, rather than other mnemonics that have only limited relevance. The key ideas that pupils will learn in this unit are that a coordinate describes an area on a grid, not the intersection of the vertical and horizontal lines, and that the convention of writing coordinates is always the horizontal value followed by the vertical value. There is potential for the skills learned here to be applied and developed in Geography lessons, as printed maps are a common context for using coordinates.

Learning pupils will have achieved at the end of the unit

- Pupils will be able to apply their knowledge of horizontal and vertical lines to the context of coordinates (Q1, Q2, Q3, Q4, Q5)
- Pupils will deepen their understanding of coordinates through experiencing situations in which coordinates are used in real life (Q1)
- Pupils will be able to generalise about the order in which the position is described (Q1, Q2, Q3, Q4, Q5)
- Pupils will have learned conventions for writing coordinates (Q3, Q4, Q5)
- Pupils' ability to work systematically and to keep track of their work will have been developed (Q1, Q5)

Resources

sticky notes; dice; counters; **Resource 4.9.5a** Map of a town; **Resource 4.9.5b** Map of the United Kingdom; **Resource 4.9.5c** Coordinate grid (stationery); **Resource 4.9.5d** World map (numerical coordinates); **Resource 4.9.5e** Coordinate grid (blank); **Resource 4.9.5f** Coordinate routes; **Resource 4.9.5g** Challenge question

Vocabulary

horizontal, vertical, coordinate, location, position

Questions 1 and 2

1 The diagram below shows the arrangement of seating positions in a cinema. Help the children find their seats. Draw a line to match each child to the correct seat.

Row 1 1 2 3 4 5 6 7 8 9 10 11
Row 2 1 2 3 4 5 6 7 8 9 10 11
Row 3 1 2 3 4 5 6 7 8 9 10 11
Row 4 1 2 3 4 5 6 7 8 9 10 11

Lou
2nd row,
seat number 6

Ella
4th row,
seat number 3

2 Think carefully and then fill in the blanks with the words 'horizontally' or 'vertically'.

When looking for the position on a location map, we first locate it _____, and then locate it _____.

What learning will pupils have achieved at the conclusion of Questions 1 and 2?

- Pupils will be able to apply their knowledge of horizontal and vertical lines to the context of coordinates.
- Pupils will deepen their understanding of coordinates through experiencing situations in which coordinates are used in real life.
- Pupils will be able to generalise about the order in which the position is described.
- Pupils' ability to work systematically and to keep track of their work will have been developed.

Activities for whole-class instruction

- Before starting work on coordinates, it is important that pupils understand horizontal and vertical lines. Show the following images and ask pupils to identify horizontal and vertical lines in each one.

- Emphasise that horizontal lines go from side to side and are parallel to the horizon. Vertical lines go up and down (and are perpendicular to horizontal lines).

- Explain that the position of things can be described by identifying their position on a grid. This is seen most often in maps. Show this map of Europe and ask pupils to describe the location of France on the map.

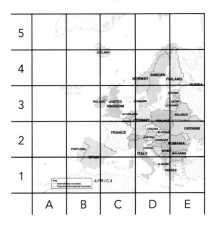

- Explain that it is more accurate and efficient to describe its position using coordinates rather than by describing it as 'next to Spain' or 'below England'. Explain that the coordinate of each country can be described by first finding its horizontal position and then its vertical position.

- Demonstrate that (most of) France is in cell (C, 2). In this example, the letters describe the horizontal position, the numbers the vertical position. Ask pupils: *Which two coordinates are there for Finland? What country is in (C, 4)? How many countries are in (D, 3)?*

- Explain that each map has its own grid lines but the way of describing position does not change: the horizontal position is written first, then the vertical one. Show pupils this map of the United Kingdom. Ask: *What towns can you see in (C, 1) and in (D, 5)?*

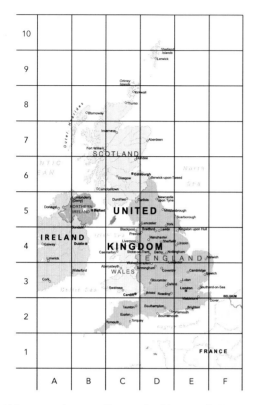

- Ask: *What are the coordinates for Liverpool? For Exeter?* Ask: *Which coordinate do we say first?*

 When describing a position on a map we first locate it horizontally, and then locate it vertically.

- Hand out copies of **Resource 4.9.5a** Map of a town. Ask pupils to work in pairs to identify coordinates, with one partner giving the horizontal coordinate and the other providing the vertical one.

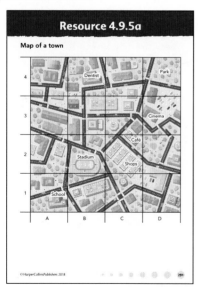

- Together, find the coordinates of a few places on the map. Ask: *Which coordinate do you write first?* Pupils should be able to explain that the horizontal position is described before the vertical position.

 When describing a position on a map we first locate it horizontally, and then locate it vertically.

- Pupils can now complete Questions 1 and 2 in the Practice Book.

Same-day intervention

- First, ensure that pupils can confidently identify horizontal and vertical lines. Pupils can use sticky notes labelled 'horizontal' or 'vertical' to label horizontal and vertical lines in the classroom. Playing a game of 'Battleships' provides pupils with further opportunities to practise reading coordinates.

Same-day enrichment

- Pupils should use **Resource 4.9.5b** Map of the United Kingdom and first add the labels for the horizontal and vertical axes.

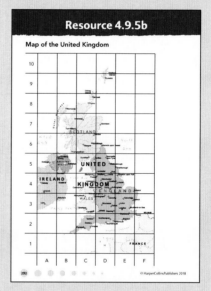

- Pupils should then find the coordinates for Portsmouth, Leeds and Cardiff. Working with a partner, pupils should take turns to ask their partner to give them the coordinates of a town. If the partner gives the correct coordinate (horizontal first, then vertical) they score a point, if they are incorrect the point goes to their partner.

Questions 3 and 4

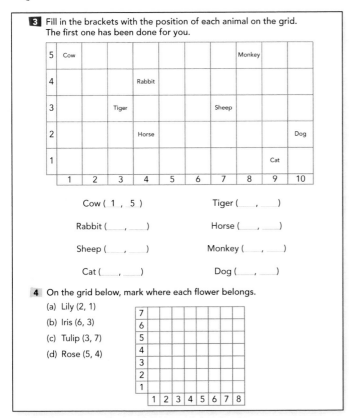

3 Fill in the brackets with the position of each animal on the grid. The first one has been done for you.

Cow (1 , 5)   Tiger (___ , ___)

Rabbit (___ , ___)   Horse (___ , ___)

Sheep (___ , ___)   Monkey (___ , ___)

Cat (___ , ___)   Dog (___ , ___)

4 On the grid below, mark where each flower belongs.
(a) Lily (2, 1)
(b) Iris (6, 3)
(c) Tulip (3, 7)
(d) Rose (5, 4)

What learning will pupils have achieved at the conclusion of Questions 3 and 4?

- Pupils will have used their knowledge of horizontal and vertical lines to find coordinates.
- Pupils will have learned conventions for writing coordinates.
- Pupils will be able to generalise about the order in which the position is described.

Activities for whole-class instruction

- Pupils' understanding of coordinates is deepened as they apply what they have learned to problems where they have to identify the coordinates and then interpret coordinates
- Show pupils the image below and ask them to identify on the grid the coordinates of the pencil, sharpener, paper clip and scissors.

 When describing a position on a map we first locate it horizontally, and then locate it vertically.

- Ask pupils questions such as: *Which cell is immediately below the pencil sharpener? Which cell is on the right of the pencil? If the paper clip were moved up two rows, what would its new coordinates be?*

- Hand out copies of **Resource 4.9.5c** Coordinate grid (stationery) and ask pupils to draw a ball in (4, 4), a book in (1, 4) and a ruler that stretches across (1,7), (2,7) and (3,7).

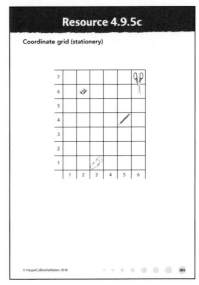

- Pupils can now complete Questions 3 and 4 in the Practice Book.

Same-day intervention

- Using the map of the world on **Resource 4.9.5d** World map (numerical coordinates), ask pupils to find Spain, Canada, Australia and Norway. Ask them to see which countries they would find if they reversed the coordinates. This should help emphasise the importance of describing the position accurately – (3, 6) and (6, 3) are very different places!

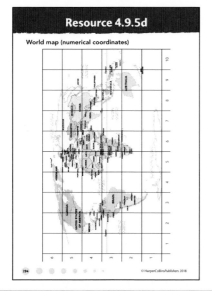

Same-day enrichment

- This activity will provide pupils with the opportunity to interpret coordinates and plot them correctly, as well as challenging them to think strategically.

- Pupils should work in pairs, sharing a copy of **Resource 4.9.5e** Coordinate grid (blank) and two different-coloured dice. Pupil A rolls both dice, one representing the horizontal position, the other the vertical position. Pupil A colours in the corresponding cell on **Resource 4.9.5e**. Pupil B then does the same and colours the corresponding cell in a different colour.

- Pupils take turns until they have coloured in four cells that touch horizontally, vertically or diagonally.

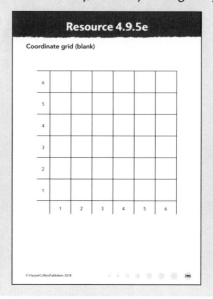

Question 5

5 A snail is at (2, 9) on the grid below. It moves first 6 squares right, then 7 squares down, then 4 squares left, and finally 3 squares up.

(a) What is the final position of the snail?

(b) What other routes could the snail have taken to reach the same final position? Describe two.

What learning will pupils have achieved at the conclusion of Question 5?

- Pupils will be able to apply their knowledge of horizontal and vertical lines to the context of coordinates.

- Pupils will be able to generalise about the order in which the position is described.

- Pupils will have learned conventions for writing coordinates.

- Pupils' ability to work systematically and to keep track of their work will have been developed.

Activities for whole-class instruction

- Pupils' understanding and use of coordinates will be developed further as they apply what they know to working systematically and planning routes on a coordinates grid. Using the grid shown below, ask pupils what the coordinates are for (i) the child, (ii) the ice cream van, (iii) the park and (iv) the beach. Check that all pupils give the horizontal coordinate first.

- Explain that the child wants to visit the ice cream van, the park and the beach. Ask: *What route would the child take from where she is (6, 6) to the ice cream van? How many cells would she travel across?* Ask: *What route would the child take from where she is (6, 6) to the park? How many cells would she travel across?*

- Compare answers and identify that there is more than one route and that some routes are the same length. Ask: *What route would the child take from where she is (6, 6) to the beach? How many cells would she travel across?*

- Agree that there is more than one route and that some routes are the same length.

- Pupils can now answer Question 5 in the Practice Book.

Same-day intervention

- Give pupils copies of **Resource 4.9.5e** Coordinate grid (blank) and ask them to mark a start point on the grid and then place a counter on the finish point. Pupils should use a pencil to mark each cell that they cross between the start point and the counter. They should then see if there is another route they can take. Using a different-coloured pencil, they should mark each cell that they cross between the start point and the counter.

- Once pupils are reliably counting the cells and are able to identify the shortest route, ask: *Can you find all the routes that are eight cells long?* This will help them to recognise that, although the routes may look different, they may be the same length and counting cells enables them to find the shortest route.

Same-day enrichment

- **Resource 4.9.5f** Coordinate routes is the same as the image above. Pupils use this to investigate which is the shortest route the child could take to travel from her starting point to the ice cream van, park and beach in one journey.

Challenge and extension question

Question 6

6 The diagram below shows a street map on a grid.

(a) If the position of the post office is described as (1, 5), then the
    position of the supermarket is (____ , ____).

(b) There are ☐ shortest routes from the post office to the
    supermarket.

Post
office

Supermarket

The challenge question provides pupils with the
opportunity to demonstrate their proficiency in
describing the location of something on a coordinate
grid. It also provides them with the opportunity to work
systematically and carefully to identify all the shortest
routes between the post office and the supermarket.
Pupils may find it helpful to use **Resource 4.9.5g**
Challenge question to keep track of their work and to
record their routes on multiple images of the grid.

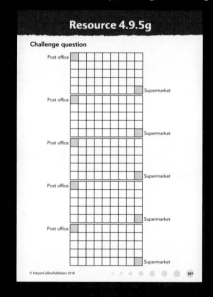

Resource 4.9.5g

Unit 9.6
Solving problems involving time and money (1)

Conceptual context

In this unit, pupils extend their understanding of time. In Book 3 they learned about equivalences between minutes and seconds, telling the 12- and 24-hour times, including those on clocks with Roman numerals, calculating durations of time and common and leap years. In Book 4, in this unit and the next, pupils will apply and develop this knowledge further.

Learning pupils will have achieved at the end of the unit

- Pupils will have consolidated their understanding of leap and common years and the number of days in each (Q1)
- Pupils will have explored equivalent units within the context of fractions and decimals (Q2)
- Pupils will have consolidated their understanding of reading and telling the time on both analogue and digital clocks (Q2)
- Pupils will have consolidated their understanding of reading and telling the time in both 12- and 24-hour formats (Q3)
- Pupils will have developed their understanding of how to solve problems involving time and money (Q4, Q5)

Resources

clock faces; mini whiteboards; **Resource 4.9.6** 24-hour clocks

Vocabulary

common year, leap year, weeks, days, hours, minutes, seconds

Questions 1 and 2

---

1 Complete the facts.

(a) There are ☐ months in a year.

(b) There are ☐ days in a common year and ☐ days in a leap year.

(c) There are ☐ days in February in a common year and ☐ days in February in a leap year.

(d) There are ☐ days in the first three months of this year.

2 Write a suitable number in each box.

(a) 1 hour = ☐ minutes = ☐ seconds

(b) 1.5 hours = ☐ minutes

(c) $\frac{3}{4}$ hour = ☐ minutes = ☐ seconds

(d) 45 minutes = ☐ hours

(e) 190 minutes = ☐ hours and ☐ minutes

(f) 2.5 days = ☐ hours

(g) 3 weeks = ☐ days = ☐ hours

(h) $\frac{1}{2}$ year = ☐ months

What learning will pupils have achieved at the conclusion of Questions 1 and 2?

- Pupils will have consolidated their understanding of leap and common years and the number of days in each.
- Pupils will have explored equivalent units within the context of fractions and decimals.
- Pupils will have consolidated their understanding of reading and telling the time on both analogue and digital clocks.

Activities for whole-class instruction

- Ask pupils to discuss with a partner the units that we use to measure time. Take feedback, agreeing years, months, weeks, days, hours, minutes and seconds. Discuss equivalences between them, drawing out that there are 60 seconds in one minute, 60 minutes in one hour, 24 hours in one day, 7 days in one week and 52 weeks in one year.
- Can they remember the difference between a common year and a leap year? If not, remind them that a leap year occurs once every four years and that it has an extra day, making 366 days. A common year has 365 days.
- On the board, write: One year is made up of 12 months.

 One year is made up of 12 months.

- On the board, write: 1 year = 12 months.

- Ask pupils to generate as many other facts as they can from this, for example: 120 months = 10 years. Time them for a minute. Invite pupils to write their facts on the board. Look out for examples of doubling, halving, multiplying and dividing, such as: 24 months = 2 years, $\frac{1}{2}$ year = 6 months, 1.2 months = 0.1 years. How many equivalences can the class find? Repeat this for other units, for example: 60 seconds = 1 minute, 7 days = 1 week.

- Ask pupils to tell you how many minutes there are in fractions of hours, for example $\frac{3}{4}$ of an hour, $\frac{1}{12}$ of an hour, $\frac{1}{3}$ of an hour and so on. Many pupils will know how many minutes there are in $\frac{1}{4}, \frac{1}{2}$ and $\frac{3}{4}$ of an hour as simple facts. Ask: *How can we find $\frac{1}{12}$ of an hour?* Agree that they can divide 60 minutes by 12.

- Also, look at a clock face together – can pupils see the twelfths? (Each 5 minutes is $\frac{1}{12}$.) Ask them what $\frac{3}{12}$ of an hour would be. Agree that they find $\frac{1}{12}$ and then multiply by three.

- Can pupils work out how many seconds there are in one hour? Agree that they multiply the number of seconds in a minute by 60. Establish that they can use what they know, for example 6 × 6 = 36, so 60 × 6 = 360 and 60 × 60 = 3600. Ask them to work out the number of seconds in different numbers of hours.

- Pupils can now complete Questions 1 and 2 in the Practice Book.

Same-day intervention

- Give pupils a fact such as 60 minutes = 1 hour. Ask them to use doubling to generate other facts. Encourage them to work systematically, for example 60 minutes = 1 hour, 120 minutes = 2 hours, 240 minutes = 4 hours, 480 minutes = 8 hours.
- Once they have done this, ask them to add and subtract for other facts, for example 3 hours = 180 minutes (60 + 120), 12 hours = 720 minutes (240 + 480).

Same-day enrichment

- Give pupils this fact: 365 days = one year. Ask them to use doubling as above and then addition and subtraction to generate other facts, for example 730 days = 2 years, 1460 days = 4 years, 2920 days = 8 years, 2190 days = 6 years. Challenge pupils to work out how many days they have been alive.

Question 3

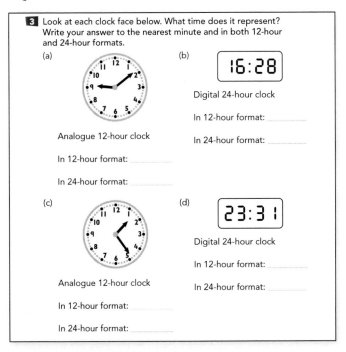

3 Look at each clock face below. What time does it represent? Write your answer to the nearest minute and in both 12-hour and 24-hour formats.

(a) Analogue 12-hour clock

In 12-hour format: _____

In 24-hour format: _____

(b) 16:28 Digital 24-hour clock

In 12-hour format: _____

In 24-hour format: _____

(c) Analogue 12-hour clock

In 12-hour format: _____

In 24-hour format: _____

(d) 23:31 Digital 24-hour clock

In 12-hour format: _____

In 24-hour format: _____

What learning will pupils have achieved at the conclusion of Question 3?

- Pupils will have consolidated their understanding of reading and telling the time in both 12- and 24-hour formats.

Activities for whole-class instruction

- Give pupils clocks and mini whiteboards. Call out different times for them to show you. Begin with times to the nearest five minutes and then move on to times to the nearest minute, for example 25 minutes past 7, 6 minutes to 4. Invite pupils to say times for a partner to show on their clocks.

- Ask: *When we are talking about time, what do analogue and digital mean?* Expect them to be able to tell you that analogue clocks have hour, minute and sometimes seconds hands and digital clocks have only numbers, no hands. Ask them to show you analogue times on their clocks and to tell you what these would be as digital times, focusing on 12-hour time. Ask: *How do we know whether these are morning or afternoon/evening times?*

- Establish that the abbreviation a.m. is used for times between midnight and noon and p.m. is used for times between noon and midnight. Remind the pupils that a.m. stands for the Latin term *ante meridiem*, which means before midday or noon, and p.m. stands for *post meridiem* meaning past midday or noon.

- Display the following clock face:

- Ask: *What do you notice about the numbers?* Expect pupils to be able to tell you that the numbers 1 to 12 show the hours on a 12-hour clock and the other numbers show the hours after midday or noon using 24-hour time.

- Ask them to show 1 o'clock on their clocks and to tell you how this time can be represented in the two digital formats (1:00 a.m., 1:00 p.m., 01:00 and 13:00). Repeat for other o'clock times, progressing to times to the nearest five minutes, then to the nearest minute.

- Ask pupils to draw analogue clock faces on paper. Call out times for them to draw onto their clock faces and then ask them to write the digital times using the two 12-hour and two 24-hour formats. For example they draw the hands to show 12 minutes to 5 and write 4:48 a.m., 4:48 p.m., 04:48 and 16:48.

- Pupils can now complete Question 3 in the Practice Book.

Same-day intervention

- Give pupils a list of times to the nearest five minutes. They find these on clock faces and then draw them on plain paper and label with 12-hour digital times, for example 10 minutes past 6, 5 minutes to 9, 20 minutes past 3.

Same-day enrichment

- Ask pupils to complete **Resource 4.9.6** 24-hour clocks, which asks them to use the digits 1, 2, 3 and 4 to make up ten possible 24-hour clock times, for example 12:34, 12:43, 13:24, 13:42.

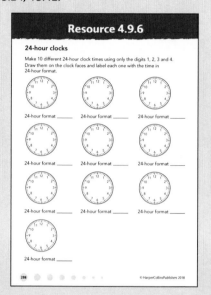

Questions 4 and 5

4 A football match started at 18:30. It lasted 135 minutes (including the half time break and some stoppage time at the end). What time did the game end?

Answer: ....

5 A bicycle shop sold 1365 bikes in 15 weeks. The same number of bikes were sold each day.

(a) How many bikes did the shop sell:

  (i) each day? ☐   (ii) each week? ☐

(b) If the price of each bike was £95, what was the total amount of money that the shop received from selling all the bikes:

  (i) each day? ....

  (ii) each week? ....

(c) The shop makes a profit of £28 on every bicycle it sells. How much profit did it make:

  (i) each day? ....

  (ii) each week? ....

  (iii) altogether over the 15 weeks? ....

What learning will pupils have achieved at the conclusion of Questions 4 and 5?

- Pupils will have developed their understanding of how to solve problems involving time and money.

Activities for whole-class instruction

- Call out different numbers of minutes for pupils to change into hours and minutes, for example 90 minutes (1 hour 30 minutes), 125 minutes (2 hours 5 minutes), 250 minutes (4 hours 10 minutes). Give pupils clocks. Ask them to show 4:40. Next, ask them to work out the time 140 minutes later than 4:40. Encourage them to first work out the number of whole hours and minutes left. They move the hands on their clocks 2 hours and then the minute hand the extra 10 minutes to show 6:50.

- Repeat several times, keeping the starting time the same and varying the number of minutes.

- Set this problem:

  – Tom started his homework at 4:15 p.m. He worked for 95 minutes. What time did he finish his homework?

- Ask pupils to use their clocks to show 4:15. They work out the number of whole hours and minutes in 95 minutes and adjust the hands of their clocks accordingly to show 5:50. Repeat the problem, varying the number of minutes Tom worked.

- Set another problem:

  – Sarah watched a film for 130 minutes. It finished at 19:35. What time did it start?

- Ask pupils to use their clocks to show 19:35. They work out the number of whole hours and minutes in 130 minutes and adjust the hands of their clocks accordingly to show 2 hours and 10 minutes earlier than 19:35.

- Repeat the problem, varying the times the film finished. You could then vary the length of the film and then the context, for example Sarah went for a bike ride. She rode for 130 minutes. She ended her ride at 19:35. What time did she set off? Each time ask: *What is the same and what is different about the problem?*

- Ask pupils this problem:

  – A baker bakes 560 loaves of bread every day of the week. How many loaves is that in one week? How many is it in 2/4/8 weeks?

- Encourage pupils to multiply the number of loaves by 7 using a method they like to use and then check using a second method. When they have the total for a week, encourage them to use doubling for 2, 4 and 8 weeks. Then ask them to find different numbers of weeks by, for example adding, subtracting and multiplying by 10.

- Ask pupils this problem:

– A shoe shop sold 1400 pairs of trainers over a period of four weeks. Their records show that they sold the same number of trainers each day over the four weeks. How many trainers did they sell each week? The shoe shop is open every day of the week. How many trainers did it sell each day?

● Discuss how pupils can find the number of trainers sold in one week. Guide pupils to a 'halving and halving again' strategy. Discuss how they can find the number in one day. Expect them to tell you that they can divide the number sold in one week by 7.

● Continue the problem by saying that each pair of trainers costs £25. Ask pupils to work out how much money the shoe shop received in one day, one week and four weeks. Tell pupils that the shop makes a profit of £5.50 on each pair of trainers that it sells. Discuss what is meant by 'profit'. Establish that the profit is the difference between the cost of the trainers when they buy them from the company that supplies them to the shop (supplier) and the price they sell them for. So the supplier would get £19.50 and the shop would get £5.50 for each pair sold.

● Ask pupils to work out the profit each day, each week and over four weeks.

● Set similar problems varying one aspect each time.

● Pupils can now complete Questions 4 and 5 in the Practice Book.

Same-day intervention

● Make a list of starting times to give pupils. Ensure these are 12-hour times to the nearest five minutes. Ask pupils to find these times on their clocks and then find and draw the times 90 minutes later. Expect them to be able to work out that 90 minutes is equivalent to 60 minutes and 30 minutes, which is an hour and a half.

Same-day enrichment

● Ask pupils to make up problems similar to those you asked in the lesson that involve time and money. They give these to a partner to solve. Towards the end of the lesson, ask pupils to share their problems with the class and for the class to evaluate how effectively they address the practice of time and money.

Challenge and extension questions

Questions 6 and 7

6 In 24 hours, how many full rotations does the hour hand move on the clock face? How many full rotations does the minute hand move on the clock face?

Hour hand: ☐   Minute hand : ☐

7 Ellie's family used 15 kilowatt-hours (kWh) of electricity per day last year.

(a) How many kilowatt-hours did her family use in the first 6 months of last year?

Answer:

(b) If the cost was 12p per kWh, how much did the family need to pay per day? How much did the family need to pay for the first 6 months of last year? Express your answers in whole pounds and pence.

Answer:

Questions 6 and 7 extend pupils' understanding of time and money. In Question 6, they have to make connections with rotation, working out the number of rotations the hour hand and minute hand make in 24 hours. Question 7 involves an understanding of the unit kilowatt-hour, which is a measure of electrical energy. You may need to explain this to pupils. The problems here require pupils to understand relationships between units of time.

Unit 9.7
Solving problems involving time and money (2)

Conceptual context

This unit is an extension of Unit 9.6. This time the focus is money, with problem solving involving time and money in real-world contexts. Pupils will convert between units of measurement for money. This includes converting fractions of pounds to pence. Pupils are asked to solve problems with money that involve multiplication and division, and making links to time, including in relation to annual salaries and hourly wages, so it is important that pupils understand what these are.

Learning pupils will have achieved at the end of the unit

- Pupils will have consolidated their understanding of the units in our monetary system and relationships between them (Q1)
- Pupils will have solved problems involving multiplication and division of money (Q2, Q3)
- Pupils will have explored solving problems about salary and hourly wages (Q4)
- Pupils will have consolidated their understanding of solving problems involving money (Q5)

Resources

selection of notes and coins

Vocabulary

annual salary, hourly wage

Question 1

1 Fill in each box below with a suitable number. The answer could be a whole number, a fraction or a decimal.

(a) £1 = ☐ pence

(b) £$\frac{1}{10}$ = ☐ pence

(c) 60p = ☐ pounds

(d) £$\frac{3}{4}$ = ☐ pence

(e) 890p = ☐ pounds and ☐ pence

(f) 1p = ☐ pounds

(g) £80.50 = ☐ pence

(h) £2.38 = ☐ pence

What learning will pupils have achieved at the conclusion of Question 1?

● Pupils will have consolidated their understanding of the units in our monetary system and the relationships between them.

Activities for whole-class instruction

● Give pairs of pupils a selection of notes and coins. Ask them to find the total of the amount that they have. How do they do this? Did anyone sort the notes and coins into those of the same value first? Did they use multiplication to find, for example the value of eight 5p coins?

● Next, ask pupils to make different values in different ways, for example £2.38, £5.49. Ask them to show you two or three alternative ways to make the values and then to show you using the fewest coins, for example £2.38 – £2 coin, 20p, 10p, 5p, 2p and 1p.

● Ask pupils to make £2.75 and £4.63. Ask: *What is the total?* Then ask: *If you bought two different items in a shop that cost £2.75 and £4.63, how much change would you get if you paid with a £10 note?*

● Repeat, making two different amounts of money, finding the total and then substituting those amounts into the questions.

● Show the following grid, which shows fractions of £1 represented by one pence coins.

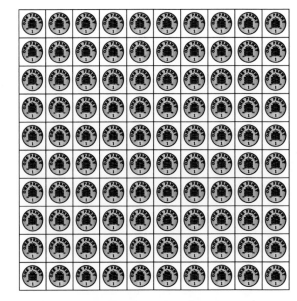

● Discuss what the image shows. Emphasise that each square shows one penny. Explain that there are 100 pennies in £1, so 1p is one hundredth of a pound. Ask questions such as: *What fraction are 6, 12, 32, 75 pennies of £1?*

● For fractions that can be reduced or simplified, ask pupils to simplify – to make the denominator as small as possible, for example $\frac{6}{100}$ could be $\frac{3}{50}$, $\frac{12}{100}$ could be $\frac{6}{50}$ or $\frac{3}{25}$.

● Pupils should focus on the 10p coins that they have. Ask: *What fraction is 10p of £1?* Agree one tenth. Ask: *How do you know?* Ask what fractions are 20p, 30p, 40p and so on of £1. Can they tell you that 20p is two-tenths, which is equivalent to one-fifth? Can they write these as decimals? Write different amounts on the board, for example 25p. Ask them to convert this to a fraction of one pound and then a decimal.

● Write different numbers of pence on the board. Pupils convert these to pounds and pence. For example 645p, 1276p, 2436p.

● Pupils can now complete Question 1 in the Practice Book.

Same-day intervention

● Give pupils a list of values, for example £1.56, £2.65, £3.14, and a container of coins. Ask pupils to make these amounts using the fewest coins. They then record the coins they have used and write the value they have made.

Same-day enrichment

- Give pupils this fact: $£\frac{1}{4}$ = 25p. Ask them to generate other facts by doubling and addition and subtraction, for example $£\frac{1}{2}$ = 50p, $£\frac{1}{4}$ = 25p, $£\frac{3}{4}$ = 75p, £1 = 100p, $£1\frac{3}{4}$ = 175p, $£3\frac{2}{4}$ = 350p.

Questions 2 and 3

> **2** Fill in the boxes.
> (a) A school bought 600 ropes. This cost £3600.
>   Each rope cost ☐ pounds.
> (b) One volleyball costs £50. With £150, Mr Lee can
>   only buy ☐ volleyballs.
> (c) Each football costs £9. Mr Lee bought 72 balls.
>   He paid ☐ pounds.
>
> **3** A gardening shop sold 12 bags of garden gravel and 4 bags of
> bark chippings in a day. Each bag of gravel was priced at £4 and
> each bag of bark chippings was priced at £75. What was the total
> amount of money received from the sales?
>
> Answer: _____

What learning will pupils have achieved at the conclusion of Questions 2 and 3?

- Pupils will have solved word problems involving multiplication and division of money.

Activities for whole-class instruction

- Ask pupils to solve this problem:
  - George was saving to buy bikes for his 4 children. The bikes cost £250 each. He has saved £875. How many bikes can he buy? How much more does he need to save for all four children to be able to have a bike?
- Use the bar model to show the problem, for example:
  - Each bike costs £250, George wants four. To find the total cost £250 must be multiplied by 4. The bar model clearly makes the link between repeated addition and multiplication.

Bike	£250	£250	£250	£250
		?		

- When the total cost is known, the difference should be found between the total and the money George saved:

Total cost of bikes	£1000	
Money saved	£875	?

- The difference can be found by subtracting £875 from £1000 or by counting on from £875 to £1000. Either way, George needs to save another £125.

- Expect pupils to be able to count in amounts of £250 to work out that George can currently buy three bikes for £750. Expect them to know the difference between £750 and £850 and then to work out that he has another £125 saved and therefore he needs to save another £125. Repeat the question, initially varying the amount that the bikes cost and then the amount that George has saved.

- Present another problem:
  - Sally wants to take her family on holiday. She has worked out that it will cost £560 per family member. Including Sally, there are 5 family members. What is the total cost of the holiday?

- Use the bar model to show the problem, for example:
  - The price per person is £560. There are five people, so £560 needs to be multiplied by 5.

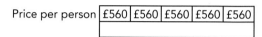

Price per person	£560	£560	£560	£560	£560

- How do the pupils work out £560 × 5? Do they use a written method? Do they use their knowledge of the relationship between 5 and 10 and multiply £560 mentally by 10 and then halve the product? This is a useful mental calculation strategy. Spend some time asking pupils to multiply different numbers by 5 using this strategy.

- Repeat the problem, varying the amount that the holiday will cost per family member.

- Present the next problem:
  - Fahmida was putting up a fence around her garden. She bought 8 fence panels and 9 fence posts. Each panel cost £125 and each post £75. What was her total spend?

- Invite a pupil to model what the problem looks like in a similar way to the way you did for the previous problems. For example:

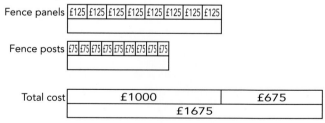

- Observe pupils as they solve this problem. Do they use a written method or a mental calculation strategy to multiply £125 by 8? Invite pupils to share their methods. What strategy do they use to multiply £75 by 9? For each calculation, ask pupils to find at least two possible strategies. Discuss which they think are the most efficient.

- Alter the problem slightly by saying that Fahmida had saved £600 and ask how many panels she can buy and then how many fence posts she can buy with her £600. Discuss ways of finding how many panels can be bought for £600.

- Encourage pupils to make jottings and use a mental calculation strategy, for example double £125 to give £250, double £250 to give £500. She can therefore buy 4 panels. Repeat this for the posts: double £75 to give £150, double £150 to give £300 and double £300 to give £600. She can therefore buy 8 posts.

- Pupils can now complete Questions 2 and 3 in the Practice Book.

Same-day intervention

- Ask pupils to make up simple problems that involve calculating with money for a partner to solve, for example:
  - Annie saved £36 a month. How much did she save in four months?

Same-day enrichment

- Ask pupils to make up their own two-step problems involving multiplication of money and finding the difference for a partner to solve, for example:
  - Freddie wanted to buy 4 computer games. Each game cost £25.75. He had saved £100. How much more money does he need?

Question 4

4 Erin graduated from university two years ago and her monthly salary is now £2512. Her younger brother Joe is still at school and works part-time during term time. He earns an hourly wage of £9.50.

(a) What is Erin's annual salary?

Answer: _____

(b) In the summer holidays, Joe works full time for 8 hours per day, 5 days per week for the same hourly wage. Estimate and then calculate how much he earns in a week. What is the difference between your estimate and the actual amount he earns?

Estimate: _____

Calculate: _____

Difference: _____

(c) Are Joe's earnings in four weeks when working full time more or less than half of Erin's monthly salary?

Answer: _____

What learning will pupils have achieved at the conclusion of Question 4?

- Pupils will have explored solving word problems about salary and hourly wages.

Activities for whole-class instruction

- Discuss what is meant by 'salary'. Establish that a salary is a fixed regular payment, usually paid every month, to someone who works for another person or company. Introduce the words 'employer' as the person someone works for and 'employee' as the worker. Explain that an annual salary is the amount paid over a full year.

- Call out a monthly payment and ask pupils to tell you what the annual salary is, for example £500, £750, £1200. Can pupils fluently multiply monthly payments by 12 to find annual salary?

- Talk about hourly wage and the difference between this and an annual salary. Establish that an hourly wage is how much a person is paid per hour. Often, if people have part time jobs, they may be paid hourly. Call out some hourly wages, for example £9, £10.50, £12, and ask pupils to work out how much a person would get per day if they work 5 hours a day, 6 hours a day and 7 hours a day.

- Ask pupils to then work out how much they would be paid in total if working for 4 days a week, 5 days a week and 6 days a week. Assess their ability to solve these calculations using their multiplication facts.

- Set this problem:
  - Bobby worked at the hardware shop for 7 hours every Saturday. His hourly wage was £10.50. How much did he earn each Saturday? He saved half of his wages. How much would he have saved after 4 weeks?

- Ask: *How can you work out how much Bobby earns each Saturday?* Discuss pupils' strategies. Repeat the problem varying Bobby's hourly wage.

- Set another problem:
  - Kelly works full time at the hardware shop. She is paid £2500 each month. What is her annual salary? Roughly how many Saturdays does Bobby have to work to earn as much as Kelly earns in one month?

- Ask pupils to explain how they would work out Kelly's annual salary. Agree that they could multiply £2500 by 12. Can they think of a quick way to do this? You could suggest multiplying £2500 by 10 (£25 000), then doubling £2500 (£5000) and add the two amounts (£30 000). If Bobby earns £73.50 each Saturday, he would earn £735 over 10 weeks, £7350 over 100 weeks. Can they use this fact to estimate roughly how many Saturdays he would need to work to make £30 000? They should be able to use doubling to get close to £30 000: 100 weeks = £7350, 200 weeks = £14 700, 400 weeks = £29 400.

- Repeat the problem varying Kelly's monthly payment.

- Pupils can now complete Question 4 in the Practice Book.

Same-day intervention

- Tell pupils that Sam's hourly wage is £12. Ask them to work out how much Sam earns if he works for different numbers of hours, for example 2, 3, 4 and 5. Observe how pupils use their knowledge of multiplication facts to work out the products, or partition £12 into £10 and £2, work out the two products and add them together.

Same-day enrichment

- Pupils make up problems similar to those you asked in the lesson that involve calculating with money to work out wages and salaries. They then give these to a partner to solve. Towards the end of the lesson, ask pupils to share their problems with the class and for the class to evaluate how effective they are for practising solving problems with money.

Question 5

> **5** Anna and her family went on holiday to Thailand for three weeks. The cost was £5418 in total.
>
> (a) If the cost for each day was the same, how much was the total cost for each day and each week?
>
> Each day: _____ Each week: _____
>
> (b) If the family had cut down their holiday to two weeks and kept the daily cost the same, how much money could they have saved?
>
> Answer: _____

What learning will pupils have achieved at the conclusion of Question 5?

- Pupils will have consolidated their understanding of solving problems involving money.

Activities for whole-class instruction

- Set this problem:
  - Sophia and her two friends spent some money on clothes. They spent £450 in total. If they each spent the same amount, how much did they spend on clothes?
- Use a bar model to show the problem, for example:

£450		
?	?	?

- Establish that £450 needs to be divided by 3 to give the amount each friend spent. Encourage pupils to divide in different ways, for example using the written method, using what they know (£45 ÷ 3 = £15, so £450 ÷ 3 = £150) and partitioning into groups that can easily be divided by 3: £300 + £150 (£100 + £50). Discuss the effectiveness of the methods used.

- Continue the problem by asking how much they would each spend if they cut their spending by one-fifth and also to find the total they spent. For example one-fifth of £150 is £30, so each would spend £120, which is a total of £360. Observe how pupils make their calculations.

- Vary the problem so that the friends spent different amounts of money on clothes. Choose amounts that are multiples of 3. You could also change the fraction to ensure that the amount each spends can be divided into that fraction.

- Set this problem:
  - Adam spent £140 on music over a week. If he spent the same amount each day, how much did he spend on Tuesday? If he spent the same amount every day for two weeks, how much did he spend each day? If he spent £2.50 a day on music, how many weeks would it take for Adam to spend £140?

- Agree that £140 is the total spent, so that to find how much he spent each day, £140 must be divided by 7 to give £20 a day. Use a bar model to illustrate this:

£140						
?	?	?	?	?	?	?

- To work out the amount spent over a two-week period, pupils could divide £140 by 14 to give £10 per day. Look out for pupils who can see the connection between doubling and halving. Two weeks is twice as many days as one week, so the same amount of money spread over twice as many days will mean that only half the amount is spent each day.

- How do pupils solve the last part of the question? Again, this could be illustrated using a bar model, for example:

£17.50						
£2.50	£2.50	£2.50	£2.50	£2.50	£2.50	£2.50

- This model shows that Adam would spend £17.50 per week. Pupils could use a doubling model to find out how long it would take him to spend £140, for example:

1 week £17.50

2 weeks £35

4 weeks £70

8 weeks £140

- Repeat the problem varying the amount that Adam spent, ensuring that the amount is a multiple of 7.
- Pupils can now complete Question 5 in the Practice Book.

Same-day intervention

- Work with pupils to represent the problems in Question 5 with pictures and diagrams.

Same-day enrichment

- Challenge pairs of pupils to make up a question similar to Question 5 about Anna and her family, who spent a different amount of money on their holiday. Ask: *Why is it difficult to make up a question?* Can pupils tell you that they must use only numbers that are multiples of 21 if they are to be able to find a daily spend and find answers in whole pounds?

Challenge and extension questions

Question 6

> **6** A pancake stall sold 6 pancakes per minute during one evening. The pancakes were 99p each. If the vendor started working from 17:45 and ended at 19:05, how much money did he make from pancake sales that evening?
>
> Answer: _____

This problem involves time and money.

Question 7

> **7** A new school plans to buy desks and chairs for 14 classes. A desk and chair set costs £15. Each class needs 30 sets of desks and chairs. If the school has a budget of £6500, is it enough? By how much is the budget more or less than the total purchase price?
>
>
>
> Answer: _____

This problem expects pupils to use multiplication and division to solve a money problem.

Chapter 9 test (Practice Book 4B, pages 88–93)

Test question number	Relevant unit	Relevant questions within unit
1a–d	9.1	1, 2
1e, f	9.2	1, 2
	9.3	1, 2
1g	9.6	1, 2
1h	9.7	1
2 a, b	9.2	3, 4, 5
	9.3	3, 4, 5
2 c	9.4	1
3	9.2	2
	9.3	2
4a	9.6	1
4b	9.7	1
4c, d	9.3	5
	9.4	5
5	9.4	2
6	9.5	5
7a–e	9.2	3, 4, 5
	9.3	3, 4, 5
	9.4	3, 4, 5
7f–h	9.6	5
	9.7	2, 3, 4, 5

Chapter 10
Four operations of whole numbers

Chapter overview

Area of mathematics	National Curriculum Statutory requirements for Key Stage 2	Shanghai Maths Project reference
Number – addition and subtraction	Year 4 Programme of Study: Pupils should be taught to: ■ solve addition and subtraction two-step problems in contexts, deciding which operations and methods to use and why.	Year 4, Units 10.3, 10.4, 10.5, 10.6, 10.7, 10.8, 10.9, 10.10, 10.11, 10.12, 10.13, 10.14, 10.15, 10.16, 10.17, 10.18
Number – addition and subtraction	Year 5 Programme of Study: Pupils should be taught to: ■ solve addition and subtraction multi-step problems in contexts, deciding which operations and methods to use and why.	Year 4, Units 10.3, 10.4, 10.5, 10.6, 10.7, 10.8, 10.9, 10.10, 10.11, 10.12, 10.13, 10.14, 10.15, 10.16, 10.17, 10.18
Number – multiplication and division	Year 4 Programme of Study: Pupils should be taught to: ■ solve problems involving multiplying and adding, including using the distributive law to multiply two digit numbers by one digit, integer scaling problems and harder correspondence problems such as n objects are connected to m objects	Year 4, Units 10.13, 10.14
	■ recall multiplication and division facts for multiplication tables up to 12 × 12	Year 4, Units 10.1 and 10.2
	■ use place value, known and derived facts to multiply and divide mentally, including: multiplying by 0 and 1; dividing by 1; multiplying together three number	Year 4, Units 10.1 and 10.2
	■ recognise and use factor pairs and commutativity in mental calculations.	

Area of mathematics	National Curriculum Statutory requirements for Key Stage 2	Shanghai Maths Project reference
Number – multiplication and division	■ solve problems involving multiplication and division, including scaling by simple fractions and problems involving simple rates.	Year 4, Units 10.1 and 10.2
Number – addition, subtraction, multiplication and division	Year 5 Programme of Study: Pupils should be taught to: ■ solve problems involving addition, subtraction, multiplication and division and a combination of these, including understanding the meaning of the equals sign	Year 4, Units 10.1, 10.2, 10.3, 10.4, 10.5, 10.6, 10.7, 10.8, 10.9, 10.10, 10.11, 10.12, 10.13, 10.14, 10.15, 10.16, 10.17, 10.18
	■ solve problems involving multiplication and division, including scaling by simple fractions and problems involving simple rates.	Year 4, Units 10.1, 10.2, 10.15, 10.16, 10.17, 10.18
Number – addition, subtraction, multiplication and division	Year 6 Programme of Study: Pupils should be taught to: ■ use their knowledge of the order of operations to carry out calculations involving the four operations.	Year 4, Units 10.3, 10.4, 10.5, 10.6, 10.7, 10.8, 10.9, 10.10, 10.11, 10.12, 10.13, 10.14, 10.15, 10.16, 10.17, 10.18

Unit 10.1
Calculating work rate (1)

Conceptual context

Pupils have previously explored mental and written methods for multiplication and division, drawing on the relationship between the two operations to check calculations and solve missing number problems.

In this unit, pupils discover a real-life application for multiplication and division as they explore 'work rates'.

They first calculate their own work rates as they engage in a practical activity, recognising that they can find this by dividing the amount of work by the time taken.

Pupils use what they know about related facts to identify the operations that are needed to calculate the time taken, having been given the work rate and the amount of work, or to calculate the amount of work, having been given the work rate and the time taken.

Pupils flexibly apply methods of multiplication and division, drawing on known facts to help them.

Learning pupils will have achieved at the end of the unit

- Pupils will have developed a conceptual understanding of 'work rate' through practical activities (Q1)
- Pupils will have applied calculation methods for multiplication and division flexibly to solve problems (Q1, Q2, Q3)
- Knowledge of the relationship between multiplication and division will have been strengthened through solving problems relating to work rate (Q2, Q3)

Resources

interlocking cubes; trays; boxes; stopwatches; **Resource 4.10.1a** Maths is fun! (1), **Resource 4.10.1b** Maths is fun! (2), **Resource 4.10.1c** Who does more? **Resource 4.10.1d** Work rate questions; **Resource 4.10.1e** What's the question?

Vocabulary

work rate, time taken, amount of work, multiply, divide

Question 1

> **1** The table below shows the numbers of toys that 3 toymakers, Mr Lee, Mrs Wood and Miss Kaur made in different numbers of days.
>
> | | Mr Lee | Mrs Wood | Miss Kaur |
> |---|---|---|---|
> | Number of toys | 252 | 215 | 360 |
> | Number of days | 6 | 5 | 8 |
>
> Please read the table carefully. From the table, do you know who was the fastest in making toys? The numbers of toys and days are all different. How can we compare them?

What learning will pupils have achieved at the conclusion of Question 1?

- Pupils will have developed a conceptual understanding of 'work rate' through practical activities.
- Pupils will have applied calculation methods for multiplication and division flexibly to solve problems.

Activities for whole-class instruction

- Split the class into equal groups and provide each group with a large tray of interlocking cubes and an empty tray. Ensure that all cubes are separate. Explain that groups will be given a number of minutes to make as many sticks of 5 cubes as possible. Each stick must be dropped into the empty tray. The number of complete sticks of 5 in the tray at the end of the time will be counted.

- Ask: *How many sticks do you think you can make by yourself in one minute?* Take responses. Ask: *So, how many will your group make in one minute? in 3 minutes?*

- Start the stopwatch, stopping groups after 3 minutes.

  Ask a team member to bring the completed sticks to the front of the class as soon as they finish.

- Show pupils the following table and ask them to complete it.

	Group 1	Group 2	Group 3	Group 4	Group 5
Number of sticks					
Number of minutes					

- Ask: *From the table, do you know which group was fastest at making sticks of cubes?* Take responses. Explain that this would be a 'work rate' – the rate or speed at which groups were working. Tell pupils that rate and speed are the same thing.

- Identify the group that worked at the greatest speed and explain that their work rate was the greatest and the rate at which they were working was the fastest.

(Use these terms interchangeably throughout the lesson so that pupils make conceptual links between them, understanding the strong connections.)

- Ask: *How could you work out what speed or rate your group was working at?* Let pupils discuss ideas. Offer prompts such as: *If you know how many sticks you made in three minutes that means you could say your rate was … sticks in three minutes. How many do you think your group had made after one minute? How would you work that out?*

Pupils should suggest dividing the number of sticks by the number of minutes to find the number of sticks made in one minute.

(i) It is helpful, at this point, to discuss similarities with speed in a car – mention 'per', explaining that 'per' means 'in every', so 40 miles per hour means travelling at a speed or rate of 40 miles in every hour (also reverse the phrasing and say that in every hour the car would travel 40 miles) – playing with the language this way forms and reinforces conceptual links.

- Repeat the sticks activity, with groups working for different lengths of time – for example 3, 4, 5 minutes.

- Establish that it is more difficult to compare the results because the times are all different.

- Ask: *How could we find out which group was most efficient?* Agree that the work rate for each group must be calculated; then they can be compared. Ask pupils to suggest how to do this?

- Each group should calculate their work rate using a division method of their choice, for example 32 sticks made in five minutes as 20 ÷ 5 = 6 r2

- Add another row to the table so that work rates can be recorded and compared.

Number of sticks per minute (work rate)					

- Agree which group was fastest at making sticks of cubes. That is, the group that made more sticks per minute.

 (All say …) *Work rate is equal to the amount of work divided by the time taken.*

Record this as:

Work rate = amount of work ÷ time taken

- Ask pupils to complete Question 1 in the Practice Book.
  [Note: Keep a copy of the table of results for the next session.]

Same-day intervention

- Pupils work together in different-sized groups to make as many sticks of eight cubes as they can in four minutes.

- Ensure they can explain whether the number of sticks made may be more or less than the number made during the whole-class instruction. Ensure they recognise that each stick will take a little longer to make as it comprises more cubes and/or that fewer people will make fewer sticks.

- They should calculate the work rates using the formula identified previously.

Same-day enrichment

- Give pupils **Resource 4.10.1a** Maths is fun! (1).

  They should each complete the activity and calculate the work rate, comparing results.

Resource 4.10.1a

Maths is fun! (1)

1. Work together as a group to explore how many times you can each write the statement 'Maths is fun!' in 2 minutes. Use the back of the sheet if you need more space.

   Maths is fun!

2. Complete the table for the group and compare the results. Calculate the work rate for each person.

Name						
Number of times statement written in total						
Time taken (minutes)	2	2	2	2	2	2
Work rate (number of times per minute)						

Who was the most efficient at writing the statements? What was their work rate?

© HarperCollinsPublishers 2018   299

Question 2

2 In the question above, the number of toys that Mr Lee, Mrs Wood and Miss Kaur made per day can be termed **work rate**. In general, **work rate** is the amount of work completed divided by the time taken. Fill in the ◯ with '×' or '÷'.

(a) work rate = amount of work ◯ time taken

(b) amount of work = work rate ◯ ....

(c) time taken = amount of work ◯ ....

What learning will pupils have achieved at the conclusion of Question 2?

- Pupils will have applied calculation methods for multiplication and division flexibly to solve problems.

- Knowledge of the relationship between multiplication and division will have been strengthened through solving problems relating to work rate.

Activities for whole-class instruction

- Remind pupils about the 'work rate' activity they carried out as part of the previous session. Show the completed table.

- Reveal another incomplete table, explaining that the same activity was carried out in another school with groups of equal size.

	Group A	Group B	Group C	Group D	Group E	Group F
Number of sticks	34	51		80		168
Number of minutes	2	3	5		6	
Number of sticks per minute (work rate)			15	20	18	24

- Ask pupils to calculate the work rate for Group A and Group B and to explain which group was faster at making sticks of cubes.

- Ask: *Which group was most efficient? ... least efficient?* Ask pupils to put the groups in order of efficiency. They should now be able to understand that:

  faster work rate = more efficient

  slower work rate = less efficient

- Now look together at the information about Group C. Discuss what is different about it, agreeing that we do not know the total number of sticks made but we do know the work rate.

- Ask: *How can we work out how many sticks were made altogether in 5 minutes?*

- Ask pupils to explore the problem, looking back at the relationship between the values for Groups A and B to help them make decisions.

- Share ideas, establishing that we need to multiply the work rate by the time taken ($15 \times 5 = 75$).

 Amount of work is equal to the work rate multiplied by the time taken.

Record this as:

'Amount of work = work rate × time taken'

- Move on to the information we know about Group D. Agree that the group made 20 sticks of cubes per minute and made 80 sticks in total. Ask: *How long did it take them? How can we work this out?*

- Again, ask pupils to explore the problem, looking back at the relationship between the values for the previous groups to help make decisions.

- Share ideas, establishing that we need to divide the amount of work by the work rate ($80 \div 20 = 4$).

 Time taken is equal to the amount of work divided by the work rate.

Record this as:

'Time taken = amount of work ÷ work rate'

- Invite pupils to now find the missing values for Groups E and F. They should record the calculations they use, explaining what each number represents (work rate, time taken or amount of work)

- Ask pupils to complete Question 2 in the Practice Book.

Same-day intervention

- Give pupils **Resource 4.10.1b** Maths is fun! (2)

- Ask pupils to complete an activity and compare results by calculating their work rates.

- Ask pupils to find missing information in a table about other pupils' work rates, using what they know about calculating the time taken, the amount of work or the work rate, as required.

Same-day enrichment

- Give pupils **Resource 4.10.1c** Who does more?

- Work together as a group to discuss the pupils' statements. Ask pupils to provide and explain answers to the questions each time.

  Answers: 1. They both filled 300 cups; 2. The girl did star jumps faster (23 jumps each minute); 3. The boy took longer (16 minutes).

Question 3

> **3** Write the number sentences and then calculate.
>
> (a) Lily has read 132 pages of a book in 4 days. How many pages did she read per day?
>
> Number sentence: _____
>
> Answer: _____
>
> (b) Tom can do 32 mental calculations per minute. Working at the same rate, how many mental calculations can he do in 5 minutes?
>
> Number sentence: _____
>
> Answer: _____
>
> (c) Asha can assemble 30 pieces of construction model per hour. With the same work rate, how many hours does it take her to assemble 480 pieces of the model?
>
> Number sentence: _____
>
> Answer: _____
>
> (d) Aaron and Meena made sweets to sell for charity. Aaron made 270 sweets in 3 hours. Meena made 400 sweets in 5 hours. Who has the higher work rate?
>
> Number sentence: _____
>
> Answer: _____

What learning will pupils have achieved at the conclusion of Question 3?

- Pupils will have applied calculation methods for multiplication and division flexibly to solve problems.
- Knowledge of the relationship between multiplication and division will have been strengthened through solving problems relating to work rate.

Activities for whole-class instruction

- (Before the session, cut up several copies of **Resource 4.10.1d** Work rate questions, ready to assign one set of the same questions to each group later on.)

Resource 4.10.1d

Work rate questions

6 drinks bottled per second	70 beats a minute
a) How many drinks can be bottled in 15 seconds?	a) How many times does this heart beat in an hour?
b) How long will it take to bottle 150 drinks?	b) How long does it take to beat 490 times?

4 buses an hour	9 flights a day
a) How many buses are there in 11 hours?	a) How many flights are there in one week?
b) How many hours does it take for 132 buses to come?	b) How many days does it take for 144 flights?

110 packs made an hour	3 deliveries a week
a) How many packs are made in 4 hours?	a) How many deliveries are there in 18 weeks?
b) How long does it take to make 550 packs?	b) How many weeks will it take to complete 72 deliveries?

© HarperCollinsPublishers 2018   101

Answers: Bottles: a) 90 b) 25 seconds; Beats: a) 4200 b) 7 minutes; Buses: a) 44 b) 33; Flights: a) 63 b) 16; Packs: a) 440 b) 5 hours; Deliveries: a) 54 b) 24.

- Show pupils the following image:

Nine flights a day

MILK

6 drinks bottled per second

70 beats a minute

SPEEDY TRUCKS

Three deliveries a week

110 packs made an hour

Biscuits

Four buses an hour

- Look together at the different statements, paying particular attention to the language used. Agree that the statements all describe different work rates.
- Work together as a group to discuss the statement '6 drinks bottled per second', explaining that this is the number of drinks that are bottled per second in a factory.
- Ask: *If drinks are bottled at the same rate, how long will it take to bottle 120 drinks?*

  Ask pupils to discuss the problem in pairs or groups.
- Share ideas, making sure that pupils recognise that we know the work rate (6 bottles per second) and the amount of work (120 bottles). We do not yet know the total time taken.
- Agree the calculation as:

  Time taken = amount of work ÷ work rate

  = 120 ÷ 6

  = 20 seconds
- Explain that at another factory, 240 drinks are bottled in 30 seconds. Ask: *Which factory has a faster work rate?*
- Give each group a set of questions from **Resource 4.10.1d**. Ask pupils to use the information to calculate as necessary and ask them to record the calculations they use each time to explain their decisions.
- Take feedback, agreeing the calculations each time and discussing the methods used to carry out the necessary multiplications or divisions.
- Ask pupils to complete Question 3 in the Practice Book.

Same-day intervention

- Look together at any of the problems that pupils found difficult in Question 3. Discuss the information that is known each time, asking pupils to select the appropriate calculation card that shows this.

> Work rate = amount of work ÷ time taken

> Amount of work = work rate × time taken

> Time taken = amount of work ÷ work rate

- Use the cards to help organise the information known and then calculate the answer.
- Look at different methods of multiplication and division, deciding whether a mental or written method is required.

Same-day enrichment

- Give pupils **Resource 4.10.1e** What's the question? Ask pupils to work out the questions each time using the given answers.

Resource 4.10.1e

What's the question?

The answer to each question has been given.
Can you fill in the missing information in the question each time?

6 drinks bottled per second
a) How many drinks can be bottled in _____ seconds?
_____192 drinks_____
b) How long will it take to bottle _____ drinks?
_____29 seconds_____

70 beats a minute
a) How many times does this heart beat in _____ minutes?
_____105 beats_____
b) How long does it take to beat _____ times?
_____35 minutes_____

4 buses an hour
a) How many buses are there in _____ hours?
_____96 buses_____
b) How many hours does it take for _____ buses to come?
_____52 hours_____

9 flights a day
a) How many flights are there in _____ days?
_____270 flights_____
b) How many days does it take for _____ flights?
_____90 days_____

110 packs made an hour
a) How many packs are made in _____ hours at the same work rate?
_____1210 packs_____
b) How long does it take to make _____ packs?
_____5½ hours_____

3 deliveries a week
a) How many deliveries are there in _____ weeks?
_____105 deliveries_____
b) How many weeks will it take to complete _____ deliveries?
_____13 weeks_____

306　　© HarperCollins Publishers 2018

Answers: Bottles: a) 32 b) 174; Beats: a) 1.5 b) 2450; Buses: a) 24 b) 208; Flights: a) 30 b) 810; Packs: a) 11 b) 605; Deliveries: a) 35 b) 39.

Challenge and extension questions

Questions 4 and 5

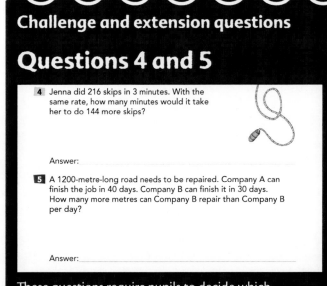

4　Jenna did 216 skips in 3 minutes. With the same rate, how many minutes would it take her to do 144 more skips?

Answer: _____

5　A 1200-metre-long road needs to be repaired. Company A can finish the job in 40 days. Company B can finish it in 30 days. How many more metres can Company B repair than Company B per day?

Answer: _____

These questions require pupils to decide which information is given each time and how it should be used to solve each work rate problem.

Encourage pupils to write the different calculations in words, for example work rate = amount of work ÷ time taken, replacing the terms with values as they identify them.

In Question 5, pupils need to recognise that the problem is not complete by simply finding the work rates, but they must identify the difference between the rates per day.

Unit 10.2
Calculating work rate (2)

Conceptual context

In this unit, pupils continue to apply their knowledge about multiplication and division to real-life examples as they deepen their understanding of 'work rates' and efficiency.

Learning pupils will have achieved at the end of the unit

- Knowledge about the relationship between multiplication and division will have been strengthened as pupils solve problems relating to work rate (Q1, Q2)
- Pupils will be able to represent 'work rate' problems in tree diagrams to help to identify the calculation required (Q1, Q2)
- Pupils will be able to apply calculation methods for multiplication and division flexibly to solve problems (Q1, Q2)
- Conceptual understanding of 'work rate' and efficiency will have been deepened through practical activities (Q2)

Resources

cubes; counters; buckets; large hoops; balls, boxes; stopwatch; **Resource 4.10.2a** Making deliveries; **Resource 4.10.2b** Tree diagrams; **Resource 4.10.2c** Three in a row

Vocabulary

work rate, time taken, amount of work, multiply, divide

Question 1

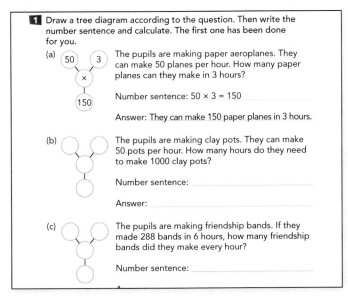

1 Draw a tree diagram according to the question. Then write the number sentence and calculate. The first one has been done for you.

(a) The pupils are making paper aeroplanes. They can make 50 planes per hour. How many paper planes can they make in 3 hours?

Number sentence: 50 × 3 = 150

Answer: They can make 150 paper planes in 3 hours.

(b) The pupils are making clay pots. They can make 50 pots per hour. How many hours do they need to make 1000 clay pots?

Number sentence: _____

Answer: _____

(c) The pupils are making friendship bands. If they made 288 bands in 6 hours, how many friendship bands did they make every hour?

Number sentence: _____

What learning will pupils have achieved at the conclusion of Question 1?

- Knowledge about the relationship between multiplication and division will have been strengthened through solving problems relating to work rate.
- Pupils will be able to represent 'work rate' problems in tree diagrams to help to identify the calculation required.
- Pupils will be able to apply calculation methods for multiplication and division flexibly to solve problems.

Activities for whole-class instruction

- Using the first image from **Resource 4.10.2a** Making deliveries, show pupils the set of questions relating to 'Three deliveries a week' used in the previous session.

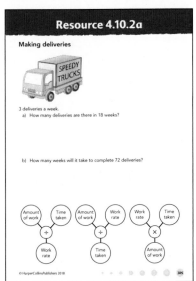

- Ask: *What information did we already know each time? What did we need to find out?*
- Agree that:
  - for the first question, we know the work rate and the time taken. We need to find out the amount of work.
  - for the second question, we know the work rate and the amount of work. We need to find the time taken.
- Revisit the following calculations needed to answer each question:
  - Amount of work = work rate × time taken. This means that, to find out how much was done altogether, we multiply the amount done in each minute (or hour, or whatever) by the number of minutes (or hours or whatever) it was done for.
  - Time taken = amount of work ÷ work rate. This means that, to find out how many minutes (or hours or whatever) it took, we divide the amount of work done altogether by the amount that was done in every minute (or hour, or whatever)
- Using the second image from **Resource 4.10.2a** Making deliveries, show pupils the following tree diagrams.

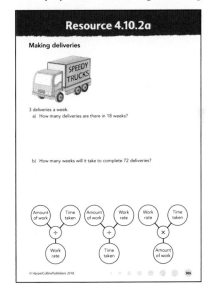

Answers: a) 54 b) 24.

- Ask: *What is the same about these tree diagrams and the number sentences used previously?* Ask pupils to identify which tree diagrams they should use to match the problems about the deliveries.

- Ask pupils to replace the labels in the tree diagrams to represent the delivery problems. Agree these for parts a) and b), respectively, as:

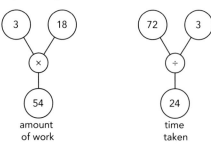

- Explain to pupils that there is another delivery company in the next town. Show pupils the following problems:

  - The company made 30 deliveries in 6 weeks. How many deliveries did they make per week?

  - The company is booked to make 120 deliveries. How many weeks will it take them?

  - The company completed 14 weeks of deliveries. How many deliveries did they make?

- Ask pupils to explain to a partner what information they already know for each of the questions and what they need to find out. Ask pupils to use tree diagrams to represent the calculations needed to solve the problems?

- Share the solutions and tree diagrams used each time.

  Record the number sentences as 30 ÷ 6 = 5, 120 ÷ 5 = 24 and 5 × 14 = 70.

Look out for … pupils who would find it useful to represent the problems using cubes or counters. Each cube can be used to represent a delivery or, when identified, each cube can represent the work rate (5 deliveries in a week) so that pupils can draw on knowledge of counting in fives to support thinking.

- Ask pupils to complete Question 1 in the Practice Book.

Same-day intervention

- Work together with pupils to represent the problems in Question 1 using cubes or counters to show the work rate, for example one cube represents 50 planes per hour in part a) and 50 clay pots per hour in part b).

- Bar models can be used to help show the relationships between the values each time, for example:

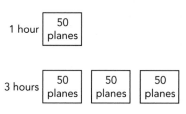

Same-day enrichment

- Give pupils **Resource 4.10.2b** Tree diagrams. Ask pupils to match the problems and the tree diagrams to help solve them. Then ask them to write a problem to match the remaining tree diagram.

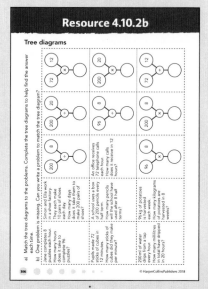

Answers: a) Puzzles: 96 ÷ 8, 24; Shoes: 200 ÷ 20, 10; Cubes: 72 ÷ 12, 6; Pencils: 200 × 8, 1600; Telephone: 72 × 12, 864; Water: 200 × 20, 4000; Potatoes: 96 × 8, 768.

b) Answers may vary for the 200 ÷ 8 tree.

Question 2

2 Application problems.

(a) A school planned to save 18 kilowatt-hours of electricity every day. They have actually saved 4 more kilowatt-hours of electricity every day than they planned. At this new rate, how many kilowatt-hours can they save in total for a month? (Note: take a month as 22 days.)

(b) Mrs Joy, Mr Lee and Mr Ellis worked in a bag factory. Mrs Joy made 18 bags in 3 hours. Mr Lee made 14 bags in 2 hours. Mr Ellis made 20 bags in 4 hours. Who made the most bags per hour?

(c) A factory receives an order to make a number of toys. They make 6480 of the toys, which is 8 times the number of toys still left to make. How many toys were ordered in total?

What learning will pupils have achieved at the conclusion of Question 2?

- Knowledge about the relationship between multiplication and division will have been strengthened through solving problems relating to work rate.

- Pupils will be able to apply calculation methods for multiplication and division flexibly to solve problems.

- Pupils will be able to represent 'work rate' problems in tree diagrams to help to identify the calculation required.
- Conceptual understanding of 'work rate' and efficiency will have been deepened through practical activities.

Activities for whole-class instruction

- Explain to the class that they are going to take part in another activity about work rate. The activity is best completed in a large space – perhaps the hall or playground.
- Ask pupils to work in equal groups of at least five to simulate a factory machine that passes a manufactured ball in a bucket along the production line to be packaged in a box. The bucket must be passed back to the beginning of the line ready to receive the next ball. Each journey on the production line also includes passing the bucket through a hoop to represent a tunnel.
- Display the image below – The Ball Factory – to show how the ball in the bucket should be passed from pupil to pupil until it reaches the box and the start of the return journey of the empty bucket.

- In this activity, all team machines have five minutes to box as many balls as possible. Once completed, each team should count the number of boxed balls and together calculate their work rate.

 Work rate equals amount of work divided by time taken.

- Show pupils the following problems. Ask pupils to answer them using what they know about their team's work rate.
  - How many minutes would it take your team machine to box 100 balls?
  - How many balls would your team machine box in 30 minutes?
  - Another team machine boxed 56 balls in 8 minutes. How does their work rate compare with your team machine?
- Encourage pupils to round numbers to avoid remainders.
- Share answers to the problems above. Pupils should explain how they calculated the answer and (in pairs) come to the front to draw tree diagrams to represent some of the problems.
- Return to the problem about the team that boxed 56 balls in eight minutes. Explain that the number of boxed balls is seven times more than the number of balls that are still to be boxed.
- Ask: *How many balls did this team machine need to box in total?* Give pupils time to discuss the problem before exploring it together. Agree that there must be 8 balls still to box, so that the team machine needed to box 56 + 8 = 64 balls in total.
- Ask pupils to complete Question 2 in the Practice Book.

Same-day intervention

- Ask pupils to draw tree diagrams to match the problems in Question 2, explaining the decisions they make each time.
- Ask pupils to write problems to match these tree diagrams.

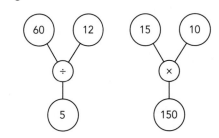

Same-day enrichment

- Give pupils **Resource 4.10.2c** Three in a row.

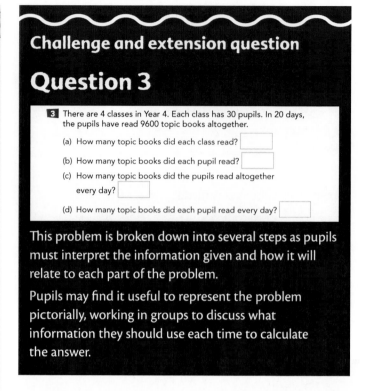

Resource 4.10.2c

Three in a row

The numbers in the grid represent work rate or the time taken.
Choose a number and decide what it will represent.
Make up a problem that will give an answer to match the number chosen.
How many groups of three numbers in a straight line can you make?

14	11	10	5	80
60	16	90	8	20
7	45	30	70	15
25	100	35	12	50
6	21	4	40	9

© HarperCollins Publishers 2018   307

- Explain that numbers in the grid represent work rate or the time taken. Ask pupils to choose a number and decide what it will represent.

- Pupils should then make up a problem that will give an answer to match the number chosen. For example, having chosen number 4 and deciding it will represent work rate, the following might be a problem that results in the number 4: 'Caleb makes 200 biscuits in 50 minutes. What is his work rate?'

- Ask pupils to record the problems they make up, or simply tell their partner who should check them.

- Ask: *How many groups of three numbers in a straight line can you make?* Lines can be horizontal, vertical or diagonal.

Challenge and extension question

Question 3

3 There are 4 classes in Year 4. Each class has 30 pupils. In 20 days, the pupils have read 9600 topic books altogether.

(a) How many topic books did each class read? ☐

(b) How many topic books did each pupil read? ☐

(c) How many topic books did the pupils read altogether every day? ☐

(d) How many topic books did each pupil read every day? ☐

This problem is broken down into several steps as pupils must interpret the information given and how it will relate to each part of the problem.

Pupils may find it useful to represent the problem pictorially, working in groups to discuss what information they should use each time to calculate the answer.

Unit 10.3
Solving calculation questions in 3 steps (1)

Conceptual context

Calculations needed in real life often contain several parts. In this unit, pupils are introduced to three-step calculations that can include any of the four operations (addition, subtraction, multiplication and division), with some calculations containing three different operations. Pupils are introduced to the concept of different operations taking precedence over others in a calculation ('order of operations'). They will learn to interpret brackets.

Learning pupils will have achieved at the end of the unit

- A hierarchy of operations (including the use of brackets) will have been introduced when answering calculations with three operations (Q1)
- The rules about the order of operations will have been learned and practised when answering questions using mental methods (Q2)
- Understanding of the order of operations will have been extended when applying these rules to solve number puzzles (Q3, Q4, Q5)
- Pupils will have explored different ways of positioning symbols into a fixed set of digits in order to make a target number (Q4, Q5)

Resources

mini whiteboards; plastic counters; coloured string or pipe cleaners; large digit cards; large paper triangle; large operation symbol cards; number cards; packs of playing cards; **Resource 4.10.3a** Calculation flowchart

Vocabulary

brackets, multiplication, division, addition, subtraction, number sentence, mixed operations, order of operations, equation

Question 1

> **1** Fill in the answers.
>
> (a) When you work on a number sentence with brackets, perform calculations inside the brackets first.
>
> For example, $(2 + 3) \times (6 - 2) = $ _____ .
>
> (b) When you work on a number sentence involving 4 operations, perform all the multiplication and division first and then perform the addition and subtraction.
>
> For example, $18 \div 2 + 3 \times 5 = $ _____ .
>
> (c) When you work on a number sentence only with multiplication and division, work from left to right.
>
> For example, $20 \div 5 \times 4 = $ _____ .
>
> (d) When you work on a number sentence only with addition and subtraction, work from left to right.
>
> For example, $18 - 2 + 11 = $ _____ .

What learning will pupils have achieved at the conclusion of Question 1?

- A hierarchy of operations (including the use of brackets) will have been introduced when answering calculations with three mixed operations.

Activities for whole-class instruction

- Write the following calculation on the board:

  $5 \times (2 + 4)$

- Ask pupils to work out the calculation without discussing it. Most will have worked through the calculation linearly and have the answer 14. Observe whether any have answered correctly (30). Ask: *What do you notice about this calculation?* Elicit that it has more than one type of operation and also that it contains brackets around one of the steps. Explain that brackets give the first clue about how to answer a mixed calculation like this.

- Show pupils **Resource 4.10.3a** Calculation flowchart.

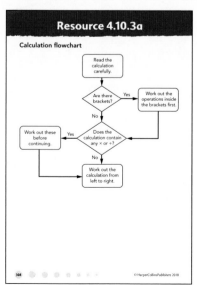

- Talk about the first question on the flow chart and encourage pupils to follow its advice, working out the brackets first. Explain that the job of brackets is to overrule the usual order in which the number sentence would be worked out. Multiplication should usually be worked out before any addition, but in this example the brackets cancel this rule because calculations inside brackets must always be solved first; this means that in this sentence the addition must be worked out first.

- Model how to cross out the calculation inside the brackets, replacing it with the answer.

$$5 \times (2 \overset{6}{+ 4})$$

- Ask: *What is the calculation now?* Go through the remaining questions on the flow chart and establish that, since there is only one symbol left, pupils can work through the calculation from left to right. Repeat for further calculations involving two operations (for example $20 \div (16 - 11)$) before moving on to those with three symbols. For example, display $(3 + 4) \times (1 + 2)$, demonstrating that it is equal to 21 as follows:

$$(3 \overset{7}{+ 4}) \times (1 \overset{3}{+ 2})$$

- Ask: *What would the answer to the same number sentence be if there were no brackets?*

  $3 + 4 \times 1 + 2 = $ ___

- Discuss and agree that, without the brackets, the multiplication would have to be done first, so it becomes:

  $3 + 4 + 2 = 9$

- Ensure that pupils understand how brackets change the solution for the following:

  $(5 + 3) \times (4 + 2) = $ ___ compared to $5 + 3 \times 4 + 2$

  $(16 - 2) \times (6 + 2) = $ ___ compared to $16 - 2 \times 6 + 2$

- Display the calculation $40 \div 5 \times 3$ and again ask pupils what they notice. Elicit that this time there are no brackets and that the calculation contains only multiplication and division.

- Go through the flow chart and consider the second question in particular. Ensure pupils understand that it means there is a hierarchy of operations and $\times$ and/or $\div$ are more important than $+$ and/or $-$ where there is a mixture of symbols (at least one from both groups). Where there is not, the calculation can be worked out from left to right.

- Explain that division and multiplication are given the same level of importance, even though we often say 'multiplication and division'.

- Model how to work out the answer as 40 ÷ 5 × 3 = 8 × 3 = 24.

ⓘ Multiplication and division take equal precedence – one is not more important than the other. The same is true for addition and subtraction. Pupils often later learn acronyms to help remember the order of operations, and these usually place D before M and A before S. This can be confusing and can lead pupils to think that division takes precedence over multiplication and addition over subtraction, but this is not true. To help teach pupils the equal value of multiplication and division, try the following strategies:

- refer to them as 'division and multiplication' too

- when completing activities such as the card triangle below, sometimes place the ÷ before the × (and the – before the +)

- provide examples where division comes before multiplication and pupils should complete it first.

- Provide pupils with their own copies of the flowchart on **Resource 4.10.3a** Calculation flowchart as well as plastic counters. Display a variety of mixed calculations (with and without brackets):

  (6 + 3) × (4 − 3)

  16 ÷ 4 + 3 × 2

  4 × 5 ÷ 2

  (14 − 2) × (8 ÷ 4)

  19 − (7 + 5)

- Encourage pupils to work out the answers by following the rules on the flow chart, moving their plastic counter along each arrow to show where they are.

- Pupils should now complete Question 1 in the Practice Book.

Same-day intervention

- Provide each pupil with a large paper triangle and a set of symbol cards (containing brackets and +, −, × and ÷ symbols). Ask pupils to fold their triangle three times to create three horizontal segments. Remind pupils of the order in which parts of a calculation need to be completed and explain that this can be shown as a pyramid – with the most important operations at the top level, then the next and so on.

- Write the calculation 20 − (4 + 2) × 2 and ask: *Which part of the calculation would you complete first?* Establish that they need to find the answer to the brackets first (to give 20 − 6 × 2). Continue with the same line of questioning and ensure that pupils understand that multiplication and division take precedence over addition and subtraction.

- Tell pupils that the next step is to multiply 6 by 2, so the calculation becomes 20 − 12. Finally, establish that pupils can work out the answer as 20 − 12 = 8.

- Ask pupils to place their symbol cards within their triangle to show the three levels of operations as follows:

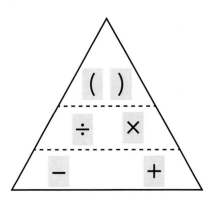

- Ask pupils to shuffle their set of cards and practise dealing them one at a time and placing them in the correct segment of their triangle.

- Give pupils calculations containing mixed operations (with and without brackets) and encourage them to use their operations triangles to help remember which part of the calculation should be answered first. Ask pupils to write out each calculation on their whiteboards and cross out each part as they answer it, noting how the calculation changes.

Same-day enrichment

- Pupils should be encouraged to devise their own questions, working backwards from clues given. Split pupils into groups of three. Pupil A should use coloured string or pipe cleaners to mark a 'flow' on the flow chart. For example:

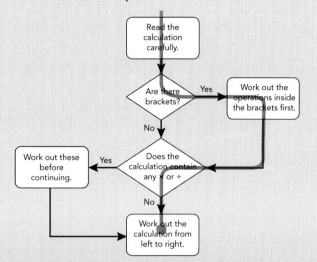

- Pupil B then writes a calculation to match the information they can see on the flow chart. In the above example, this might be (13 − 5) + (15 − 2). Finally, they pass this to Pupil C who answers the question without looking at the flow chart for help.
- Ask pupils to check that they have completed the operations in the correct order. Pupils should repeat for different calculations and swap roles each time.

Question 2

> **2** Work these out mentally. Write the answers.
>
> (a) 4 × 5 + 4 = ☐   (b) 6 ÷ 3 + 12 = ☐
>
> (c) 12 + 12 ÷ 4 = ☐   (d) 10 × 2 − 7 = ☐
>
> (e) 13 − 5 × 2 = ☐   (f) (7 − 3) × 6 = ☐
>
> (g) 9 ÷ 9 + 12 = ☐   (h) 9 + 8 + 7 = ☐
>
> (i) 10 ÷ (5 + 5) = ☐

What learning will pupils have achieved at the conclusion of Question 2?

- The rules about the order of operations will have been learned and practised when answering questions using mental methods.

Activities for whole-class instruction

- Remind pupils of the rules about the order of operations that they have learned:
  - anything inside a bracket must be worked out first as it takes precedence over other operations
  - any multiplication and/or division is more important than addition and/or subtraction, and so they need to be completed before continuing.
- Choose pupils to come to the front and hold up a combination of digit cards and operation cards to model the calculation 18 − 3 × 3. Ask: *Which part of the calculation do you think needs to be calculated first? Why?*
- Establish that there are no brackets and multiplication takes precedence over subtraction, so 3 × 3 must be worked out first. Encourage pupils holding the cards showing 3 × 3 to hold their cards high and the other two pupils to turn theirs away.

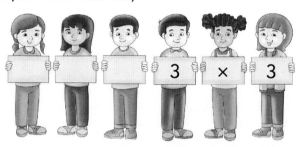

- Pupils with the multiplication should work out the product and replace their three cards with one (9). Any pupils without cards should sit down. Show the first cards again to reveal the number sentence as:

- Provide pupils with a variety of questions involving mixed operations (some with brackets, some without). For example:

  10 × 3 − 4

  (5 − 2) × 9

  12 ÷ 4 + 4

  15 + 15 ÷ 5

- Ask pupils to model each question using cards in the same way. Ask: *Which part of the calculation will you work out first? Why?* Next, ask pupils to calculate each answer mentally, without the support of cards, first agreeing which part of the sentence should be solved first.

- Pupils should now complete Question 2 in the Practice Book.

Same-day intervention

- Give pairs of pupils a set of digit and symbol cards. Display the calculation 10 × 3 − 8 ÷ 4 and ask them to represent this with cards. Ask: *Which part of the calculation should you solve first?* Remind pupils of the flow chart and triangles they used before. Pupils should use mental methods to work out the multiplication and then the division (work from left to right because they have equal precedence) and then swap their cards for the answer.

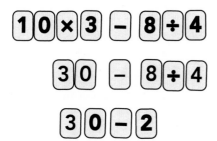

- Finally, pupils should subtract 2 from 30.
- Provide pupils with further calculations to model. Encourage them to use mental methods to find each part before replacing their cards.

Same-day enrichment

- Pupils should work in pairs or small groups. Each pupil should write a number sentence containing three numbers from one to 13, together with two operations. These may or may not contain brackets. They should then use mental methods to work out two possible strategies to answer their question, one correct and one wrong. For example, the calculation 2 + 8 × 5 could have the following two responses:

$$2 + 8 \times 5$$

2 + 8 = 10	8 × 5 = 40
10 × 5 = 50	2 + 40 = 42

- Pupils should share their calculations and strategies to see whether peers can decide which is the correct. They should repeat for different calculations. Encourage pupils to extend the activity by including four numbers and three operations.

Question 3

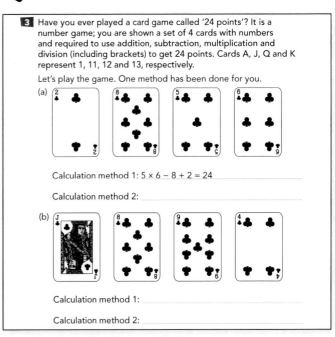

3 Have you ever played a card game called '24 points'? It is a number game; you are shown a set of 4 cards with numbers and required to use addition, subtraction, multiplication and division (including brackets) to get 24 points. Cards A, J, Q and K represent 1, 11, 12 and 13, respectively.

Let's play the game. One method has been done for you.

(a)

Calculation method 1: 5 × 6 − 8 + 2 = 24

Calculation method 2: _____

(b)

Calculation method 1: _____

Calculation method 2: _____

What learning will pupils have achieved at the conclusion of Question 3?

- Understanding of the order of operations will have been extended when applying these rules to solve number puzzles.

Activities for whole-class instruction

- Show pupils four cards, showing the numbers 4, 8, 2 and 10. In pairs, pupils should use the numbers to make up calculations (each number used once), which can contain any of the four symbols (+, −, × and ÷) as well as brackets. For example:

8 × 10 + 4 × 2 = 88

(10 − 2) × (8 + 4) = 96

- Share pupils' calculations, discussing possible answers and strategies.

- Introduce the idea of making the number 24 by reading the game instructions in Question 3. Play the game, taking four cards at random (ensuring that these are not the same as those in Questions 3a and 3b) and asking pupils to find a solution. If an example is needed, show pupils the cards Q, 4, 3 and 5. Since the Q is worth 12, one possible solution is:

12 ÷ 3 + 5 × 4.

- As pupils play the game, discuss the different number bonds that equal 24 as well as multiplication facts that they could use to help. Encourage them to explain how they found each solution.

(i) With this game, and in variations of it in later questions, trial and error will be a popular strategy. Pupils will often use this approach, but with more experience of the game they should begin to look for number facts and particular combinations to assist them. 24 is a number with eight factors, and knowledge of these will be important. Time spent reviewing multiplication and division facts that make 24 prior to playing will be worthwhile.

- Pupils should now complete Question 3 in the Practice Book.

Same-day intervention

- Write the numbers 1 to 13 on the board. These can be linked to the values of playing cards later in the activity. Describe an example of how to make the number 24 using any of the cards, for example four plus two lots of 10. Ask: *How would you write this as a calculation? Do you need to use brackets to show which part needs to be calculated first?*

- Ensure pupils understand that two lots of ten is shown as 2×10 and that as multiplication takes priority over addition this part does not require brackets to determine the order of operations: $4 + 2 \times 10$.

- Ask: *Can you rearrange the calculation so that it still makes 24?* (for example $2 \times 10 + 4$).

- Lead pupils through other ways to make 24 by first swapping the expressions. For example, ask: *Can you think of a different way to make 20 instead of 2×10? How can you make 4 instead of using + 4?* Consider solutions ranging from the simpler $12 + 8 + 1 + 3$ to the more complex $4 \times 5 + 8 \div 2$.

- As pupils become more confident, encourage them to think about how to make 24 in other ways. Ask them to write a simple, one-step calculation that equals 24 (for example $30 - 6$) and then encourage them to think about how one (or both) of the numbers can be made using another expression. For example:

$$30 - 6 = 24$$
$$5 \times 6 \qquad 12 \div 2$$

So,
$$5 \times 6 - 12 \div 2 = 24$$

- Discuss pupils' calculations (and how they found them) with the group.

Same-day enrichment

- Provide pupils with an opportunity to play '24 points' for themselves. Give each pair a full pack of cards. Remind them of the values of the A, J, Q and K cards.

- Pupils should deal out 4 cards at random, with the aim of attempting to make 24 by choosing their operations carefully. Where they can find a solution, encourage pupils to make a note of it and then show other pairs the same cards as a challenge to see if they can also make 24 points.

Questions 4 and 5

4 Insert +, −, ×, ÷ and ( ) in each set of numbers below so that the result is 24. The order of the numbers should not be changed.

(a) 4 ◯ 2 ◯ 6 ◯ 3

(b) 3 ◯ 6 ◯ 4 ◯ 2

(c) 3 ◯ 6 ◯ 2 ◯ 4

(d) 2 ◯ 6 ◯ 3 ◯ 4

5 Use +, −, ×, ÷ and ( ) and the four numbers in each set below to write a number sentence so that the result is 24. (Each number can be used only once.)

(a) 7, 7, 1, 2 _____

(b) 6, 2, 7, 4 _____

(c) 12, 8, 6, 4 _____

(d) 1, 12, 10, 13 _____

What learning will pupils have achieved at the conclusion of Questions 4 and 5?

- Understanding of the order of operations will have been extended when applying these rules to solve number puzzles.

- Pupils will have explored different ways of positioning symbols into a fixed set of digits in order to make a target number.

Activities for whole-class instruction

- Display number cards showing 2, 9, 1 and 5. Ask: *If all these numbers were in a calculation, how many symbols might we need in between them? What symbols could we use?* Display cards showing each of the possible symbols (+, −, × and ÷), as well as bracket symbols. Ask: *Why might you use brackets in a calculation?*

- Remind pupils of the game they played when answering Question 3. Challenge them to make the number 24 using only the number cards and any of the symbols they choose. Give pupils time to consider this in pairs. For those who require support with the task, give them the symbols they can use (for example one × and two + symbols as one possible solution is 2 × 9 + 1 + 5.

- In pairs, pupils should share their calculations. Ask: *What methods did you use to find the answer?* Discuss the ways that pupils can use known facts to help – for example looking for multiplication facts that get close to 24 and then adjusting the answer with the remaining digits.

- Display the digits 4, 8, 5 and 2 and repeat the activity. In pairs, give pupils different challenges:

  - Make a calculation that includes division (for example (8 × 5) ÷ (2 + 4)).

  - Make a calculation that includes subtraction (for example: (8 − 5) × (2 × 4)).

  - Make a calculation and then rearrange it so that the numbers are in a different order, but still makes 24.

- Ask pupils if the same symbols are required. Discuss calculations and strategies with the class. Repeat for different groups of digits.

- Pupils should now complete Questions 4 and 5 in the Practice Book.

Same-day intervention

- Write the number 24 in a circle on the left-hand side of a large piece of paper and have a 'pen relay' (where pupils pass the pen to the next writer) where they are given a few minutes to write as many number facts as they can with 24 as the answer. Ensure this is fairly comprehensive, so provide more time (or more pens!) if further facts are needed. Explain that these facts will come in useful later.

- Display the digits 3, 4, 7 and 5. Ask pupils to think of the different facts they can make using these digits. For example 3 × 4 = 12, 7 + 3 = 10 and so on. A useful way of working through these possibilities is asking questions like: *How can you make the numbers 1/2/3 and so on?* (for example 2 can be made by 7 − 5, 5 − 3 and even more complicated (5 + 3) ÷ 4).

- Write these facts on the right-hand side of the piece of paper, which now should look something like this:

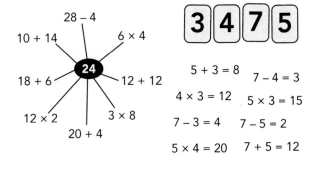

- Explain that pupils will be trying to use some of their 3, 4, 7, 5 facts to help make 24. Encourage them to identify links between the facts on the left- and right-hand sides of the piece of paper.

- For example, point to 12 × 2 on the left-hand side. Ask: *Can we make the two factors in this calculation (12 and 2) using only the numbers 3, 4, 7 and 5?* Pupils should use their calculations on the right-hand side to help them locate possible answers quickly. In this case, the answer could be:

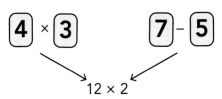

- This can be written 4 × 3 × (7 − 5).

- Ask pupils to model this calculation using number and symbol cards. Encourage them to move their digits around to see whether they can make the same answer with the digits in a slightly different order (for example (7 − 5) × (3 × 4) or (3 × 4) × 7 − 5).

- Repeat the activity for different sets of digits with at least one known solution (for example 10, 2, 2 and 2, where one possible solution is 2 + 2 + 10 × 2; another is 2 × 2 + 10 × 2).

- For each example, encourage pupils to draw links between the numbers that make 24 (the facts on the left-hand side) and the different possibilities they can make using the digits they have available (the facts on the right-hand side).

Same-day enrichment

- Split pupils into groups of three. Pupil A should write down an expression on their whiteboard that equals 24. They should then pass the whiteboard to Pupil B who should draw the calculation pictorially on their own whiteboard or model it, using base 10 blocks. For example:

- Pupil A should then rub out the symbols from their whiteboard, leaving only the digits, and pass their whiteboard to Pupil C.

8 4 (5 3)

- Pupil C should then attempt to work out how to create 24 by placing symbols in between 8, 4, 5 and 3. Pupil B can reveal their drawing as a pictorial clue if it is needed.

- Pupils should repeat the activity several times, using different digits and swapping roles each time.

Challenge and extension questions

Questions 6 and 7

6 Can the 4 numbers in each set below make 24 using 4 operations and brackets? If so, write a number sentence so the result is 24. Otherwise, write a No in the space provided.

(a) 4, 4, 4, 4 ....

(b) 5, 5, 5, 5 ....

(c) 8, 8, 8, 8 ....

(d) 9, 9, 9, 9 ....

(e) 12, 12, 12, 12 ....

7 Fill in the nine boxes with the numbers 1–9 to make the equations true. Each number can be used only once.

(a) 6 × (☐ − 8) = 6   (b) (☐ + 6) ÷ 2 = 5

(c) ☐ ÷ 3 + 1 = 3   (d) 3 × ☐ + ☐ = 16

(e) ☐ × ☐ − 15 = 9   (f) 2 × (☐ − ☐) = 10

The two questions require pupils to apply their knowledge of mixed operation calculations and insert symbols and brackets (Question 6) or digits (Question 7) to ensure given calculations make the necessary answers.

Pupils may rely on a degree of trial and error, but will need to lean heavily on the skills they have developed during the unit.

Unit 10.4
Solving calculation questions in 3 steps (2)

Conceptual context

This unit reinforces and develops understanding about the order of operations. Tree diagrams visually represent the steps needed. Pupils are encouraged to read each diagram and identify the number sentence they represent.

Learning pupils will have achieved at the end of the unit

- Tree diagrams will have been used to explore the concept of two- and three-step calculations (Q1)
- Pupils will have improved fluency when solving three-step calculations (Q1, Q2)
- Pupils will have had further opportunities to explore and practise the order of operations (Q2, Q4)
- Pupils will have investigated the steps involved in answering a number sentence, using this to derive the original sentence (and vice versa) (Q3, Q4)

Resources

mini whiteboards; large digit cards; large operation symbol cards; strips of paper; sticky notes; boxes; **Resource 4.10.4** Blank tree diagrams

Vocabulary

brackets, multiplication, division, addition, subtraction, number sentence, mixed operations, order of operations, equation, tree diagram

Question 1

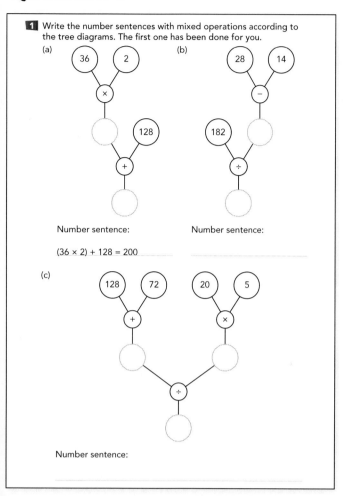

1 Write the number sentences with mixed operations according to the tree diagrams. The first one has been done for you.

(a)

36 × 2 → 128 +

Number sentence:

(36 × 2) + 128 = 200

(b)

28 − 14, 182 ÷

Number sentence:

(c)

128 + 72, 20 × 5, ÷

Number sentence:

What learning will pupils have achieved at the conclusion of Question 1?

- Tree diagrams will have been used to explore the concept of two- and three-step calculations further
- Pupils will have improved fluency when solving three-step calculations

Activities for whole-class instruction

- Display the following blank tree diagram from **Resource 4.10.4** Blank tree diagrams:

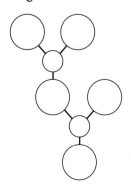

- Remind pupils that the smaller circles contain operation symbols and the larger circles contain numbers. Ask pupils to describe how they think the tree diagram flows.
- Write the calculation 45 × 3 − 78 on the board. Ask: *How many steps are there to the calculation? What are they? Which part of the calculation would you work out first and why?* Ask pupils to insert the different numbers and symbols into the tree diagram to reflect the two steps and their order.

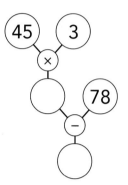

- Encourage pupils to use their fingers to trace the route that they need to follow to work out the final answer. Give them time to work out each step and complete the tree diagram. Use **Resource 4.10.4** to provide further examples for pupils to practise (including those where the tree diagram is a horizontal reflection of the one above). Include examples of three-step calculations too. For example:

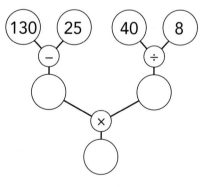

- Ask: *What is different and what is the same about this tree diagram compared with the ones you have looked at already?* Encourage pupils to provide three facts about the number sentence this is based on. Ask: *What can you say is certain about the number sentence?* For example, it contains three operations (subtraction, division and multiplication), it includes brackets and so on.
- Pupils should now complete Question 1 in the Practice Book.

Same-day intervention

(i) It is not generally the aim of same-day intervention activity to provide similar questions with easier numbers. However, in this instance it may be worthwhile to begin by providing pupils with one or two examples of multi-step tree diagrams where they do not need to concentrate too much on the calculations themselves. By lightening the cognitive load in this way, the focus can be directed to understand the process itself, rather than on finding the answer. Once pupils have grasped the concept, the numbers can then be altered to raise the calculations to a more challenging level.

- Prepare an enlarged tree diagram on a piece of paper (from **Resource 4.10.4** Blank tree diagrams).

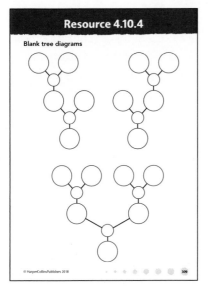

- Partially complete it as follows:

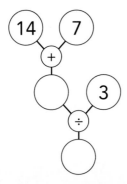

- Cut up the tree diagram into the two calculations and get pupils to arrange them in the order that they think they appear in the number sentence. Remind them that they do not need the empty circle as this is the answer to 14 + 7. Choose a pupil to draw brackets around the part they think is answered first.

 We use brackets when we want to override the usual order of operations.

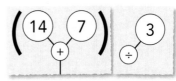

- Write the corresponding number sentence, (14 + 7) ÷ 3. Display a copy of the original tree diagram and choose pupils to point to each part of the tree diagram, the cut-up tree diagram and the number sentence so that they can follow the process. Finish by asking pupils to work out the answer. Repeat the activity using different tree diagrams.

Same-day enrichment

- Encourage pupils to devise their own tree diagrams for their peers to solve. Provide them with copies of **Resource 4.10.4** to use as templates if they wish. After setting challenges for their friends, pupils should write a two- or three-part number sentence and pass it to a partner to devise a tree diagram that represents it. For example:

$56 \times (9 + 3) - 14$ can be written as →

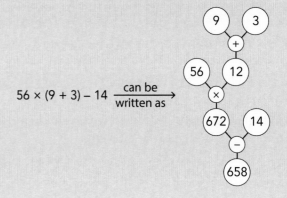

Question 2

> **2** Circle the correct answer.
>
> (a) The correct order of operations to calculate 600 + 600 ÷ 25 × 4 is
>
>   A. Addition → division → multiplication
>
>   B. Division → addition → multiplication
>
>   C. Multiplication → addition → division
>
>   D. Division → multiplication → addition
>
> (b) The result of 492 − 66 ÷ 3 × 22 is
>
>   A. 491   B. 8   C. 157   D. 2904

What learning will pupils have achieved at the conclusion of Question 2?

- Pupils will have improved fluency when solving three-step calculations.

- Pupils will have had further opportunities to explore and practise the order of operations.

Activities for whole-class instruction

- Shuffle several symbol cards showing ( ), +, –, × and ÷. Choose two pupils to take a card each then walk towards a door or opening in the classroom. They should reveal their cards to the class and then go through the door in the order of operations. Pupils can have fun at emphasising the 'politeness' of letting one symbol go before another. For example, if the cards are ( ) and +, the pupil holding the + card could wait and say *After you!* Or perhaps they could place it in between brackets and push rudely in front of a multiplication symbol! Ask: *If symbols were people, which would be the quietest and shyest? Which would push past and want to be first every time?*

- Where pupils take two like symbols (for example + and +) or two symbols with the same priority (for example ÷ and ×), use the opportunity to revise the fact that pupils should simply work out the calculation from left to right.

- Without showing it, write the calculation 400 + 200 × 2 – 350. Explain that the hidden calculation contains multiplication, addition and subtraction. Do not say whether there are any brackets. Ask: *What are some of the possible orders you could complete each operation in?*

- Prepare three whiteboards with the words multiplication, addition and subtraction, one word on each whiteboard. Ask the class to suggest different orders in which the operations might need to be completed.

- **Look out for** … pupils who think that there is only one possible operation that comes first (multiplication because it always takes precedence over the others).

- Remind pupils that if there are brackets, then any operation in a calculation could be first.

- Choose different pupils to come to the front and rearrange the words (for example addition → subtraction → multiplication, multiplication → addition → subtraction and so on).

- Reveal the calculation (400 + 200 × 2 – 350) to pupils and discuss which of the suggested orders is the correct one (multiplication → addition → subtraction) and why.

- Pupils should work out the answer and discuss the steps needed to find it. Ask: *Can you add brackets to the calculation so that the order becomes addition → multiplication → subtraction?* This will be (400 + 200) × 2 – 350.

- Repeat for different two- and three-step calculations without brackets.

- Pupils should now complete Question 2 in the Practice Book.

Same-day intervention

- Give four pupils operation cards with the words addition, multiplication, division and subtraction. Ask: *If you had to split these into two pairs, how would you do it? Why have you chosen this way?* Remind pupils that in a calculation where there is more than one type of operation and no brackets, the multiplication and division are worked out before the addition and subtraction.

- Remind pupils of the role that brackets play in overriding this order.

- Set up four boxes at the front of the class, labelled A, B, C and D. Write a number sentence on the board. For example, 300 – 100 × 2 ÷ 4. Write four different possibilities for the order of operations and label these A, B, C and D. For example:

    A: division → multiplication → subtraction

    B: multiplication → subtraction → division

    C: multiplication → division → subtraction

    D: subtraction → multiplication → division

- Ensure that a cube is secretly placed into the box representing the correct answer (in this example, Box C). Encourage pupils to consider the order of operation rules they have learned and to discuss in pairs which of the three orders is correct. Choose a pair to make their decision and check the corresponding box to see whether they are correct. Work out the answer as a group by following the steps in option C.

- Repeat for different number sentences, including those with brackets. As pupils become more confident, ask extension questions that allude to the use of brackets. For example, ask: *How could we tweak the number sentence so that option D becomes true?*

Same-day enrichment

- Split pupils into groups of three and give each group a piece of paper. Pupil A should write a sequence of operations at the top of the piece of paper (for example addition → multiplication → subtraction) and then fold the paper to cover it.

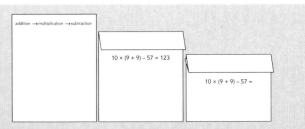

- Pupil B should then take the paper, look at the order of operations and devise a number sentence that matches it, complete with the answer. In this example, this could be 10 × (9 + 9) – 57 = 123. They should then fold the paper again before writing their number sentence one more time (this time without the answer) and passing it to Pupil C.

- Pupil C should then answer the number sentence and write down the order of the operations. They can check whether they are correct, by opening up the folded paper to see what is written on it. Repeat the activity several times, swapping roles.

Question 3

3 In each question below, put the calculations in 3 steps into one number sentence with mixed operations and then calculate.

(a) 650 ÷ 50 = 13
13 + 45 = 58
58 + 60 = 118

Number sentence: _____

(b) 35 × 6 = 210
121 ÷ 11 = 11
210 – 11 = 199

Number sentence: _____

What learning will pupils have achieved at the conclusion of Question 3?

- Pupils will have investigated the steps involved in answering a number sentence, using this to derive the original sentence (and vice versa).

Activities for whole-class instruction

- Complete the following 'If this is the answer, what was the question?' activity with pupils. Explain that in the activity, pupils will need to take on the role of being the teacher.

- Tell them that one of the skills a good teacher has is being able to look over a pupil's work and try to understand what was meant – not every pupil explains their thinking very well.

- Display the following series of calculations as an example of a child's work:

530 – 90 = 440

440 × 2 = 880
880 ÷ 4 = 220

- Explain that the answers are all correct and ask: *What do you notice?* (Each calculation feeds the next.) Ask: *Can you explain what you were thinking when you worked through these calculations? What does this tell you about the number sentence you were trying to answer?*

- Establish that the number sentence must contain a subtraction in brackets as it is worked out before the multiplication and the division. Ask: *Which numbers are definitely in the number sentence?* (530 – 90, ×2, and also ÷ 4) Ensure that pupils understand the number sentence that they are working towards: (530 – 90) × 2 ÷ 4.

- Repeat for different examples of pupils' work. Ensure that these include some where the first calculation does not automatically feed into the second (see example B below).

Example A:

26 – 24 = 2
65 × 2 = 130
130 ÷ 10 = 13

Original number sentence: 65 × (26 – 24) ÷ 10 = __

Example B:

46 + 29 = 75
60 ÷ 12 = 5
75 ÷ 5 = 15

Original number sentence: (46 + 29) ÷ (60 ÷ 12) = __

- Ensure pupils can explain the train of thought behind the calculations and can derive the original number sentence.

- Pupils should now complete Question 3 in the Practice Book.

Same-day intervention

- Give pupils opportunities to physically manipulate steps to make a number sentence. Write out the following three steps on large strips of paper:

460 – 20 = 440
25 – 21 = 4
440 ÷ 4 = 110

- Explain that these show a pupil's working when answering a three-step number sentence and that 110 is the final answer. Ask: *What do you think are the three operations that are in the number sentence? Why do the subtractions come before the division?* Establish that there are brackets in the sentence because the usual order of operations would be division first.

- Take the first number sentence and ask: *Does the answer to this flow into the next step or is it separate?* Establish that it is separate, so move the step to one side and draw brackets around it (rip off the answer).

- Discuss both of the remaining number sentences and choose pupils to move each piece of paper into position, ripping the parts that they do not need.

$$\left(\;460 - 20\;\right) \div \left(\;25 - 21\;\right) = 110$$

- Look at the completed number sentence and choose a pupil to describe how they would answer it. Ask the rest of the class to check that this corresponds to the original steps on the strips.

- Repeat for further calculations with and without brackets, including those where the first answer directly feeds into the next (see example A below):

Example A:

$351 + 34 = 385$

$385 \div 5 = 77$

$77 + 68 = 145$

Original number sentence: $(351 + 34) \div 5 + 68$

Example B:

$86 - 37 = 49$

$28 \div 4 = 7$

$49 \div 7 = 7$

Original number sentence: $(86 - 37) \div (28 \div 4)$

Same-day enrichment

- Provide pupils with four strips of paper. Each pupil should create their own three-step challenge by first constructing a number sentence containing three operations and writing this on one of the strips. They should turn this upside down and write the three steps needed to answer it on the remaining strips of paper. Pupils should share their strips with peers who should work out what the original number sentence was.

- As a further challenge, pupils could try shuffling their strips and seeing whether peers can work out the order before identifying the number sentence. Only some pupils will be able to do this as it is difficult, but it is possible to do it if pupils consider which numbers are repeated and where they are used.

Question 4

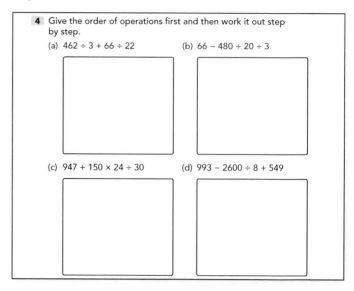

4 Give the order of operations first and then work it out step by step.

(a) $462 \div 3 + 66 \div 22$

(b) $66 - 480 \div 20 \div 3$

(c) $947 + 150 \times 24 \div 30$

(d) $993 - 2600 \div 8 + 549$

What learning will pupils have achieved at the conclusion of Question 4?

- Pupils will have had further opportunities to explore and practise the order of operations.

- Pupils will have investigated the steps involved in answering a number sentence, using this to derive the original sentence (and vice versa).

Activities for whole-class instruction

- Display the calculation $324 \div 3 + 46 \times 2$. Ask: *In what order would you work this out?* Prompt pupils to think about the way they recorded their working out of the main activity in Question 3. Provide pupils with sticky notes labelled 1, 2 and 3 and ask pupils to place the notes next to the part of the calculation they think should be worked out first, second and third. It may be helpful to highlight the parts of the calculation to colour code the order.

$$\boxed{1}\quad\boxed{3}\quad\boxed{2}$$

$$324 \div 3 + 46 \times 2$$

- Ask: *How many different calculations will you need to work out? Will they feed from one into the next every time or do you need to work out two parts before you do anything with the answers? If this were a tree diagram, what would it look like?*

- Split pupils into pairs and ask them to work out the answer to the number sentence in three steps. Can they explain why the steps are:

  $324 \div 3 = 108$

  $46 \times 2 = 92$

  $108 + 92 = 200$

- Repeat for different number sentences with three parts (without brackets). Ensure that pupils are given examples where division comes before multiplication or where subtraction comes before addition so that they become used to the fact that they have equivalent weighting and (if there are no brackets) it is the operation that comes first when working from left to right that is completed first.

- Pupils should now complete Question 4 in the Practice Book.

Same-day intervention

- Remind pupils of the hierarchy of operations they have been taught. Take three cards from a set of operation symbol cards (+, −, × and ÷) and place them in the order they were taken. Ask: *If this is the order these symbols appear in a number sentence, in what order should they be worked out?* Observe whether any pupils answer that it depends on whether there are any brackets in the sentence. Explain that there are no brackets in this example and discuss the answer. Ask: *How do you remember which operations take priority over others? What helps you?*

- Write $50 − 100 \div 10 + 29$. Pupils should copy this and write 1, 2 or 3 in circles above the symbols to show the order in which they should be solved. Share ideas and discuss how they decided which should come first. Write each calculation out separately to show the order:

  $100 \div 10 = \_\_\_$

  $50 − \_\_\_ = \_\_\_$

  $\_\_\_ + 29 = \_\_\_$

- Go through the steps, completing the missing values.

- Repeat for different calculations. Using a strip of paper, torn into sections, will allow pupils to physically order the different parts.

Same-day enrichment

- Pupils should work in groups of two or three. Each pupil should devise a three-step number sentence and work out the answer. Pupil A should share their number sentence and give three different possibilities of the order of operations. For example:

  $58 − 120 \div 4 \div 5$ could be:

  A: $\div − \div$

  B: $− \div \div$

  C: $\div \div −$

- Others in the group should decide on the correct order and find the answer. Points are scored for guessing the correct order and for calculating correctly. Pupils should repeat the activity for each of their number sentences.

Challenge and extension questions

Questions 5 and 6

5 Put the calculations in 4 steps into one number sentence with mixed operations and then calculate.

$7 \times 9 = 63$ $142 \div 2 = 71$ $71 − 63 = 8$ $8 + 2 = 10$

Number sentence: _____

6 A vertical pole is used to measure the depth of the swimming pool. The part above the water is 120 cm long, which is 20 cm less than twice the part in the water. How deep is the water in the pool?

_____

In the first of these questions, pupils are provided with four steps involved when solving a number sentence. Pupils should trace the flow of the calculations, looking carefully to see how each answer is then used in the next step. At first glance, the first two calculations do not look related, so pupils will need to consider how both answers are then used in the third calculation.

In the second question, pupils are given a multi-step word problem to solve. They should draw a labelled diagram to represent the problem scenario and read the question several times. Pupils need to break the question into sections, so they should be encouraged to write out the problem as a number sentence before finding the answer (if 120 is 20 cm less, then 120 + 20 gives the amount that is twice the part in the water; half of 140 gives the length of the part in the water). This can be written as $(120 + 20) \div 2$.

Unit 10.5
Solving calculation questions in 3 steps (3)

Conceptual context

This is the third in a series of units about using mixed operations and brackets involving understanding about the order of operations. Pupils should now be more familiar with solving multi-step problems. This is further developed in this unit. Brackets containing two operations are introduced. Word problems are included.

Learning pupils will have achieved at the end of the unit

- Having previously broken down number sentences into component parts, pupils will have been able to use reasoning to combine three steps to construct one number sentence with mixed operations (Q1)
- Pupils will have consolidated their understanding of how to solve calculation questions containing three operations (Q2)
- Further opportunities will have been given to explain the order of operations, including when deriving general rules (Q2, Q3, Q4)
- Application of multi-step calculations will have been extended to include word problems (Q4)

Resources

mini whiteboards; sticky labels; large digit cards; large operation symbol cards; **Resource 4.10.3a** Calculation flowchart (from earlier unit); **Resource 4.10.5a** The great number sentence challenge; **Resource 4.10.5b** At the supermarket

Vocabulary

brackets, multiplication, division, addition, subtraction, number sentence, mixed operations, order of operations, equation

Question 1

> **1** Put the calculations in 3 steps into one number sentence with mixed operations and then calculate.
>
> (a) $650 \div 50 = 13$
> $45 - 20 = 25$
> $25 + 13 = 38$
>
> Number sentence: _____
>
> (b) $35 - 23 = 12$
> $121 + 11 = 132$
> $132 \div 12 = 11$
>
> Number sentence: _____

What learning will pupils have achieved at the conclusion of Question 1?

- Having previously broken down number sentences into component parts, pupils will have been able to use reasoning to combine three steps to construct one number sentence with mixed operations.

Activities for whole-class instruction

- Show pupils the following three calculations in order:

  $87 - 77 = 10$

  $378 + 132 = 510$

  $510 \div 10 = 51$

- Explain that these are the three steps to working out the answer to a number sentence that they have not seen. Encourage pupils to give one fact that they can derive about the number sentence. Ask: *What else do you know?*

- Begin with the final step. Use two different colours to circle each number in the final calculation and then ask pupils where these numbers come from. Use the same two colours to colour code the previous calculations. For example:

  $\boxed{87 - 77} = 10$

  $\boxed{378 + 132} = 510$

  $\boxed{510} \div \boxed{10} = 51$

  $378 + 132 \div 87 - 77$

  $(378 + 132) \div (87 - 77)$

- Discuss the order in which each calculation is completed. Ask: *If the subtraction and addition are completed before the division, what does this tell us?* Elicit that there must be two pairs of brackets in the number sentence and that the second pair was calculated first. Ask: *In this number sentence, does it matter which of the two brackets is worked out first? Why/why not?* Repeat the colour coding activity

for further three-step calculations, working backwards from the final step to establish where each number comes from.

- Pupils should now complete Question 1 in the Practice Book.

Same-day intervention

- Display the following calculations:

  $120 \div 10 = 12$

  $68 - 36 = 32$

  $32 + 12 = 44$

- Ensure that pupils understand that these are three steps leading to the final answer 44. Place three chairs at the front of the class and chose three pupils to hold whiteboards with the numbers 32, 12 and 44. Position pupils with + and = symbol cards in between so that the final calculation is represented.

- Point to the first pupil (holding 32). Ask: *How can we make 32?* Direct pupils' attention to the second number sentence and establish that $68 - 36 = 32$. Replace the pupil on the first chair with another holding a new whiteboard with $68 - 36$ written on it. The calculation should now read $68 - 36 + 12 = 44$.

- Point to the second pupil (holding 12). Ask: *How can we make 12?* Direct pupils' attention to the first number sentence and establish that $120 \div 10 = 12$. Replace the pupil on the second chair with another holding a new whiteboard with $120 \div 10 = 12$ written on it. The calculation should now read $68 - 36 + 120 \div 10$.

- Discuss with pupils whether any brackets are needed. In this particular example the number sentence can be worked out without them in the correct order.

- Repeat for different sets of three-step calculations. Begin with the final calculation and encourage pupils to physically replace the different parts in order to build the original number sentence.

Same-day enrichment

- Provide pupils with the following calculations in three steps, containing missing numbers:

  $14 \times \boxed{} = 700$

  $700 + \boxed{} = 770$

  $770 - \boxed{} = 198$

- Pupils should work backwards in each calculation to find the missing numbers and then derive the number sentence these calculations come from.

• Pupils should invent their own similar problems by first creating a number sentence with three operations, writing each of the three steps and then erasing one of the numbers in each step. Encourage pupils to share their problems for each other to solve.

Question 2

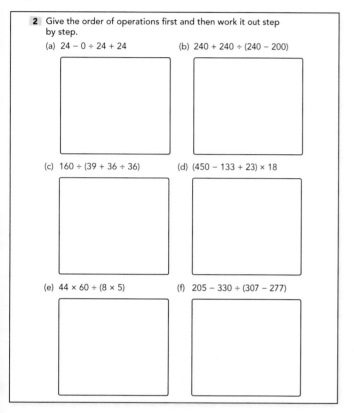

2 Give the order of operations first and then work it out step by step.

(a) $24 - 0 \div 24 + 24$ (b) $240 + 240 \div (240 - 200)$

(c) $160 \div (39 + 36 \div 36)$ (d) $(450 - 133 + 23) \times 18$

(e) $44 \times 60 \div (8 \times 5)$ (f) $205 - 330 \div (307 - 277)$

What learning will pupils have achieved at the conclusion of Question 2?

• Pupils will have consolidated their understanding of how to solve calculation questions containing three operations.

• Further opportunities will have been given to explain the order of operations, including when deriving general rules.

Activities for whole-class instruction

• Display the following calculations: $28 - 8 \times 2$ and $5 + 11 \times 2$. Explain that the number sentences come from previous work completed in Year 2 (Book 2, Unit 5.10). Remind pupils that at the time they were asked to think about the different ways they could be answered, but that they were not taught about the order of operations or

which way was correct. Ask: *How would you explain how to answer these number sentences to your Year 2 self?*

• Write the following number sentence on the board:

$56 \times (4 + 20 \div 20)$

• Ask: *Can you split this number sentence into the three operations that need to be calculated?* Show pupils that these are:

$56 \times$?

$4 +$?

$20 \div 20$.

Choose three pupils to hold whiteboards at the front displaying these different parts.

• Ask: *What do you notice about the brackets in this number sentence? How do you think this affects the order of operations?* Ensure that pupils understand that where there are two operations inside a pair of brackets, they should be worked out in the usual order of operations (in this case, division and then addition).

• Ask the class to think about which operation should be worked out first, second and then third. Call out *First!*, *Second!* and *Third!* For each number, the pupil holding the relevant part of the number sentence should hold their whiteboard above their head. Show how each part to the number sentence can then be listed, ready to complete:

$20 \div 20 =$ ___

$4 +$ ___ $=$ ___

$56 \times$ ___ $=$ ___

• Work through the three steps, completing each missing value.

• Repeat the activity for different number sentences, particularly those containing two operations inside brackets where pupils need to consider which should be calculated first.

• Pupils should now complete Question 2 in the Practice Book.

Same-day intervention

• Revise the rules for the order of operations. Provide pupils with quick instances of two-step, then three-step number sentences without brackets. For example:

Two-step:

$93 + 57 \div 2$

$34 \times 3 + 11$

Three-step:

$36 + 14 \times 5 \div 10$

$83 - 7 \times 3 + 9$

- Ask pupils to explain the order in which each operation should be worked out (without asking them to calculate anything). Move on to considering number sentences containing brackets.

- Display the number sentence $140 + 140 ÷ (57 − 55)$ on a strip of paper. Ask: *Which is the first operation that needs to be worked out? Why?* Pupils should be able to explain that as the subtraction is in brackets it takes priority over the normal order of operations and should be calculated first. Write the calculation $(57 − 55)$ and then use a sticky label to cover over the bracketed calculation with the answer:

$$140 + 140 ÷ \boxed{2}$$

- Ask: *Which is the second operation that needs to be worked out?* Ensure pupils understand that division takes priority over addition when there are no brackets. Again, write the calculation $(140 ÷ 2)$ so pupils can see the step and cover the original number sentence with a further sticky label:

$$140 + \boxed{70}$$

- Ask pupils to complete the final step to find the answer. Repeat for further number sentences. Ensure pupils understand that by covering up each part of the calculation as it is worked out, they are replacing each expression with its equivalent value (for example $57 − 55$ is the same as 2, so it can just be replaced with 2).

Same-day enrichment

- Use **Resource 4.10.5a** The great number sentence challenge to set pupils a series of challenges where they are asked to write number sentences to match given clues.

Resource 4.10.5a

The great number sentence challenge

Can you write the following number sentences?

A number sentence that contains addition, multiplication and subtraction, but the subtraction is worked out first.

A number sentence that should be worked out as it is written, from left to right.

A number sentence that should be worked out from right to left.

A number sentence that contains no brackets.

A number sentence that contains two different operations within a pair of brackets.

A number sentence that contains division and multiplication, which are worked out in that order.

Share each number sentence with a partner. Can they solve them?

- Pupils should choose a challenge and then share their number sentences for peers to split into steps and answer.

Question 3

3 Fill in the spaces.

(a) If a number sentence contains multiplication and division, as well as addition and subtraction but without brackets, then we

first do _____ and then do _____ .

(b) If a number sentence contains brackets, then we first

do _____ .

(c) For $(6400 − 800 × 20) ÷ 4$, the correct order of operations

is to do _____ first, then _____ and

finally _____ .

What learning will pupils have achieved at the conclusion of Question 3?

- Further opportunities will have been given to explain the order of operations, including when deriving general rules.

Activities for whole-class instruction

- Split pupils into pairs. Ask them to write rules that they use when deciding the order of operations. Ask: *What do you use to help you remember the order?* Use the opportunity to revisit these strategies as a class.

- Choose a pupil to come to the front and show them a number sentence involving three steps. For example:

$530 − 120 ÷ 60 + 29$

- Ask the pupil to describe the number sentence without mentioning any of the numbers and without giving any hints about the order in which to answer the question. For example, pupils might say, *There is a subtraction, a division and an addition and there are no brackets.*

- Ask: *Do you have enough information to be able to say the order of the operations?* Explain to pupils that as there are no brackets, they can say that the order of operations is the same as the usual order of operations – division will come first and then either addition or subtraction depending on where they are in the number sentence. Ask: *What if the order in the number sentence is an addition, subtraction and then division?* Pupils should give the order correctly.

- Repeat the activity for further number sentences, including those that are more complex (for example with two operations within brackets or a number sentence containing all four operations). For each example, encourage pupils to give a general rule for the order of operations based on the information they are given.

- Pupils should now complete Question 3 in the Practice Book.

Same-day intervention

- Use the following activity to devise rules for the order of operations, planning each set of steps rather than going on to work out each answer.

- Split pupils into pairs and give each pair one of the following number sentences on a strip of paper:

$34 \times 2 + 20 \div 2 =$___

$14 \times 4 + 16 \div 2 =$___

$12 \times 2 + 28 \div 2 =$___

- Agree on a colour scheme for representing which operation should be completed first, second and third.

- As a group, discuss their strategies for remembering the order of operations when there are no brackets. Ask them to write out the operations in order. Collect the calculations together and look at them as a group. Use them to form a more general rule. Ask: *If a number sentence contains multiplication, then addition, then division and there are no brackets, in what order should the operations be worked out?*

- Repeat the activity for different sets of number sentences that have a common theme. For example, number sentences with brackets, number sentences with two operations inside a pair of brackets and so on.

Same-day enrichment

Remind pupils of the flow chart they used when introduced to the order of operations (**Resource 4.10.3a** Calculation flowchart). Ask them to devise a new flow chart that also includes their knowledge of number sentences with three steps and also those where two operations are within a pair of brackets.

Question 4

4 Application problems.

(a) A school is organising a trip for 42 teachers and 567 pupils. Each coach can seat 40 people. Everyone must be seated. How many coaches are needed for the trip?

(b) In a supermarket, 22 boxes of apples were sold in the morning and 34 boxes in the afternoon. The weight of the apples that were sold in the afternoon was 360 kilograms more than that of the apples sold in the morning.

(i) How many kilograms does each box of apples weigh?

(ii) How many kilograms of apples have been sold in total?

(iii) If the price for each box of apples is £80, how much did the supermarket receive on that day from selling these boxes of apples?

What learning will pupils have achieved at the conclusion of Question 4?

- Application of multi-step calculations will have been extended to include word problems.

- Further opportunities will have been given to explain the order of operations, including when deriving general rules.

Activities for whole-class instruction

- Display the following word problem:
  - A factory is packaging popcorn into boxes. There are 324 packets of sweet popcorn and 150 packets of salty popcorn. Each box can hold 50 packets altogether. How many boxes are needed to pack all the popcorn?

- Give pupils time to read the problem several times. Encourage them to explain it using their own words. Ask: *What is the same and what is different about this problem and the number sentences you have been working with?*

- Get pupils to identify the numbers that are important within the problem. Ask: *What are the steps you need to work out to find the answer?*

- For each step, encourage pupils to explain what it is they are finding out. For example, they need to begin by adding 324 and 150 to find the total packets of popcorn. They then need to divide the answer by 50 to find out how many boxes are needed. Pupils should express this as a number sentence, for example $(324 + 150) \div 50$.

- Pupils should then calculate the answer, writing each step on their whiteboards. Ask: *What should be done with the remainder?* Establish that the leftover packets of popcorn will need an extra box. Ensure that pupils understand that the answer needs to be rounded up by 1 box.

- Repeat for further word problems, allowing pupils to apply their knowledge of multi-step calculations in different contexts. For each example, encourage them to express the problem as a number sentence before continuing.

- Pupils should now complete Question 4 in the Practice Book.

Same-day intervention

- Read the following word problem:
  - Jack has 26 stickers. He buys 14 more. He then gives $\frac{1}{4}$ of the stickers to his brother. How many does he give his brother?

- Provide pairs with a set of approximately 50 cubes or similar. Read the problem further times and encourage pupils to model the problem using the cubes. Ask: *What are the different operations you need to do to find the answer? What order do you need to work them out?* Show pupils how the problem can be represented as the number sentence $(26 + 14) \div 4$.

- Repeat for further application problems. For each problem, encourage pupils to model the steps using manipulatives before sharing their ideas about the order of operations.

Same-day enrichment

- Provide pupils with the title 'At the supermarket'. Encourage them to devise their own word problems that require two- or three-step calculations to work out the answer. Provide pupils with **Resource 4.10.5b** At the supermarket to help them frame their questions initially.

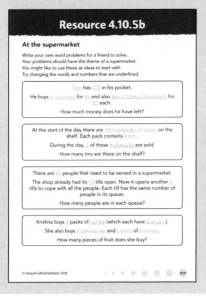

- Pupils should share these problems with peers who should first express them as a number sentence and then perform the two or three calculations needed to solve them.

Challenge and extension questions

Questions 5 and 6

5 Put brackets in each of the following number sentences to make the equation true.

$480 - 360 \div 12 + 8 = 6$ $480 - 360 \div 12 + 8 = 462$

6 There were 724 books in a school library. Year 1 pupils borrowed 88 books. Year 2 pupils borrowed half of the remaining books. The other half of the remaining books were shared equally by Year 3, Year 4 and Year 5. How many books did Year 4 pupils receive?

Pupils are given two questions in order to further develop their knowledge and understanding of three-step calculations. The first question provides pupils with two identical number sentences that have differing answers. They are expected to apply their knowledge of the order of operations and insert brackets so that each calculation becomes true.

The second question tests pupils' abilities to read through a multi-step word problem and break it down into parts so that it can be solved. Pupils should be encouraged to take the problem a step at a time, rather than aim to express it as a single number sentence to begin with (for example first consider how to find the number of books borrowed by Year 2 and then how to find the remaining year groups).

Unit 10.6
Solving calculation questions in 3 steps (4)

Conceptual context

This is the final in a series of units about using mixed operations and brackets. Pupils are now introduced to the idea of nesting one bracketed operation within another. For this purpose, square and rounded brackets are used, for example $10 \times [45 \div (5 + 4)]$. The principle behind such nested brackets is to allow a further layer of order within a number sentence (in the above example, to show that the division must be completed before the multiplication).

Pupils are encouraged to work 'from the inside, out' and so calculate anything within the inner (round) brackets first, before moving on to anything within the outer (square) brackets, then go through other operations according to the order they have previously learned.

Pupils have learned that the inner (round) brackets should only be used when they are needed – that is, when the order of operations is ambiguous without them. However, now that calculations are becoming more complex, pupils will at first be encouraged to include both sets of brackets in order to be absolutely clear, even where the outer (square) brackets are not strictly necessary. This will help them to make the conceptual and procedural progression that is needed at this stage. In time (and for some particularly high-performing pupils, even at this stage) they will make decisions about when the outer brackets are required.

Learning pupils will have achieved at the end of the unit

- Fluency with three-step calculations will have been consolidated through the use of tree diagrams to represent them (Q1)
- Conceptual understanding will have been strengthened as links between a number sentence and the steps needed to find its answer have been explored (Q2, Q4)
- The concept of brackets will have been extended to include nested brackets (Q3, Q4)
- Knowledge of the general rules of the order of operations will have been consolidated, deepening number concepts (Q2, Q3 Q4)

Resources

mini whiteboards; a small round tray or container; a large square/rectangular tray or container; digit and symbol cards (small and large); strips of paper; cards

Vocabulary

brackets, multiplication, division, addition, subtraction, number sentence, mixed operations, (order of) operations, equation

Question 1

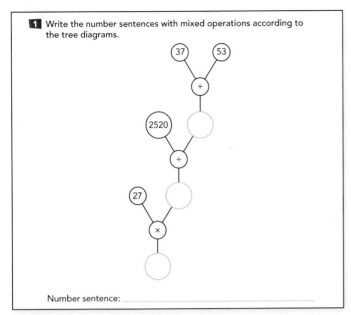

1 Write the number sentences with mixed operations according to the tree diagrams.

Number sentence: _____

What learning will pupils have achieved at the conclusion of Question 1?

- Fluency with three-step calculations will have been consolidated through the use of tree diagrams to represent them.

Activities for whole-class instruction

- Display the following tree diagram:

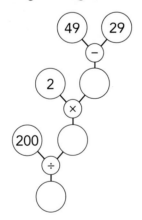

- Ask: *How many steps are in the number sentence that this tree diagram is based on? In what order are they completed?* Agree that the number sentence has three operations; they are completed in the order –, × and ÷.

- Ask: *If we are doing the subtraction first when there is multiplication and division to be done as well, what do we know about the number sentence – does it have brackets or not?* Pupils should be able to tell you that there must be brackets around the subtraction segment if it appears first in the tree (in the sequence).

- Write (49 – 29) with space on both sides to indicate that its position in the sentence is not yet known.

- Ask pupils to copy the tree, filling in the missing values where they can. They should be able to complete all of them.

- As a group, write the complete number sentence. Pupils will probably suggest:

  $200 \div 2 \times (49 - 29) =$ ____

- Ask: *Is there only one answer?* Pupils might offer 2000 and 5.

- Explore pupils' routes to the different answers:

  2000 is the answer if the sentence is read from left to right as pupils have been taught to do because ÷ and × are equal in the order of operations, so $200 \div 2$ is calculated as the second part of the calculation to give $200 \div 2 \times (49 - 29) = 100 \times 20 = 2000$.

  5 is the answer if $2 \times (49 - 29)$ is calculated as the second part of the calculation to give $200 \div 40 = 5$.

- Explain that, to be really clear, we can add a second set of brackets and that these are square brackets so that they look different to the first set of brackets. Write the sentence again with square brackets:

  $200 \div [2 \times (49 - 29)] =$ ____

- Ask: *What does this show you?* Explain that the rounded brackets (49 – 29) are nested within the square brackets. and so these are sometimes called nested brackets. Model the new number sentence as $200 \div [2 \times (49 - 29)]$.

- Pupils should draw tree diagrams for:

  $2 \times [100 \div (56 - 6)] =$ ____
  $500 \div [4 \times (14 + 11)] =$ ____

- Discuss with pupils the fact that two sets of brackets are used as signposts to guide them through the process of working through number sentences when they become complicated. Explain that sometimes the answer with them is still the same as without: $2 \times 100 \div (56 - 6)$ gives the same answer as $2 \times [100 \div (56 - 6)]$. However, having the extra brackets means that pupils do complete the operations in the required order. Then, when they meet more complicated number sentences (where the square brackets have more of an effect on the answer), they will know what to do.

- Pupils should draw tree diagrams for:

  $6 \times [20 \div (36 - 32)] =$ ____ (This is another example where the square brackets do not affect the answer.)
  $500 \div [4 \times (14 + 11)] =$ ____

- Pupils should now complete Question 1 in the Practice Book.

Same-day intervention

- Build concrete links between number sentences and the tree diagrams that represent them. Draw a large tree diagram (the same layout as that in Q1).

- Display the following number sentence: $12 \times [80 \div (6 + 4)]$. Use the idea of a 'tray within a tray' to demonstrate the effect of brackets within brackets. Model the sentence by placing number and symbol cards on the desk, with the calculation $6 + 4$ placed inside a round tray or container inside a larger, rectangular container holding the calculation $80 \div$. These represent the round and square brackets, respectively.

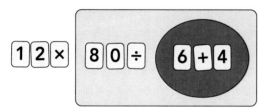

- Ask: *Which operation would you work out first and why?* Ensure pupils understand that as the round brackets are inside the square brackets, the addition should be calculated first. Choose pupils to take the relevant cards $(6 + 4)$ and place them onto the tree diagram. Continue for the remaining operations so that pupils understand where each part of the tree diagram comes from. Repeat the activity and also work backwards, giving pupils the tree diagram and asking them to move the cards to form a number sentence. Use the two trays to represent the two forms of brackets as a visual aid.

Same-day enrichment

- Ask pupils to write their own number sentence problems containing three operations and round brackets within square brackets. To begin with, encourage pupils to use the example in Question 1 as a template. As they grow in confidence using the two types of brackets they can vary the order in which they appear.

- Pupils should draw tree diagrams on their whiteboards to represent their number sentences and erase each of the answers to the steps. They should share their partially completed tree diagrams for peers to solve and to write the number sentences that they represent. Pupils can compare their answers with the original number sentences to check whether they were correct.

Question 2

> 2 Put the calculations in 3 steps into one number sentence with mixed operations and then calculate.
>
> (a) $247 - 82 = 165$
> $165 \times 2 = 330$
> $660 \div 330 = 2$
>
> Number sentence: _____
>
> (b) $70 + 20 = 90$
> $1000 - 90 = 910$
> $910 \times 2 = 1820$
>
> Number sentence: _____

What learning will pupils have achieved at the conclusion of Question 2?

- Conceptual understanding will have been strengthened as links between a number sentence and the steps needed to find its answer have been explored.

- Knowledge of the general rules of the order of operations will have been consolidated, deepening number concepts.

Activities for whole-class instruction

- Place three chairs at the front of the class and choose three pupils to hold whiteboards showing the following three steps of a calculation:

  $149 - 144 = 5$

  $4 \times 5 = 20$

  $320 \div 20 = 16$

- Encourage pupils to consider the final step. Ask: *Can we replace any numbers in this division with a calculation that gives the same value?* Direct their attention to the second step and point out that 4×5 equals the 20 in the final step, and so the number 20 can be rubbed out and replaced as follows: $320 \div (4 \times 5)$. Ask: *Why is it important to include brackets around the subtraction $(149 - 144)$?*

- Again, encourage pupils to consider the new number sentence. Ask: *Are there any numbers in this number sentence that we can replace with an operation that gives the same value?* Direct their attention to the first step and point out that $149 - 144$ equals 5, and so the number 5 can be rubbed out and replaced.

- Discuss the need to use different types of brackets. Ask: *Which is the first step?* Agree that round brackets are needed around the subtraction (as it is the first step) and square brackets around the multiplication (as it is the second step).

- Show how the number sentence can also be derived by starting with the first step and working forwards to get the same answer.

- Provide further sets of three steps and choose different pupils to come to the front and explain how they can find each number sentence the steps are related to. Include examples such as:

  $37 + 82 = 119$

  $119 - 115 = 4$

  $268 ÷ 4 = 67$

- Pupils may choose to derive the number sentence for this example as $268 ÷ [(37 + 82) - 115]$. Ask: *Are the two sets of brackets actually required?* As addition and subtraction have equal priority in the order of operations, $37 + 82 - 115$ will be calculated from left to right as it is written, and so only one set of brackets around this string is needed: $268 ÷ (37 + 82 - 115)$.

- Pupils should now complete Question 2 in the Practice Book.

Same-day intervention

- Display the following on three strips of paper:

  $12 + 13 = 25$

  $2 × 25 = 50$

  $500 ÷ 50 = 10$

- Ask: *Does each answer feed into the next calculation or are they separate?* Consider the final calculation to begin with. Point to the number 50 in the third step and ask: *What is this the same as?* Fold the second strip of paper and use the subtraction to cover over the number 50 with $2 × 25$. Write the corresponding calculation next to it, as below:

   $500 ÷ (2 × 25)$

- Point to the number 25. Ask: *What is this the same as?* Fold the first strip of paper and replace 25 with $12 + 13$.

- Ask: *What can we do in the number sentence to show that the addition needs to be completed before the multiplication?* Write the new calculation, using round and square brackets.

   $500 ÷ [2 × (12 + 13)]$

- Repeat for different three-step calculations, where possible based on number sentences with both round and square brackets. For example:

  $42 ÷ 7 = 6$

  $3 × 6 = 18$

  $10 × 18 = 180$

Number sentence: $10 × [3 × (42 ÷ 7)] = 180$

  $24 + 16 = 40$

  $40 × 3 = 120$

  $240 ÷ 120 = 2$

Number sentence: $240 ÷ [(24 + 16) × 3] = 2$

- Each time, ensure pupils are able to explain how to build up the number sentence by replacing numbers with the expressions that equal them.

Same-day enrichment

- Split pupils into groups of three and provide each pupil with a piece of card. Pupil A should devise their own number sentence, where possible containing both round and square brackets. They should turn their card over and write 1 on it.

- Pupil B should now look at card 1 and write down the three steps needed to solve it, in order. They should turn their card over and write 2 on it. Pupil C must then look at card 2 and put the calculations in three steps into one number sentence. They should then compare their answer with card 1. If it is the same, they get a point.

- Pupils should play the game several times, swapping roles each time.

Question 3

3 Write the correct answers in the spaces.

(a) If a number sentence has round brackets inside square brackets, then you perform the calculation first within

_____ and then _____ .

For example, $10 + [5 × (6 ÷ 3)] =$ ☐ .

(b) In $29 × [1440 ÷ (328 - 280)]$, the correct order of calculations is to do the subtraction first, then the _____ and finally the _____ .

(c) In $[(1400 ÷ 2) - (328 + 280)] × 2$, the correct order of calculations is to do the _____ , the _____ , then the _____ and finally the _____ .

(d) In $4200 - (650 + 50 × 3)$, the correct order of calculations is to do the _____ first, then the _____ and finally the _____ . The answer is ☐ .

(e) In $2 kg + 550 g - 1100 g =$ ☐ g, the correct order of calculations is first to calculate _____ , then calculate _____ and finally calculate _____ .

The answer is ☐ g.

What learning will pupils have achieved at the conclusion of Question 3?

- The concept of brackets will have been extended to include nested brackets.
- Knowledge of the general rules of the order of operations will have been consolidated, deepening number concepts.

Activities for whole-class instruction

- Display symbol cards (representing +, −, ×, ÷, () and []) in a random order at the front of the class. Read a description of a number sentence as a clue. For example, a number sentence that has round brackets within square brackets.

- Choose pupils to come to the front and tap each symbol card in the order the number sentence should be completed (in this case, the round brackets followed by the square brackets). Refrain from asking pupils to calculate the answer so that they can focus on the order of operations.

- Continue the activity, ensuring that the clues become progressively more complex. Include both those represented using words as well as numbers and symbols, for example:

  - a number sentence with no brackets that contains an addition, followed by a division, followed by a multiplication

  or

  - $[820 \div 2 - (130 + 89)] \times 3$

- Turn the activity into a game by choosing two pupils to come to the front. Explain that one pupil should tap the operation that should be completed second and the other should tap the operation that should be completed third. Display different number sentences, and the pupil that taps their correct operation quickest stays at the front, while the other pupil is replaced by another.

- Pupils should now complete Question 3 in the Practice Book.

Same-day intervention

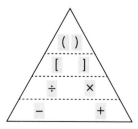

- Remind pupils of the three-layered order of operations pyramid they have used before. Provide pairs of pupils with a large piece of paper. Ask them to draw a triangle, this time split into four horizontal layers. Provide pupils with symbol cards (including both round and square brackets) and ask them to place them on this operations pyramid to show the order in which they should be worked out.

- Display different number sentences containing three operations and encourage pupils to use their pyramids to help recall the rules for the order of operations. For example:

$$45 \times (10 + 2) - 9 \quad \text{[Order: +, then ×, then −]}$$
$$(15 + 85) \div (5 \times 5) \quad \text{[Order: +, then ×, then ÷]}$$
$$18 \div [3 \times (26 - 23)] \quad \text{[Order: −, then ×, then ÷]}$$

- As with the main activity, do not ask pupils to work out the answer. Instead, ask them to give the order in which they would solve the parts. Include number sentences where an operation within round brackets is within square brackets.

Same-day enrichment

- Give pupils five minutes to write as many three-step number sentences as they can on small pieces of paper. They should fold these up and place them into a bowl. Encourage pupils to include examples containing two forms of brackets as well as brackets containing two operations and a variety of operations overall.

- Each pupil should write any five operation symbols (from +, −, × and ÷) on their whiteboard. These represent the first step that needs to be completed in a calculation. Pupils may use any of the four operations and can repeat them as often as they like (for example they might write ×, +, + and −).

- Pupils should take it in turns to take one of the number sentences and reveal it to the group. They should decide which operation should be completed first. If they have written this symbol on their whiteboard they may cross it off. Play should repeat until one student has crossed off all four symbols.

- A variation of this activity could be played where pupils predict four symbols and their positions in the order of operations. For example, they might write × (first), − (second), ÷ (first) and ÷ (third). They can only cross off a symbol when it appears in the correct position in the order of operations.

Question 4

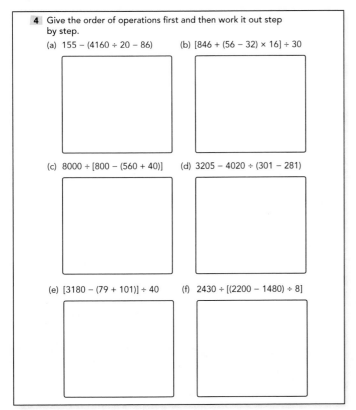

4   Give the order of operations first and then work it out step by step.

(a) $155 - (4160 \div 20 - 86)$

(b) $[846 + (56 - 32) \times 16] \div 30$

(c) $8000 \div [800 - (560 + 40)]$

(d) $3205 - 4020 \div (301 - 281)$

(e) $[3180 - (79 + 101)] \div 40$

(f) $2430 \div [(2200 - 1480) \div 8]$

What learning will pupils have achieved at the conclusion of Question 4?

- Conceptual understanding has been strengthened as links between a number sentence and the steps needed to find its answer have been explored.
- The concept of brackets will have been extended to include nested brackets.
- Knowledge of the general rules of the order of operations will have been consolidated, deepening number concepts.

Activities for whole-class instruction

- Display the calculation $237 \times [(67 - 41) \div 2]$
- Discuss the three steps in this calculation and the order in which the operations should be worked out. Select three pupils and explain that they are going to make a human 3-D number sentence to show this. Ask the group to direct the three pupils forwards or backwards so that the first operation is standing at the front, then the second and then the third. In this example, the pupil holding the subtraction should come to the front, followed by the division and then the multiplication.

- Ask: *Can you explain why you have put the operations in this order?*

- Give pupils time to calculate each part of the number sentence. As each part is worked out, it can be erased from the whiteboard, replaced with its answer and each pupil can move forwards. For example:

$$67 - 41 = 26$$

$$26 \div 2 = 13$$

$$237 \times 13 = 3081$$

- Repeat the activity to help order and solve further number sentences, particularly those with two types of brackets.
- Pupils should now complete Question 4 in the Practice Book.

Same-day intervention

- Use the following activity as a way to physically reinforce the order of operations needed to solve a three-step number sentence. In an open space, chalk the following design on the ground:

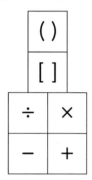

- Explain that the squares on the grid represent the order of operations (from top to bottom). Ask pupils to draw the relevant symbols in each square.
- Display a number sentence containing three steps and at least one pair of brackets. For example, 9 × (764 − 521) − 45. Ask pupils to recall the order of operations and decide on the order they should use to calculate the answer. Choose different pupils to hop across the grid to show the three operations (in this case, the subtraction inside the brackets, followed by the multiplication outside of the brackets, followed by the subtraction outside of the brackets).

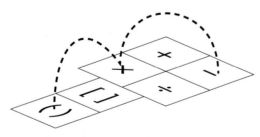

- Discuss with pupils the strategies they would use to complete each step. Model how to complete each step and cross out each part of the number sentence as it is calculated, replacing it with the answer.
- Repeat for different number sentences and encourage pupils to work in pairs to find each solution after planning the correct route their working should take using the grid.

Same-day enrichment

- Display the following calculations:

   $340 ÷ 10 − 8 ÷ 2 =$ ___

   $4258 − 1342 + 1014 ÷ 6 =$ ___

- Challenge pupils to explore the number of different answers they can make by completing the calculations as they are and also by placing brackets in different positions. Remind them that they may use square brackets as well as round. Pupils can write out the calculations and use symbol cards to rearrange the brackets.
- Remind them that not all combinations of numbers will be solvable.

Challenge and extension question

Question 5

> 5 A barrel of oil weighs 21 kilograms, including the weight of the barrel. After using $\frac{1}{3}$ of the oil, it weighs 15 kilograms, including the barrel. What is the weight of the barrel?

In this question, pupils are presented with a word problem requiring mixed operations and multiple steps in order to solve it. Pupils should represent the problem pictorially as well as modelling it, using beakers of water to establish a more thorough understanding of what is required and the order of operations needed to solve it.

Pupils are expected to first calculate the weight of the oil that has been used by first working out the answer to 21 − 15 (the before and after weights). As this represents $\frac{1}{3}$ of the oil, it can be multiplied by three to find the total weight of the oil. By subtracting this from 21, pupils are left with the weight of the barrel. The corresponding number sentence can be written as $21 − [3 × (21 − 15)] = 3\,\text{kg}$.

Unit 10.7
Working forwards

Conceptual context

This unit builds on pupils' understanding of calculations with mixed operations and encourages them to view them as a series of forward steps where each answer is changed in some way following an operation.

Each step feeds directly into the next, allowing pupils to view calculations serially.

The concept of a given input leading to an output is one that pupils will be familiar with from previous chapters and topics. Here, this is extended to include several steps before it results in an output. The next unit is 'Working backwards'.

Learning pupils will have achieved at the end of the unit

- Multi-step calculations will have been interpreted from number machine diagrams, tree diagrams and chains of operations (Q1, Q2)
- Fluency with number sentences will have been developed to include the idea of 'working forwards' from an input to find an unknown output (Q1, Q2, Q3)
- Understanding of three-step calculations will have been developed – moving from vertical to horizontal representations (Q2)
- Starting with a problem presented in words, pupils will have represented this as a diagram (Q3)
- Pupils will have solved multi-step word problems (Q3, Q4)

Resources

mini whiteboards; envelopes; digit cards; operation symbol cards; a ball; counting objects; **Resource 4.10.4a** Blank tree diagrams (from earlier unit); **Resource 4.10.7a** Changing positions; **Resource 4.10.7b** Chains of operations (1)

Vocabulary

brackets, multiplication, division, addition, subtraction, number sentence, (order of) operations, equation, number machine, forwards, backwards, input, output, inverse

Question 1

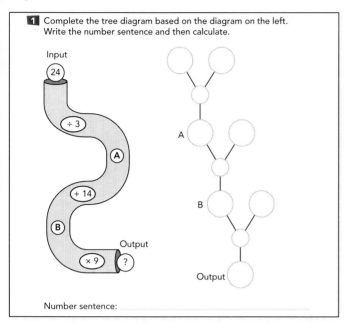

> **1** Complete the tree diagram based on the diagram on the left.
> Write the number sentence and then calculate.
>
> Input
> (24)
> ÷ 3
> (A)
> + 14
> (B)
> × 9
> Output
> (?)
>
> A
> B
> Output
>
> Number sentence: _____

What learning will pupils have achieved at the conclusion of Question 1?

- Multi-step calculations will have been interpreted from number machine diagrams, tree diagrams and chains of operations.

- Fluency with number sentences will have been developed to include the idea of 'working forwards' from an input to find an unknown output.

Activities for whole-class instruction

- Remind pupils of the function machine diagrams they have worked with in the past, where an input enters at one end, an operation is carried out and an output leaves at the other end. Explain that this involves working forwards – where pupils are given a number to begin with and the unknown number is the one at the end.

(i) It may be useful to introduce what is meant by 'working backwards' too. Although pupils will not be using this concept until the next unit, it does add context to the idea of 'working forwards'. Explain to pupils that sometimes they are given the answer and have to work backwards to find what the first number was. Give a very simple example to establish that working backwards involves using the inverse operations (for example ☐ + 6 = 10 requires subtraction), whereas working forwards involves using the operations as they are written (for example 4 + 6 = ☐).

- Choose a pupil to stand at the front holding an envelope with the operation ÷ 2 written on it. Ask: *What number will leave the envelope if various numbers are put in?*

- Ask: *How can we change this number machine so that it represents a three-step calculation?* Agree that more operations should be added.

- Choose two more pupils to also sit with envelopes, one on a chair in front of the first pupil and one sitting on the floor. The operations should be + 7 and then – 9. This will give the effect of a vertical number machine allowing pupils to later make cognitive links between what they see and a tree diagram.

- Ask: *What number will come out of the first envelope if the input is 24? What number will go into the second envelope?* Ensure pupils understand that the second operation relies on the answer to the first and so on.

- Display **Resource 4.10.4** Blank tree diagrams and discuss with pupils how to use them to represent the number machine. Pupils should draw and complete the appropriate tree diagram so that it reflects the three given operations.

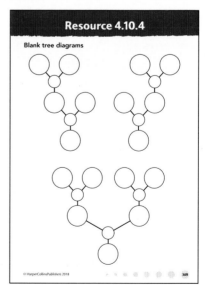

Resource 4.10.4

Blank tree diagrams

© HarperCollinsPublishers 2018   309

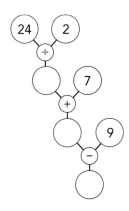

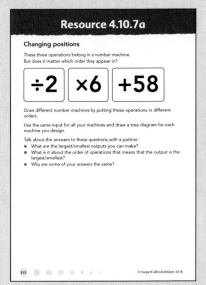

- Ask: *Which order would you do the calculation in if there were no brackets at all? How can we use brackets so that the order is from left to right?* Represent the number sentence as (10 × 2 − 11) × 3.

- Finally, encourage pupils to consider how to write their three-step calculation as a number sentence. Ask: *What is the first step? Do you need to use brackets to show that it is the first step? Why/why not?* Point out that pupils need to work forwards to find the answer – to complete each operation as it is written.

- Repeat for further combinations of steps in number machines, always working forwards from a given input to an unknown output.

- Pupils should now complete Question 1 in the Practice Book.

Same-day intervention

- Display a blank tree diagram (see **Resource 4.10.4** Blank tree diagrams) and ensure that pupils are familiar with what it represents.

- Choose three pupils to represent the three operations in a number machine. Give them whiteboards on which the following operations are written: × 2, − 11 and × 3. They should not show these to any others in the group. Ask each of the three pupils: *Where will you get the number you need to use as your input?* Relate this to the tree diagram, pointing out that pupils are working forwards and the answer to the first calculation feeds into the second and so on.

- Show the first pupil the number 10. Ask them to work out what the answer will be and then complete the tree diagram with their calculation. Ask the second pupil: *How can you work out your calculation? What is it?* (20 − 11). Again, they should complete the calculation on the tree diagram. Repeat for the third pupil.

- Use the cutting-up method used in previous units to help construct the number sentence.

Same-day enrichment

- Provide pupils with a copy of **Resource 4.10.7a** Changing positions.

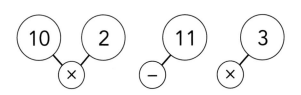

- Pupils should explore whether the position of an operation in a number machine has an effect on the output. Pupils should be given three operations: ÷ 2, × 6 and + 58. Encourage pupils to draw number machines and their related tree diagrams for these three operations in different orders. Pupils should use the same input (for example 32) and work forwards each time.

- **Resource 4.10.7a** prompts pupils to work with a partner, discussing the largest and smallest outputs they can make and what it is about the order of operations that means the output is largest/smallest. Pupils should use reasoning to explain their results.

Question 2

> **2** Fill in the boxes. Then write the number sentence with mixed operations and calculate.
>
> (a) $1000 \xrightarrow{\div 5}$ [ ] $\xrightarrow{-118}$ [ ] $\xrightarrow{\times 2}$ [ ]
>
> Number sentence: _____
>
> (b) $1285 \xrightarrow{-892}$ [ ] $\xrightarrow{-369}$ [ ] $\xrightarrow{\div 8}$ [ ]
>
> Number sentence: _____

What learning will pupils have achieved at the conclusion of Question 2?

- Multi-step calculations will have been interpreted from number machine diagrams, tree diagrams and chains of operations.
- Fluency with number sentences will have been developed to include the idea of 'working forwards' from an input to find an unknown output.
- Understanding of three-step calculations will have been developed – moving from vertical to horizontal representations.

Activities for whole-class instruction

- Choose four pupils to sit in a row at the front – slightly apart. Explain that they are part of a three-step calculation where they are given an input at one end and work forwards to find out what the output will be.
- Ask: *How does this differ from the tree diagrams you have already worked with?* Pupils should realise that chains of operations like this are simply horizontal representations of the same information featured in vertical tree diagrams. Using a horizontal, rather than vertical, representation is a way of providing conceptual variation and consolidating pupils' understanding.
- Place operations in between each pupil to show what each step will be.

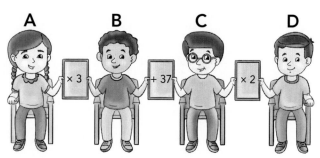

A   B   C   D

- Show how the chain of operations can be modelled as follows:

$$10 \xrightarrow{\times 3} \boxed{} \xrightarrow{+37} \boxed{} \xrightarrow{\times 2} \boxed{}$$

- Ask: *How can this be written as a number sentence? Will we need to use brackets? Why?* Establish that brackets are needed to show that + 37 comes before × 2.

  $(10 \times 3 + 37) \times 2$

- Repeat for different chains of operations, swap pupils and allow them to choose their input. Each time, represent the chain with its equivalent number sentence.
- Pupils should now complete Question 2 in the Practice Book.

Same-day intervention

- Give pupils the example of a computer game – where they might start a level with 22 points, then score 64 points as they achieve more tasks, have their score halved when they lose a life and finally score 18 bonus points. They end the level with a new score. Ask: *What is the input in this example? What are the three different operations that happen?* (+ 64, ÷ 2 and + 18).
- Ask: *What are the different scores that appear on the screen during the game?* Choose three pupils to represent the three different steps and pass the first pupil a whiteboard with the number 22 written on it. Go through each step and encourage each pupil to alter the score according to what happens. Model this as a chain of operations using arrows:

$$22 \xrightarrow{+\,64} \boxed{86} \xrightarrow{\div\,2} \boxed{43} \xrightarrow{+\,18} \boxed{61}$$

- Write as a number sentence with no brackets: 22 + 64 ÷ 2 + 18 and ask: *If this has no brackets, which order would you have to use to work out the answer? How can we use brackets to show that 22 + 64 must come first?* Pupils should add brackets and be able to explain the new order, working from left to right: (22 + 64) ÷ 2 + 18.
- Repeat for different three-step calculations. To ensure pupils stay above zero with these examples, explain that the game ends if their score reaches zero and choose the inputs to avoid this.

Same-day enrichment

- Provide groups of four pupils with the set of instructions provided on **Resource 4.10.7b** Chains of operations (1).

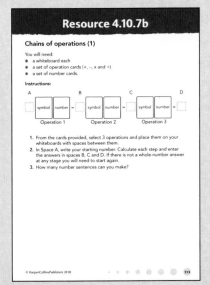

Resource 4.10.7b

Chains of operations (1)

You will need:
- a whiteboard each
- a set of operation cards (+, –, × and ÷)
- a set of number cards.

Instructions:

A   B   C   D

| symbol | number | = | symbol | number | = | symbol | number | = |

Operation 1   Operation 2   Operation 3

1. From the cards provided, select 3 operations and place them on your whiteboards with spaces between them.
2. In Space A, write your starting number. Calculate each step and enter the answers in spaces B, C and D. If there is not a whole-number answer at any stage you will need to start again.
3. How many number sentences can you make?

© HarperCollinsPublishers 2018   313

- One pupil should place an operation card and number cards in between each pupil to represent three steps to a calculation. For example:

  ▢ + 14 _ ▢ _ × 3 ▢ – 25 ▢ _

- Pupil A should begin with an input, write it on their whiteboard and show it to Pupil B. Pupil B should complete the first operation, then show their answer to Pupil C. Pupil C should do the same and, finally, Pupil D should complete the third operation and display the answer.

- Pupils should then write down the number sentence that they think their chain of operations can be written as. If there are differences in where pupils decide to place brackets, they should discuss these as there may be different possibilities.

Question 3

> **3** Write the number sentence and then calculate.
> (a) First add 2 to 17, then multiply the result by 2, and finally subtract 2.
>
> What is the result?
>
> Number sentence: _____
>
> (b) Subtract 2 times 15 from 71, and then multiply by 24.
>
> What is the result?
>
> Number sentence: _____

What learning will pupils have achieved at the conclusion of Question 3?

- Fluency with number sentences will have been extended to include the idea of 'working forwards' from an input to find an unknown output.
- Starting with a problem presented in words, pupils will have represented this as a diagram.
- Pupils will have solved multi-step word problems.

Activities for whole-class instruction

- Discuss the different ways pupils have used to represent calculations with three steps – number machines, tree diagrams and number sentences. Remind pupils that, so far, in each of these they have been working forwards – starting with a number, completing several operations and then ending with the answer.

- Display the following set of instructions, written using words:
  - First multiply 8 by 5, then add 24 and finally divide by 4.

- Ask: *What is the result? What are the three operations in this set of instructions?* (×, + and ÷).

- Split the class into three groups and ask them to represent the multi-step calculation in different ways. Group A should represent the calculation as a chain of operations, Group B as a tree diagram and Group C as a number sentence. Each group should solve the calculation.

- Choose pupils from each group to share their answers and compare the ways in which they have modelled the same calculation. Check that pupils understand that they have moved forwards through the calculation, starting with a known number, completing the operations as they are written to find the answer at the end.

- Repeat for further instructions, remembering to alternate each group's role so that pupils experience different ways of representing multi-step problems. Include instructions where operations are grouped together, for example 4 times 10 is added to 38 and then multiplied by 2.

- Ask: *What is the result?*

(i) It is essential that group rotation occurs with the above activity. The representations (the chain, the tree diagram and the number sentence) provide different ways of showing the same mathematical idea (conceptual variation). The aim is to develop learners who can glide seamlessly between representations, building connections between concepts and spotting patterns. Students should be able to move fluently between representations and, by having practice at this stage, pupils are being given mental tools and visual pictures to deepen their understanding.]

- Pupils should now complete Question 3 in the Practice Book.

Same-day intervention

- Give pupils a set of instructions written on a piece of paper as follows:

  - First subtract 16 from 39, then multiply the result by 2, and finally add 19.

- Ask: *What is the result?*

- Provide pupils with scissors and ask them to cut the instructions into three parts – one for each step they need to do to work out the answer. They should arrange the phrases vertically in order. Ask: *What is the number that the calculation begins with?* Encourage pupils to read through the phrase 'subtract 16 from 39' several times to ensure that, in this example, the starting number is 39.

- Give pupils cards to write each instruction using numbers and symbols and then ask them to place these next to the relevant phrase.

- Ask: *Can you rearrange these steps into a number sentence? Do you need brackets to help show the order of operations?* Pupils should rearrange their cards to derive the number sentence $(39 - 16) \times 2 + 19$. Give pupils time to work out the answer by working forwards through each of the steps.

- Repeat the activity for further sets of written instructions, with pupils physically ordering them, converting the instructions into numbers and symbols and rearranging them into a number sentence before solving.

Same-day enrichment

- Pupils should work in groups of four. Each pupil should have a piece of paper and, at the top, should write a starting instruction. For example, 'first add 19 to 36'. They should fold the top of the piece of paper to cover their instruction and then pass it to the left. Pupils should then write a second instruction, fold the paper down and pass it to the left again. They should repeat this one more time and pass on their paper.

- Each pupil should then open their folded paper and write the number sentence that the instructions represent. If it is solvable (some resulting calculations may not be) they should work out the answer and share their findings with the group.

- Pupils should repeat the activity. If an extra layer of challenge is required, encourage pupils to write initial instructions that combine two operations together (for example half of 28 is added to 73).

Question 4

> 4 Application problems.
>
> (a) There were 12 passengers on a bus when it departed. At the first stop, 2 passengers got off and 6 passengers got on the bus. At the second stop, 3 passengers got off and 4 passengers got on. How many passengers were then on the bus?
>
> (b) A farm has 360 geese. The number of chickens is 32 more than 3 times the number of geese. How many chickens does the farm have?

What learning will pupils have achieved at the conclusion of Question 4?

- Pupils will have solved multi-step word problems.

Activities for whole-class instruction

- Display the following problem:

  - There are 47 people watching a game of football. 14 people leave at half-time. During the second half, 8 people arrive and 12 people leave to go home. How many people are still watching the match when it ends?

- Encourage pupils to read through the problem several times. Ask them to rephrase it using their own words. Ask: *What is the starting number in the calculation? What do you need to do to it to find the answer?* Write the three steps as follows:

$$47 \xrightarrow{-14} \square \xrightarrow{+8} \square \xrightarrow{-12} \square$$

- Ask: *How would you represent this as a number sentence?* Ensure pupils understand that as they are starting with a given number and performing operations to get a final answer, they are working forwards. The number sentence can be written as $47 - 14 + 8 - 12$. Ask: *Why aren't brackets needed in this number sentence?*

- Ask pupils to calculate the answer. Ensure that pupils do not simply regard this as a number sentence that needs solving. It is important that they retain the context for the calculation and can see that 29 is the number of people who are watching the football match when it ends.

- Repeat for further word problems, allowing pupils to apply their knowledge of multi-step calculations in different contexts. For example:

  – Sam does a word count on a story he is typing. It is 480 words long. Josh is also writing a story. He has typed 42 more than double the number of Sam's words. How long is Josh's story?

- For each example, encourage them to express the problem as a chain of operations and as a number sentence before continuing.

- Pupils should now complete Question 4 in the Practice Book.

Same-day intervention

- Show pupils the following word problem:

  – There are 48 cars in a long-stay car park on Monday. On Tuesday, 29 cars leave and another 25 cars arrive. How many cars are in the car park on Tuesday?

- Provide pairs of pupils with a set of around 50 counters or similar. Read the problem again (and again) and encourage pupils to model the problem using the counters. Ask: *What are the different operations you need to do to find the answer? What order do you need to work them out in?* Show pupils how the problem can be represented as the number sentence 48 – 29 + 25. Ask: *How can you show that you are working forwards to find the answer?*

- Repeat for further application problems. For each problem, encourage pupils to model the steps using manipulatives or bar models before sharing their ideas about the order of operations.

- Include problems with more complex wording, for example *There are 36 people standing on Platform 1. The number of people on Platform 2 is 8 more than half of the number of people on Platform 1. How many people are on Platform 2?*

- Encourage pupils to change instructions into numbers and symbols and rearrange them into a number sentence before solving.

Same-day enrichment

- Pupils should devise their own chains of operations, for example:

$$65 \xrightarrow{+\ 47} \square \xrightarrow{\div\ 4} \square \xrightarrow{\times\ 5} \square$$

- Pupils should write these as number sentences, in this case $(65 + 47) \div 4 \times 5$, and then create application problems based on them. For example, *Krishna has 65 shells in her collection. She collects an extra 47 and then shares her collection into four equal piles. Her brother counts one of the piles and states he has five times as many. How many shells does her brother have?*

- Pupils should then share their problems in the group. They should award up to 3 points for peers who can express the problem as the correct chain of operations, write it correctly as a number sentence and give the correct answer (in context).

Challenge and extension questions

Questions 5 and 6

5 Grandpa is 68 years old. Half of Grandpa's age plus 8 is 3 times Min's age. How old is Min?

6 City score 54 goals in a season. Double this total and subtract 36 is 4 times the goals that Wanderers score. How many goals do Wanderers score?

Pupils are given two word problems that involve working forwards and solving three steps. These problems are more complex in the sense that the operations may seem less clear than in previous questions.

Pupils should be encouraged to use a chain of operations to represent each problem in order to deepen understanding of what is required. Once they have done this, they should write each problem as a number sentence and solve each problem.

Unit 10.8
Working backwards

Conceptual context

In the previous unit, pupils considered multi-step calculations as a series of serial steps forward, where a given input went through a series of mixed operations before leaving as an output. This unit continues the same theme, but this time gives pupils the output and encourages them to work backwards to establish what the original input was.

Pupils will need to draw on their knowledge of inverse operations in order to work from output back to input.

Learning pupils will have achieved at the end of the unit

- Multi-step calculations with inverse operations will have been interpreted from number machine diagrams, tree diagrams and chains of operations (Q1, Q2)
- Fluency with number sentences will have been developed to include the idea of 'working backwards' from an output to find an unknown input (Q1, Q2, Q3)
- Understanding of three-step calculations will have been consolidated, moving from vertical to horizontal representations (Q2)
- Pupils will have 'translated' a problem presented in words into a diagrammatic representation (Q3)
- Multi-step word problems will have been solved (Q3, Q4)

Resources

mini whiteboards; envelopes; digit cards; operation symbol cards; a ball; base 10 blocks; counters; **Resource 4.10.4** Blank tree diagrams (from earlier unit); **Resource 4.10.8a** Working backwards; **Resource 4.10.8b** Chains of operations (2)

Vocabulary

brackets, multiplication, division, addition, subtraction, number sentence, (order of) operations, equation, number machine, forwards, backwards, input, output, inverse

Question 1

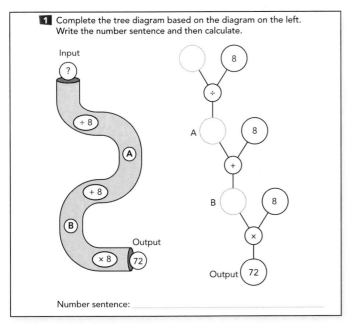

1 Complete the tree diagram based on the diagram on the left. Write the number sentence and then calculate.

Input
?
÷ 8
A
+ 8
B
Output
× 8   72

8
÷
A   8
+
B   8
×
Output   72

Number sentence: _____

What learning will pupils have achieved at the conclusion of Question 1?

- Multi-step calculations with inverse operations will have been interpreted from number machine diagrams, tree diagrams and chains of operations.
- Fluency with number sentences will have been developed to include the idea of 'working backwards' from an output to find an unknown input.

Activities for whole-class instruction

- Choose a pupil to represent a simple number machine by holding an envelope with × 10 written on it. Remind pupils that the common way to use this would be to put a number into the machine, multiply it by 10 and write the answer.
- Ask: *If all we know is that 90 comes out, is there a way to work out what went in?* Pupils should know that, if 90 came out, 9 must have gone in. Agree that what actually needs to happen is 'working backwards', performing the inverse operation.

(i) Each operation has its inverse. It is important to spend time reiterating to pupils that addition and subtraction are not wholly separate operations; in fact they are linked. Combining amounts is the opposite to separating them, and so addition and subtraction are inverse operations. The same is true of multiplication and division (combining equal groups to form a larger number is the opposite of splitting a larger number into equal groups).

- Revise the concept of inverse operations (see above) and remind pupils that to find the answer to ☐ × 10 = 150, they need to work backwards and divide by 10 to find the answer.
- Choose two further pupils to also sit with envelopes – one on a chair in front of the first pupil and one sitting on the floor to form a vertical number machine. The operations on each envelope should be × 10, followed by + 16 and finally ÷ 2. Explain that the output of the number machine is 43.
- Display an appropriate blank tree diagram (see **Resource 4.10.4** Blank tree diagrams) and discuss with pupils how to use it to represent the number machine.

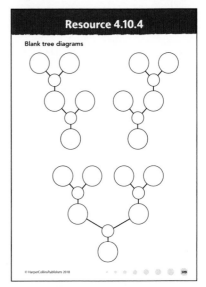

Resource 4.10.4

Blank tree diagrams

© HarperCollins Publishers 2018

- Complete it together so that it reflects the three given operations and the output.
- Explain that pupils could write this as a number sentence in one of two ways:
  - working forwards, with an unknown value at the start: $(? × 10 + 16) ÷ 2 = 43$, or
  - working backwards, using inverse operations. Explain that this number sentence will be more useful as it will find the missing number. Encourage pupils to use this second method to derive the number sentence, which should be:

  $(43 × 2 − 16) ÷ 10$

- Pupils should use their inverse number sentence to find the answer. Ask: *How can we check that our answer is correct?* Pupils should work forwards through the operations to see whether the input results in the number they started with (the output).
- Repeat for further combinations of steps in number machines, always using inverse operations to work backwards from a given output to find an unknown input.

- Pupils should now complete Question 1 in the Practice Book.

Same-day intervention

- Choose pupils to represent the three operations in a number machine. Write the following operations on whiteboards: × 3, + 17 and ÷ 2. Explain that the input to the machine is not known, but that the number that comes out of the machine is 28.

- Display a blank tree diagram (see **Resource 4.10.4** Blank tree diagrams) and complete as much of it as is known. Ask: *How can we work backwards to find the starting number?* Relate this to the tree diagram, ensuring that pupils understand that each operation needs to be the inverse as they are working backwards.

- Show the third pupil the number 28. Ask them to work backwards, multiplying by 2, and then to complete the tree diagram. Ask the second pupil: *How can you work out your calculation? What is it?* (56 – 17). Again, they should complete the calculation on the tree diagram. Repeat for the first pupil.

- Ask: *How can we write a number sentence to show the different steps?* Ensure that pupils start with 28 and record the inverse operations as (28 × 2 – 17) ÷ 3, discussing why brackets are needed.

- Repeat for different multi-step calculations.

Same-day enrichment

- Give pairs of pupils a copy of **Resource 4.10.8a** Working backwards, which provides them with activity instructions as well as a blank template to use.

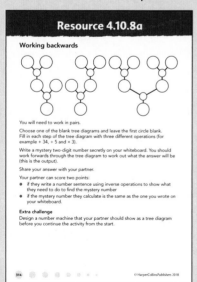

- Pupils should play the following mystery number game. Before starting, they should take a blank tree diagram (**Resource 4.10.4** Blank tree diagrams), partly completing it with three operations (for example + 34, ÷ 5 and × 3). Pupil A should write a mystery two-digit number secretly on their whiteboard. They should work forwards through the tree diagram to work out what the answer will be. Pupil A should then share this answer (the output) with their partner. Pupil B can score two points as follows:

  - if they write a number sentence using inverse operations to show what they need to do to find the mystery number, they earn a point

  - if the mystery number they calculate is the same as is on Pupil A's whiteboard, they earn a second point.

- Each pair should play the game several times, swapping roles. To add a further level of complexity, Pupil A could design a number machine that Pupil B should represent as a tree diagram before continuing as before.

Question 2

2 Fill in the boxes. Then write the number sentence with mixed operations and calculate.

(a) [   ] $\xrightarrow{+\ 34}$ [   ] $\xrightarrow{\times\ 3}$ [   ] $\xrightarrow{-\ 190}$ 149

Number sentence: _____

(b) [   ] $\xrightarrow{\div\ 23}$ [   ] $\xrightarrow{-\ 76}$ [   ] $\xrightarrow{\times\ 50}$ 750

Number sentence: _____

What learning will pupils have achieved at the conclusion of Question 2?

- Multi-step calculations with inverse operations will have been interpreted from number machine diagrams, tree diagrams and chains of operations.

- Fluency with number sentences will have been developed to include the idea of 'working backwards' from an output to find an unknown input.

- Understanding of three-step calculations will have been consolidated, moving from vertical to horizontal representations.

Activities for whole-class instruction

- Choose four pupils to sit in a row at the front, slightly apart. Explain that they are part of a three-step calculation where there is an unknown input at one end, but they know the output at the other. Place operations in between each pupil to show what each step will be. Ask: *How will you work out what the input is?*

- Remind pupils that what they are working with is simply a horizontal representation of the same information featured in vertical tree diagrams. This provides conceptual variation and helps consolidate their understanding. Ask: *Why do you think it is important to show calculations in lots of different ways?*

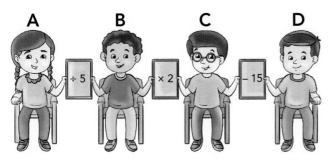

- Give a ball to Pupil D. They should call out the number 9 as the starting number (the output). Before progressing, discuss with pupils how they need to work backwards through the chain of operations and what the inverse of each operation will be.

- Pupil D should pass the ball to Pupil C. In this example, Pupil C should add 15 to the output (the inverse of − 15) and call out the answer. They should then pass the ball on to Pupil B and so on until Pupil A calls out the final number (the input).

- Show how the chain of operations can be modelled:

$$? \xrightarrow{\div 5} \boxed{} \xrightarrow{\times 2} \boxed{} \xrightarrow{-15} \boxed{9}$$

- Ask: *How can we write a number sentence showing how to find the input?* Establish that brackets are needed to show that + 15 comes first. For example, $(9 + 15) \div 2 \times 5$.

- Repeat for different chains of operations, swap pupils and allow them to choose their output. Each time, represent working backwards through the chain with its equivalent number sentence.

- Pupils should now complete Question 1 in the Practice Book.

Same-day intervention

- Three pupils should sit at a table, representing a conveyor belt where each of them does something different to the numbers that come past them. Give pupils the operations − 25, × 2 and + 19, respectively. Practise using the 'conveyor belt' in a forward direction by passing the first pupil a number modelled out of base 10 blocks.

- Each pupil should then complete their particular operation, altering the blocks until there is an output. Ask: *How can this be written as a chain of operations? How does the number change with each step?*

$$22 \xrightarrow{+\ 64} \boxed{86} \xrightarrow{\div\ 2} \boxed{43} \xrightarrow{+\ 18} \boxed{61}$$

- Once pupils have revised how to work forwards, give the third pupil base 10 blocks equalling 41. Ask: *If this is what comes at the end of the conveyor belt, how can we work out what went on at the start?* Discuss the inverse of each operation separately by asking: *If this number is what it looks like after your operation, how can we work backwards to find out what it was like before your operation?*

- Write the chain of operations as a number sentence showing the inverse of each operation. Pupils should pass the blocks backwards along the conveyor belt to demonstrate the inverse of their operations. Repeat for different three-step calculations and encourage pupils to devise similar 'conveyor belts' of their own.

Same-day enrichment

- Provide groups of four pupils with the set of instructions provided on **Resource 4.10.8b** Chains of operations (2).

- One pupil should place an operation card and number cards in between each pupil to represent three steps to a calculation. For example:

$$\boxed{} − 10 \boxed{} + 28 \boxed{} \times 2$$

- Pupil D should write an output on their whiteboard – the aim of the activity is for the other pupils to work backwards to find the unknown input (Pupil A's number). Pupil D should reveal their number to Pupil C, who should consider how to work backwards using the inverse operation. Pupils B and A should do the same, with Pupil A displaying their answer (the input).

- Pupils should check their input is correct by working forwards through the operations as they are written.

- Pupils should then write down the inverse number sentence. If correct, they get a point. If there are differences in where pupils decide to place brackets, they should discuss these as there may be different possibilities.

Question 3

> **3** Write the number sentence and then calculate.
>
> (a) After a number is added to 8 and then multiplied by 8, it is 160. What is the number?
>
> Number sentence: _____
>
> (b) Five times a number is equal to 20 less than 8 times 45. What is the number?
>
> Number sentence: _____

What learning will pupils have achieved at the conclusion of Question 3?

- Fluency with number sentences will have been developed to include the idea of 'working backwards' from an output to find an unknown input.

- Multi-step word problems will have been solved.

- Pupils will have 'translated' a problem presented in words into a diagrammatic representation.

Activities for whole-class instruction

- Write the number 36 secretly on a piece of paper. Explain that you have thought of a mystery number and give the following set of instructions:

  - *If you divide my number by 4, add 19 and then multiply by 5 you get the answer 140. What is my mystery number?*

- Ask: *Which direction do you need to work to find out the mystery number? Why?*

- Split the class into three groups, asking them to represent the multi-step calculation differently. Group A should represent the calculation as a chain of operations, Group B as a tree diagram and Group C as a number sentence. Each group should solve the calculation by working backwards.

- Choose pupils from each group to share their answers and discuss how they modelled the same calculation.

- Repeat for further sets of instructions, alternating each group's role. Include practice for instructions where operations are less linear, for example *Three times a number is equal to 43 more than 10 × 5. What is it?*

- This sort of question is more complex as working backwards in this case does not mean all the operations mentioned need to be the inverse. Simplify the problem (*What would the number be if it were equal to 10 × 5?*) and gradually add in each operation until pupils understand that they need to work out 10 × 5 first, then add 43, and finally divide by three (the only inverse operation) to find the mystery number: $[(10 \times 5) + 43] \div 3$.

(i) Conceptual variation is where the same mathematical idea is represented in different ways. In the above activity, pupils will experience this conceptual variation as they move between representing multi-step problems as chains of operations, tree diagrams and number sentences. In order to develop mental tools and visual pictures, it is important that pupils are given opportunities to consider concepts in these different ways and move from one to the other.

- Pupils should now complete Question 3 in the Practice Book.

Same-day intervention

- Give pupils a set of instructions written on a piece of paper as follows:

  - 58 is subtracted from a mystery number, the answer is divided by three, and finally multiplied by six. The answer is 66. What was the mystery number?

- Provide pupils with scissors and ask them to cut the instructions into three parts – one for each step they need to consider to work out the answer. Ask: *Do you know the input or the output in this calculation? Are you working forwards or backwards?*

- They should arrange the phrases vertically in the order that they need to find the mystery number (reverse order).

- Discuss what the inverse of each operation is and ask pupils to alter each strip of paper to reveal the new operation.

- Give pupils cards to write each instruction using numbers and symbols and then ask them to place these next to each altered phrase.

- Ask: *Can you rearrange these steps into a number sentence? Do you need brackets to help show the order of operations?* Pupils should rearrange their cards to derive the number sentence 66 ÷ 6 × 3 + 58.

- Give pupils time to work out the answer. Ask: *How can you check that you have found the mystery number correctly?*

- Repeat the activity for other sets of written instructions.

Same-day enrichment

- Pupils should work in groups of four. Each pupil should have a piece of paper and, at the top, should write a starting instruction about a mystery number, for example 'Add 84 to a mystery number'. They should fold the top of the piece of paper to cover their instruction and then pass it to their left.

- Pupils should then write a second instruction, fold the paper down and pass it left again. They should repeat this one more time, this time also writing down what the answer to the sequence is before passing on their paper. For example, 'Multiply by four and the answer is 100.'

- Each pupil should then open their folded paper and write the inverse number sentence that is necessary to work out the mystery number. If it is solvable (some resulting calculations may not be), they should work backwards to find the mystery number and share their findings with the group.

- Pupils should test whether they are correct by working forwards from the mystery number to see whether it equals the output.

Question 4

> **4** Application problems.
> (a) In a maths activity, the teacher said to the pupils: 'If you add 4 to my age, then divide by 3, then subtract 14 and finally multiply by 20, you have 100.' How old is the teacher?
>
> Answer: _____
>
> (b) There are many apples on an apple tree. If 7 is subtracted from the number of apples, then the number is multiplied by 7, then 7 is added and finally that number is divided by 7, the result is 7. How many apples are there on the tree?
>
> Answer: _____

What learning will pupils have achieved at the conclusion of Question 4?

- Multi-step word problems will have been solved.

Activities for whole-class instruction

- Display the following problem:
  - Leah takes her house number and adds 17 to it, divides the answer by 5 and then multiplies the answer by 3. She ends with the number 39. What number house does Leah live at?

- Encourage pupils to rephrase the problem. Ask: *Do you need to work forwards or backwards to find the answer? Why?* Write the three steps as follows:

$$\boxed{?} \xrightarrow{+\ 17} \boxed{} \xrightarrow{\div\ 5} \boxed{} \xrightarrow{\times\ 3} 39$$

- Ask: *How would you represent this as a number sentence?* Ensure pupils understand that as the question starts with an unknown number and operations are performed to get a final answer, they need to work backwards. Ask: *How would you change the three operations to work backwards?* They should write the inverse number sentence as 39 ÷ 3 × 5 − 17. Ask: *Why aren't brackets needed in this number sentence?*

- Pupils should calculate the answer. Ask: *How can you check that your answer is correct?* Pupils should go through their chain of operations forwards, using the house number they worked out as the input.

- Repeat for further word problems where pupils are required to work backwards, for example:
  - There are a number of chocolate bars on a shop shelf. 18 of them are sold during the morning. The number of

bars is then doubled and another 25 are sold during the afternoon. At the end of the day there are 57 bars on the shelf. How many were there to begin with?

- For each example, encourage pupils to express the problem as a chain of operations and as a number sentence (containing inverse operations) before continuing to solve the calculation and then check their answer by working forwards.

- Pupils should now complete Question 4 in the Practice Book.

Same-day intervention

- Show pupils the following word problem:
  - There are many sheep in a field. If the number of sheep is multiplied by 2, added to by 14 and then 3 is subtracted from it, the result is 47. How many sheep are in the field?

- Provide pairs with a set of around 50 counters or similar. Encourage pupils to model the problem using the counters.

- Ask: *Do you need to work forwards or backwards to find the answer? Why? What are the different operations you need to do to find the answer?*

- Show pupils how the problem can be represented using inverse operations as $(47 + 3 - 14) \div 2$. Ask: *How can you check whether the number of sheep is correct?*

- Repeat for further application problems. For each problem, encourage pupils to explain why each problem needs to be solved by working backwards, model the backward steps using manipulatives before sharing their ideas about the order of operations as a number sentence.

Same-day enrichment

- Pupils should devise their own chains of operations, for example:

$$? \xrightarrow{+\ 45} \boxed{} \xrightarrow{\times\ 7} \boxed{} \xrightarrow{-\ 92} \boxed{356}$$

- They should write these as the number sentences required to solve them (in this case, $(356 + 92) \div 7 - 45$) and then create application problems based on them. These may be mystery number-type problems or those that represent a scenario with an unknown starting point, for example:
  - There are a number of books on a library shelf. If 45 is added to the number, it is then multiplied by seven and 92 is taken away, the result is 356. How many books are on the shelf?

- Pupils should then share their problems with peers. They should award up to 3 points for peers who can express the problem as the correct inverse chain of operations, write it correctly as a number sentence and give the correct answer (in context).

Challenge and extension questions

Questions 5 and 6

5 In $\blacksquare \times 8 \div 5 - 24 = 48$, what number should be in the $\blacksquare$?

6 Sufyaan was reading a storybook. On the first day, he read 6 pages more than half of the book. On the second day, he read 5 pages more than half of the remaining part of the book. There were 13 pages left. How many pages were there in the book?

Answer: _____

Pupils are given two problems (one number sentence and one word-based) that involve working backwards and solving three inverse steps to find the starting number.

Pupils should be encouraged to use a chain of operations to represent each problem in order to deepen understanding of what is required. This will be particularly useful when considering the second problem. Once they have worked backwards to find the answer, pupils should check whether their starting number was correct, by working forwards.

Unit 10.9
Word calculation problems (1)

Conceptual context

In this unit, pupils continue to develop their fluency with problems containing more than one operation by exploring word calculation problems. Rather than word problems based on real-life scenarios, these problems describe a calculation in words using terms such as sum, product, quotient, divisor and difference. Pupils may need to revisit describing single-step problems before moving on to the concept of multi-step descriptions.

Learning pupils will have achieved at the end of the unit

- Pupils will have practised interpreting calculations involving mixed operations described in mathematical words (Q1)
- Pupils will have reinforced their knowledge of key descriptive words (Q1)
- Pupils will have practised interpreting and solving calculations involving mixed operations described in mathematical words (Q2, Q3)
- Numerical reasoning will have been practised when explaining the number sentence being described by a particular word calculation problem (Q1, Q2, Q3)

Resources

mini whiteboards; flashcards with key words on; large digit cards; large operation symbol cards; **Resource 4.10.9a** Phrase cards; **Resource 4.10.9b** Match up! **Resource 4.10.9c** Calculation strips

Vocabulary

sum, addend, difference, minuend, subtrahend, product, multiplier, quotient, dividend, divisor, half, double, equation, word calculation problem, number sentence

Question 1

> **1** Think carefully. Fill in the brackets, write the number sentences and calculate.
>
> (a) The quotient of 150 divided by 6 is multiplied by 12. What is the product?
>
> Product = (_____) × (_____).
>
> Number sentence: _____
>
> (b) The sum of 288 and 42 is divided by 30. What is the quotient?
>
> Quotient = (_____) ÷ (_____).
>
> Number sentence: _____

What learning will pupils have achieved at the conclusion of Question 1?

- Pupils will have practised interpreting calculations involving mixed operations described in mathematical words.
- Pupils will have reinforced their knowledge of key descriptive words.
- Numerical reasoning will have been practised when explaining the number sentence being described by a particular word calculation problem.

Activities for whole-class instruction

- Display the following words on flash cards: product, sum, difference, total, dividend, divisor, quotient, addend, minuend, subtrahend. Include any similar key words used when describing any of the four operations. Ask: *What do these words have in common?*

- Split pupils into pairs and ask: *If you were to organise them into groups, how would you group them and why?* Ask pairs to share their groupings and their reasoning. Ensure pupils understand the meaning of each term.

- Choose different pupils to come to the front and ask a question using any of the key words in context. For example, *What is the product of 4 and 12? What is the quotient if the dividend is 120 and the divisor is 10?*

- Encourage the rest of the class to write the number sentence (in words) for each question. Check that pupils are able to use each term correctly.

- Combine 'product' and 'difference' in a word problem, for example, *What is the product of 20 and the difference between 16 and 8?* Read it again, pausing after '20'. (Pausing will separate the two parts of the question for pupils as they hear it.)

(i) Each of these word problems has a single over-arching operation at its heart. In the above

example, pupils are essentially being presented with a multiplication problem, having been asked to multiply one value (20) by another (the difference between 16 and 8). It is important that pupils understand and can recognise this. Explain that this clue is often found in the first few words of a word calculation problem (What is the sum of …? What is the quotient of …? and so on), but can sometimes can be found elsewhere ('20 is multiplied by the difference between 16 and 8. What is the product?').

- Provide pupils with opportunities to practise identifying these central operations. For example, which operation is at the heart of the difference between the product of 40 and 10, and 80?

- Ask pupils to read the problem several times and then ask them which part they would work out first. Establish that the difference between 16 and 8 is 8 (16 − 8 = 8), and so the question is asking what is the product of 20 and 8. To give pupils a structure in which to provide their answer, display two whiteboards either side of a multiplication sign and ask: *How can we write each part of the product?* Model this as:

$$\boxed{20} \times \boxed{(16 - 8)}$$

- Repeat for further two-step word calculation problems. For example, ask:

  - *The quotient of 90 divided by 9* (pause) *is multiplied by 14. What is the product?*

  - *The difference between 45 and 89* (pause) *is added to 520. What is the sum?*

- Use the whiteboards to provide pupils with a structure each time and then encourage them to solve each problem using the correct order of operations.

- Pupils should now complete Question 1 in the Practice Book.

Same-day intervention

- Provide pupils with a set of digit cards and a set of operation cards. Practise the different mathematical terms they will be using by calling them out and asking pupils to hold up the relevant operation card – sum (+), quotient (÷), product (×) and so on. This will help to build up speed and fluency.

- Display the following word calculation problem on a strip of paper: 'What is the quotient of 56 divided by the difference between 18 and 11?'

- Ask: *Which are the key words in the problem? What sort of operation do you think is at the heart of this problem?* Elicit that it is a division question where one value (56) is being divided by another (the difference between 18 and 11).

- Fold the paper so that each part of the problem is separate. To begin with, only show the first part:

> What is the quotient of 56 divided by

- Discuss what this means and ask pupils to model what it is asking using their cards (56 ÷). Explain that instead of a number in the second part of the problem, there is a phrase. Show pupils the second part of the strip:

> the difference between 18 and 11?

- Again, discuss what is meant by this and ask pupils to model it (18 − 11). Ask pupils to read the whole question out loud, putting the pause in the right place. Ask: *What can you tell me about the pause when you read the question and the fold in the question strip?* Ensure pupils can tell you the fold and the pause happen in the same place.

- Represent the problem as __ ÷ ( ) = __ . Ask: *Do you agree that this is the correct representation?* Read the question aloud again and ask: *The fold in the paper strip and the pause and the brackets in the number sentence all have a connection – what is it?* Elicit that they all show how to break up the sentence into different parts and help to show in which order to do different parts of the calculation.

- Pupils should complete each part of the calculation using their cards. Ask: *Which part of the problem do you need to work out first?* Model how to solve the problem, writing each number sentence to show their working: 18 − 11 = 7, then 56 ÷ 7 = 8.

- Repeat for further two-step word calculation problems. For example:

  – What is the product of 10 and the sum of 8 and 9?

  (in this case, the fold in the question strip should come after the number 10).

Same-day enrichment

- Provide pupils with a set of phrase cards from **Resource 4.10.9a** Phrase cards.

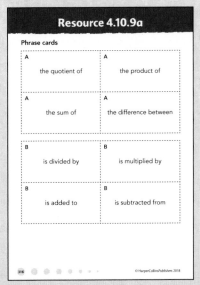

- Pupils should arrange them into A and B piles. They should take one card from each set and devise their own word calculation problems based on them, inserting their own numbers, for peers to solve. When solving calculations, pupils should complete two parts on either side of a symbol, for example:

the product of **3 0** and the sum of **1 1** and **4** =

$$30 \times (11 + 4)$$

- Pupils should then write number sentences showing the order of operations as in the whole class activity. They should repeat for different combinations of cards.

Question 2

> **2** Multiple choice questions. Read each question carefully. Fill in each box with the letter of the correct number sentence.
>
> **A.** 108 × (32 + 23) **B.** (108 + 32) × 23
>
> **C.** 108 + 32 × 23 **D.** 108 ÷ (32 − 23)
>
> (a) What is the sum of 108 and the product of 32 and 23?
>
> Answer: ☐
>
> (b) What is the product of the sum of 108 and 32 multiplied by 23?
>
> Answer: ☐
>
> (c) What is the product of 108 multiplied by the sum of 32 and 23?
>
> Answer: ☐
>
> (d) What is the quotient of 108 divided by the difference between 32 and 23?
>
> Answer: ☐

What learning will pupils have achieved at the conclusion of Question 2?

- Pupils will have practised interpreting and solving calculations involving mixed operations described in mathematical words.
- Numerical reasoning will have been practised when explaining the number sentence being described by a particular word calculation problem.

Activities for whole-class instruction

- Write the numbers 120, 10 and 8 on the board. Give pupils two minutes to use different operations (and brackets if they wish) and write as many different calculations as they can, keeping these numbers in the same order.
- Ask pupils to share their number sentences and write four different examples on the board. Label these A, B, C and D. For example:

  A) 120 × (10 − 8)

  B) 120 ÷ 10 − 8

  C) 120 + (10 − 8)

  D) (120 − 10) × 8

- Describe any one of the number sentences as a word calculation problem, inserting a pause (or pauses) in the appropriate place when reading the sentence, for example

  – *What is the sum of 120 (pause) and the difference between 10 and 8? (C)*

  – *What is the product of 120 (pause) and the difference between 10 and 8? (A)*

  – *What is the product of (pause) the difference between 120 and 10 (pause) and 8? (D)*

  – *What is the quotient of 120 (pause) divided by the difference between 10 and 8? (B)*

- Read the description several times and ask pupils to vote for the number sentence that they think it describes by writing A, B, C or D on their whiteboard. If correct, they get a point. Ask: *What operation is at the heart of the calculation – what do we need to do in this calculation? Add things together to find a sum? Multiply things to find a product?*
- Repeat for some of the other number sentences involving these numbers. Ask pupils to choose one of the number sentences and calculate the answer.
- Repeat the activity for different number sentences.

- Pupils should now complete Question 2 in the Practice Book.

Same-day intervention

- Display the number sentence 8 × (43 + 29). Ask: *In what order would you complete the operations?*
- Establish that the addition should be worked out first and then followed by the multiplication. Point to the last operation that needs to be done (the multiplication) and ensure pupils understand that this is a multiplication question at heart – albeit one where the second factor is found by using addition.
- Choose pupils to label the two parts using enlarged copies of the key phrase cards (**Resource 4.10.9a** Phrase cards) as follows:

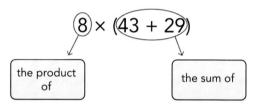

- Establish that the sentence can be described by the following word calculation problem:

  – What is the product of 8 multiplied by the sum of 43 and 29? Repeat the activity so that pupils draw links between further number sentences and word calculation problems that describe them.

Same-day enrichment

- Provide pupils with **Resource 4.10.9b** Match up!

Resource 4.10.9b

Match up!

Number sentences	Word calculation problems	Answers

You will need:
some coloured counters, a playing grid and a partner.

How to play:
1. Complete the playing grid as follows:
   a) Write four different number sentences in Column 1.
   b) Think carefully about how to describe your number sentences using words. In Column 2, write word calculation problems to match them, but in a jumbled order!
   c) Finally, work out the answers to your number sentences and write these in Column 3 (again in a jumbled order).
   So, your grid should contain the information that matches your four number sentences, but not in the right places.
2. Put one coloured counter on any of your number sentences in Column 1.
3. Your partner should read the information in the square and then find the correct squares in the remaining two columns that match it. They should put coloured counters on these squares.
   For example:
   - You might place a counter on a square that says 36 × 3 ÷ 6 (the number sentence).
   - Your partner might then place their counters on a square that says 'What is the quotient of the product of 36 and 3, and 6?' (the word calculation problem that goes with the number sentence) and also on a square that says '18' (the answer to the number sentence).

© HarperCollinsPublishers 2018 · · · · · · · · 117

- Pupils should use the sheet to devise their own quiz. In the first column, they should write four word calculation problems. In the second column, they should write the four corresponding number sentences, but in a random order. In the final column, they should write the answers to each of their number sentences – again in a random order. Pupils may wish to complete the middle column first.

- Pupils should read the instructions on **Resource 4.10.9b** and play the matching game they have created.

- To increase the difficulty of the challenge, pupils may choose number sentences that have the same numbers in them with very similar (but differing) operations.

Question 3

> **3** Write the number sentences and then calculate.
>
> (a) What is the sum of the quotient of 600 divided by 20 and 187?
>
> Answer: _____
>
> (b) What is the quotient of the product of 500 and 32 divided by 100?
>
> Answer: _____
>
> (c) What is the difference between the product of 470 and 15 and the product of 17 and 104?
>
> Answer: _____
>
> (d) The dividend is 244. The divisor is 118 less than half of the dividend. What is the quotient?
>
> Answer: _____
>
> (e) What is the difference between 1098 and half of 756?
>
> Answer: _____

What learning will pupils have achieved at the conclusion of Question 3?

- Pupils will have practised interpreting and solving calculations involving mixed operations described in mathematical words.

- Numerical reasoning will have been practised when explaining the number sentence being described by a particular word calculation problem.

Activities for whole-class instruction

- Split pupils into four teams, with each team representing a different operation (+, −, × and ÷). Each team should have two large operation symbol cards with their team's symbol on it. Display a word calculation problem. For example:

  - What is the quotient of the product of 10 and 3 divided by 5?

- Ask pupils to consider what operation the word calculation problem has at its centre (this particular example is a division question, albeit one where the dividend is found by multiplying 10 and 3 together).

- If teams think that the corresponding number sentence will feature their particular operation, they should send a representative to the front holding their particular symbol card. Ask them to arrange themselves into the order that they think they need to work out the answer. In this example, the product of 10 and 3 needs to be calculated before the division, so the two team symbols should be × then ÷.

- Ask: *How would you write the number sentence for this problem?* In this example, pupils should give the number sentence 10 × 3 ÷ 5. Ask pupils to calculate the answer.

- Repeat for different word calculation problems. Use examples where

  (a) the order of symbols as they need to be calculated is different from the order they appear in the number sentence. For example:

  What is the product of 252 multiplied by (pause) *the difference between 14 and 6?*

  In this example the number sentence is 252 × (14 − 6). Therefore, the order in the sentence is × then −, but the order they need to be worked out is − then ×.

  (b) there are three steps. For example:

  What is the difference between (pause) *the product of 370 and 13 and* (pause) *the sum of 1450 and 1300?*

  (c) the wording includes less obvious descriptions. For example:

  The dividend is 452. The divisor is 902 less than double the dividend. What is the quotient?

  In this example, pupils will need to recognise that they need to multiply the dividend by 2 then subtract 902 to find the divisor, so the number sentence is 452 ÷ (452 × 2 − 902).

- Pupils should now complete Question 3 in the Practice Book.

Same-day intervention

- Provide pupils with strips containing word calculation problems from **Resource 4.10.9c** Calculation strips.

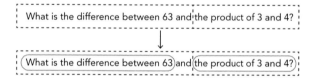

Resource 4.10.9c

Calculation strips

What is the difference between 63 and the product of 3 and 4?

What is the sum of 47 and the product of 7 and 7?

What is the quotient of the product of 8 and 4 divided by 2?

What is the product of the sum of 10 and 10, multiplied by 3?

The difference between 15 and 3 is added to 25. What is the sum?

56 is added to the quotient of 35 divided by 5. What is the sum?

318   © HarperCollinsPublishers 2018

- Choose one of the problems to focus on initially and encourage pupils to read it through several times. Ask: *What are the different parts to this problem?* Ask pupils to draw around the separate parts that they are being asked to complete. For example:

> What is the difference between 63 and the product of 3 and 4?

> What is the difference between 63 and the product of 3 and 4?

- Ask pupils to cut their strip and arrange the phrases vertically to establish the order of operations. In this example, the product of 3 and 4 needs be completed before using it to find the difference with 63.

> the product of 3 and 4?

> What is the difference between 63 and   ?

- Ask: *What sort of a problem is this at heart – addition, subtraction, multiplication or division?* Establish that it is a subtraction ('What is the difference…') where the subtrahend is found first by using multiplication.

- Pupils should then use their knowledge of the order of operations to write the problem as a number sentence, using brackets to overrule the natural order of operations where appropriate.

$$63 - 3 \times 4$$

- Finally, they should calculate the answer to the problem.
- Repeat for further word calculation strips taken from **Resource 4.10.9c** Calculation strips.

Same-day enrichment

- Split pupils into groups of three or four. Challenge pupils to devise their own word calculation problems for peers to solve. On one side of a piece of card they should write their problem. On the other side they should write the corresponding number sentence and its answer. Pupils should aim to create around four or five cards each.

- Pupils should place their completed cards on the table in a grid formation with the word calculation problem face up.

- One by one, pupils should choose a card (not one of their own problems!) and attempt to predict what is on the reverse (by inferring the number sentence and then working out the answer).

- They should look at the card's reverse. If they are correct, they can keep the card. If they are incorrect, they must replace the card back where it was.

- The winner is the pupil at the end with the most cards.

Challenge and extension questions

Questions 4 and 5

4 There are three numbers 0, 2 and 8. They form a greatest 3-digit number and a least 3-digit number. What is their product?

Answer: _____

5 Errol is 9 years old. His father is 37 years old. How old will Errol be when his father's age is 3 times his age?

Answer: _____

Pupils are given two multi-step word problems to solve. The first is the kind of word calculation problem pupils have been practising during the unit. Although only one operation is needed (×), it requires pupils to consider the place value of three-digit numbers and to multiply two three-digit numbers to find the answer.

The second problem provides pupils with a scenario where they should consider the relationship between two ages in order to solve it. This is likely to be solved by trial and error, although pupils should be encouraged to write a number sentence to show their answer.

Unit 10.10
Word calculation problems (2)

Conceptual context

In the previous unit, pupils were introduced to word calculation problems describing multi-step calculations using key terms. Here this is developed, extending to three-step calculations and including more complex language. Pupils will need to break down each problem into steps, identify what the key terms mean and place the operations in the correct order. Fluency with multi-step calculations will develop as pupils are able to identify and describe calculations more confidently using words.

Learning pupils will have achieved at the end of the unit

- Fluency with calculations described in words will have been extended to include simple three-step calculations (Q1)
- Pupils will have practised interpreting and solving calculations involving more complex three-step operations, and those that require inverse operations, described in mathematical words (Q2, Q3)

Resources

mini whiteboards; large digit cards; large operation symbol cards; blank cards; coloured pens; luggage tags; string; **Resource 4.10.9a** Phrase cards (from previous unit)

Vocabulary

sum, addend, difference, minuend, subtrahend, product, multiplier, quotient, dividend, divisor, half, double, equation, word calculation problem, number sentence,

Question 1

> **1** Think carefully. Fill in the brackets, write the number sentences and calculate.
>
> (a) The quotient of 210 divided by 7 is multiplied by the difference between 120 and 80. What is the product?
>
> Product = (＿＿＿＿＿) × (＿＿＿＿＿).
>
> Number sentence: ＿＿＿＿＿＿＿＿＿＿
>
> (b) What is the sum of the product of 34 and 12 and the quotient of 48 divided by 12?
>
> Sum = (＿＿＿＿＿) + (＿＿＿＿＿).
>
> Number sentence: ＿＿＿＿＿＿＿＿＿＿

What learning will pupils have achieved at the conclusion of Question 1?

- Fluency with calculations described in words will have been extended to include simple three-step calculations.

Activities for whole-class instruction

- Write the sentence: 'What is the ＿＿＿ of 68 and 2?' Discuss the possible words that could fill the gap and the effect these words might have on the answer. Some tweaks may be needed to the phrasing (for example 'What is the quotient of 68 divided by 2? What is the difference between 68 and 2?'). Possible answers are: product = 136, quotient = 34, sum/total = 70, difference = 66). Remind pupils of their use of mathematical terms in the last unit and spend time revising these if necessary.

- Choose three pupils to come to the front and sit on chairs. Pupils A and C (on the ends) should have whiteboards. Pupil B (in the centre) should have a set of large operation symbol cards. Display a word calculation problem containing three steps on the board. For example, what is the product of (pause) the difference between 52 and 46 (pause) multiplied by the sum of 3 and 4? Give pupils time to read through this several times. Ask: *What is it about this problem that makes it tricky to answer?* Discuss the fact that it describes several steps and several key words.

- Cover up the problem and reveal the first phrase: 'What is the product of...' Establish that this shows that the calculation is a multiplication calculation and that both factors need to be calculated before it can be worked out. Pupil B should show the relevant operation symbol card (×).

- Reveal the next part of the problem: '... the difference between 52 and 46...' Ask: *What calculation should Pupil A write on their whiteboard?* (52 − 46).

- Repeat for the final phrase: '... and the sum of 3 and 4?', which Pupil C should represent as 3 + 4.

- Ask: *How would you write this as a number sentence? Which part should you calculate first?* Encourage pupils to come to the front and rub off the various calculations on each whiteboard, replacing them with a number until they eventually find the answer.

- Repeat the activity with further word calculation problems where two calculations are needed either side of an operation symbol in order to find the answer.

- Pupils should now complete Question 1 in the Practice Book.

Same-day intervention

- Provide pupils with copies of the following word calculation problem written on a strip of paper:

  – The sum of 4 and 6 is multiplied by the quotient of 360 divided by 6. What is the product?

- Ask pupils to make as many cuts in the strip as is necessary to separate the different steps in the question. For example:

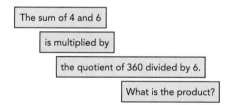

- Ask: *How many steps are in the problem?* Ensure pupils understand that there are three separate steps (the question 'what is the product?' is referring to the solution, the answer).

- Ask pupils to think about the operations they think each step needs (these should be addition, multiplication and division). Under each strip, ask them to write down the calculation being described:

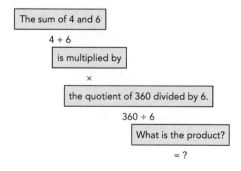

- Pupils must consider the order in which they need to work out the answer. Establish that the final step is the multiplication of two numbers. The previous two steps are to find those two numbers. Ask: *Where would you put brackets into this number sentence to show the steps that need to be completed first?*
  $(4 + 2) \times (360 \div 6)$ Pupils should complete each step and work out the answer.

- Provide further similar problems on paper strips. Move from problems with a central operation and two calculations either side (as above) to less obvious problems. For example:

  – What is the difference between the product of 56 and 9 and the quotient of 645 and 5?

  In this problem the arrangement is still symmetrical: ( ) – ( ), but the wording is such that 'what is the difference' appears at the start of the problem, rather than in the centre.

Same-day enrichment

- Provide pupils with several sets of key phrase cards (see **Resource 4.10.9a** Phrase cards, from previous unit).

Resource 4.10.9a

- Pupils should remove Set B and only use the cards labelled A. They should shuffle the cards and take out three cards, arranging them in a pyramid formation (one on the top, two on the bottom) in front of them. They should turn over the top card. This will give them the central operation in the number sentence. The other two cards will give them the two calculations they need

to do to find each number either side. For example:

- Pupils should then use this framework to devise their own problems for peers to solve. After they have swapped (and answered) their problems, they should shuffle the cards and deal a new problem framework.

Question 2

2 Write the number sentences and then calculate.
  (a) The sum of 66 twenty-fives is divided by the sum of 6 fives. What is the quotient?

  Answer: _____

  (b) Number B is 2940, which is 20 times Number A. How much more is Number B than Number A?

  Answer: _____

  (c) A number is divided by 50. The quotient is 128 and the remainder is 36. Find the number.

  Answer: _____

  (d) How much less is the quotient of 6300 divided by 60 than two times 72?

  Answer: _____

What learning will pupils have achieved at the conclusion of Question 2?

- Pupils will have practised interpreting and solving calculations involving more complex three-step operations, as well as those that require inverse operations, described in mathematical words.

Activities for whole-class instruction

- Display the following word calculation problem:
  – The sum of 42 eighteens is divided by the difference between 51 and 48. What is the quotient?

- Ask pupils to come to the front and underline each word that shows a different step to the problem. Ask: *How many steps are there?* In this example there are three steps, represented by the words sum, divided by and difference (the word quotient simply means the answer to the division). Ask: *Which symbols would you expect to find in the number sentence?* (+, ÷ and −). Note whether any pupils suggest multiplication instead of addition.

- Discuss with pupils what 'the sum of 42 eighteens' means. Ask: *Does it make sense to work out 18 + 18 + 18 + 18 + ... forty-two times or is there a quicker way to work out the answer?*

- Establish that, despite the use of the word 'sum', this is best solved using multiplication, not addition.

- Working in pairs, ask pupils to decide how they should order the three underlined words to show how to work out the answer. Pupils should write large 1st, 2nd and 3rd underneath to denote this. Establish that pupils should first find the sum of 42 eighteens (×), second, they should find the difference between 51 and 48 (−), and third, they should divide the two numbers (÷).

- Ask: *How would you write this as a number sentence?* Pairs should derive the number sentence as 42 × 18 ÷ (51 − 48). Give pupils time to solve their number sentence and share their methods.

- Repeat the ordering exercise for further examples of three-step word calculation problems, particularly those with less obvious wording. For example:

  – Number B is 3672, which is 4 times Number A. How much more is Number B than Number A?

  – A number is divided by 20. The quotient is 52 and the remainder is 13. What is the number?

- Pupils should now complete Question 2 in the Practice Book.

Same-day intervention

- Provide pupils with large cards showing the four operation symbols.

- Read out a three-step word calculation problem twice. The first time, pupils should listen carefully to each part. The second time, they should hold up the operation symbols that they hear in the problem. For example, the product of [pupils hold up ×] 32 and 10 is divided by [pupils hold up ÷] the difference between [pupils hold up −] 42 and 37. Ask: *What is the quotient?*

- Ask: *Which operation symbols did you show? In which order would you need to do them to work out the answer?* (in this example, the multiplication and the subtraction need to be completed before the division can be worked out). Ask: *How would you write this as a number sentence?* Split pupils into pairs to devise and solve the corresponding number

sentence (in this example, 32 × 10 ÷ (42 − 37). Ensure pupils remember the order of operations and can substitute the bracketed calculations for their answers before continuing.

- Repeat for further three-step word calculation problems, encouraging pupils to represent them using symbol cards before finding the number sentence and calculating each answer.

Same-day enrichment

- Challenge pupils to invent their own three-step word calculation problems for peers to solve. Provide pupils with two luggage tags and a length of string. On the first luggage tag, pupils should invent a word calculation problem. On the second luggage tag, pupils should write the corresponding number sentence and answer. They should tie each end of their piece of string to each luggage tag. Pupils should then place their piece of string into a container so that one tag is in the container and the other dangles outside.

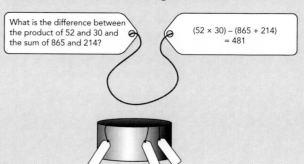

Pupils should take it in turns to 'go fishing' for a pair. They should take a tag and work out what will be on the corresponding tag before removing it to check. Points are scored for correct pairings.

Question 3

3 Multiple choice questions. Read each question carefully. Fill in the boxes with the letter of the correct number sentence.

A. (78 − 20 ÷ 2) × 6	B. 6 × (78 − 20) ÷ 2
C. 6 × 78 − 20 ÷ 2	D. (6 × 78 − 20) ÷ 2

(a) What is the difference between the product of 6 and 78 and the quotient of 20 divided by 2? ☐

(b) The difference between 78 and half of 20 is multiplied by 6. What is the result? ☐

(c) The difference between the product of 6 and 78 subtracted from 20 is divided by 2. What is the quotient? ☐

(d) The product of 6 and the difference between 78 and 20 is divided by 2. What is the result? ☐

What learning will pupils have achieved at the conclusion of Question 3?

- Pupils will have practised interpreting and solving calculations involving more complex three-step operations, as well as those that require inverse operations, described in mathematical words.

Activities for whole-class instruction

- Place four chairs at the front of the class with gaps in between. On each chair, place number cards to show the numbers 420, 3, 10 and 41.

- Place large operation symbol cards in between each chair (perhaps on more chairs) to model the calculation 420 ÷ 3 × 10 + 41. Ask pupils in which order they would work out the answer and remind them that the use of brackets can make the answer to a calculation very different.
- Ask pupils to suggest ways brackets could be placed in the number sentence. Remind pupils that brackets should be used appropriately to overrule the natural order of operations (for example the brackets in (420 ÷ 3) × 10 + 41 are not needed as they make no difference to the order of operations). Examples are:

    420 ÷ 3 × (10 + 41)

    420 ÷ (3 × 10) + 41

    420 ÷ 3 × 10 + 41

- Write three or four of these examples on the board and label them using letters. Encourage pupils to silently think about how they would describe these examples using words. Describe one of the sentences using the terminology of a word calculation problem and ask pupils to vote for the number sentence that they think it describes. In this example, these might include:

    – What is 41 added to the quotient of 420 divided by the product of 3 and 10?

    – What is the product of the quotient of 420 divided by 3 and the sum of 10 and 41?

- To add a physical element to the task, the four walls of the classroom could be labelled A, B, C and D. Pupils could vote with their feet by standing next to the wall corresponding to the answer they think is correct.
- Ask pupils to work in pairs and solve any two of their number sentences. This allows them to leave any calculations where the answer is more complicated – for example 420 ÷ [3 × (10 + 41)], which results in a long decimal! It may be worthwhile discussing with pupils which number sentences look like they may be more difficult to solve and why.
- Repeat for different sets of three-step number sentences and word calculation problems.
- Pupils should now complete Question 3 in the Practice Book.

Same-day intervention

- Display the number sentence (65 − 10 ÷ 2) × 3. Ask: *How many steps are there in this calculation? In what order would you complete the operations?* Establish that the calculation inside the brackets should be completed first and, out of the two operations, the division should be worked out before the subtraction.
- Provide pupils with enlarged copies of the key phrase cards (from **Resource 4.10.9a** Phrase cards) and ask them to label each step using appropriate phrases. For example:

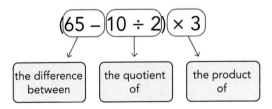

- Point to the last operation that needs to be done (the multiplication) and ensure pupils understand that this is a multiplication question at heart – albeit one where the multiplicand is found by using division and then subtraction.
- Ask: *What is dividing by 2 otherwise known as?* Establish that the sentence can be described by the following word calculation problem: 'What is the product of the difference between 65 and half of 10 multiplied by 3? Ask pupils to point to each corresponding part of the number sentence as the problem is read out.
- Repeat the activity so that pupils draw links between further three-step number sentences and word calculation problems that describe them.

Same-day enrichment

• Pupils should work in pairs. Pupil A should deal three cards from a set of key phrase cards (from **Resource 4.10.9a** Phrase cards), using these to generate a word calculation problem where they also work out the answer. For example:

| the difference between | the quotient of | the product of |

could be used to generate the problem:

– What is the sum of the product of 5 and 9 added to the difference between 524 and 476?

• Pupil B should then derive the number sentence associated with the problem $5 \times 9 + (524 - 476) = \_\_$ and use this to find the answer. Pupils should repeat the activity, swapping roles each time.

Challenge and extension questions

Questions 4 and 5

4 Express the following number sentences in words and then calculate.

(a) $403 \times (213 - 90) - 13$

In words: _____

Answer: _____

(b) $864 \div [(2193 - 1473) \div 90]$

In words: _____

Answer: _____

5 The sum of 4 times a number and 456 is 1000. What is the number?

Number sentence: _____

Answer: _____

Pupils are provided with two extension questions to further develop their understanding of word calculation problems and the order of operations. The first question contains two number sentences that pupils are expected to express, using words (in the same style as the word calculation problems they have been working with), before solving. Encourage pupils to consider the order in which each operation is completed and the order in which they are referred to in the description (the last operation is referred to first and so on).

In the second question, pupils are challenged to work backwards using a three-step 'mystery number' type statement in order to derive what the starting number is. As they are working backwards, they will need to implement their understanding of inverse operations.

Unit 10.11
Laws of operations (1)

Conceptual context

With the aim of calculating efficiently and accurately, pupils have already learned and practised the order of operations in Chapter 10. In this unit, pupils review and formalise two mathematical laws, continuing to help them solve problems efficiently.

These two laws – commutative and associative – apply to addition and multiplication. Pupils will initially learn their general meaning and apply them more specifically when checking or simplifying calculations. Understanding the concepts in this unit will help pupils to make useful, efficient calculating decisions. The use of letters and picture symbols to represent numbers in the unit is developed, continuing to help pupils build a foundation for thinking algebraically.

Unlike previous units where brackets have only been used to override the order of operations to reach a different solution, in this unit they are used to denote the part of a calculation that can be worked out first to reach the same solution, but more easily. This is a subtle difference in concept, but one that pupils should be aware of.

Learning pupils will have achieved at the end of the unit

- The commutative and associative laws will have been introduced (Q1, Q2)
- Numbers and symbols will have been manipulated in calculations as preparation for thinking algebraically (Q1, Q2)
- Calculations will have been checked by applying the commutative law (Q3)
- Column methods of addition and multiplication will have been practised (Q3)
- The associative law will have been applied to simplify calculations before solving them (Q4)
- Pupils will have begun to develop strategies to solve calculations efficiently (Q2, Q3, Q4)

Resources

mini whiteboards; interlocking cubes; counters; base 10 blocks; blank cards; small boxes;
Resource 4.10.11 Prove it! (1)

Vocabulary

addition, multiplication, brackets, commutative law, associative law

Question 1

> **1** Fill in the answers.
>
> (a) When adding 2 numbers, we can swap the _____ of
>
> the 2 addends and their sum remains _____.
>
> This is known as the **commutative law of addition.**
>
> Using letters *a* and *b* to represent the 2 addends, it is:
>
> *a* + *b* = ☐ + ☐.
>
> (b) When multiplying 2 numbers, we can swap the _____
>
> of the 2 factors and their product remains _____.
>
> This is known as the **commutative law of multiplication.**
>
> Using letters *a* and *b* to represent the 2 factors, it is:
>
> *a* × *b* = ☐ × ☐.
>
> (c) When adding 3 numbers, we can add the first 2 numbers first
> and then add the third number or add the last 2 numbers first
>
> and then add the first number. The sum remains _____.
>
> This is known as the **associative law of addition.**
>
> Using letters *a*, *b* and *c* to represent the 3 numbers, it is:
>
> (*a* + *b*) + *c* = *a* + (_____).
>
> (d) When multiplying 3 numbers, we can multiply the first 2
> numbers first and then multiply by the third number or multiply
> the last 2 numbers first and then multiply by the first number.
>
> The product remains _____.
>
> This is known as the **associative law of multiplication.**
>
> Using letters *a*, *b* and *c* to represent the 3 numbers, it is:
>
> (*a* × *b*) × *c* = *a* × (_____).

What learning will pupils have achieved at the conclusion of Question 1?

- The commutative and associative laws will have been introduced.

- Numbers and symbols will have been manipulated within calculations as preparation for thinking algebraically.

Activities for whole-class instruction

- Split the class into two groups. Ask Group A to write down all the additions (with two addends) that have the sum 20. Group B should do the same for multiplications (two factors with a product of 20). Pupils should share their results as a class. Ask: *Can you order these to show you have found all the possibilities?* List both the additions and the multiplications in order.

- Ask: *What do you notice about the calculations now that they are written like this?* Although pupils may notice vertical patterns, also encourage them to recognise that each of the calculations has its opposite (for example 10 × 2 and 2 × 10 both equal 20, 5 + 15 and 15 + 5 both equal 20). Ask: *Does this work for subtraction and division?*

- Give pupils time to briefly explore this question in pairs (25 − 5 equals 20 but 5 − 25 does not, 40 ÷ 2 equals 20 but 2 ÷ 40 does not). Go back to the pairs of bonds found in the addition and multiplication calculations. Ask: *Can you remember the name of the law that explains why this happens?* Elicit it is the commutative law.

> **All say …** *The commutative law means that the numbers in an addition or multiplication can be swapped around and still give the same answer.*

ⓘ The commutative law of addition states that where two numbers are added together, the addends may be reversed and the sum remains unchanged (*a* + *b* = *b* + *a*). The commutative law of multiplication expresses the same rule, but for multiplication (*a* × *b* = *b* × *a*). This idea of being able to reverse numbers is useful for several reasons. For example, the commutative law can be a way of simplifying calculations (267 + 925 is easier if you start with the larger number first) or checking answers (the answer to 45 × 23 can be checked by working out 23 × 45 and seeing whether it is the same). A useful way to remember the name for this is the idea of a 'commuter' travelling to and from work (the numbers travel one way and the other). Pupils have learned this previously, so this is revision.

- Remind pupils of the role of brackets in calculations. Write (4 + 7) + 5 and 4 + (7 + 5). Ask: *Which part of each calculation should be worked out first? Why?* Model both calculations using interlocking cubes:

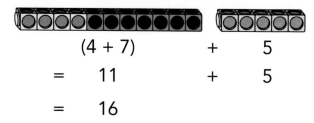

$$(4 + 7) \quad + \quad 5$$
$$= \quad 11 \quad + \quad 5$$
$$= \quad 16$$

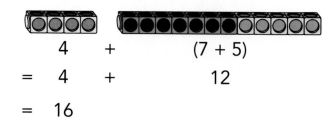

$$4 \quad + \quad (7 + 5)$$
$$= \quad 4 \quad + \quad 12$$
$$= \quad 16$$

- Ask: *Think about the order of operations you already know – does it matter which part of the addition is in brackets and is worked out first? Is the answer affected?*

- Write: (2 × 3) × 6 and 2 × (3 × 6). Again, ask pupils to consider which part of each calculation should be answered first. Model using arrays of counters:

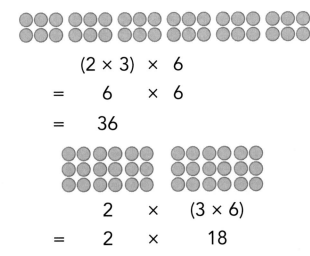

$(2 \times 3) \times 6$

$= \quad 6 \quad \times \ 6$

$= \quad 36$

$2 \quad \times \quad (3 \times 6)$

$= \quad 2 \quad \times \quad 18$

$= \quad 36$

- Introduce the rule name for this: the associative law of addition/multiplication.

All say ... *The associative law means that the numbers in an addition or multiplication can be grouped in different ways and the answer is unchanged.*

(i) The associative law of addition states that where several numbers are added together, it does not matter which part of the addition is worked out first – usually denoted by brackets $((a + (b + c) = (a + b) + c))$. Again, the law can also be applied to multiplication. $((a \times (b \times c) = (a \times b) \times c))$. As with the commutative law, the associative law can be a useful way of simplifying calculations.

- Ensure pupils are familiar with both rules at this basic level before continuing. Discuss and model further examples if necessary.

- Pupils should now complete Question 1 in the Practice Book.

Same-day intervention

- Choose different pupils to come to the front and write and ask them to model an addition (using manipulatives of two different colours) or multiplication (using manipulatives to show an array). Ask others to use the commutative law to write the calculation another way. Ask them to then reverse the model to show that the alternative order gives the same answer.

- After several examples, split pupils into pairs where they can devise their own similar challenges for each other to solve.

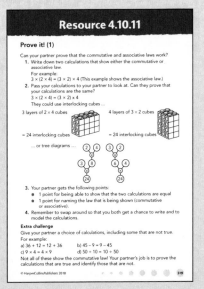

- Pupils should read through the instructions independently and then play the game described.

Question 2

> **2** Fill in the blanks using the laws of operations.
>
> (a) $732 + 488 = 488 +$ ....
>
> (b) $379 + 248 + 621 = 379 +$ .... $+$ ....
>
> (c) $26 \times 14 =$ .... $\times 26$
>
> (d) $250 \times 27 \times 4 = 27 \times ($ .... $\times$ .... $)$
>
> (e) $\blacktriangle + \bigstar =$ .... $+$ ....
>
> (f) $\bullet \times \blacklozenge =$ .... $\times$ ....
>
> (g) $x + y + z = x + ($ .... $+$ .... $)$
>
> (h) $j \times k \times l = j \times ($ .... $\times$ .... $)$

What learning will pupils have achieved at the conclusion of Question 2?

- The commutative and associative laws will have been introduced.

- Pupils will have begun to develop strategies to solve calculations efficiently.

- Numbers and symbols will have been manipulated within calculations as preparation for thinking algebraically.

Activities for whole-class instruction

- Choose three pupils to write three-digit numbers on whiteboards and to sit on chairs facing the class. Write their numbers as an addition:

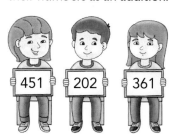

451 + 202 + 361

- Agree that the sum is 1014.

- Ask: *Can you rearrange these numbers so that they make a different total?* Pupils could reorder themselves, and the class should agree that the sum is always the same. They should be able to predict that the sum will always be the same when other additions are changed in the same way.

- Ask: *What is the name of the law that says that you can change the order of addends and the total is unchanged?* Practise the same for a similar multiplication fact:

10 × 4 × 6 = 240

- Agree that the product is 240.

- Ask: *Can you rearrange these numbers so that they make a different product?* Pupils could reorder themselves, and the class should agree that the product is always the same. They should be able to predict that the product will always be the same when other multiplications are changed in the same way.

- Ask: *What is the name of the law that says that you can change the order of factors and the product is unchanged?*

321 + (239 + 108) = (321 + 239) + 108
321 + 347 = 560 + 108
668 = 668

- Repeat the same activity, this time showing the associative law (the numbers stay in the same order, but

one part of the calculation is completed first). This could be representing by pupils moving forwards or backwards to stress their order of operations. For example:

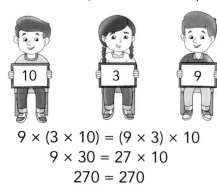

9 × (3 × 10) = (9 × 3) × 10
9 × 30 = 27 × 10
270 = 270

- Give pupils further questions, including those using letters or symbols instead of numbers. For example:

● × (■ × ▲) + (×   )   ×

On the left the product of the other two factors is multiplied by 10 to reach 270. On the right, the product of the other two factors is multiplied by 9 to reach 270. Either way, the answer is the same. Encourage pupils to consider which is easiest and choose that way to find the solution.

- Pupils should now complete Question 2 in the Practice Book.

Same-day intervention

- Ask two pupils to make any three-digit number out of base 10 blocks. Write these as an addition. For example, 501 + 157 = ☐. Place each set of blocks into two small boxes and ask pupils various questions that lead them to consider the commutative law more generally. For example:

  [Swap the boxes around] *501 + 157 equals 157 plus what? Can you prove it?*

  What if we give each box a name? SAM'S NUMBER plus HATHAM'S NUMBER equals what plus SAM'S NUMBER?

  Or a symbol? ● + ■ = ■ + ?

  Or a letter? a + b = b + ?

- Do the same for the associative law so that pupils develop their basic understanding of both laws and how to represent them in different ways.

Same-day enrichment

- Give each pupil several strips of paper. On each strip, they should write a pair of equivalent number sentences demonstrating the commutative or associative laws. These should include one or two blank spaces and could include sentences written using shapes or letters too. For example:

    652 + ___ = 472 + 652

    ■ × ● = ___ × ■

    $a \times (b \times c) = ($ ___ $\times$ ____ $) \times c$

- Each strip should be folded and placed into a container. Pupils should then take it in turns to take a random strip and then decide how to fill in the blanks. They get a point for each blank completed and an extra point if they can say the name of the law of operations that they are demonstrating.

Question 3

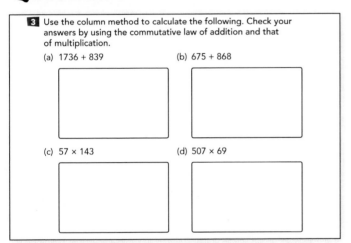

3 Use the column method to calculate the following. Check your answers by using the commutative law of addition and that of multiplication.

(a) 1736 + 839   (b) 675 + 868

(c) 57 × 143   (d) 507 × 69

What learning will pupils have achieved at the conclusion of Question 3?

- Calculations will have been checked by applying the commutative law.
- Pupils will have begun to develop strategies to solve calculations efficiently.
- Column methods for addition and multiplication will have been practised.

Activities for whole-class instruction

- Write the following two calculations on the board: 738 + 156 and 348 × 52. Ask: *Is there a way that we can arrange these to make them easier to calculate?* Give pupils

time to remind themselves in pairs of how to use column methods to work out both calculations. Model each method as a revision, firstly:

$$
\begin{array}{r}
7\ 3\ 8 \\
+\ 1\ 5\ 6 \\
\hline
8\ 9\ 4 \\
\small 1
\end{array}
\quad = \quad
\begin{array}{r}
1\ 5\ 6 \\
+\ 7\ 3\ 8 \\
\hline
8\ 9\ 4 \\
\small 1
\end{array}
$$

- Discuss whether pupils found one way easier than the other and why.

- Ask: *What mistakes are easy to make?* Take feedback. Ask: *How could you check whether you have answered correctly?* Elicit that we should subtract one addend from the sum to check that the difference is the second addend.

- Shift the focus to multiplication. Together with the class, work through the column method for multiplying 348 × 52 = __ using the following method:

$$
\begin{array}{r}
3\ 4\ 8 \\
\times \quad 5\ 2 \\
\hline
6\ 9\ 6 \\
\small 1 \\
1\ 7\ 4\ 0\ 0 \\
\hline
1\ 8\ 0\ 9\ 6
\end{array}
\begin{array}{l}
\ \\
\ \\
(348 \times 2) \\
\ \\
(348 \times 50) \\
\ \\
\ \\
\end{array}
\quad = \quad
\begin{array}{r}
5\ 2 \\
\times \quad 3\ 4\ 8 \\
\hline
4\ 1\ 6 \\
\small 1 \\
2\ 0\ 8\ 0 \\
1\ 5\ 6\ 0\ 0 \\
\hline
1\ 8\ 0\ 9\ 6
\end{array}
\begin{array}{l}
\ \\
\ \\
(52 \times 8) \\
\ \\
(52 \times 40) \\
(52 \times 300) \\
\ \\
\end{array}
$$

- Ask: *Could we multiply these numbers the other way around?* Pupils should know that multiplication is commutative but will not be familiar with seeing the two-digit number written above the three-digit number. Show them that the answer is the same. Ask: *Which is the more efficient way to multiply these two numbers together? Why?* Elicit that when the three-digit number is on the bottom, there are three part products that need to be added together, so it is more efficient to put the two-digit number on the bottom. Point out that it would be a way to check a calculation; however, as not all pupils may be confident about an answer.

- Ask: *Could we use the commutative law to check any calculation?* Pupils should be able to tell you that it can be used to check addition and multiplication, but not subtraction or division because those operations are not commutative, so you would not get the same answer 'both ways'.

- Pupils should now complete Question 3 in the Practice Book.

Same-day intervention

- Split pupils into two groups, A and B. Write the numbers 415 and 274 on the board. Ask each group to add the numbers in a different order – for example Group A might calculate 415 + 274 and Group B might calculate 274 + 415. Provide base 10 blocks should pupils wish to model each addition more concretely, but also use the vertical method in parallel.
- Compare each answer as well as each part (column by column) of the additions. Ask: *What is the same? What is different?*
- Repeat for multiplication questions, where each group multiplies in a different order.

Same-day enrichment

- Pupils should devise and then solve three calculations (addition and/or multiplication), then alter their answers so that only one is correct. They should rewrite their calculations horizontally and pass them to their partner. For example:

    $427 \times 51 = 22\,778$ [altered from 21 777]

    $583 + 209 = 783$ [altered from 792]

    $364 \times 23 = 8372$ [correct answer]

- Their partner should then use the commutative rule to identify the right answer and also to correct the two answers that are wrong.

Question 4

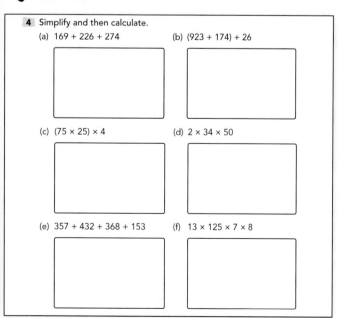

4 Simplify and then calculate.

(a) $169 + 226 + 274$

(b) $(923 + 174) + 26$

(c) $(75 \times 25) \times 4$

(d) $2 \times 34 \times 50$

(e) $357 + 432 + 368 + 153$

(f) $13 \times 125 \times 7 \times 8$

What learning will pupils have achieved at the conclusion of Question 4?

- The associative law will have been applied to simplify calculations before solving them.
- Pupils will have begun to develop strategies to solve calculations efficiently.

Activities for whole-class instruction

- Briefly remind pupils of the two laws of operations that they have learned. Ask: *What do you think is the point of knowing these rules?* Pupils should recognise that the commutative law can be applied to check calculations (following Question 3). Explain that a further benefit of understanding both these laws is to simplify calculations.
- Display the calculation $2 \times 39 \times 50$. Ask: *If you had to work this out as it was written, how would you find the answer?* Establish that they would need to start with 2, multiply it by 39 and then multiply the answer by 50.
- Ask: *What does it mean to 'simplify' a calculation?* Write 325×47 on the board and discuss what might be a simpler calculation than this to solve. Pupils may well begin by suggesting something like 'using easier numbers'. Encourage them to consider what makes a number easier – is it always a lower number?
- Remind pupils of their previous work rounding numbers in estimation (see Unit 2.8) and ask them why they think working with multiples of 10 or 100 makes a calculation simpler to deal with. Explain that the aim of the next activity is for pupils to use the commutative and associative laws to look for multiples of 10 or 100.
- Ask: *Can you identify a simpler way to multiply the numbers?* Refer to the original multiplication and elicit that they can start with 2×50 to make 100 and then multiply 39 by this:

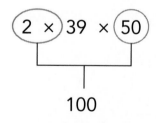

$$39 \times 100 = 3900$$

- Explain that pupils can only simplify in this way because it doesn't matter which part of the multiplication is worked out first. Ask: *Which law makes this possible?*

- Model the original method (2 × 39, then 78 × 50) to demonstrate that the simplified method is much quicker.
- Repeat for further examples. Ask pupils to come to the front and write each number on whiteboards so that they can physically adjust their order and discuss ways of combining them in order to simplify the calculation. For example:
  - 18 × 125 × 6 × 8
  - 125 times 8 makes 1000 and we can start with this to help simplify the rest of the calculation
  - 1000 times 18 makes 18 000. 18 000 times 6 is the same as 18 × 6 with three zeros on the end (108 000).
- Pupils should now complete Question 4 in the Practice Book.

Same-day intervention

- Begin by showing pupils groups of three numbers on the board and asking them to identify a pair within each set that could be added to make a multiple of 10 or 100 (e.g. out of the numbers 13, 9 and 7, the number 20 can be made by combining 13 and 7).
- Ensure that pupils spend time using this skill to deepen their understanding of the associative law. Write the calculation 28 + 16 + 4 so that each number is written on a separate whiteboard. Ask: *Which two whiteboards would you add together first? Why?* Remind pupils that identifying a pair that makes a tens number makes a calculation quicker (in this case, it becomes 28 + 20).
- Repeat for further additions and then practise identifying ways to simplify multiplications (for example revising a fact like 4 × 25 = 100 to help with 25 × 7 × 4).

Same-day enrichment

- Provide pairs with several blank cards. They should work together to devise 'complicated calculations' that can then be simplified using the associative law. Display some examples to help pupils remember that simplified calculations often involve tens numbers.
- Pairs should swap cards so that they have a set to simplify and answer. They should get one point for solving the calculation and another for being able to explain how they simplified it.

Challenge and extension question

Question 5

5 Simplify each of the following calculations and then find the answer.
(a) 385 − 173 + 615 − 227

Answer: _____

(b) 16 × (125 × 6)

Answer: _____

(c) 9 + 98 + 997 + 9996 + 99 995 + 999 994 + 21

Answer: _____

Pupils are given three calculations to simplify and solve. In order to do this, they need either an understanding of the associative law or the ability to identify number patterns.

The first two calculations require pupils to identify pairs that equal tens numbers and then use the associative law to complete the calculation in this simpler order.

In the final challenge, pupils should be encouraged to look at each of the 'near ten' numbers being added and identify a way to add them quickly (i.e. add 10, 100, 1000, 10 000, 100 000 and 1 000 000 and then adjust the answer to cater for the 'near tens'). Pupils should notice that the difference equals 21 (the last number in the addition), and so they simply need to round and add the first six numbers, ignoring the seventh. Pupils might like to invent similar challenges for peers to try.

Unit 10.12
Laws of operations (2)

Conceptual context

Pupils should now be secure with the commutative and associative laws of addition and multiplication. As well as understanding what each law means, it is important that pupils can utilise them (and, importantly, identify opportunities to utilise them) to calculate more efficiently. So, this unit consolidates pupils' abilities to apply these laws – when completing equivalent statements, simplifying and solving calculations and in word-based problems.

Learning pupils will have achieved at the end of the unit

- Knowledge of the commutative and associative laws will have been consolidated (Q1)
- Calculations will have been simplified and then solved using knowledge of the commutative and associative laws (Q2)
- The commutative and associative laws will have been applied when solving word-based problems (Q3)
- Pupils' fluency when using strategies will have developed as they consider different approaches to the same problem (Q3)
- Pupils will be able to perceive opportunities to apply commutative and associative laws in order to make calculation and problem solving simpler (Q2, Q3)

Resources

mini whiteboards; interlocking cubes; large 100 square; a buzzer/whistle/tambourine or similar; pieces of card; **Resource 4.10.12** Name that strategy!

Vocabulary

addition, multiplication, brackets, commutative law, associative law

Question 1

> **1** Fill in the spaces using the laws of operations.
>
> (a) ⬜ + 270 = 270 + 80
>
> (b) 25 × 976 = 976 × ⬜
>
> (c) ⬜ + 56 = ⬜ + 44
>
> (d) $a +$ ⬜ $= b +$ ⬜
>
> (e) $(a +$ _____$) + c = a + (b +$ _____$)$
>
> (f) $(a ×$ _____$) × c = a × (b ×$ _____$)$
>
> (g) $(33 + 16) + 84 =$ ⬜ $+ (16 +$ _____$)$
>
> (h) ⬜ × ▲ = ⬜ × ■
>
> (i) $75 × 8 × 2 × 125 = ($ _____ × _____$) × ($ _____ × _____$)$

What learning will pupils have achieved at the conclusion of Question 1?

- Knowledge of the commutative and associative laws will have been consolidated.

Activities for whole-class instruction

- Write the names of the two laws pupils have been introduced to – the commutative law and the associative law. Give pupils time in pairs to discuss what each rule means. Write examples of each as a reminder:
- The Commutative Law:

  251 + 95 is the same as 95 + 251

  7 × 9 is the same as 9 × 7

  ● + ★ is the same as ★ + ●
- The Associative Law:

  26 + (42 + 31) is the same as (26 + 42) + 31

  (2 × 6) × 10 is the same as 2 × (6 × 10)

  ■ × (▲ × ✹) is the same as (■ × ▲) × ✹
- Ask pupils to write, draw or model a simple example to prove that each rule is true. For example, pupils might model the associative law of multiplication by making cuboids out of interlocking cubes:

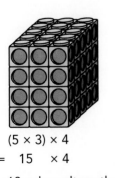

(5 × 3) × 4   5 × (3 × 4)

= 15 × 4   = 5 × 12

= 60 cubes altogether   = 60 cubes altogether

- ... or write the commutative law using letters:

  $a + b = b + a$
- Choose four or five pupils to share their examples with the class. Ask: *Which rule does this illustrate? Why? How could you show it another way?*
- Pupils should now complete Question 1 in the Practice Book.

Same-day intervention

- Provide pupils with something to make a short, sharp noise with (a buzzer or small whistle would work well). Each pupil should take it in turns to read out a pair of equivalent number sentences demonstrating the commutative law. They should include at least one unknown number (a 'blank'). When they read their number sentences, they should replace the blank with a noise! For example, *28 times [BUZZ!] equals 13 times 28.*
- The rest of the group should write the missing number on their whiteboards.
- Encourage pupils to explain how they know what the answer is and use the opportunity to reinforce the commutative law. Repeat for examples that consolidate knowledge of the associative law also.

Same-day enrichment

- Pupils should work in small groups, writing calculations that show the commutative and associative laws on strips of paper. They should cover up at least one number or symbol in each calculation with sticky notes. The group's strips should be placed in the centre of the table.
- Pupils should then take it in turns to choose one of the strips of paper to guess what is underneath the sticky notes and identify the rule being shown.

Question 2

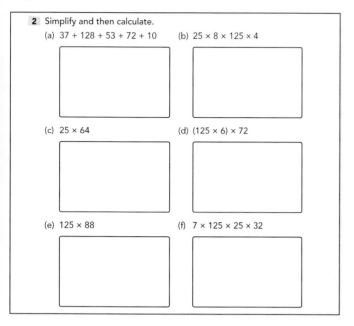

2 Simplify and then calculate.
(a) 37 + 128 + 53 + 72 + 10   (b) 25 × 8 × 125 × 4

(c) 25 × 64   (d) (125 × 6) × 72

(e) 125 × 88   (f) 7 × 125 × 25 × 32

Example	Possible strategy
548 + 63 + 52 + 27 + 10	48 and 52 make 100, so 548 + 52 = 600. 63 needs 37 to equal 100. 27 and 10 make 37, so 63 + 27 + 10 = 100. Simplified calculation: 600 + 100 = 700
25 × 84	84 can easily be split into 80 and 4. 25 multiplied by 4 makes 100. Simplified calculation: 100 × 80 = 8000
(17 × 125) × 8	125 multiplied by 8 equals 1000. So, it can be worked out as 17 × (125 × 8). Simplified calculation: 17 × 1000 = 17 000

- Ensure that pupils can relate their strategies to the commutative or associative laws where they have used them. This may not always be the case, but should be noted where appropriate. For each example, ask: *What did you look for first? Did anyone use a different strategy?* Demonstrate that there are many ways to approach a calculation and encourage pupils to consider whichever seems the most efficient strategy to use.

Pupils should now complete Question 2 in the Practice Book.

What learning will pupils have achieved at the conclusion of Question 2?

- Calculations will have been simplified and then solved using knowledge of the commutative and associative laws.

- Pupils will be able to perceive opportunities to apply the commutative and associative laws in order to make calculation and problem solving simpler.

Activities for whole-class instruction

- Ensure pupils are able to explain the meaning of both the commutative and the associative laws.

- Give the example of 75 × 5 × 2 and ask pupils to quickly find the answer to 75 × 5. Demonstrate that this isn't a fact that springs to mind quickly at all. Ask: *What do you notice about the numbers that might help you find the answer more quickly?* Remind pupils that the key to a simpler calculation is often about making tens or hundreds numbers as these are easier to add or multiply. So, working out 75 × (5 × 2) is a more efficient method because 75 × 10 = 750. Explain that 'efficient' methods are those that reach correct answers more quickly.

- Write several number sentences on the board and ask pupils to use a 'Think, Pair, Share' approach to consider how to simplify them. First, pupils should think individually, then pair up with a partner to discuss any patterns they can identify, and finally share their ideas as a class. Possible number sentences might include the following:

Same-day intervention

- Write the calculation 4 × 7 × 25, where the numbers have been covered with sticky notes (but the multiplication symbols are still visible). Explain that you are going to ask pupils to simplify the calculation before solving it.

- Ask: *What pairs of numbers might you be looking for if you want to simplify the calculation? Why?* Ensure that pupils understand that they are looking to find combinations that make multiples of 10 or 100 as these are easier numbers to multiply with. Possible answers might be '5 and 2', '2 and 50', '5 and 20' and so on.

- Reveal the 7 and the 25. Ask: *Does this seem like a simple multiplication to start with? What would you like the first number to be in order to help you answer the question more quickly?* Establish that 25 × 4 = 100, and so 4 would be a good number to see. Reveal the starting number. Ask: *How can we work out the answer?*

- Repeat for further examples where part of the calculation is revealed and pupils are asked to predict what might be a helpful final number in order to simplify and then solve it.

Same-day enrichment

- Display the following grid:

8 × 125	20 × 5	2 × 50
36 + 14	146 + 354	87 + 13
25 × 4	243 + 257	50 × 20

- Challenge pupils to work as quickly as possible to find the answers to each calculation and to identify why those calculations have been chosen. Ask: *If there were an extra row, what other calculations might you include?*

- Having established that these are all combinations of numbers that make multiples of 10 and/or 100, pupils should then choose one of these squares and write a calculation based on it for their partner to solve. For example, the first square could be used to devise 8 × 13 × 125. Pupils should then pass their calculations to their partner, who should look for the relevant combination of numbers to simplify and then solve it.

Question 3

3 Application problems.

(a) Each piece of cake costs £6. Each box has 4 pieces of cake. How much do 25 boxes of cake cost? (Use 2 methods to calculate.)

_____

(b) Five boxes of model cars cost £40. Each box has 4 cars. How much does each car cost? (Use 2 methods to calculate.)

_____

(c) A flower team organises a rectangular carnival parade consisting of 25 rows, with 8 people in each row. Each person holds 2 flowers. How many flowers are needed for the flower team?

_____

What learning will pupils have achieved at the conclusion of Question 3?

- The commutative and associative laws will have been applied when solving word-based problems.

- Pupils' fluency when using strategies will have developed as they consider different approaches to the same problem.

- Pupils will be able to perceive opportunities to apply commutative and associative laws in order to make calculation and problem solving simpler.

Activities for whole-class instruction

- Explain that the aim of the following activity isn't just for pupils to solve the problem, but to find two ways of working it out. Ask: *Why is it useful to have more than one way to solve a problem?*

- Display the following problem on the board:
  - A burger van sells burgers for £4 each. It sells 9 every hour. How much money does the burger van make in 8 hours?

- Give pupils time to consider the scenario and ask them to explain it using their own words – this might entail acting out the scenario. Ask pupils what they think they would need to do to solve the problem. They might suggest a linear approach (using each number in the order it features). One such explanation might be something like: *Multiply 4 by 9 to find out how much the van makes in 1 hour. Then multiply the answer by 8 to find out how much it makes in 8 hours.*

- Ask: *How would you write this as a number sentence?*

(i) Although the point of the activity is for pupils to apply the associative law and also to consider the placement of brackets, it is important to remember that calculations involving only one type of symbol are always completed from left to right. So, 4 × 9 × 8 (without any brackets) is a perfectly correct notation for the above problem. It may be worth asking pupils who answer this to explain their reasoning.

- Write the number sentence (4 × 9) × 8 on the board and ensure that pupils understand what it represents in terms of the problem: (cost of burgers per hour) × total number of hours. Choose pupils to model this method:

  (4 × 9) × 8
  = 36 × 8
  = £288

- Ask: *How else could we work out the answer?* Point to the original bracketed number sentence and ask pupils to consider which law might apply. Write the number sentence 4 × (9 × 8) and ensure that pupils understand that this time it represents the cost of each burger × (total number of burgers sold in eight hours). Again, choose pupils to model the method:

  4 × (9 × 8)
  = 4 × 72
  = £288

The associative rule means that it doesn't matter which part of a multiplication we do first.

- Discuss how the brackets were not strictly necessary in these calculations but that they can still be helpful to break down the problem or to help represent the situation clearly.

- Go through further two-step examples where pupils should suggest two different methods of working out the answer. For example:

  - A racing team replaces 4 tyres on each of its cars. Each tyre costs £160. There are 5 cars in the team. How much do the tyres cost altogether?

- Within these, also include examples where the associative law is not applicable (for example because the calculation involves division). For example:

  - Seven packs of books cost £42 altogether. Each pack has 3 books in it. How much does each book cost?

- Encourage pupils to first consider the operations they might use to find the answer, then express this as a number sentence and then finally explain their number sentence using words. This will aid them in finding a second strategy to use.

  $(42 \div 7) \div 3$ = (price of each pack of books) ÷ number of books in a pack

  = $6 \div 3$

  = £2 per book

  $42 \div (7 \times 3)$ = total price of packs ÷ (total number of books)

  = $42 \div 21$

  = £2 per book

 … pupils who see brackets and automatically presume that the associative rule can be applied.

- Challenge them to consider that $(42 \div 7) \div 3$ is not the same as $42 \div (7 \div 3)$. This is because the associative law only applies to addition and multiplication.

- Pupils should now complete Question 3 in the Practice Book.

Same-day intervention

- Prior to the activity, set up different stations for pupils to explore different ways of solving problems and then support pupils as they work at them. The stations may include:

  - interlocking cubes and counters (to model a strategy)

  - whiteboards (to write a strategy numerically)

  - a large 100 square (or number line)

  - a role-play table.

- Display the following problem for pupils to consider:

  - There are 46 boys in the park and 37 girls. How many children are there altogether?

- Pupils should use their station's resources to model two different ways of finding the answer. For example, by modelling a chain of 46 cubes and then 37 cubes and a similar chain of 37 cubes and then 46 cubes. Ask: *Which law of operations have you used to help you?* (commutative law)

- Repeat for further word-based problems, building up from one-step problems (where the commutative law can be applied) to two-step problems (where the associative law can be applied). After each problem, pupils should share their answers and then move to a new station in order to model the calculation using a different resource.

Same-day enrichment

Provide pupils with **Resource 4.10.12** Name that strategy! in order to challenge small groups of pupils to write their own application problems for peers to solve.

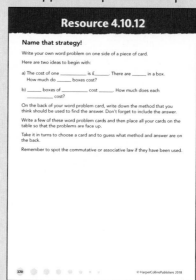

Challenge and extension question

Question 4

4   Calculate smartly.

(a) $625 \times 8 \times 8 \times 2 \times 2 \times 2$

Answer: _____

(b) There are ☐ zeros at the end of the product
$1 \times 2 \times 3 \times 4 \times 5 \times ... \times 28 \times 29 \times 30$.

Answer: _____

Pupils are given two multiplications, each containing several numbers. They are expected to calculate efficiently (or 'smartly'), identifying ways to combine them to find their products. In the first calculation, pupils may choose to multiply 2 by 2 by 2 to make 8, multiply 625 by 8 to make 5000 and then work out the rest from this point. Or, knowing that $2 \times 2 \times 2$ equals 8 can also be used to turn the whole multiplication into a doubling exercise, where the first number simply needs to be doubled 9 times.

Although there are several ways pupils might approach the second question, encourage pupils to use the associative law and look for ways to multiply the numbers in a different order. They should break the multiplication into manageable chunks, identifying pairs that will make multiples of 10 (or 100) when multiplied. Pupils should understand that multiplying 10 by a number will yield a number with a zero on the end and multiplying 5 by an even number will do the same. The other numbers will not make multiples of 10, and so there will be seven zeros at the end.

Unit 10.13
Laws of operations (3)

Conceptual context

In this chapter, pupils' knowledge of the laws of operations is extended to include the distributive law. As with the two previous units, the focus is placed on the concept of efficient calculation techniques, and so pupils will eventually use the distributive law to simplify and then solve calculations. Pupils will be encouraged to apply the law in different contexts, including using shapes or letters instead of numbers. Understanding of the distributive law lays secure foundations for much of the manipulation that pupils will encounter later, with algebra.

Learning pupils will have achieved at the end of the unit

- The distributive laws of multiplication over addition and over subtraction will have been introduced (Q1)
- Pupils will have generalised the distributive law, using shapes and letters instead of numbers (Q2)
- Knowledge of the distributive law will have been applied in order to complete and correct number sentences (Q2, Q3)
- Calculations will have been simplified and solved using the distributive law (Q4)

Resources

mini whiteboards; interlocking cubes; sticky notes (in two colours); plastic counters (in two colours); **Resource 4.10.13a** Prove it! (2); **Resource 4.10.13b** Distributive puzzles; **Resource 4.10.13c** Jigsaw pairs

Vocabulary

distributive law, commutative law, associative law, brackets

Question 1

> **1** Calculate and then draw a line to match each pair.
> (a) 10 × 3 + 10 × 9   A. 23 × (7 + 8 + 5)
> (b) 42 × 8 − 4 × 42   B. (8 − 4) × 42
> (c) 23 × 7 + 23 × 8 + 23 × 5   C. 10 × (3 + 9)
> (d) Please write two more pairs of number sentences like these.
>
> _____
>
> _____
>
> _____
>
> (e) Please use letters to express the **distributive law of multiplication over addition** and the **distributive law of multiplication over subtraction**.

What learning will pupils have achieved at the conclusion of Question 1?

- The distributive laws of multiplication over addition and over subtraction will have been introduced.

Activities for whole-class instruction

- Remind pupils of the two laws of operations that they have learned already – the commutative and associative laws – and explain that they are going to learn about a third law to help them simplify calculations – the distributive law. Ask: *What does it mean to 'distribute' something?* Elicit the definition of something being given out or shared out.

- Show pupils three trays. Place five pencils and two rulers in each.

 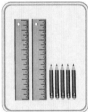 

- Ask: *How could you work out the number of items there are altogether?* Show pupils that they could calculate the total number of items in two ways:

1. By multiplying the number of trays (3) by the total number of items (5 + 2) in each tray.

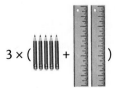

$3 \times (\quad + \quad)$

or

2. By working out three trays worth of five pencils and three trays worth of two rulers, then adding the two together.

$(3 \times \quad) + (3 \times \quad)$

- Show how these methods can be written as number sentences and solved:

Method 1:

trays × (pencils + rulers) 3 × (5 + 2) = 3 × 7 = 21 items altogether

Method 2:

(trays × pencils) + (trays × rulers) (3 × 5) + (3 × 2) = 15 + 6 = 21 items altogether

- Show the trays with pencils and rulers again, arranging and rearranging them until pupils are completely assured that 3 × (5 + 2) = (3 × 5) + (3 × 2)

- Ask: *Which number is common to each part of the addition?* Show how both addends are multiplied by the number three. The number three is distributed across the calculation, so we can multiply everything in the brackets by three or we can get rid of the brackets and write 3 × next to each part of the calculation. This is the distributive law.

 The distributive law means that multiplying something by those numbers inside the brackets is the same as doing each multiplication separately.

(i) The distributive law of multiplication over addition states that where an addition in brackets is multiplied by a number, each part of that addition can be written as a separate multiplication and then those two products added together. For example, in the calculation 5 × (6 + 2), both the 6 and the 2 are being multiplied by 5. This can then be written as (5 × 6) + (5 × 2). Note that, while it is common in algebra to write a number immediately next to brackets to imply multiplication (without the need for a symbol), at this level multiplication, symbols should be used at all times to avoid confusion.

The distributive law works in the opposite direction too. In the following calculation, the number 6 is common: (6 × 23) + (6 × 12). It can therefore be rewritten with brackets as 6 × (23 + 12) to show the 6 being 'distributed' across both parts of the addition. The distributive law of multiplication over subtraction works in the same way. For example, 7 × (10 − 3) is the same as (7 × 10) − (7 × 3), where the 7 is 'distributed' across the subtraction.

The distributive law is particularly useful in helping pupils to simplify tricky multiplications. For example, if they can see that 73 × 12 is the same as 73 × (10 + 2) then they can use the distributive law to form two easier multiplications to find the total of 73 × 10 and 73 × 2.]

- Write: (54 × 15) − (10 × 54). Point out that this is a subtraction where both the minuend and subtrahend are multiplied. Ask pupils whether they can spot the term that has been distributed across both parts of the subtraction. Circle '54 ×' and '× 54' and explain why the calculation can be written as 54 × (15 − 10). Ask: *Would you rather work out (54 × 15) − (10 × 54) or 54 × (15 − 10)? Which is the simpler calculation? Why?* Demonstrate that, for the second number sentence, pupils just need to know 54 × 5, and so the distributive law has simplified the calculation.

- Provide further examples using simple numbers to familiarise pupils with the law. Give examples of both bracketed number sentences (where pupils should write the calculation by multiplying each term) and non-bracketed calculations (where pupils should identify the common multiplier and use brackets to simplify the number sentence). For example:

$$6 × 2 + 6 × 10$$
$$⊙6 ×⊙2 + ⊙6 ×⊙10 = 6 × (2 + 10)$$
$$6 × (12 − 9) = 6 × 12 − 6 × 9$$

- Encourage pupils to devise their own examples before continuing.

- Pupils should now complete Question 1 in the Practice Book.

Same-day intervention

- Provide further opportunities to model the distributive law using concrete materials and by investigating multiplication facts to 10 × 10. This can be a useful entrance point for pupils to learn about the distributive law – tricky calculations such as 6 × 7 can be made easier with the realisation that 6 × 7 can be written as 6 × (5 + 2) and then worked out as two simpler multiplications: (6 × 5) + (6 × 2).

- For example, ask pupils to make four chains of interlocking cubes, each containing three blue and five yellow cubes. Ask: *What number sentence would you use to work out the number of blue cubes altogether? Can you break your chains to show this? What about the number of yellow cubes? How would you combine these to find the total number of cubes?* Show how this can be written as 4 × 3 + 4 × 5. It may be useful to briefly show the number sentence using brackets (4 × 3) + (4 × 5) to demonstrate that it is an addition where both addends are being multiplied by 4.

- Ask: *Is there a simpler way to find the total number of cubes? What multiplication do we need to do?* Show how the number of chains can just be multiplied by the total of each chain: 4 × (3 + 5) or 4 × 8.

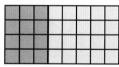　　　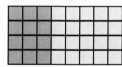

4 × 3 + 4 × 5　　is the same as　　4 × (3 + 5)

- Repeat for further calculations, remembering to work in the opposite direction and include the distributive law over subtraction. As pupils grow in confidence, encourage them to use the manipulatives less and begin to rely more on identifying the common terms.

- Give more complex examples for pupils to work with. Write two columns containing the following six calculations:

12 × 5 + 12 × 10 + 12 × 2	(4 − 2) × 52
52 × 4 − 2 × 52	14 × (2 + 3)
14 × 2 + 14 × 3	12 × (5 + 10 + 2)

- Discuss which pairs (one calculation from each column) demonstrate the distributive law. Encourage pupils to use the knowledge they have gained through using the manipulatives when explaining why the second calculations match the first.

Same-day enrichment

- Provide pairs of pupils with a copy of **Resource 4.10.13a** Prove it! (2).

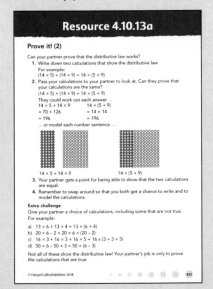

- Pupils should read through the instructions and then play the following game in pairs. The structure of the game will be familiar from Unit 10.11. Understanding of the distributive law will be consolidated.

Question 2

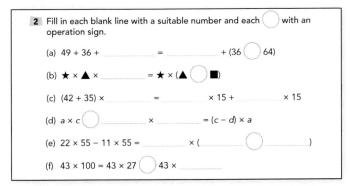

What learning will pupils have achieved at the conclusion of Question 2?

- Knowledge of the distributive law will have been applied in order to complete and correct number sentences.
- Pupils will have generalised the distributive law, using shapes and letters instead of numbers.

Activities for whole-class instruction

- Remind pupils of the definition of the distributive law – that when they are multiplying a sum or a difference of terms, they can multiply each addend or part of the subtraction separately. For example:

Multiplying a sum:

$16 \times (9 + 4)$

$= (16 \times 9) + (16 \times 4)$

Multiplying a difference:

$18 \times (15 - 2)$

$= (18 \times 15) - (18 \times 2)$

- Display the following statement along with three sticky notes (using different colours to represent the missing numbers and symbol):

$$15 + 67 + \boxed{} = \boxed{} + (67 \boxed{} 19)$$

- Ask: *Does this look like the distributive law we have been learning about? What is different?* Ask pupils to suggest the missing numbers and symbol, explaining their answers. Do pupils notice that:

  - The missing number is an addend, not a factor
  - The missing symbol must be + because the three numbers are added together on the left
  - The distributive law does not apply here because the number outside of the brackets is an addend; it does not need to be 'distributed' to each number inside the bracket separately
  - The law that applies to this calculation is the associative law – 'When adding three numbers, we can add any two numbers first and then add the third number; the sum remains unchanged.'

$$15 + 67 + \boxed{19} = \boxed{15} + (67 \boxed{+} 19)$$

- Show how this also applies to a number sentence that contains only multiplication:

  $4 \times (2 \times 3)$ is the same as $4 \times 2 \times 3$.

- **Look out for** … pupils who automatically assume that all calculations containing an operation before brackets obey the distributive law. Encourage pupils to examine calculations carefully before assuming that, just because there are brackets, the distributive law applies.

- Give pupils examples of number sentences that do illustrate the distributive law. These should include the following:

  a) where pupils are given the expanded version and need to work out the version containing brackets;

b) … and vice versa;

c) where shapes have been used instead of numbers;

d) where letters have been used instead of numbers.

- Spread the missing numbers and symbols across the number sentences to encourage pupils to use reasoning to fill each blank. For example:

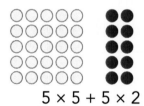

a) $27 \times 67 - \boxed{} \times 27 = \boxed{} \times (\boxed{} \boxed{} 18)$

b) $29 \times (4 + \boxed{}) = \boxed{}\ \boxed{}\ \boxed{}\ \boxed{}\ \boxed{}\ 12$

c) $\bigcirc \times (\square - \varowedge) = \boxed{}\ \boxed{}\ \boxed{}\ \boxed{}\ \boxed{}$

d) $a \times b + a \times c = \boxed{} \times (\boxed{}\ \boxed{}\ )$

- Pupils should now complete Question 2 in the Practice Book.

Same-day intervention

- Provide pupils with a set of counters. Display $(5 \times 5) + (5 \times 2)$ and ask them to make two arrays with a small gap in between to model the number sentence.

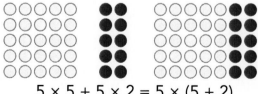

$$5 \times 5 + 5 \times 2$$

- Ask: *What is the same about the two arrays that you made?* Write an equivalent number sentence containing blanks: $(5 \times 5) + (5 \times 2) = 5 \times (\_ + \_)$. Model how to complete this by taking the '5 ×' expression and placing the remaining addition inside brackets: $5 \times (5 + 2)$. Ask pupils to demonstrate this equivalence using their counters:

$$5 \times 5 + 5 \times 2 = 5 \times (\underline{5} + \underline{2})$$

- Ask: *What is 5 times 5 + 2 as a simple multiplication fact?* Repeat for further illustrations of the distributive law, with pupils moving from the above structured approach to being encouraged to fill the gaps in each example without needing to model it. Ask them to explain why they have chosen to fill the blanks in this way.

Same-day enrichment

- Provide pupils with **Resource 4.10.13b** Distributive puzzles.

- Working in small groups, each pupil should devise two number sentences where the distributive law is demonstrated. Although these should generally consist of numbers, encourage some examples of shapes and letters too, as in the whole-class activity.

- Pupils should use blank cards to cover up some of the numbers and symbols in order to make a puzzle for their peers to solve.

- The others in the group should then make predictions about what is underneath each card, using their knowledge of the distributive law to help.

- To add an extra layer of challenge, encourage pupils to also include some red herrings (for example number sentences that contain only addition or multiplication symbols and so the distributive law need not apply).

Question 3

> **3** True or false? (Put a ✓ for true and a ✗ for false in each box.)
>
> (a) $46 + 54 \times 77 = (46 + 54) \times 77$ .... ☐
>
> (b) $25 \times 125 + 4 \times 8 = 25 \times 4 + 125 \times 8$ .... ☐
>
> (c) $24 + 6 \times 36 = 6 \times (4 + 36)$ .... ☐
>
> (d) $(125 + 71) \times 8 = (125 \times 8) + 71$ .... ☐
>
> (e) $100 - 33 - 55 = 100 - (33 + 55)$ .... ☐
>
> (f) $99 \times 99 + 99 = 99 \times 100$ .... ☐

What learning will pupils have achieved at the conclusion of Question 3?

- Knowledge of the distributive law will have been applied in order to complete and correct number sentences.

Activities for whole-class instruction

- Write: $39 + 28 \times 15 = \underline{\ \ \ }$
- Ask: *In which order would you complete the different operations in this number sentence?* Ensure that pupils answer by referring to the order of operations (where there are no brackets, multiplication comes before addition).
- To the right of the number sentence, write: $(39 + 28) \times 15$. Ask: *How would you work out the answer now?* Pupils should understand that they need to add the bracketed numbers to get 67 and then multiply by 15. Write an equals sign in between the two number sentences and then ask: *Is this true or false?* Give pupils time to discuss in pairs whether the number sentences are equal.

$$39 + 28 \times 15 \qquad (39 + 28) \times 15$$
$$= 39 \times 15 + 28 \times 15$$

So $39 + 28 \times 15 = (39 + 28) \times 15$ is not true.

- Guide pupils to see that, in the first version the 28 is multiplied by 15 and in the second version, both 28 and 39 are multiplied by 15. Together, rewrite the second number sentence as $39 \times 15 + 28 \times 15$ to remind them of this. Agree that the two sentences could be written as an inequality:

$39 + 28 \times 15 < (39 + 28) \times 15$.

- Write further examples of pairs of number sentences for pupils to decide whether they are true or not. For example:

$35 \times 19 + 35 = 35 \times 20$

$30 + 3 \times 17 = 3 \times (10 + 17)$

$400 - 34 - 12 = 400 - (34 + 12)$

$64 \times 200 + 5 \times 2 = 64 \times 2 + 200 \times 5$

- Provide time for pupils to consider these as a 'Think, Pair, Share' activity – where they begin by individually considering each example, then pair up with a partner to discuss their ideas, and finally share their thoughts with the class. Most of the examples will benefit from shared consideration in this way as pupils will need to reason carefully about how the relationships in each number sentence compare.

- Pupils should now complete Question 3 in the Practice Book.

Same-day intervention

- Ask: *Can you draw an array to model $6 \times (5 - 2)$?* For example:

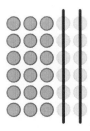

- Establish that this shows 5 minus 2 repeated 6 times (equal to 6 lots of 3).

- Ask: *Can you draw an array to model $6 \times 5 - 2$?* Pupils might draw something like this:

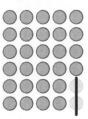

- Establish that this shows 6×5 minus 2.

- Ask: *Is it true or false to say that $6 \times (5 - 2) = 6 \times 5 - 2$? How can we change the second statement to make it true?* Repeat for further true or false statements, with pupils modelling or drawing each part as an array. Link each to the distributive law.

Same-day enrichment

- Ask pairs to devise their own True or False statements based on the distributive rule. They should write three statements, one of which is correct and the other two are not.

- They should then join with another pair and challenge them to identify the true statement and correct the two false statements. They should get a maximum of three points for doing so.

Question 4

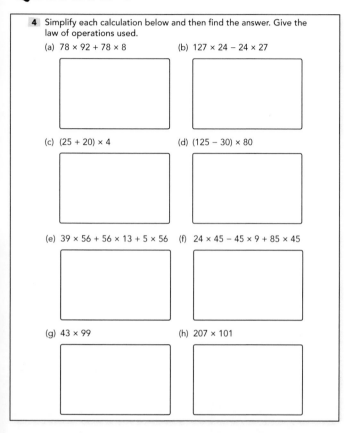

4 Simplify each calculation below and then find the answer. Give the law of operations used.

(a) 78 × 92 + 78 × 8

(b) 127 × 24 − 24 × 27

(c) (25 + 20) × 4

(d) (125 − 30) × 80

(e) 39 × 56 + 56 × 13 + 5 × 56

(f) 24 × 45 − 45 × 9 + 85 × 45

(g) 43 × 99

(h) 207 × 101

What learning will pupils have achieved at the conclusion of Question 4?

- Calculations will have been simplified and solved using the distributive law.

Activities for whole-class instruction

- Ask: *Which laws of operations have you learned about?* Revisit these, encouraging pupils to share examples of them in action.

- Ask pupils to consider how each of these laws could help to simplify a calculation. Collect ideas. For example:

  - the commutative law could help if the second number is larger in an addition and it makes sense to start with this, rather than the smaller number (e.g. 578 + 32 instead of 32 + 578)

  - the distributive law could help simplify a calculation where each term in an addition (or subtraction) is being multiplied by the same amount (e.g. (45 + 36) × 3 instead of 45 × 3 + 36 × 3).

- Pupils should then add further ideas.

- Write: (35 + 20) × 3. Ask: *How could you simplify this number sentence?* Although pupils might suggest using the distributive law to 'multiply out' the bracket (35 × 3) + (20 × 3), establish that a simpler way of finding the answer is to work out the addition inside the bracket so they just need to solve 55 × 3.

- Repeat for further calculations. For each one, encourage pupils to explain how it might be made simpler and then solve using their chosen method. For example:

  - 57 × 99 = __ recognise that this is one lot of 57 less than 100, and so work out (57 × 100) − 57.

  - 34 × 28 + 34 × 5 = __ identify that both addends are being multiplied by 34 and use the distributive law to simplify as 34 × (28 + 5) and then as 34 × 33.

- Ensure that pupils understand that sometimes it may be quicker to expand brackets than to work out the calculation within them. For example, in the calculation (25 + 30) × 4, expanding the brackets gives the calculations 25 × 4 + 30 × 4. Pupils may instantly recognise that 25 × 4 is equal to 100, so all they need to do is to work out the second multiplication and add 100. This may be quicker for them than working out 25 + 30 and then having to multiply the answer by 4.

- Pupils should now complete Question 4 in the Practice Book.

Same-day intervention

- Display the calculation 130 × 30 − 50 × 30. Ask: *In which order would you work this out?* Remind pupils of the order of operations they already know and that they would need to do the two multiplications first, then the subtraction. Ask: *What do you notice about both parts to the subtraction?* (They both have 30 as a factor).

- Write the number sentence (_ − _) × 30 on the board and ask pupils to complete it. Compare this with the original calculation and ask pupils to say which looks the simpler and why. Ask: *What can we do next to simplify the calculation?* Agree 80 × 30. Remind pupils that they can use a known multiplication fact to help (8 × 3 = 24). Give pupils further opportunities to simplify similar calculations.

Same-day enrichment

- Provide pupils with **Resource 4.10.13c** Jigsaw pairs, which contains instructions for the following activity.

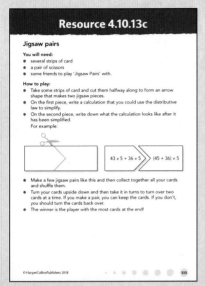

- Pupils should take strips of card and cut them halfway along to form an arrow shape making two 'jigsaw' pieces. On the first piece, pupils should write a calculation that the distributive law can be applied to. On the second piece, they should write a simplified version of the same calculation.

- They should use the cards that they make to play a game of pairs, turning over two cards at a time to try to match calculations with their simplified versions.

- If time allows, pupils could work out the answers to their calculations at the end.

Challenge and extension question

Question 5

5 Someone made a mistake in maths and calculated (☐ + 50) × 4 as ☐ × 4 + 50. Do you know what the difference between the correct answer and the wrong answer is?

In this question, pupils are given the scenario where a calculation has been solved incorrectly by wrongly applying the distributive law. Pupils are asked to calculate the difference between the correct answer and the wrong answer. They should also be encouraged to explain why this is so (pupils will need to apply the distributive law correctly and then compare the second addends).

The challenge may be extended by giving pupils the original number sentence (? + 50) × 4 and then the slightly altered ? + 50 × 4. This time, the difference will change each time. Pupils should identify that the difference is equal to three lots of whatever number they used as the unknown.

Unit 10.14
Laws of operations (4)

Conceptual context

Having learned and practised the three laws of operations, pupils are now provided with further opportunities to consolidate and apply their knowledge. It is possible that the commutative, associative and distributive laws could remain as theoretical concepts on a textbook page, but it is important that pupils understand that these are actually very useful tools to use when simplifying and solving calculations. In this unit, pupils will apply what they have learned in the preceding three chapters in a variety of problems.

Learning pupils will have achieved at the end of the unit

- Knowledge of each of the laws of operations will have been consolidated (Q1)
- Pupils will have continued to build connections between symbolic, numerical and pictorial representations of the laws of operations (Q1)
- Pupils will now appreciate the usefulness of knowing about commutative, associative and distributive laws through repeated opportunities to exploit them to simplify and solve calculations (Q2, Q3)
- Calculations will have been answered using different strategies as pupils look for opportunities to simplify numbers in different ways (Q2, Q3)
- Pupils will have developed their working knowledge of the laws of operations by applying them to word problems set in the real world (Q4)
- Further practice with word problems will have improved problem-solving skills (Q4)

Resources

mini whiteboards; three large hoops; base 10 manipulatives; **Resource 4.10.14a** Calculation cards; **Resource 4.10.14b** Simplifying challenge; **Resource 4.10.14c** Distributive word problems

Vocabulary

commutative law, associative law, distributive law, multiplication, addition, simplify, efficient (strategy)

Question 1

> **1** Fill in each space with the correct law of operations.
>
> (a) In 315 + 438 + 185 + 562 = (315 + 185) + (438 + 562), _____
>
> _____ are used.
>
> (b) In 857 × 25 × 4 = 857 × (25 × 4), _____
>
> _____ is used.
>
> (c) In 8 × 36 + 89 × 8 = 8 × (36 + 89), _____
>
> _____ is used.
>
> (d) In (71 − 36) × 20 = 71 × 20 − 36 × 20, _____
>
> _____ is used.

What learning will pupils have achieved at the conclusion of Question 1?

- Knowledge of each of the laws of operations will have been consolidated.
- Pupils will have continued to build connections between symbolic, numerical and pictorial representations of the laws of operations.

Activities for whole-class instruction

- Write the names of the three laws of operations on the board. Ensure that these are written horizontally, with spaces in between. Remind pupils of the three definitions.

  - *The commutative law means that the numbers in an addition or multiplication can be swapped around and the answer is unchanged.*
  - *The associative law means that it doesn't matter which part of an addition or multiplication we do first.*
  - *The distributive law means that multiplying something by each of the numbers inside the brackets and adding those products together is the same as adding the numbers in the brackets together and then multiplying that by the number outside the brackets.*

- Write: (49 − 32) × 21 = 49 × 21 − 32 × 21. Ask: *Which law of operations is being used?* Choose pupils to point to the law they think is correct. Ensure pupils can explain why. Repeat for further pairs of equivalent number sentences, including those where both the commutative and associative laws are being used (for example 503 + 230 + 824 + 770 = (824 + 503) + (770 + 230).

- Pupils should now complete Question 1 in the Practice Book.

Same-day intervention

- Set up three large hoops, labelling each with the name of one of the laws of operations. Ask pupils to suggest ways to model each law using manipulatives or by sketching. One example of these should be placed inside each hoop.
- Then ask for an example of each law using numbers. Again, one example should be placed inside each hoop.
- Finally, ask pupils how the law can be written using letters. These should be the final addition to each hoop. This will produce an aide memoire for pupils:

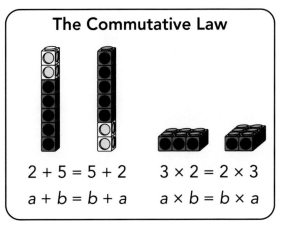

The Commutative Law

$2 + 5 = 5 + 2$ $3 × 2 = 2 × 3$

$a + b = b + a$ $a × b = b × a$

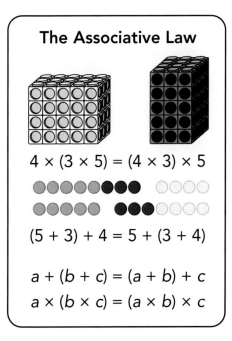

The Associative Law

$4 × (3 × 5) = (4 × 3) × 5$

$(5 + 3) + 4 = 5 + (3 + 4)$

$a + (b + c) = (a + b) + c$

$a × (b × c) = (a × b) × c$

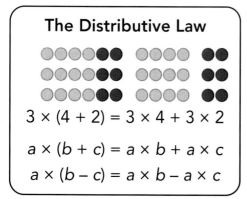

The Distributive Law

$$3 \times (4 + 2) = 3 \times 4 + 3 \times 2$$
$$a \times (b + c) = a \times b + a \times c$$
$$a \times (b - c) = a \times b - a \times c$$

- Provide pupils with examples of further pairs of equivalent number sentences written on strips of paper and ask them to place these in the correct hoops. Ask: *Which laws do they illustrate? How do you know?*

Same-day enrichment

- Challenge pupils to come up with as many different ways as they can to illustrate/model/explain the three laws they have been learning about. Provide them with access to all the maths resources the classroom has to offer (number lines, 100 squares, base ten blocks and so on).

- As a mini-plenary, it might be useful for pupils in the same-day enrichment group to take their peers around the examples they have made, commentating on them (and thus providing further scaffolding for those who require same-day intervention).

Question 2

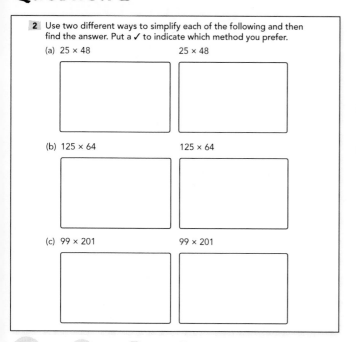

2 Use two different ways to simplify each of the following and then find the answer. Put a ✓ to indicate which method you prefer.

(a) 25 × 48   25 × 48

(b) 125 × 64   125 × 64

(c) 99 × 201   99 × 201

What learning will pupils have achieved at the conclusion of Question 2?

- Pupils will now appreciate the usefulness of knowing about commutative, associative and distributive laws through repeated opportunities to exploit them to simplify and solve calculations.

- Calculations will have been answered using different strategies as pupils look for opportunities to simplify numbers in different ways.

Activities for whole-class instruction

- Challenge pupils to take on the role of 'number detectives'. Remind them that calculating efficiently is often about being able to spot clues in the numbers and opportunities to use different strategies. Give the analogy of a toolkit, where pupils identify opportunities where they can use different tools (and include the laws they have learned about) to help.

- Display: 302 × 99. Give pupils time to discuss in pairs how they would find the answer. Set the target of finding at least two efficient ways. Ask: *What do you notice about the numbers? How can they help?* Elicit that they are near multiples of 100. Ask: *Do we need to round both or just one number?* Methods might include:

$$302 \times 99 = (302 \times 100) - 302$$

or

$$= (300 \times 99) + (2 \times 99)$$

- Ask pupils to shut their eyes (to ensure an unbiased vote) and to raise their hand to vote for their preferred method. Share the results and discuss why the class think that particular calculation is preferable. Bring in the idea of efficiency – often the favoured calculation is the one that can be simplified enough to be a quick way of getting to the answer. Ask: *Is your favourite method the first one you would have thought of?*

- Provide further multiplications to explore using two methods to simplify and solve.

- Pupils should now complete Question 2 in the Practice Book.

Same-day intervention

- Introduce the concept of identifying different strategies to solve problems by using simple applications of the associative law of addition and multiplication. Display the addition 37 + 145 + 96. Ask: *Without actually working out the answer, can you think of two ways to solve this calculation?*

- Give pupils time to talk about this in pairs and then regroup to share their ideas. Ensure also that they are clear about the specific strategy they would use (for example writing down the addition vertically or using partitioning to help). Remind pupils that the associative law says that they do not have to add the numbers in the order shown. So, two different methods might be:

  (37 + 145) + 96   or   37 + (145 + 96)

- Give pupils time to work out the answer both ways. Ask: *Which method do you prefer? Why?*

- Repeat for further examples where the associative law can be applied, in particular multiplication questions where, arguably, one method is often more obviously preferable than another. An example of this is 5 × 2 × 35 where (5 × 2) × 35 (or 10 × 35) is much quicker to work out than 5 × (2 × 35) or any other alternative.

Same-day enrichment

- Provide pairs of pupils with **Resource 4.10.14a** Calculation cards, cut into cards.

Resource 4.10.14a

Calculation cards

52 × 25	101 × 48
125 × 72	99 × 101
29 × 98	55 × 125
25 × 102	150 × 86

- Pupils should take a calculation card and then both attempt to simplify and solve it. After each calculation, they should ask themselves the following questions:
  - Did we use the same method?
  - If yes, why did the method we used spring to mind? Can we think of a different method to use?
  - If no, what is the same and what is different about our methods? Is one of them quicker to use?

Question 3

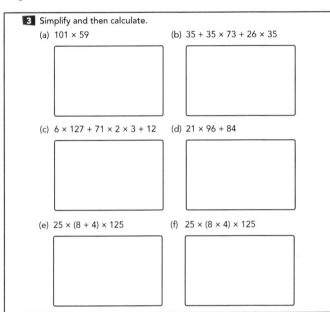

3 Simplify and then calculate.
(a) 101 × 59
(b) 35 + 35 × 73 + 26 × 35
(c) 6 × 127 + 71 × 2 × 3 + 12
(d) 21 × 96 + 84
(e) 25 × (8 + 4) × 125
(f) 25 × (8 × 4) × 125

What learning will pupils have achieved at the conclusion of Question 3?

- Pupils will now appreciate the usefulness of knowing about commutative, associative and distributive laws through repeated opportunities to exploit them to simplify and solve calculations.

- Calculations will have been answered using different strategies as pupils look for opportunities to simplify numbers in different ways.

Activities for whole-class instruction

- Display the following calculations:

  1000 × 58   300 × 30   13 × 29

- Ask: *Which calculation do you think will be the most complicated to solve? Which do you think will be the simplest?* Discuss how the multiplication with the largest numbers can possibly be the simplest (and why the multiplication with the smallest numbers can be the most complicated).

A calculation that involves tens numbers is simple to work out.

- Ask: *Can you explain why this is?*

- Explain that pupils are going to see several calculations and their task is to make them simpler. Ask: *How can we use the laws of operations to do this?* Remind pupils that they should be constantly looking for ways to make the all-important tens/hundreds numbers.

- Write: 99 × 71. Ask: *How would you work out the answer to this as it is? How can we turn the calculation into something simpler? Do we need to alter both numbers or only one? Why?* Elicit that pupils can find the answer quickly by rounding 99 up to 100 and subtracting one lot of 71 to adjust the answer:

$$99 \times 71 = (100 \times 71) - 71$$
$$= 7100 - 71$$
$$= 7029$$

- Demonstrate that this became a calculation pupils could easily do mentally – all because they saw an opportunity to simplify it.

- Provide further calculations to practise simplifying, drawing attention to any of the laws of operations that are applied to help. For example:

Number sentence	Strategy to simplify
125 × (7 + 1) × 25	Work out the brackets: 125 × 8 × 25 (order of operations). Calculate 125 × 8 (associative law). Simplified calculation: 1000 × 25
8 × 42 + 160 × 4 × 2 − 16	Recognise that 4 × 2 = 8, so rewrite as: 8 × 42 + 160 × 8 − 16. Identify that 8 is distributed across both addends. Rewrite as 8 × (42 + 160) − 16 (distributive law). Work out the brackets: 8 × 202 − 16 (order of operations). Recognise that this can be simplified further as the 16 on the end cancels out the 8 × 2 in the calculation. Simplified calculation: 8 × 200

- Each time, compare the simplified calculation with the original complex calculation to show how much easier it has become.

- Pupils should now complete Question 3 in the Practice Book.

Same-day intervention

- Practise simplifying calculations that clearly illustrate specific laws of operations. For example, write the calculation 28 × 51 + 49 × 28. Draw boxes around each addend to show that this is, basically, an addition. Ask: *What do you notice about this calculation?* Pupils should note that the factor 28 features in both addends. Ask: *What does the distributive law say we can do when this happens?* Choose a pupil to cross out the calculation and rewrite it as 28 × (51 + 49).

- Ask: *How can we simplify the number sentence further?* Encourage pupils to note that 51 and 49 are a pair that equal 100. Choose a pupil to cross out the calculation and rewrite it as 28 × 100.

- Compare this simplified multiplication with the original. Ask: *Which would you rather be asked?*

  28 × 51 + 49 × 28 = ___, or

  28 × (51 + 49) = ___ ?

- Repeat for pairs of multiplications with pupils crossing out calculations themselves. For example:

  (19 + 21) × 45 = ___, or

  19 × 45 + 21 × 45 = ___?

Same-day enrichment

- Set pupils challenges to write complex calculations that can be simplified in different ways. Provide them with a copy of **Resource 4.10.14b** Simplifying challenge, which gives them several examples.

Resource 4.10.14b

Simplifying challenge

Your task is to design several complex questions for your friends to simplify before they solve.
You need to make sure that you know how you want them to simplify each question, so think carefully about how you write them.
Here are some design challenges for you with an example for each:

Design a complex calculation that …	What question could you design?	How do you expect them to simplify it?
… your partner can use the distributive law to simplify	25 × 18 − 25 × 12	By using the distributive law to write 25 × (18 − 12) and then work out 25 × 6
… is easier to work out if the numbers are multiplied in a different order (associative law)	7 × 10 × 7	By finding the answer to 7 × 7 and then multiplying the answer by 10
… equals 31 × 100 when finally simplified	31 × 86 + 31 × 14	By using the distributive law to write 31 × (86 + 14) and then working out 31 × 100
… contains two numbers that can be combined to make a multiple of 100	367 + 482 + 133	By seeing that 367 + 133 equals 500 and then working out 500 + 482
… contains four or more numbers, but can be simplified to a calculation with only two numbers.	9 × 13 + 11 × 13	By using the distributive law to write (9 + 11) × 13 and then writing it as 20 × 13

Now try your own examples for each challenge.
See whether your partner simplifies in the way you want them to!

- The challenges include asking them to design calculations that:
  - they can use the distributive law to simplify;
  - are easier to work out if the numbers are multiplied in a different order (associative law);
  - equal 31 × 100 when finally simplified;
  - feature two numbers that can be combined to make a multiple of 100;
  - contain four or more numbers in the complex calculation and can be simplified to a calculation with only two numbers.
- Pupils should read and think through each example before attempting the challenge.
- Pupils should then share their complex calculations for peers to simplify and solve.

Question 4

4   Application problems.

(a) The passenger information at a coach station is shown in the table below.

Type of coach	Number of trips per day	Number of passengers on board per coach
Regular coach	12	32
Mini coach	12	18

How many passengers were sent off from the coach station per day?

Answer: _____

(b) There are 30 boxes of bananas and 4 boxes of apples in a fruit store. Each box weighs 25 kilograms. How many kilograms of fruit does the store have in total?

Answer: _____

What learning will pupils have achieved at the conclusion of Question 4?

- Pupils will have developed their working knowledge of the laws of operations by applying them to word problems set in the real world.
- Further practice with word problems has improved problem-solving skills.

Activities for whole-class instruction

- Remind pupils that they can apply the laws of operations to help solve real-life problems. Show this table and explain that it represents the deliveries that a lorry makes taking packs of water to a shop.

Day	Number of packs delivered	Number of bottles in each pack
Monday	12	6
Tuesday	16	6

Ask pupils to write down as many questions as they can that they can ask, using the information in the table. Explain that they do not need to answer these, just to frame the questions. Give them an example to begin with:

- How many bottles were delivered on Monday altogether?

- Share examples as a class and then focus particularly on the question: How many bottles will be delivered in total over both days?

- Ask: *What would you do to work out the answer to this question?* Establish that they would need to multiply 12 by 6 and then add this to 16 multiplied by 6 (note whether any pupils express this by applying the distributive law as the total of 12 plus 16 multiplied by 6 or even 28 multiplied by 6).

- Display the following table:

Subject	Number of questions on test	Number of pupils taking test
English	18	25
Maths	30	25

- Explain that the table shows the amount of marking a teacher needs to do after their class takes two tests. Ask: *Based on the table, what question do you think I am going to ask you?*

- Ask pupils to suggest how to find out the total number of questions the teacher needs to mark. Elicit that this can be written as:

18 × 25 + 30 × 25

(total number of English questions) + (total number of Maths questions)

- Allow pupils time to study the number sentence before asking them whether they think one of the laws of operations might help them simplify it. Establish that the factor 25 is 'distributed' across both addends, and so the distributive law of multiplication over addition can be used to simplify it to (18 + 30) × 25 and then 48 × 25. Display this as an array:

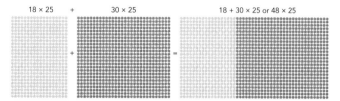

- Pupils should then calculate the answer. Note whether any pupils use a 'double one number, halve the other' approach to simplify the calculation further with this particular question, which can be altered to 24 × 50 and then 12 × 100. It is not necessary for pupils to use this method (and most will not), but it is certainly worth looking to see whether any pupils have the numerical awareness to do so.

- Give pupils further word-based problems to solve using their knowledge of the laws of operations to simplify and solve. For example:

  - 20 cars and 18 motorbikes cross over a toll bridge. They each buy a ticket for £3. What is the total amount of money the bridge takes?

  - A decorator uses 51 tins of wall paint and 42 tins of ceiling paint every month. How many tins of paint does she use in a year? In a year, how many more tins of wall paint than ceiling paint does she use?

  - There are 11 racks of T-shirts in a shop. On each rack there are 8 surf T-shirts and 4 skate T-shirts. How many T-shirts are there altogether?

Same-day intervention

- Give pupils the scenario of an imaginary student – Georgia – who has been struggling to work out multiplication facts. Write the calculation 7 × 12 on the board. Ask: *How can the number 12 be partitioned?* Encourage pupils to look for numbers that are 'easier' times tables – so, for example, 10 and 2 is a good combination.

- Rewrite the calculation as 7 × (10 + 2). Ask: *How can we use the distributive law to help Georgia write the calculation another way?* (7 × 10) + (7 × 2) *How would you explain this method of making times tables simpler to Georgia?*

- Give pupils opportunities to allow further practice of this method. Include the distributive law of multiplication over subtraction too (for example partitioning 8 × 8 as 8 × (10 − 2) and simplifying).

Same-day enrichment

- Pupils should work in small groups to generate and then solve their own problems based on the distributive law. Each pupil should use the writing frames provided on **Resource 4.10.14c** Distributive word problems, to help generate these.

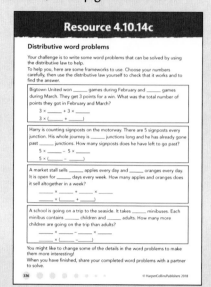

- Encourage pupils to consider how they might write their calculation as a number sentence and then how the distributive law might be used to simplify it. They should share their completed word problems with peers to solve.

Challenge and extension question

Question 5

> **5** Calculate smartly.
>
> (a) 280 × 36 + 360 × 72
>
> Answer: _____
>
> (b) 1999 + 999 × 999
>
> Answer: _____

As an extension of their work with the laws of operations, pupils are given two questions and asked to calculate them 'smartly'. Remind pupils that this is another way of saying that they do so 'efficiently' (i.e. quickly and accurately, simplifying where they are able).

The first calculation consists of an addition where each addend is found by multiplying two numbers. Pupils should look for opportunities here to apply the distributive law. This is possible if they adjust one of the addends (e.g. 72 is double 36, so if it is halved and 360 doubled, the second addend will still equal the same number). The calculation will read 280 × 36 + 720 × 36 and pupils can then use the distributive law as normal.

The second calculation involves the multiplication and addition of several 'near multiples'. Pupils need to consider how to round one of the factors upwards and then adjust, in particular thinking about how the addend can be used in the adjustment process.

Unit 10.15
Problem solving using four operations (1)

Conceptual context

This is the first of four units where pupils are encouraged to apply all they have learned over the course of Chapter 10, including the order of and laws of operations. The problems featured in this unit focus on multi-step questions relating to work rate. Pupils revisit the concept of rate (previously introduced in Units 10.1 and 10.2) and apply this knowledge to word-based problems. Pupils are expected to be able to work out the planned efficiency of a particular situation and to compare it with the actual efficiency as a result of some change. Problems that involve efficiency and rate require pupils to apply a range of calculation strategies, particularly those involving multiplication and division.

Learning pupils will have achieved at the end of the unit

- Word problems will have been systematically broken down into steps, with pupils identifying strategies to achieve each step (Q1)
- The concepts of planned and actual work rate will have been applied to word problems (Q1, Q2)
- Pupils will have practised dividing work planned/completed by the time planned/taken and then using this concept of work rate to solve more complex problems (Q1, Q2)
- Several opportunities will have been provided to express problem-solving strategies in different ways (Q2)

Resources

mini whiteboards; small manipulatives (beads, counters or similar); large 100 squares; **Resource 4.10.15** Work rate challenge cards

Vocabulary

rate, efficiency, how many more? how many fewer? average, per

Question 1

> **1** Think carefully, and fill in the spaces.
>
> A company planned to build a 1200-metre auto-racing track in 40 days. It actually completed 10 more metres of the race track each day than planned.
>
> (a) From the given condition 'to build a 1200-metre auto-racing track in 40 days', we can find the planned work rate.
>
> Number sentence _____
>
> (b) From the given condition 'it actually completed 10 more metres of the race track each day than planned', we can find the actual work rate.
>
> Number sentence _____
>
> (c) Finally, from the given length of the auto-racing track and the actual work rate, we can find the actual amount of time taken to complete the work.
>
> Number sentence _____

What learning will pupils have achieved at the conclusion of Question 1?

- Word problems will have been systematically broken down into steps, with pupils identifying strategies to achieve each step.
- The concepts of planned and actual work rate will have been applied to real-world contexts.
- Pupils will have practised dividing work planned/completed by the time planned/taken and then using this concept of work rate to solve more complex problems.

Activities for whole-class instruction

- Begin by clarifying the meaning of the word 'efficient', which has been used in the context of 'a quick and accurate' way of calculating in recent units.
- Remind pupils of their previous work considering work rate (Units 10.1 and 10.2). It may be worth directing pupils to these units in their Practice Book to remind themselves of the sorts of scenarios where the rate of something can be calculated and how to do so. Ask: *What operations do we tend to use to find out the efficiency of something?*
- Place two chairs at the front of the class and label one 'MORE EFFICIENT' and the other 'LESS EFFICIENT'. As a revision of the concept of efficiency, call out different scenarios and ask pupils to come and sit on the chair that applies to each scenario. For example:
  - if you read the same book as your friend, but in less time
  - if your car travels the same distance as mine, but it uses more petrol to get there
  - if a factory manages to produce more yoghurts than they planned, but in less time.

- Display the following scenario on the board:

- A chocolate factory planned to make 2400 Easter eggs in the 30 days leading up to Easter.
- It actually managed to make 20 more eggs every day than it had planned.
- Ask: *Is the factory more or less efficient than it planned?*
- Point to the first sentence. Explain that this shows what was planned – the number of Easter eggs that the factory planned to make in 30 days. Ask pupils how they might use this information to find the number of eggs per day.
- Revise the method and the term used to describe the solution: the planned work rate.

  Total number of eggs ÷ total number of days planned to make them = number of eggs every day (planned)

  = 2400 ÷ 30 = 80. Agree that this means the factory planned to make eggs at the rate of 80 per day.

- Point to the second sentence. Explain that this tells us that the factory made 20 more eggs each day than it had planned. Ask: *How do you think you could work out the actual work rate?* Discuss and agree that this means how many eggs the factory actually made every day.
- Discuss how 'planned work rate' (80 per day) + the change in work rate (20 per day) = 'actual work rate' (100 per day)?
- Ask: *Considering that the actual work rate was 100 eggs per day, how long did it take the factory to make 2400 eggs?* Pupils should discuss in pairs and write an appropriate number sentence. Ensure that pupils understand the following:

  Total number of eggs ÷ actual work rate = number of days needed

  = 2400 ÷ 100 = 24

- Put this information into context – because the chocolate factory managed to produce more each day than they expected, they finished making their eggs 6 days before Easter – 6 days before they had planned.

- Give pupils further scenarios – this time asking them to work in pairs to find:
  - the planned work rate
  - the actual work rate
  - the difference in the time taken.

- For example:

  A delivery driver has a 300 mile journey to make. He plans to make it in 5 hours.

  He actually travels 10 miles less each hour than he planned.

  How much longer does it take him to reach his destination?

- Pupils should now complete Question 1 in the Practice Book.

Same-day intervention

- Use manipulatives to model each part of a rate-based scenario so pupils make concrete links with planned/actual rate. Display the following problem and give pupils time to read and understand it:
  - A car factory plans to make 60 cars. They plan to do this in 15 days. They actually manage to make 2 more cars every day than they had planned.

- Begin by going through each part of the scenario and asking pupils to model it using the manipulatives:

The factory plans to make 60 cars	[Count out 60 manipulatives]
They plan to do this in 15 days	[Share into 15 groups, each representing 1 day – there will be 4 in each group]
They actually make 2 more cars every day	[Redistribute the 60 'cars' to make groups of 6, representing the actual daily rate of 6, rather than 4.

- Discuss how many groups there are now.
- If time allows, provide further examples to model concretely.

Same-day enrichment

- Provide pupils with **Resource 4.10.15** Work rate challenge cards.

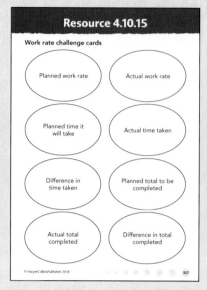

- Give pupils a list of challenges based on the cards. They should move them around on their whiteboards, writing symbols in between to show the different ways that answers can be found. For example:
  - How would you find the planned work rate of a factory making toy cars?

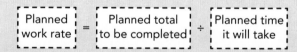

  - How would you find the actual work rate of a builder laying bricks?

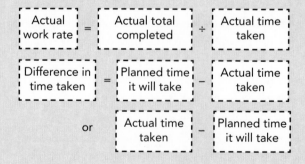

- Ask pupils to find the difference between the planned time it was going to take to read a book and the actual time it took.

- To extend pupils further, encourage them to invent their own scenarios and use the cards to cover over information. Their partner should reveal any two numbers in the calculation and use the information shown to predict what the third is.

Question 2

2 Application problems.

(a) A road construction company planned to build a section of motorway. According to the plan, it would build 91 metres of the motorway per day and complete the work in 10 days. It was actually completed in 7 days. How many metres of the motorway were actually built each day? How many more metres were built each day than planned?

Answer: _____

(b) A road construction company planned to build a section of motorway. According to the plan, it would build 81 metres per day and complete the work in 10 days. It actually built 9 metres more of the motorway each day than it planned. How many days did the company actually take to complete the work? How many day(s) earlier did it complete the work than planned?

Answer: _____

(c) An author needs to type a 360-page manuscript. She planned to type 60 pages per day, but in fact she typed 90 pages per day. With this faster work rate, how many days earlier did she complete the task than planned?

Answer: _____

(d) An author needs to type a 360-page manuscript. She planned to finish the work in 6 days, but in fact she finished the work in 4 days. How many more pages did she type per day than planned?

Answer: _____

(e) A school kitchen has 3000 kg of rice, which was planned to last for 20 days, but it actually lasted for 30 days. How many fewer kilograms of rice were consumed each day than originally expected?

Answer: _____

(f) In 3 minutes, Jordan can bounce a basketball 126 times and Caila can bounce a basketball 135 times. How many more bounces than Jordan can Caila manage per minute?

Answer: _____

What learning will pupils have achieved at the conclusion of Question 2?

- The concepts of planned and actual work rate will have been applied to word problems.

- Pupils will have practised dividing work planned/ completed by the time planned/taken and then using this concept of work rate to solve more complex problems.

- Several opportunities will have been provided to express problem-solving strategies in different ways.

Activities for whole-class instruction

- Explain that pupils will now be applying their knowledge of work rate to solve problems. Ask: *Who might need to work out the planned and actual work rates in real life?*

- Give pupils the following as a real-life illustration of the importance of this area of maths. In the spring of 2017, the Tottenham Hotspur football ground began to be demolished and rebuilt. It was planned to take a further year to complete and the team needed to move out and play at Wembley during this time. The builders had a planned work rate. Discuss how the actual work rate might be different and what effect might it have. For example, if the actual work rate is faster than expected, it will take less time and the stadium will be completed earlier than planned. The opposite is true if the actual work rate is less (slower) than planned (and, in this example, the team will need to carry on playing at Wembley for longer).

- Give pupils the following scenario:

  – A football club is installing seats at its new stadium. It plans to install 87 seats every day for 10 days. Instead, the club actually finishes the job in only 6 days.

- Ask the following questions:

  – *How do you think the builders' work rate has changed?*

  – *Is the actual work rate more or less than the planned work rate? How do you know?*

  – *How many more seats every day do the builders fit, compared with what they planned to do every day?*

  – *How would you work out the number of seats altogether that they need to fit?*

  – *If the builders decided to continue to work for 10 days, how many more seats could they fit than the number they planned?*

- Go through each of these questions. Where a calculation is needed, encourage pupils to describe how to find the answer (this does not necessarily need to involve numbers as it is more important that they recognise the strategy needed). For instance:

  – To find the total number of seats, we need to multiply the number of seats installed in a day by the number of days that are needed.

  – The actual work rate is found by dividing the total number of seats by the actual time it took to fit them.

- Give pupils similar scenarios to solve. For each one, choose pupils to take the role of the tradespeople involved and ask them to act out an explanation of how they might find each answer.
- Example questions might include:
  - You are sorting out the lighting for a rock concert. Your original plan is to fit 9 lights per hour for 4 hours. Your actual rate is 3 lights fewer per hour. The lead singer in the rock group comes to ask how long it will take to get the lights fitted.
  - What do you tell him? How much longer will it take than you originally planned?
  - The Queen has requested that 400 meringues be baked for a royal banquet. The plan says that they can be baked at a rate of 20 per hour. However, the royal ovens are bigger than expected and can actually fit in 25 every hour.
  - You are the chef. The Queen comes down to ask you personally when the meringues will be completed.
  - What good news can you tell the Queen? Using your actual efficiency, how much sooner will you finish cooking all 400 meringues?
- Pupils should role-play each scenario in pairs, including a description of their working out in their scene. Share these as a class.
- Pupils should now complete Question 2 in the Practice Book.

Same-day intervention

- Use the following activities to help pupils build links between the concepts of efficiency and work rates and the maths involved in calculating them. Give pupil pairs a large 100 square and two counters. Explain that the aim is to get to 100 first and pupils should take it in turns to move their counter. Pupil A can move their counter only five squares at a time. Pupil B can move their counter only four squares at a time. Pupils should quickly realise that this is a pointless race! Ask: *Who is going to reach 100 first? How do you know? How many goes will it take both of you to reach 100? Can you work this out without counting each step?*
- Progress to considering a scenario that illustrates a similar problem. Explain that pupils are bakers with a target of 40 cakes to bake. Their work rate is different – Baker A bakes 8 cakes every day. Baker B bakes 10 cakes every day. Ask: *How much more/less time will it take Baker B?*

- Pupils should use their 100 square to model the problem, moving their plastic counters at these two different rates. Ask: *How long did it take you to reach 40? Can you explain how to work this out as a calculation?* Agree that Baker B is more efficient than Baker A because Baker B has a higher work rate, so Baker B will, of course, reach the target first.
- Give pupils further examples where they have a choice whether to use the 100 square or simply work out the answer using the numbers given. Encourage them to move from modelling the answer concretely to understanding that the higher work rate means greater efficiency and so will mean that targets are achieved more quickly. They should also be able to describe the scenario in number sentences such as:

$40 \div 8 = 5$. Baker A will need 5 days to bake 40 cakes

$40 \div 10 = 4$. Baker B will need 4 days to bake 40 cakes

Same-day enrichment

- Use the following to encourage pupils to explore more deeply how the numbers in efficiency problems work together. Display the following problem:
  - Two pigeons are racing home, which is a distance of 19 kilometres away. The first flies at a rate of 2 kilometres per hour. The second flies at a rate of 3 kilometres per hour. How long will it take each one to arrive home?
- Ask: *Why is this problem difficult to work out, compared with the others you have looked at? Which number would you change to make it easier?* Challenge pupils to alter the distance so that the problem becomes less complicated to calculate. Ask: *What sort of a number does it need to be?* (a multiple of 2 and 3 in order to be more easily solved)
- Pupils should then devise efficiency problems of their own, using what they have learned about the numbers involved to ensure that they are easier to answer.

Challenge and extension questions

Questions 3 and 4

3 A factory needs to produce 3600 car parts. If the job is given to worker A, it will take 30 days. If it is given to worker B, it will take 20 days. If they work together to produce the parts, then in how many days can they finish the task?

Answer: _____

4 25 workers were initially deployed to complete a construction project in 15 days. Three days after the project had started, they were informed that the project must be completed 2 days earlier than planned. How many more workers were then needed in order to meet the new requirement? (Assume that all the workers have the same work rate.)

Answer: _____

Pupils are given two further problems where their knowledge of efficiency is extended to include more complex scenarios. In the first question, they are provided with the times two workers take and asked to calculate the time it will take them to produce a given total if they work together. It is these latter four words that add the element of challenge to the problem. Pupils need to utilise what they know of the workers' times to calculate their work rates per day. They can then combine these to find their joint work rate per day and, from this, calculate how long it will take them working together.

The second question is particularly challenging as a key piece of information is missing. Pupils are not given a total amount of something to aim for, so they may initially be confused as to how to find each worker's rate. Pupils should be encouraged to invent a simple rate per day for each worker (1 of something is the simplest!) and use this to help find the answer.

Unit 10.16
Problem solving using four operations (2)

Conceptual context

In this unit, pupils are given further opportunities to apply their knowledge of calculations involving the four operations. As with the previous unit, the focus again is placed on problems that deal with efficiency and work rate. The concept is extended to encourage pupils to describe the steps needed to complete calculations and to express these as number sentences. Here, their prior knowledge of the order of operations is applied. Pupils are challenged to explore more than one way to find an answer, recording each separate strategy they use as a number sentence (containing mixed operations and brackets).

Learning pupils will have achieved at the end of the unit

- An understanding of problem-solving strategies as a series of purposeful steps will have been developed and described (Q1, Q3)
- Pupils will have explored and applied two different strategies when solving problems (Q2)
- Number sentences will have been derived from given word problems and then solved (Q2, Q3)
- Fluency when working with application problems containing mixed operations will have been developed (Q1, Q2, Q3)

Resources

mini whiteboards; manipulatives (small beads, counters or similar); a stopwatch/timer

Vocabulary

efficiency, rate, pace, per

Question 1

> **1** Think carefully and then draw a line to match each pair. 144 balloons are equally shared by 6 groups. Each group has 4 children. If all children get the same number of balloons, how many is that?
>
> (a) 144 ÷ (6 × 4)
>
> (b) 144 ÷ 6 ÷ 4
>
> A. First find the number of balloons each group will get, and then divide it by 4 children in each group. The result is the number of balloons each child will get.
>
> B. First find the total number of children in the 6 groups, and then divide the total number of balloons by the total number of children. The result is the number of balloons each child will get.

What learning will pupils have achieved at the conclusion of Question 1?

- An understanding of problem-solving strategies as a series of purposeful steps will have been developed and described.
- Fluency when working with application problems containing mixed operations will have been developed.

Activities for whole-class instruction

- Prior to the activity, count out 120 plastic counters or similar into a container. Place four chairs at the front of the class and three pieces of paper on each chair. Display the following problem:
  - 120 sweets are shared equally between four groups of children. Each group has three children sitting around it. If each child gets the same number of sweets, how many is that?
- Tell pupils that you will be asking them how they might find the answer and give them time to think about this either on their own or in pairs. Collect pupils' ideas and encourage them to model them using the counters, the chairs (which represent the four groups) and the pieces of paper (which represent the children in each group).
- Establish that the answer can be found in different ways:

Strategy 1	Calculations
Find the number of sweets each group will get (by dividing total sweets by number of groups)	120 ÷ 4 = 30 sweets per group
Find the number of sweets each child will get (by dividing one group's sweets by the number of children in it)	30 ÷ 3 = 10 sweets each

Strategy 2	Calculations
Find the total number of children that will be getting sweets (by multiplying the number of groups by the children in them)	4 × 3 = 12 children altogether
Find the number of sweets each child will get (by dividing total sweets by total number of children)	120 ÷ 12 = 10 sweets each

- Display the following number sentences on the board:

  120 ÷ (4 × 3) = ___

  120 ÷ 4 ÷ 3 = ___

- Ask: *Which number sentence goes with which strategy?* Call out parts of each strategy (for example the total number of children') and ask pupils to point to that particular part of the number sentence.

- Repeat for similar problems. Choose a pupil to describe the method they have used (for example 'I first found the total number of … Then I divided by the total number of … to find each individual ...') Again, display two number sentences and ask the class which number sentence is the method that has been described. Ask: *Has anyone used a different method?*

- (i) Pupils have explored recording strategies in different ways already in this chapter. However, it is important that the focus here is placed firmly on their ability to describe what it is they are doing. This does not mean a generalised, almost abstract, description of a calculation, such as:

  'I divided 150 by the product of 5 and 3.'

  Instead, pupils should be encouraged to use a more specific context-based description of what is happening:

  'I divided the total number of stickers by the total number of children, which I had already worked out by multiplying the number of tables by the number of children sitting at each table.'

  Pupils' fluency with calculation strategies depends on their ability to talk like this. There is a context to their number work – being able to describe each step is essential and should be encouraged generally, not only in this question.

- Pupils should now complete Question 1 in the Practice Book.

Same-day intervention

- Provide further opportunities for pupils to physically model each method they use to solve problems involving sharing. For example, display the following calculation:
  - There are 80 plants in a garden centre. They are shared equally between 10 rows of pots. Each row contains 4 pots. How many plants are in each pot?

- Provide pupils with access to manipulatives (beads or similar) and ask them to model how they would find the answer. Many pupils will work through the calculation serially (dealing with each number as it appears) – starting with 80 beads, sharing them into 10 rows and then splitting each row into 4 equal groups of 2. Ask: *How would you write this as a number sentence?*

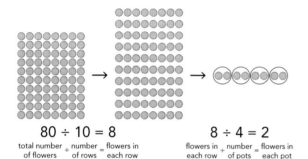

$80 \div 10 = 8$	$8 \div 4 = 2$
total number ÷ number = flowers in of flowers of rows each row	flowers in ÷ number = flowers in each row of pots each pot

- Establish that it can be written as $80 \div 10 \div 4$. Establish whether pupils can spot a second method of finding the answer. Model it as before.

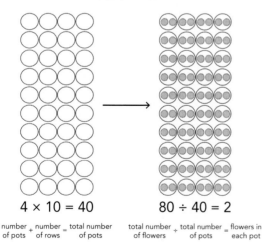

$4 \times 10 = 40$	$80 \div 40 = 2$
number + number = total number of pots of rows of pots	total number ÷ total number = flowers in of flowers of pots each pot

- Ensure pupils understand how this can be written as a different number sentence: $80 \div (4 \times 10)$.

- Repeat for similar problems, with the emphasis being placed on pupils modelling each strategy physically and describing what they are doing for each step.

- Display the following pairs of calculations:

  $144 \div (6 \times 4) = \underline{}$ and $144 \div 6 \div 4 = \underline{}$

  $100 \div (5 \times 10) = \underline{}$ and $100 \div 5 \div 10 = \underline{}$

  $240 \div (8 \times 5) = \underline{}$ and $240 \div 8 \div 5 = \underline{}$

  $270 \div (3 \times 30) = \underline{}$ and $270 \div 3 \div 30 = \underline{}$

- Point out that the first pair corresponds to Question 1 in the Practice Book. Give pupils time to remind themselves of the word problem that was represented by these sentences and the different approaches that each describes.

- Challenge pupils to write word problems for the other three pairs of calculations. Pupils should not only devise the problem but rehearse how they would describe two ways that each can be solved in.

- As a further extension, ask pupils to come up with one more word problem, this time using numbers of their choice.

Question 2

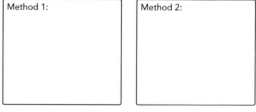

2 Write 2 different number sentences with mixed operations and then calculate.

(a) A toy factory plans to produce 60 teddies per day, with a target to produce 1620 teddies in total. The plan has been carried out for 9 days. How many more days are needed to meet the target?

Method 1:	Method 2:

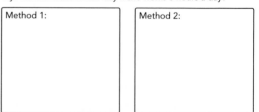

(b) Mrs Lee made 56 toys in 4 hours. At this work rate, how many toys can she make in one day if she works 8 hours a day?

Method 1:	Method 2:

What learning will pupils have achieved at the conclusion of Question 2?

- Pupils will have explored and applied two different strategies when solving problems.

- Number sentences will have been derived from given word problems and then solved.

- Fluency when working with application problems containing mixed operations will have been developed.

Activities for whole-class instruction

- Remind pupils of their previous work calculating and comparing work rates. Ask: *If you wanted to know the efficiency of a factory that makes toy cars, what information might you need to know?* For example, pupils might need to know the total number of toy cars made and divide it by the time taken to make them to find out the number that were produced per day or per week.

- Display the following problem:

  - Jamie reads 75 pages of his book in 3 hours. At this rate, how many pages can he read in a day if he reads for 6 hours a day?

- Ask: *What is Jamie's reading rate?* Ensure pupils see that it is 25 pages per hour or 150 pages per day. Ask: *How do you know?* Discuss the two methods pupils could use:

Strategy 1	Calculations
Total number of pages ÷ total number of hours = pages per hour	75 ÷ 3 = 25 pages per hour
Pages per hour × hours he reads in a day = pages per day	25 × 6 = 150 pages in a day

Strategy 2	Calculations
Number of hours he reads in a day ÷ number of hours he reads 75 pages in = number of 'lots of 75' he reads in a day	6 ÷ 3 = 2 lots of 75 pages read in a day
Total number of pages × the number of 'lots of' those pages in a day = pages read in a day	75 × 2 = 150 pages in a day

- Ask: *How can we write these strategies as number sentences? Where should we use brackets to show which part is completed first?*

- Give pupils further examples to practise exploring different methods:

  - A football player practises 20 penalties each day with the target of kicking 1480 penalties altogether. She has been doing this for 7 days so far. How many more days are needed to reach her target?

- Again, ensure pupils can explain each step of the methods they suggest and write these as number sentences with mixed operations.

- Pupils should now complete Question 2 in the Practice Book.

Same-day intervention

- Display the following problem for pupils to consider:

  - Amy is reading a book with 340 pages. She plans to read 20 pages every day. Her plan has been carried out for 5 days. How many more days does she need to finish the book?

- Ask: *What information do we need to find the answer?* Encourage pupils to describe in words what they need to do (e.g. divide the number of pages in the book by 20 to see how many days it will take her, then subtract 5 from this number to see the number of days she has left). Ask: *How could we draw this as a tree diagram?* Label parts of the diagram that pupils derive:

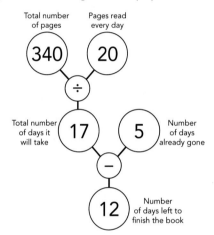

- Elicit that this can be written as 340 ÷ 20 − 5. Ask: *Can you think of another method we could use to find the answer?* Prompt pupils if necessary to start by working out the number of pages read already. Show how this can be modelled as:

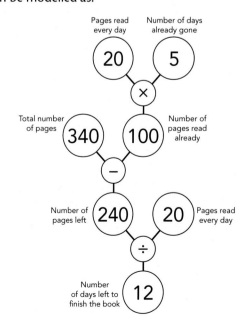

- Show how this can be written as $(340 - 20 \times 5) \div 20$. Ask: *What do you notice about the two methods? Which would you choose if you were asked a similar question? Why?*
- Repeat for further questions if time allows.

Same-day enrichment

- Set pupils a 10 second challenge – for example, how many times can you flip a coin in 10 seconds? Pupils should predict the rate at which they can flip a coin and then ask a partner to time them so that they find an actual rate.
- They should then use the information they have garnered to write their own rate-based problems. For example:
  - I thought I would be able to flip a coin at a rate of 4 every 10 seconds. My actual score was 3 every 10 seconds. At my new 'flip rate', how many fewer times will I be able to flip the coin in 1 minute than I originally thought?
- Pupils should explore different ways to find the answers to their rate-based problems. For example, in the above example, they could find the answer in the following ways:

Method 1:

$4 - 3 = 1$ (to find the difference between the predicted and actual rates)

$60 \div 10 = 6$ (to find the number of 10 seconds in a minute)

$1 \times 6 = 6$ (to find the overall difference in a minute)

Number sentence: $60 \div 10 \times (4 - 3)$

Method 2:

$4 \times 6 = 24$ (to find the total number of planned flips in a minute)

$3 \times 6 = 18$ (to find the total number of actual flips in a minute)

$24 - 18 = 6$ (to find the difference between the planned and actual)

Number sentence: $4 \times 6 - 3 \times 6 = 6$

- Pupils should share their rate-based problems for peers to solve.

Question 3

> **3** Application problems.
>
> (a) A storybook has 460 pages. Errol read 120 pages in the first 6 days. At this pace, how many more days are needed for him to finish reading the whole book?
>
> Answer: _____
>
> (b) A landscape company plans to complete the lawn treatment for the 82 800 square metres of lawns at a botanic garden in 60 working days. According to this plan, how many square metres of the lawns are still to be treated after 44 working days?
>
> Answer: _____
>
> (c) A road construction team was repairing a 4920-metre road. They repaired 2400 metres in 20 days. At this work rate, after how many more days would the team finish the job?
>
> Answer: _____
>
> (d) Four workers can produce 100 TV parts in five hours. At this work rate, how many workers are needed to produce 600 TV parts in 8 hours?
>
> Answer: _____

What learning will pupils have achieved at the conclusion of Question 3?

- Number sentences will have been derived from given word problems and then solved.
- An understanding of problem-solving strategies as a series of purposeful steps will have been developed and described.
- Fluency when working with application problems containing mixed operations will have been developed.

Activities for whole-class instruction

- Display the following problem:
  - Isla is trying to save £350. She manages to save £150 in the first 6 weeks. If she carries on saving at the same rate, how many more weeks are needed to save the entire £350?
- Ask: *Which operations will you need to use to find the answer?*

- Ask pupils to draw a set of stairs on their whiteboard and write each step that is needed to solve the problem. For example:

Step 1: Start with the amount Isla has saved already and divide it by 6 to find the rate she is saving (per week).

Step 2: Subtract 150 from 350 to find out how much money Isla still needs to save to get to £350.

Step 3: Divide the amount she still has to save by the rate she saves each week to find the number of weeks she has left.

150 ÷ 6 = £25 per week

350 – 150 = £200 left to go

200 ÷ 25 = 8 weeks left

- Ask: *How can you write your strategy as a number sentence?* The above example can be written as (350 – 150) ÷ (150 ÷ 6).

- Ask: *Did anyone use the same strategy? Did anyone use a different strategy? What steps did you take?* Although pupils should not be required to generate more than one strategy, it is important that time is given to share their methods and draw attention to the different ways they have arrived at the same solution.

- Provide pupils with further application problems to answer, describing their strategies as a series of steps, a series of calculations and finally as a number sentence. Problems might include:

  - The passport office has a pile of 3000 passports to send out. They manage to send out 1200 in 20 days. At this work rate, after how many more days will they have sent out all the passports?

  - Four farm workers can pick 60 punnets of strawberries in 3 hours. At this work rate, how many farm workers are needed to pick 150 punnets in 5 hours?

- Pupils should now complete Question 3 in the Practice Book.

Same-day intervention

- Use bar models to help pupils visualise problems involving efficiency. Display the following problem:

  - 100 miles of train track need to be laid and two companies say they can do the job.

    FastTrack will complete 20 miles of track every week.

    RapidRail says that it will complete 5 more miles every week than FastTrack.

    How much quicker can RapidRail finish the job?

- Establish three things that pupils need to know:

  1. the number of weeks it will take FastTrack to lay 100 miles of track

  2. the number of weeks it will take RapidRail to lay 100 miles of track

  3. the difference between 1 and 2.

- Ask: *Do you expect RapidRail to take more or fewer weeks altogether than FastTrack. Why?*

- Ask: *How can we work out the number of weeks it will take FastTrack to lay 100 miles? Can you draw a bar diagram to show this?* Establish that this is a division question and can be shown as follows:

100				
20	20	20	20	20

100 ÷ 20 = 5 weeks

- Ask: *How can we work out the number of weeks it will take RapidRail to lay 100 miles? Can you draw another bar diagram to show this?*

100			
25	25	25	25

100 ÷ 25 = 4 weeks

- Finally, refer pupils back to the list of the three things they needed to find out. Ask: *How much quicker can RapidRail finish the job?*

- Encourage pupils to consider what a more efficient work rate looks like on a bar model (same total, fewer bars along the bottom, each with higher value). If time allows, give them further opportunities to model simple efficiency problems in this way.

Same-day enrichment

- Challenge pupils to solve the following open-ended problem:

  - Kyle has a total of 240 points on a computer game. He has completed 10 levels and has scored the same number of points on each level.

- Charlotte has also got a total of 240 points and has scored the same number of points on each level. However, she is a better player because she has completed fewer levels. What are the different numbers of levels Charlotte might have completed? For each number of levels that she might have completed, work out the number of points she must have scored.

- Pupils should work out the answer using whatever method they find most useful and should compare their answers with peers. They should then devise a similar problem, considering how they can alter the numbers so that it still makes sense.

Challenge and extension questions

Questions 4 and 5

4 Alice needs to type up a 4800-word story. She types 1800 words in the first 2 hours. Then she gets tired and her typing speed falls to 400 words less every hour.

Ben is also typing up a 4800-word story. His typing speed is a constant 600 words every hour. Which of these statements is true?

A. Alice finishes first.

B. Ben finishes first.

C. They both take the same time.

5 A school bought 20 desks and 40 chairs at a total cost of £2400. The cost of 1 desk was equal to the cost of 3 chairs. How much each did a desk and a chair cost respectively?

Answer: _____

Pupils are given two questions to extend their problem-solving skills. The first requires them to calculate the typing work rate of two authors, comparing the time they will take to complete a given story. Additional difficulty is provided for in this challenge by the fact that the typing rate of one of the authors changes. Pupils need to incorporate this change in their answer, working out the time taken at both speeds and combining to find the overall time.

The second problem asks pupils to calculate the individual costs of a desk and a chair where they are given the total cost of a set of 20 desks and 40 chairs and the relationship between them (1 desk = 3 chairs). Pupils can find the answer by allocating a simple value to the cost of a chair (the simplest value is £1) and then work from this to find out how much 20 desks and 40 chairs will cost. Pupils can then use this answer to adjust the original price (using division to see how many £100s are in the total cost of £2400 and using this information to alter the prices).

Unit 10.17
Problem solving using four operations (3)

Conceptual context

This unit continues to develop the theme of 'real-life' problems where pupils need to apply their knowledge of all four operations in order to solve them. Pupils will become increasingly aware of the need to read problems slowly and carefully before attempting these problems as the scenarios are more complex than in the previous unit and mostly involve three steps. It is important that pupils continue to practise recording calculations as three-step number sentences and, where appropriate, three-operation tree diagrams. This allows them to consolidate their knowledge of the order of operations, applying this concept in a meaningful problem-solving context. Pupils will need to use brackets to denote the order in which the three operations should be carried out.

Learning pupils will have achieved at the end of the unit

- The particular skill of using division to derive unit costs from a given quantity and its cost will have been practised (Q1)
- Further opportunities to apply knowledge of the four operations when solving problems will have been provided (Q1, Q2)
- Pupils will have continued to develop their reasoning skills, explaining how they arrived at a particular solution (Q2)

Resources

mini whiteboards; examples of food and drink in multipacks; manipulatives (plastic counters, beads, cubes); **Resource 4.10.17a** 'Use your brain' shop; **Resource 4.10.17b** Blotted out!

Vocabulary

unit price, rate, tree diagram

Question 1

> **1** A 'use your brain' shop never simply tells its customers the unit price of each item it sells. If you want to buy something, you are first expected to use your brain to think mathematically.
>
> This table shows the information about the cost and quantity of purchase for some of the items it sells.
>
> | Items | Pencil | Eraser | Pen | Pencil box |
> |---|---|---|---|---|
> | Quantity of purchase | 8 | 3 | 5 | 10 |
> | Cost | £16 | £12 | £25 | £270 |
>
> (a) Aaron wants to buy 10 pencils; how much does he need to pay?
>
> Answer: _____
>
> (b) Ms Akintola wants to buy pencil boxes for 36 pupils, 1 pencil box for each person. How much does she need to pay?
>
> Answer: _____
>
> (c) Yee wants to buy 2 erasers and 3 pens. How much does he need to pay?
>
> Answer: _____
>
> (d) Asha wants to buy 4 pencils and 2 erasers. How much does she need to pay?
>
> Answer: _____

What learning will pupils have achieved at the conclusion of Question 1?

- The particular skill of using division to derive unit costs from a given quantity and its cost will have been practised.
- Further opportunities to apply knowledge of the four operations when solving problems will have been given.

Activities for whole-class instruction

- Prior to the activity, collect several packs of food (or other objects) in clearly labelled multipacks – where possible in a variety of group sizes. Allocate prices to these packs so that they are divisible by the number of items in them (prices do not need to be realistic!).
- For example:

- Explain that, in this shop, items are sold in multipacks; they are also sold individually by splitting up the multipacks. Ask: *If the cans of lemonade are split up and sold individually, how much should a single can cost? How did you work out the answer?* Establish that, to find the individual prices, pupils should divide the pack price by the number of items in the pack.
- Ask: *If I want to buy 9 mini breakfast cereals how would I find out the price?* Give pupils time to share their ideas. They should divide the price of the pack by the number of cereals in it to find the price of an individual pack and then multiply by 9 to find the total cost for 9 boxes. Ask: *How could you show this as a tree diagram? What about a number sentence?*
- Ask further single-step and multi-step problems based on the items in your 'shop'. Pupils can role-play these scenarios and then discuss the strategies they would use to find the answers:
  - *Year 4 are having a party and will need to buy enough crisps for everyone to have a packet. How much will it cost to buy packets for everyone.*
  - *Someone wants to buy two chocolate bars and three cans of fizzy pop. How much should they be charged?*
  - *I have £15. Do I have enough money to buy five boxes of cereal and two packets of crisps? Why/why not?*
- For each problem, ask pupils to sketch each method as a tree diagram and then as a number sentence containing mixed operations (using brackets where they are appropriate).
- Pupils should now complete Question 1 in the Practice Book.

Same-day intervention

- Begin by giving pupils further practice at calculating a unit price when they are given the quantity in a pack and the cost of that pack. For example, show pupils three exercise books and explain that they cost £21 altogether. Ask: *How would you find out how much each book costs?*
- Pupils should recognise that they need to calculate 21 ÷ 3. Ask them to then model the answer as a bar model.

£21		
£7	£7	£7

- Ask further questions, such as: *A pack of ten rulers costs £40 altogether. How much does one ruler cost? Three rulers? Seven rulers?*

- Challenge pairs to design their own 'Use your brain' shops. Provide them with a copy of **Resource 4.10.17a** 'Use your brain' shop to set the task and give pupils initial ideas.

Resource 4.10.17a

'Use your brain' shop

In a 'Use your brain' shop the prices need to be worked out before you can pay!
Design your own shop by making up <u>nine</u> different items to sell. Instead of writing the prices, you could:
1. give a price for a pack so that the customer needs to do some maths to find out what different amounts cost
   (for example, a pack of 5 pens that costs £6.00. How much do 4 pens cost?)
2. give a price that is based on the price of something else
   (for example, a pack of pencils that is labelled 'Half the price of 5 pens'.)
3. give a price that is written as a calculation:
   (for example, a book that is labelled 'three-quarters of £12.00').
Once you have invented your nine items, use them to ask your friends questions based on them.
For an extra challenge, include challenges that involve calculating in pounds and pence.

- **Resource 4.10.17a** provides ideas for pupils to use when creating the prices for the items in their shop. Ensure pupils work through their statements to check that they make numerical sense before setting challenges for their peers to answer.

- To add an extra layer of challenge, pupils can choose prices that involve calculating in pounds and pence.

Question 2

2 Application problems.

(a) A company needed to assemble a batch of computers. 120 computers were assembled in the first 8 working days. At this rate, 24 more working days were needed to finish the job. How many computers did the company need to assemble?

Answer:

(b) An arts and crafts manufacturer planned to produce 680 crafts items. It had produced 65 crafts items per day for the first 4 days. The remaining items needed to be produced in the next 6 days. How many items did it need to produce each day?

Answer:

(c) A new motorway is under construction. 240 km of it has been completed. The remaining part is 8 km longer than twice the completed part. What is the total length of the new motorway?

Answer:

(d) There are 150 apple trees in an orchard. There are 50 more pear trees than apple trees. The number of orange trees is 20 fewer than 3 times the number of pear trees. How many orange trees are there in the orchard?

Answer:

What learning will pupils have achieved at the conclusion of Question 2?

- Further opportunities to apply knowledge of the four operations when solving problems will have been provided.
- Pupils will have continued to develop their reasoning skills, explaining how they arrived at a particular solution.

Activities for whole-class instruction

- Explain to pupils that they will now be working with problems that all require multiple steps to find the answer. Ask: *What is the best way to make sure that you know the steps that need to be done and keep track of them as you work out each answer?*
- Share suggestions, which might include writing down a plan of what needs to be done, describing what needs to be done to a friend, recording the steps as a tree diagram or as a number sentence containing mixed operations.
- Display the following problem:
  - A school uniform company has been asked to provide sweatshirts for the whole school. They manage to produce 80 in the first 4 working days. 8 more working days are needed to complete the job. How many pupils are in the school?

- Ask pupils to discuss in pairs what steps they should work through to find the answer. For example:

  1. Add the number of days taken so far to the number of days left to find the total number of days it will take.

  2. Find the work rate by dividing the number produced already by the number of days taken to make them.

  3. Multiply the total number of days (the answer to step 1) by the work rate (the answer to step 2) to find the total number of sweatshirts needed and, therefore, the number of pupils in the school.

- Ask: *How could you sketch this as a tree diagram? What about as a number sentence?* Model these.

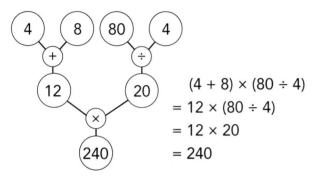

$(4 + 8) \times (80 \div 4)$
$= 12 \times (80 \div 4)$
$= 12 \times 20$
$= 240$

- Ensure that pupils are able to explain how to use brackets to ensure that the number sentence is one where the addition is completed first, then the division, then the multiplication. Write it without brackets and ensure pupils understand what would happen without them.

- Ask: *Where should brackets be placed to overrule the order of operations?* Share any different strategies pupils may have found. Ask: *How are they different? How are they similar?*

- Provide further multi-step number problems for pupils to solve. For example:

  - A farmer is building a fence around one of his fields. 150 metres of it have already been fixed. The rest of it is 20 m longer than half of the completed part. What is the total length of fence that is used?

  - A boat is in a race that is 390 km long. To begin with, it travels 50 km per day for the first 3 days. To beat the world record, it needs to travel the rest of the distance in 4 days. How many kilometres does it need to travel each day?

- Pupils should now complete Question 2 in the Practice Book.

Same-day intervention

- Encourage pupils to visualise application problems by giving further opportunities to use manipulatives or sketches to represent a scenario before calculating it. Display the following problem:

  - A gardener needs to plant a number of trees before the bad weather comes. 18 trees are planted in the first 6 days. At this rate, 12 more days are needed to finish the job. How many trees does she need to plant in total?

- Go through each sentence in the problem, asking a series of questions to establish understanding and guiding pupils towards a visual representation of the problem:

Problem sentence	Possible questions	Model
A gardener needs to plant a number of trees before the bad weather comes.	Which part of this sentence is not important? What could we use to represent the trees when we model the problem?	
18 trees are planted in the first 6 days.	How can you show this using objects or a sketch? What information can we use this to find out? How would you write this as a calculation? What operation does it show?	18 ÷ 6 = 3
At this rate, 12 more days are needed to finish the job.	At what rate? How many trees will she plant in 12 more days? How would you show this using objects or a sketch? How would you write this as a calculation?	12 × 3 = 36
How many trees does she need to plant in total?	What do you need to do to find the overall total? Go back to the second sentence, step 2. Is there a way to use this to help work out the answer in a different way? [This second question is alluding to the following alternative method: If 18 trees are planted in 6 days and the total number of days is equal to 3 lots of 6 (the original 6 days and then 2 more lots of 6 to represent the 12 more days needed), then 18 × 3 will find the overall total].	18 + 36 = 54

- Collect the various calculations and show how these can be used to derive a single number sentence that represents the entire problem: 18 + 18 ÷ 6 × 12.

- Repeat the activity with similar application problems to help pupils build links between concrete, pictorial and abstract representations. Ensure that these problems consist of simple sentences (each giving a single fact and displayed in a separated layout) to help pupils to work through them systematically. For example:

  – A bridge is being built across a river.

  – 380 m of it have been completed.

  – The part that still needs to be built is 50 m more than twice the part that is completed.

  – How long will the bridge be when it is finished?

- Encourage pupils to underline or highlight the facts that they think are important.

Same-day enrichment

- Provide pupils with copies of **Resource 4.10.17b** Blotted out! which contains a selection of multi-step word problems where the numbers have been blotted out.

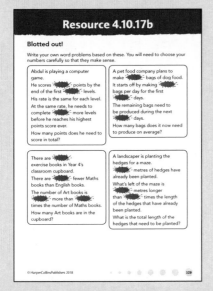

- Pupils should use these to devise their own problems, checking that the numbers they select 'work'. It is this checking process that will enhance pupils' problem-solving skills as they consider the links between the different variables in the problem. Pupils should then share their rewritten problems for peers to solve.

Challenge and extension questions

Questions 3 and 4

3 When Ella was doing an addition problem, she mistakenly read 0 in the ones place in one of the addends as 6 and the digit 2 in its tens place as 5. Therefore, her answer was 156. What is the correct answer?

Answer: _____

4 Jamal and his parents went apple picking in an orchard. They picked 78 apples in total. Dad picked 11 more apples than Mum. Jamal picked 2 fewer apples than Mum. How many apples did each of them pick?

Answer: _____

Pupils extend their problem-solving skills by answering two further questions. Both questions require a degree of logical thinking in order to solve them.

The first question gives the scenario of a pupil who has misread an addition problem, leading her to end up with an incorrect answer. Pupils are given the two errors she has made when reading the ones and units digits and are challenged to use these to find the correct answer. They can do this by taking the misread digits, considering what has been added to them to end with the given answer and then replacing them with the correct digits, altering the answer as appropriate.

The second question gives a total number of apples and asks pupils to divide them between three people according to two clues – these express Jamal's and Dad's totals of apples in relation to Mum's. Mum's total acts as a reference – a central starting point that pupils need to find in order to work out the other two amounts. The strategy pupils need to use here is to use the clues to adjust the overall total (by −11 and +2) so that each person's amount is now the same. They can then use division to find Mum's total, which they can then use as a starting point to find the two remaining totals.

Unit 10.18
Problem solving using four operations (4)

Conceptual context

This unit is the final one of four that consolidate problem-solving skills using all four operations. As it is the last unit in the chapter and the book, it also provides opportunities for general consolidation. Pupils should put into practice all they have learned about calculating using four operations – when to use them, in what order, using what strategies and according to what laws. Each problem involves multiple steps, which pupils should now be able to identify and calculate efficiently.

Learning pupils will have achieved at the end of the unit

- Problem-solving skills involving the four operations will have been extended to deal with more complex multi-step problems (Q1, Q2)
- Pupils will have compressed the steps involved in answering a problem into a single number sentence (Q1)

Resources

mini whiteboards; **Resource 4.10.18a** Question cards; **Resource 4.10.18b** At the airport

Vocabulary

number sentence, order of operations, rate, per, tree diagram

Question 1

> **1** Application problems.
>
> (a) In a printer's, 160 newspapers are printed in 8 minutes on its production line. Assuming the same rate, how many minutes would it take for 600 newspapers to be printed?
>
> Answer: _____
>
> (b) 126 tiles of the same size have been used to cover a 9 square metre floor. If 12 more square metres need to be covered, how many tiles are used altogether?
>
> Answer: _____
>
> (c) Dillon borrowed a 255-page science book from his school library. He planned to finish reading the book in a week. He read 37 pages per day in the first 5 days. He wanted to read the remaining pages over the weekend. How many pages did he still need to read each day?
>
> Answer: _____
>
> (d) A car can drive 60 km in 30 minutes. At this speed, how many kilometres can the car drive in 7 hours?
>
> Answer: _____

What learning will pupils have achieved at the conclusion of Question 1?

- Problem-solving skills involving the four operations will have been extended to deal with more complex multi-step problems.
- Pupils will have compressed the steps involved in answering a problem into a single number sentence.

Activities for whole-class instruction

- Explain to pupils that they are going to put into practice all they have learned on the subject of solving problems with four operations. Split pupils into pairs and give each pair a question card from **Resource 4.10.18a** Question cards. The questions relate to the various elements of solving problems with more than one operation and should act as a revision tool.

Resource 4.10.18a

Question cards

What is the first thing you think you should do when you are given a word problem?	What is the best way you know of remembering the order of operations?
What is the order of operations? Does it always stay the same?	A calculation has an addition and a subtraction in it. Which should you work out first?
Why do some number sentences have brackets and some do not?	How would you explain the order of operations to someone who has difficulty remembering it?
Are there any calculations where it doesn't matter which way around the numbers go? How do you know?	A calculation has a division and an addition in it. Is it always true to say that the division should be worked out first?
How do you know what to do to solve a word problem?	What methods do you find most helpful to help you understand what a problem is asking?

330 © HarperCollinsPublishers 2018

- Give time for each pair to consider their question and decide on an answer. Call the class back together and ask each pair to share their questions and answers. Ask the class to respond in case they have anything further to add.

- Display the following problem for pupils to consider:
  - A bird catches 30 worms in 10 minutes to feed its chicks. If the bird continues at the same rate, how many minutes would it take for it to catch 72 worms?

- Ask: *What do you need to find out in order to solve the problem?* Establish that pupils need to identify what the 'worm-catching rate' is and then use this to find out how long it would take to catch 72 worms. Allow pupils time to work independently and then share their answers as a class. Ask: *How many steps did it take to work out the answer? What was the worm-catching rate? How would you write your method as a number sentence?*

- Agree that it can be written as 72 ÷ (30 ÷ 10), in other words:

  the total number of worms caught ÷ (the worm-catching rate) = the time taken

- Extend pupils' learning by asking them how many minutes it would take the bird to catch 72 worms if the rate increased to 4 worms per minute.

- Further examples might include the following:
  - 140 vehicles cross over a river bridge every 7 minutes. If this rate stays the same, how many minutes will it take for 640 vehicles to cross the river?
  - Molly's dad is laying a patio. He uses 96 paving slabs to cover an area of 8 square metres. If another 2 more square metres need to be paved, how many slabs will be used altogether?
- For each example, pupils should not only answer the question, but represent the problem and solution as a number sentence that best depicts the method they have used.
- Pupils should now complete Question 1 in the Practice Book.

Same-day intervention

- Write the following two-sentence framework on the board:

  'First I … to find …'

  'Then I … to find …'
- Explain that these sentences can be used to explain the steps involved in solving a problem. Each step begins with the maths that has been done ('First I multiplied 10 by 4 …') and then importantly also explains why ('… to find out how many apples there were altogether').
- Display the following problem:
  - A recycling machine sorts through 20 plastic bottles in 4 seconds. If the rate stays the same, how many seconds does it take to sort through 75 bottles?
- Ask pupils to work in pairs, drawing large speech bubbles on their whiteboards. They should write, 'First I …' and 'Then I …' sentences to explain their methods. For example:

> First I divided 20 by 4 to find the number of bottles the machine sorts through per second.

> Then I divided 75 by the answer (which is 5) to find the time it takes to sort through 75 bottles.

- Use their answers to construct the accompanying number sentence – in this case 75 ÷ (20 ÷ 4) = 15.

- Repeat for further multi-step problems. For example:
  - A vet has 134 animals to vaccinate in a week. She vaccinates 22 animals per day for the first 5 days and then needs to see the rest over the weekend. How many animals does she still need to see each day?
  - The local council uses 24 bags of grass seed to plant 8 football pitches. If 3 more football pitches need to be planted, how many bags of grass seed will be used altogether?

Same-day enrichment

- Provide pupils with a copy of **Resource 4.10.18b** At the airport.

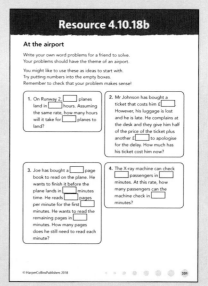

- Pupils should use the airport theme given and the framework questions provided to devise their own two- or three-step questions for peers to solve. As they grow in confidence, pupils should move away from the framework and begin to write their own calculations. When answering each question, pupils should write down their method as a number sentence, checking that it represents the correct order of operations.

Question 2

> 2 Read each problem carefully before working out the answer.
>
> (a) Mrs Chan went shopping with £200. She spent £137 on a set of English books. Pens cost £10 each. What is the largest number of pens she could buy with the money left over?
>
> Answer: _____
>
> (b) Three lorries of the same type can deliver 75 000 kg of goods in 5 trips. A supermarket needs 100 000 kg of goods to be delivered in 2 trips. How many of these lorries does it need?
>
> Answer: _____
>
> (c) 900 kg of rice is delivered to a store. The rice is in 5 more sacks than the flour the store had received earlier. Each sack of rice weighs 30 kg and each sack of flour weighs 25 kg. How many kilograms of flour has the store received?
>
> Answer: _____
>
> (d) A clothing store received a delivery of 480 sweaters, which were packed in 2 plastic boxes and 8 cardboard boxes. If the number of sweaters in 2 cardboard boxes is the same as the number of sweaters in 1 plastic box, how many sweaters are there in each plastic box and how many are in each cardboard box?
>
> Answer: _____

What learning will pupils have achieved at the conclusion of Question 2?

- Problem-solving skills involving the four operations will have been extended to include more complex multi-step problems.

Activities for whole-class instruction

- Remind pupils of the importance of reading through a problem several times in order to decide on the steps that are needed to find the answer. Display the following problem on the board. Explain that the numbers have been removed to allow pupils to think about how to find the answer without considering what it is:
  - In a car factory, _____ identical robots are able to spray _____ cars in _____ hours.
  - The factory owners have a target of being able to spray _____ cars in _____ hours. How many robots do they need?
- Give pupils time to read through the problem more than once and discuss it with a partner. Ask: *Can you use your own words to describe what the problem is asking? Do you have an idea how you might work out the answer?*

- Agree that pupils first need to find the number of cars that one robot can spray in an hour. They can then use this information to decide how many robots are needed to meet the owners' target.
- Complete the problem with the following numbers:
  - In a car factory, 4 identical robots are able to spray 40 cars in 5 hours.
  - The factory owners have a target of being able to spray 30 cars in 3 hours. How many robots do they need?
- Give pupils time to solve the problem in pairs. Share methods, discussing why each step is needed. For example:

Find the number of cars sprayed per hour by 4 robots.	40 ÷ 5 = 8 cars per hour
Find the number of cars sprayed per hour by 1 robot	8 ÷ 4 = 2 cars per hour per robot
Find the number of cars needed to be sprayed every hour in the target	30 ÷ 3 = 10 cars per hour are needed
Find the number of robots needed to meet the target	10 ÷ 2 = 5 robots are needed

- Ask: *How would you write this as a number sentence?* Establish that it can be written as 30 ÷ 3 ÷ (40 ÷ 5 ÷ 4). Go through each step to check that the number sentence matches the steps that have been carried out.
- Provide further complex problems for pupils to work through, using reasoning to explain each step:
  - Tom has £68. He spends £16 on a sweatshirt. If he decides to spend the rest of his money on as many T-shirts as possible costing £8 each, how many T-shirts could he buy?
  - A supermarket has a delivery of 200 tins of tomato soup and some tins of chicken soup. There are four more boxes of tomato soup than chicken soup. If each box of tomato soup contains 20 tins and each box of chicken soup contains 25 tins, how many boxes of chicken soup are delivered to the supermarket?
  - 320 children arrive at a theme park in 6 coaches and 4 minibuses. Each of the vehicles is full. All the coaches hold the same number and all the minibuses hold the same number.

    The number of children on 2 minibuses is the same as the number on 1 coach.

    How many children are on each minibus and how many are on each coach?

233

- Pupils should now complete Question 2 in the Practice Book.

Same-day intervention

- Draw links between concrete, pictorial and abstract representations. Choose two pupils to role-play the following scenario:

  - Pupil A should pretend to be a delivery driver, delivering a batch of football kits to a sports shop. As they 'arrive' at the shop, reveal that they have 80 kits and that they are in 3 plastic boxes and 10 cardboard boxes. As Pupil B begins to mime lifting each box off the lorry, ask if they feel heavy; after all, each plastic box holds twice as many kits as a cardboard box.

- Display the problem using words:

  - A lorry is delivering 80 football kits in 3 plastic boxes and 10 cardboard boxes. Each plastic box holds twice as many kits as a cardboard box. How many kits fit in each type of box?

- Ask: *What are 10 cardboard boxes the same as? How do you know?* Establish that the whole delivery is the same as having 8 plastic boxes. Encourage pupils to sketch or model their working. For example:

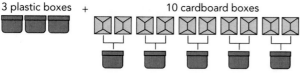

3 plastic boxes   +   10 cardboard boxes

= 8 plastic boxes in total

- Ask: *How can we find out how many kits fit into one plastic box?* Establish that, now that pupils know the equivalence of 10 cardboard boxes in terms of plastic boxes, this is simply 80 ÷ 8.

- Ask: *Now that we know how many kits one plastic box holds, how can we work out how many kits one cardboard box holds?* Encourage pupils to work independently on this step and then share their working.

- Ask pupils to write down the series of calculations that they used to solve the problem and aim to write two number sentences – one for finding the number of kits that fit in a plastic box and one for finding the number of kits that fit into a cardboard box.

Same-day enrichment

- As Question 2 extends pupils' logical as well as numerical skills, provide them with further opportunities to solve problems of the same type. Provide pupils with pieces of card with which to create their own problem cards.

Challenge pupils to rewrite the problems in Question 2, changing whatever elements they wish as well as the numbers. Pupils may also wish to add a further question onto the end of an existing problem. Their newly devised problems should be written on one side of a piece of card, with the answer (and working) written on the reverse. These cards should form a bank of problems for peers to solve.

Challenge and extension questions

Questions 3 and 4

3 If 6 plates and 3 bowls cost £87, and 2 plates and 3 bowls cost £39, then how much does 1 plate cost? How much does 1 bowl cost?

Answer: _____

4 Three children, A, B and C, have 108 pictures in total. Given that Child A has 18 fewer pictures than Child B, and Child C has 12 more pictures than Child B. How many pictures does each child have?

Answer: _____

Pupils are given two problems, both having similarities with algebraic problems pupils will be solving in future years. As such, they provide a useful precursor to algebra.

For Question 3, pupils should be encouraged to write each set of costs as number sentences and then compare the two equations side by side. They should notice that in both calculations there are three bowls being bought – the only difference is four extra plates. Pupils can then use this information to work out the cost of one plate and, from this, the cost of a bowl.

In Question 4, pupils are given a set of clues about the number of pictures that three children (A, B and C) have. The key to solving this problem is understanding that Child B's total is the key number to find out, from which both of the other children's totals can be calculated. Pupils can do this by altering the total number so that every child now has the same number (for example, Child A has 18 fewer pictures than Child B, then by adding 18 to the overall total both children have an equal number). The same strategy can be used for Child C. Once pupils have altered the overall total, they can then use this to derive the number of pictures that Child B has.

Chapter 10 test (Practice Book 4B, pages 154–159)

Test question number	Relevant unit	Relevant questions within unit
1	10.3	2
2	10.11	3
3	10.11	4
	10.12	2
	10.13	4
	10.14	2, 3
4	10.1	2
	10.5	3
	10.6	3
	10.11	1, 2
	10.12	1
	10.13	2
5	10.4	2
	10.13	3
6	10.7	1
	10.8	1
7	10.7	3
	10.8	3
	10.9	1, 2, 3
	10.10	1, 2, 3
8	10.1	1, 2, 3
	10.2	1, 2
	10.5	4
	10.7	4
	10.8	4
	10.12	3
	10.14	4
	10.15	1, 2
	10.16	1, 2, 3
	10.17	1, 2
	10.18	1, 2

Growth of a sunflower graph

Look at this line graph showing the growth of a sunflower and answer the questions.

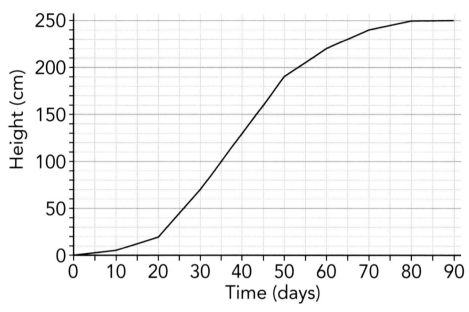

1. What is being measured on the vertical axis?

   _____

2. What numbers are labelled on the vertical axis?

   _____

3. What is being measured on the horizontal axis?

   _____

4. What is the height of the sunflower on:

   ● Day 20? _____   ● Day 40? _____

   ● Day 70? _____

5. Estimate the height of the sunflower on:

   ● Day 25 _____   ● Day 55 _____

6. Why are there no readings before Day 10?

   _____

7. Make up and answer a question of your own.

   _____

Growth of sunflowers in light and shade graphs

Look at this line graph showing the growth of sunflowers in full and partial sunlight and answer the questions.

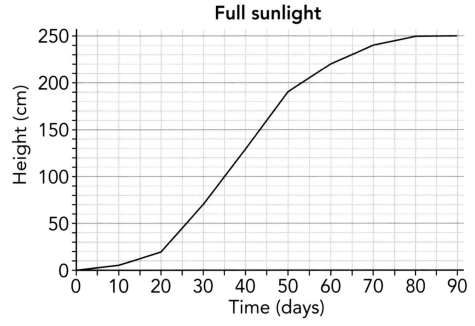

Full sunlight

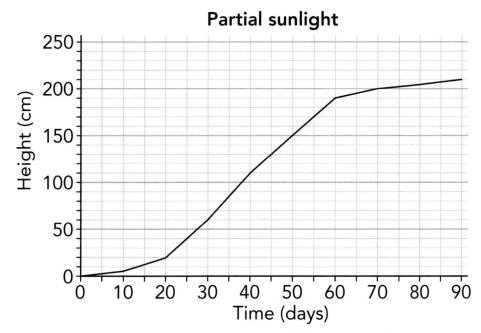

Partial sunlight

1. What is being measured on the vertical axis?

_____

2. What numbers are labelled on the vertical axis? What is a unit worth?

_____

3. What is being measured on the horizontal axis? What is a unit worth?

_____

4. What is the height of the sunflowers on:

- Day 20? Full sunlight _____   Partial sunlight _____

- Day 40? Full sunlight _____   Partial sunlight _____

- Day 70? Full sunlight _____   Partial sunlight _____

5. Estimate the height of the sunflower on:

- Day 25? Full sunlight _____   Partial sunlight _____

- Day 55? Full sunlight _____   Partial sunlight _____

6. Describe the difference between the growth in full and partial sunlight.

_____

7. Why are there no readings before Day 10?

_____

8. Make up and answer a question of your own.

_____

Reading and interpreting line graphs

The four line graphs show the maximum daily temperatures during four consecutive weeks. Cut out the statements. Read each one carefully and match it to the line graph for the correct week. (Three statements match each line graph).

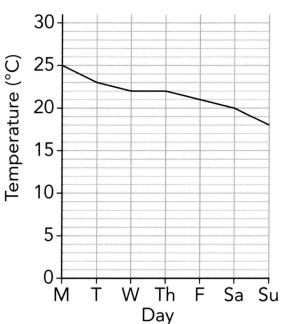

Maximum temperatures during Week 1 (°C)

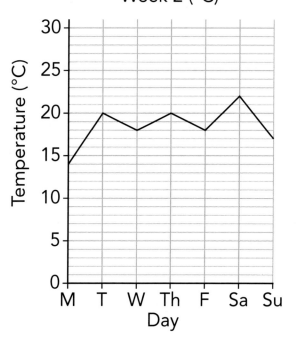

Maximum temperatures during Week 2 (°C)

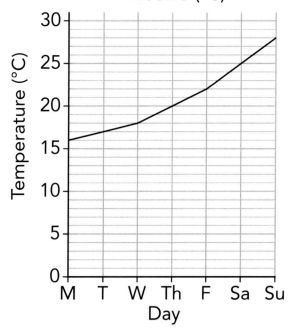

Maximum temperatures during Week 3 (°C)

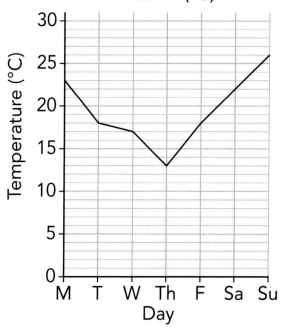

Maximum temperatues during Week 4 (°C)

A
The daily temperatures gradually decrease over the week.

B
The temperature on Tuesday is 20°C.

C
The lowest temperature in this week is 13°C

D
The highest temperature in this week is 28 °C.

E
The temperature on Monday is 25°C.

F
The daily temperatures rise and fall several times over the week.

G
The highest temperature in this week is 25°C.

H
The daily temperatures gradually fall until the middle of the week and then rise.

I
The temperature on Saturday is 25°C.

J
The daily temperatures gradually increase over the week.

K
The lowest temperature in this week is 14°C.

L
The temperature on Thursday is 13°C.

Visitors to Black Castle

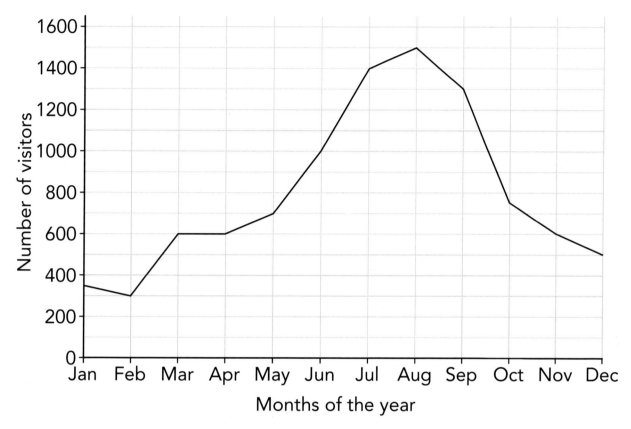

The line graph shows the number of visitors to Black Castle each month.
Study the graph and circle whether the following statements are true or false.

1. There is no downward tendency on the graph.
   TRUE/FALSE

2. The month showing the greatest number of visitors is August.
   TRUE/FALSE

3. There is no change in the number of visitors in February and March.
   TRUE/FALSE

4. The steepest gradient showing the greatest increase in numbers is between May and June.
   TRUE/FALSE

5. The steepest gradient showing the greatest decrease in numbers is between September and October.
   TRUE/FALSE

6. This data could also be represented by a bar chart.
   TRUE/FALSE

Matching graphs

Graph 1
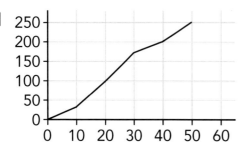

Graph 2
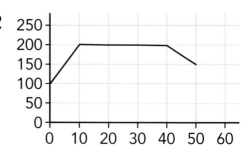

Graph 3
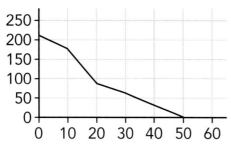

Graph 4
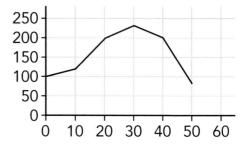

1. Match each letter with the correct graph.

   A – This line graph increases to a maximum value and then decreases. Graph _____

   B – This line graph shows an upward tendency, with values gradually increasing. Graph _____

   C – This line graph shows a downward tendency, with values gradually decreasing. Graph _____

   D – This line graph shows a section where there is no change. Graph _____

2. Sketch four more graphs to match the four statements A–D.

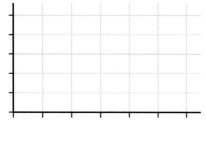
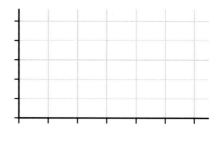
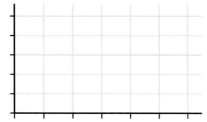
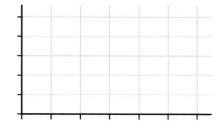

Snowfall in New York and Chicago

Snowfall in New York and Chicago

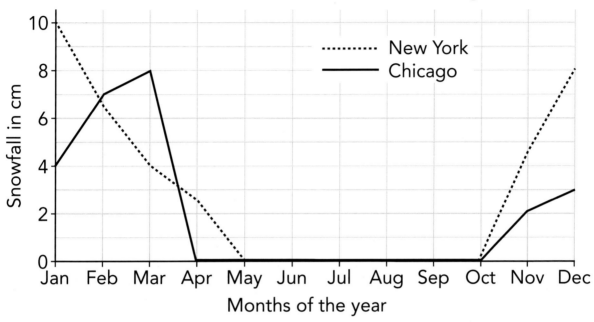

Look carefully at the line graph comparing the snowfall each month in New York and Chicago.

Write five questions about the data shown on the graph for a friend to answer. Try to use the following vocabulary: axis, scale, upward/downward tendency, difference.

Question 1 _____

Answer _____

Question 2 _____

Answer _____

Question 3 _____

Answer _____

Question 4 _____

Answer _____

Question 5 _____

Answer _____

Ice cream sales

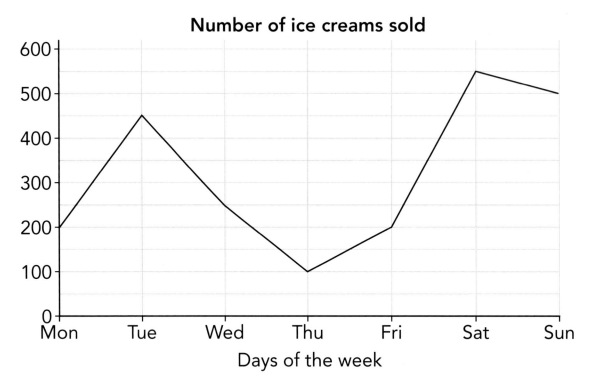

Number of ice creams sold

Days of the week

Look at the line graph and answer the questions.

1. On which two days were the same number of ice creams sold? What number were sold?

    _____

2. How many ice creams were purchased on Wednesday?

    _____

3. Which day during the week has the highest sales? Which has the next highest? Why do you think most ice creams were bought on these two days?

    _____

4. One day was very hot; which day do you think it was? Explain your reasoning.

    _____

5. One day it rained all day; which day do you think that was? Explain your reasoning.

    _____

Temperatures in London and Sydney

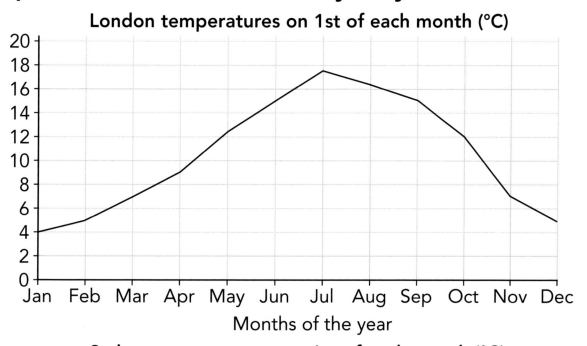

London temperatures on 1st of each month (°C)

Months of the year

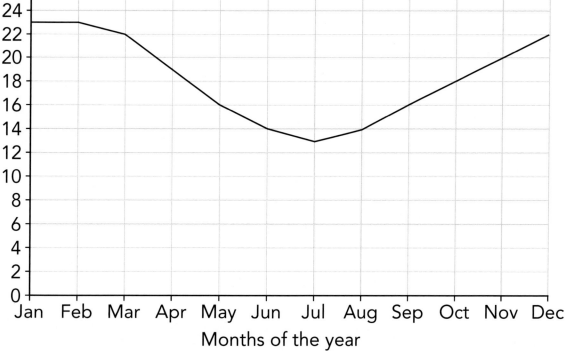

Sydney temperatures on 1st of each month (°C)

Months of the year

The line graphs show the temperatures on the first day of each month in London and Sydney.

1. Describe the trends shown in each graph.

_____

_____

2. Why do the two graphs show opposite trends?

_____

3. Make up three questions comparing the two graphs. Try to include the following words: highest, lowest, difference.

_____

_____

_____

Graphs

1. Three graphs with different scales have been drawn showing the distance travelled by a car over five hours.

   Think about which version is best. Explain your reasoning.

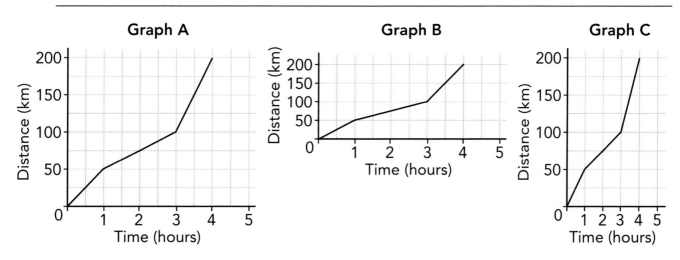

2. Finish marking the axes for these line graphs.

   Graph 1

   Complete the sentences describing the scales.

   The horizontal scale is marked in _____. Each interval is _____.

   The vertical scale is marked in _____. Each interval is _____. A small square on the vertical axis is worth _____.

Graph 2

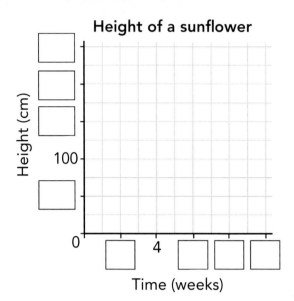

Height of a sunflower

Height (cm)

100

0

4

Time (weeks)

Complete the sentences describing the scales.

The horizontal scale is marked in _____. Each interval is

_____.

The vertical scale is marked in _____. Each interval

is _____. A small square on the vertical axis is worth

_____.

Line graph or bar chart?

1. Look at each set of data and decide whether it would be represented best by a line graph or by a bar chart, or whether both would be effective. Circle your answer.

2. Fill in suitable titles and units for the axes. One has been done for you.

A. Growth of a runner bean plant

line graph / bar chart / (both)

Height (cm)

Number of weeks

B. Favourite colour of 25 children

line graph / bar chart / both

C. Temperature on first day of each month in New York

line graph / bar chart / both

D. Weight of a blue whale from birth to adult

line graph / bar chart / both

E. How pupils travel to school

line graph / bar chart / both

Length of a baby

The table shows the length of a baby at different ages. Look at the data and answer the following questions.

Age (months)	0	3	6	9	12
Length (cm)	20	23	26	28	30

1. What should be plotted on the horizontal axis?

   _____

2. What should be plotted on the vertical axis?

   _____

3. What is the length of the baby at a year old?

   _____

4. Decide on suitable scales for the axes. Use this graph paper grid to draw the graph. Plot the points carefully, with a small dot. Join the points to make a line graph.

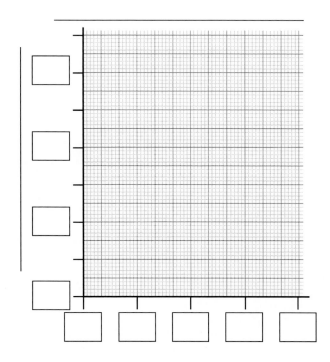

5. Use the graph to estimate the length of the baby at 5 months.

   _____

Some pupils heated a beaker of water in their Science lesson and collected the following data.
Look at the data and answer the following questions.

Time (mins)	0	1	2	3	4	5	6	7	8
Temp. (°C)	20	40	57	75	87	96	100	100	100

1. How many measurements were made? _____

2. How often was the temperature taken? _____

3. What is the highest temperature recorded? _____

4. What should be plotted on the horizontal axis? _____

5. What should be plotted on the vertical axis? _____

6. Decide on suitable scales for the axes and complete the labels, using the prepared graph paper.
   Plot the points carefully, with a small dot.
   Join the points with a ruler to make the line graph.

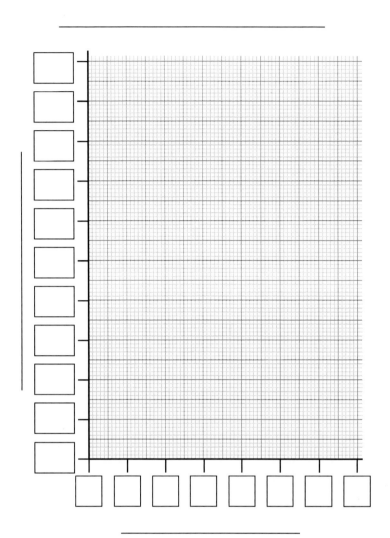

7. Describe the shape of the graph, explaining what is happening.

_____

Identifying angles in buildings

Angles all around us

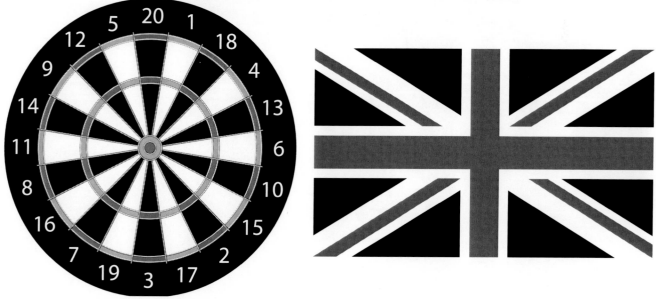

Identifying angles

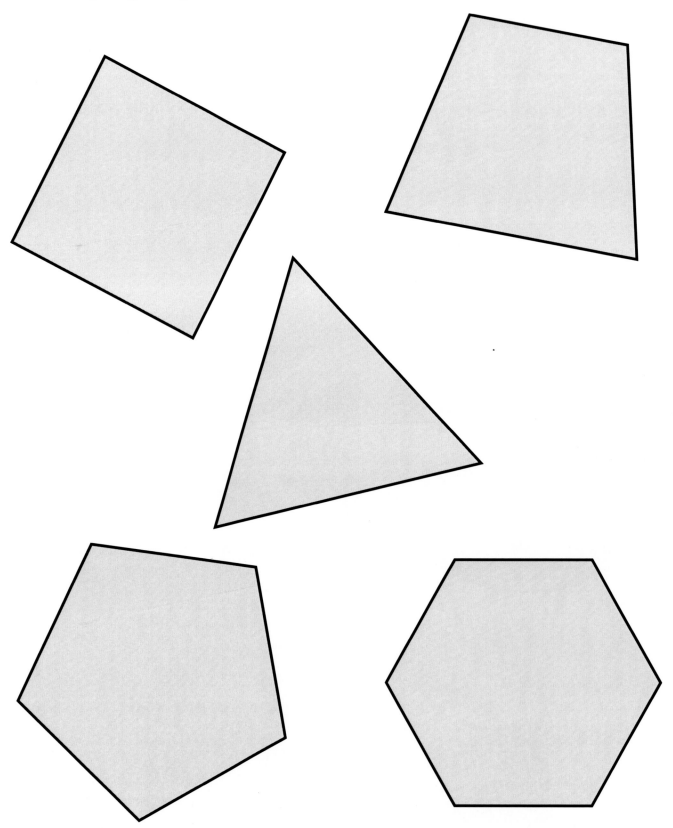

Floor tiles

259

Isometric paper

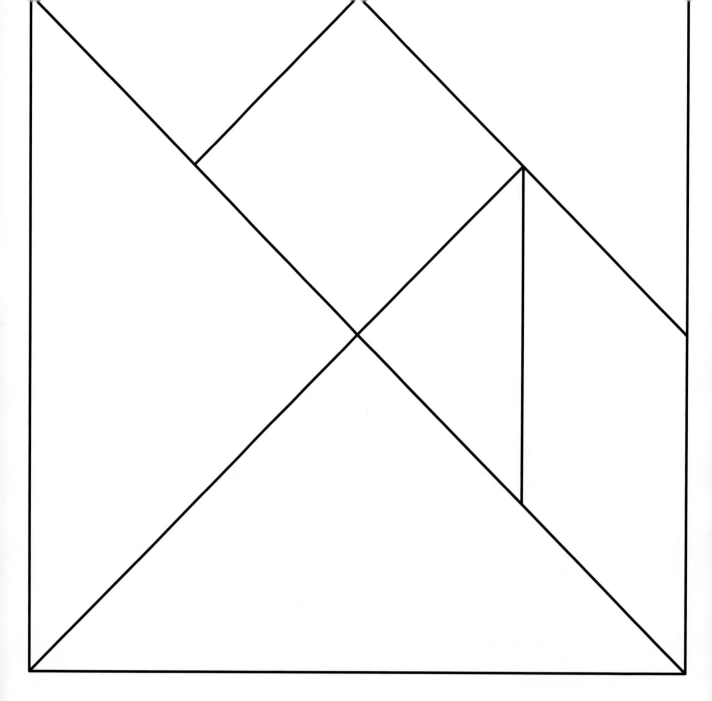

Tangram animals

Tangram duck

Tangram rabbit

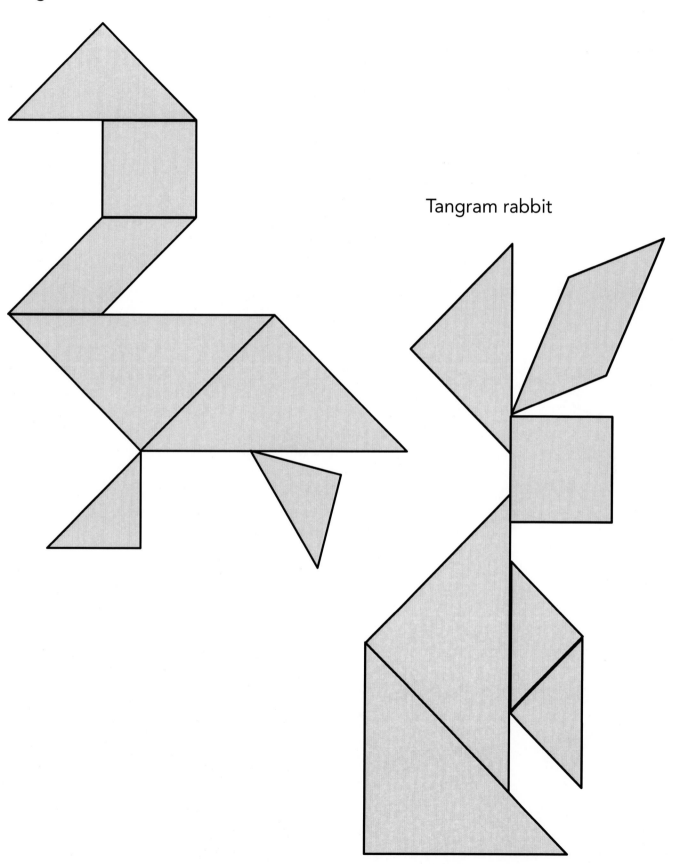

Triangles

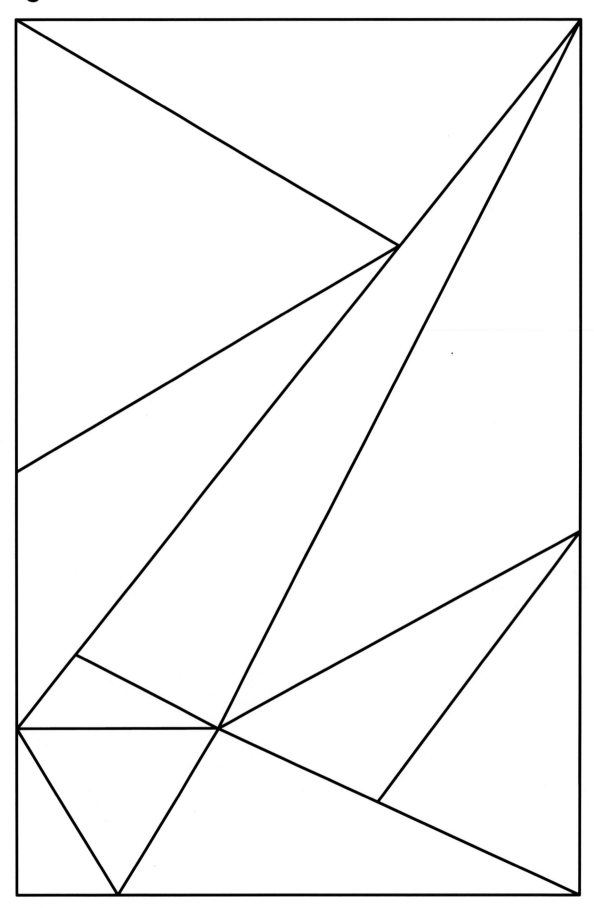

Triangles to sort

Venn diagram

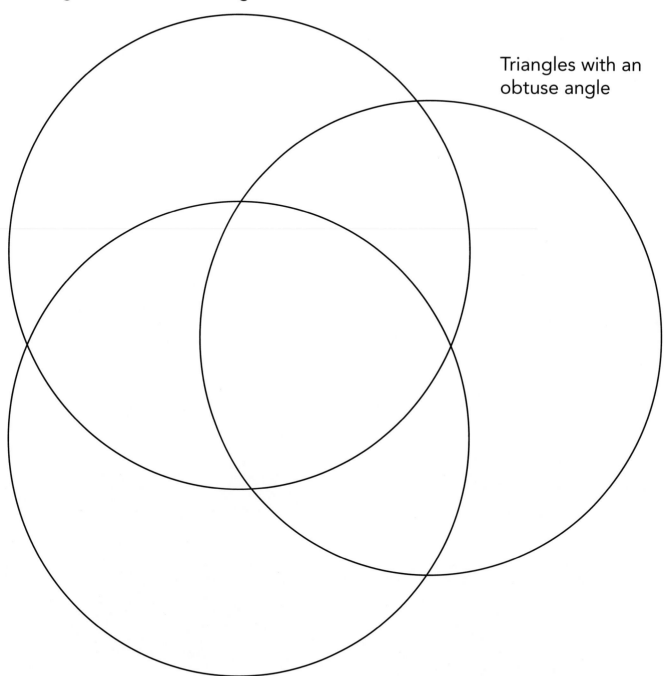

Triangles with an acute angle

Triangles with an
obtuse angle

Triangles with a right angle

How many triangles?

How many triangles can you find?

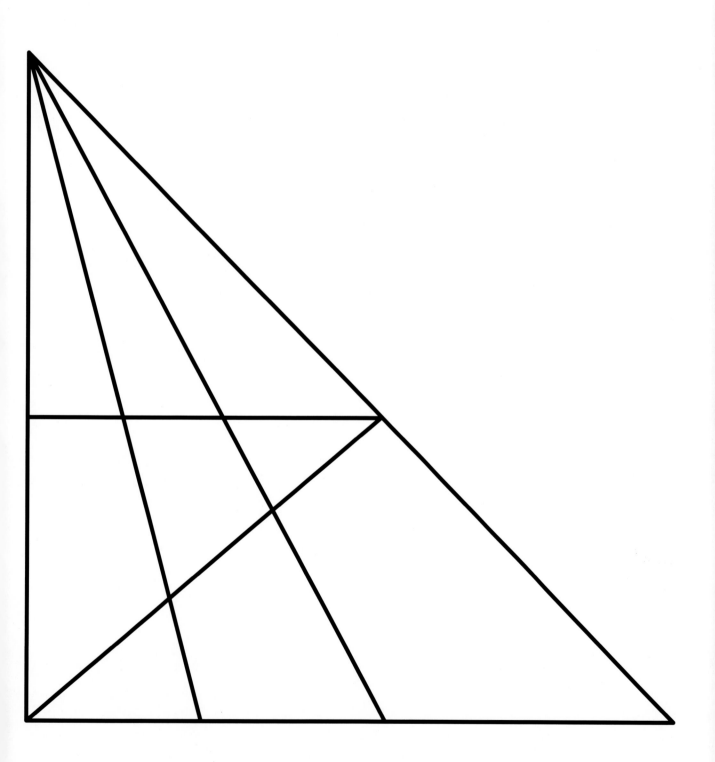

Quadrilaterals to split into triangles

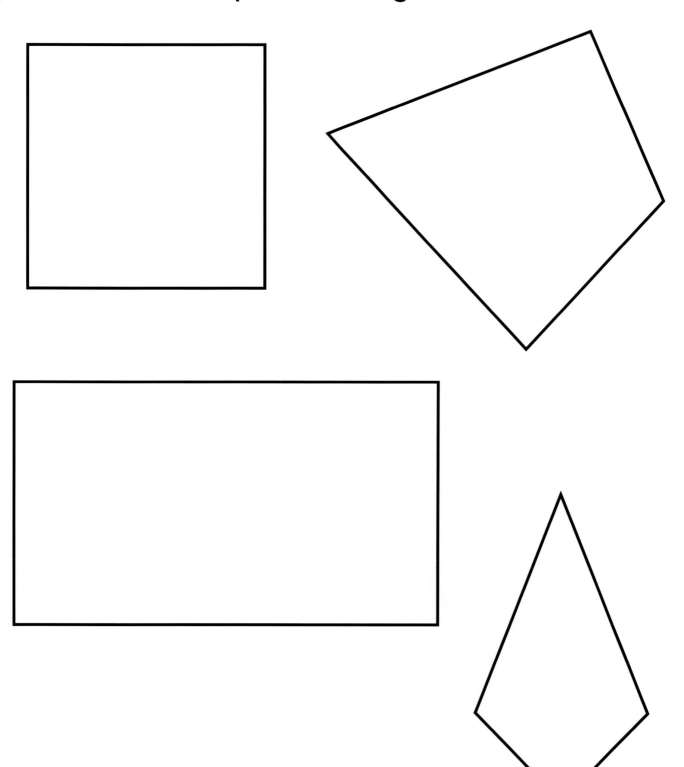

Always, sometimes or never

Obtuse-angled triangles have a right angle	Acute-angled triangles have obtuse angles	A triangle can have 3 obtuse angles
A triangle can have one right angle, one obtuse angle and one acute angle	An obtuse-angled triangle can have 2 equal angles	Triangles must have the point at the top
All 3 sides of an acute-angled triangle are the same length	2 triangles can be put together to make a square	Obtuse-angled triangles have 2 acute angles

Triangle diagram

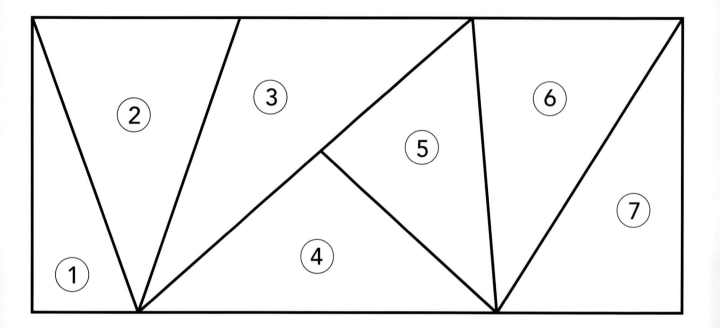

Combining triangles and exploring angles

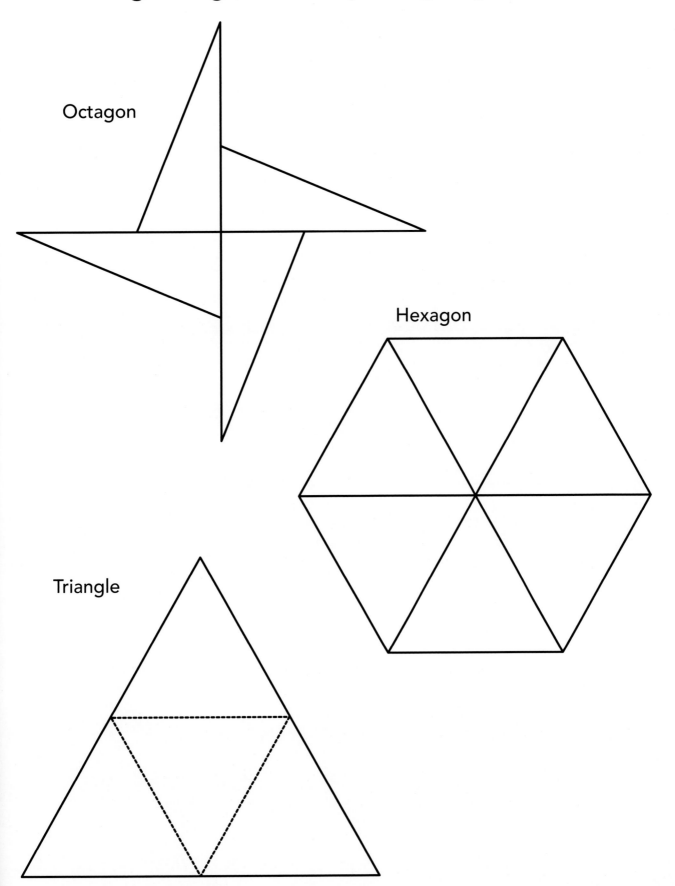

Octagon

Hexagon

Triangle

How many triangles?

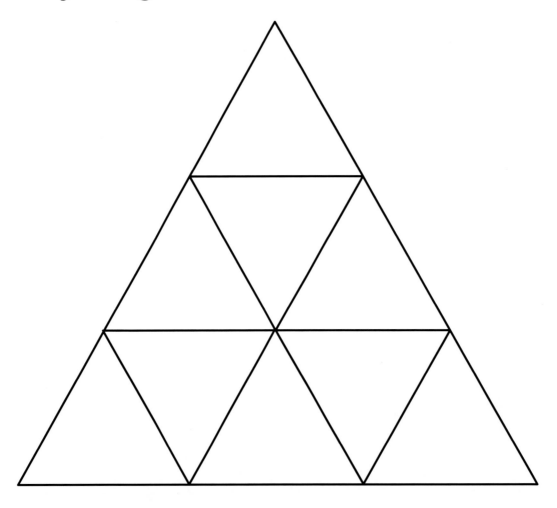

Shapes to demonstrate line symmetry

More shapes to demonstrate line symmetry

Grids to shade

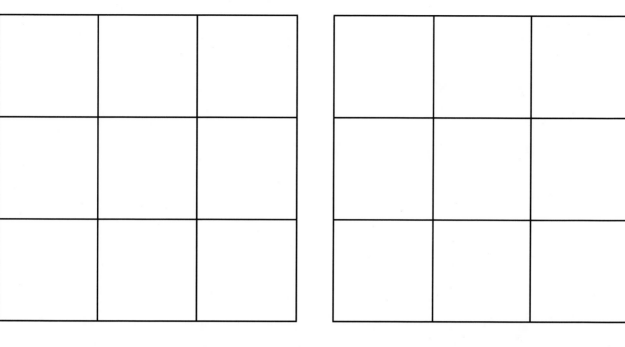

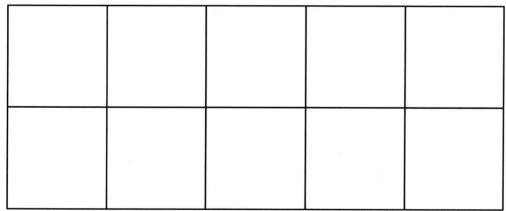

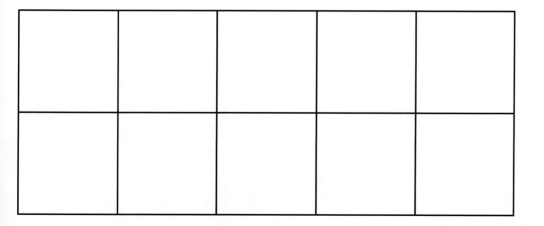

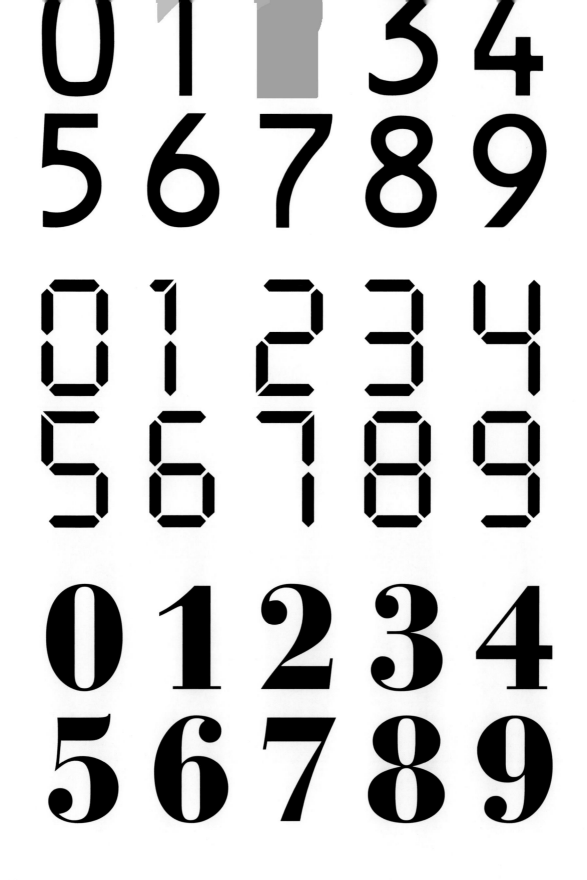

Descriptions of triangles to create

Create a triangle with 3 sides of equal length.	Create a triangle with 2 equal angles but no right angles.
Create a triangle with 1 right angle and 2 equal acute angles.	Create a triangle with sides of different lengths.
Create a triangle with 3 equal angles.	Create a triangle with angles of different sizes.

Triangles in the real world

Identifying triangles within another shape

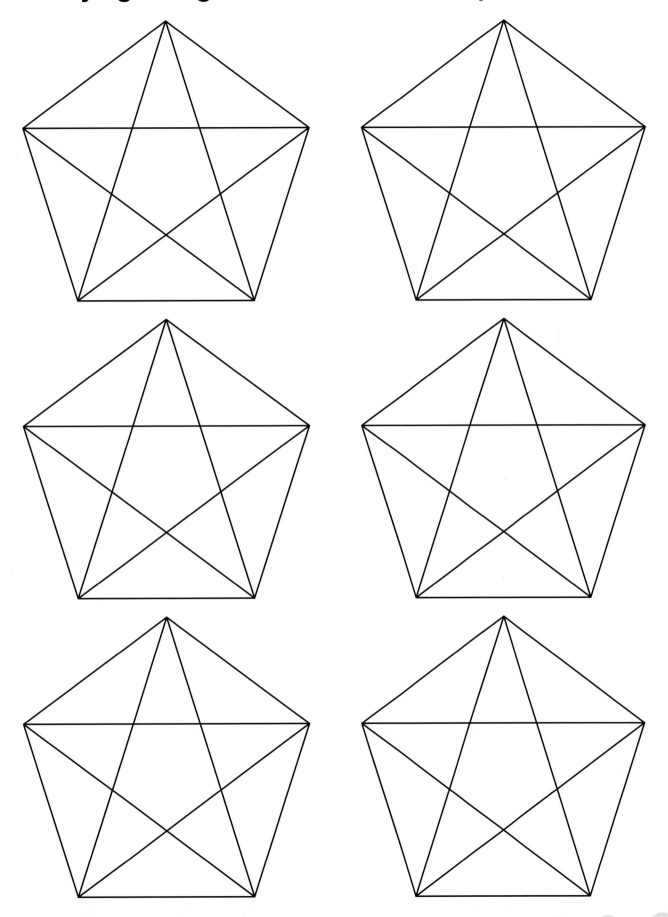

Apartment floor plan

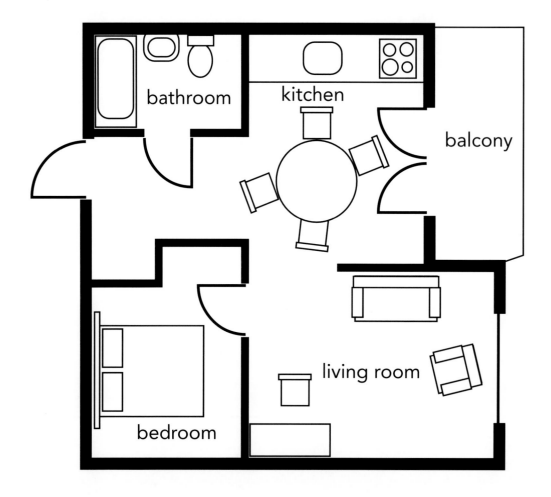

This is the floor plan of an apartment.

● Which units would you use to measure the area of the floor of the bedroom?

● Which units would you use to measure the area of the surface of the bed?

● What else in the flat would be measured in these units?

● Which units would you use to measure the area of the seat of one of the kitchen chairs?

● Which units would you use to measure the size of the television screen?

● What else in the flat would be measured in these units?

Distance

We can represent distances in kilometres and metres, in metres or in kilometres.

Here is an example:

1 km 500 m = 1500 m = 1.5 km

Fill in the missing numbers.

1. 3.25 km = _____ km _____ m = _____ m

2. 2750 m = _____ km _____ m = _____ km

3. 5 km 625 m = _____ km = _____ m

4. 8.48 km = _____ km _____ m = _____ m

5. 9725 m = _____ km _____ m = _____ km

6. 10 km 125 m = _____ km = _____ m

Answer these:

1. Dana drove from London to Oxford. She drove 87.23 km.

How many metres is that? _____ m

How many kilometres and metres is that? _____ km _____ m

2. Dana then drove from Oxford to Coventry. The distance was 90 250 m.

How many kilometres is that? _____ km

How many kilometres and metres is that? _____ km _____ m

3. After this, Dana drove from Coventry to Loughborough. The distance she travelled was 74 km 930 m.

How many metres is that? _____ m

How many kilometres is that? _____ km

	London	Paris	Cairo	New York	Sydney
London		344 km	3510 km	5585 km	16 983 km
Paris	344 km		3209 km	5834 km	16 950 km
Cairo	3510 km	3209 km		9016 km	14 407 km
New York	5585 km	5834 km	9016 km		15 979 km
Sydney	16 983 km	16 950 km	14 407 km	15 979 km	

Distance digit games

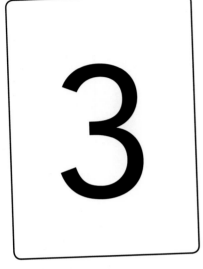 

3 7 8

- Make all the possible 2-digit numbers from these digits.
- Do this systematically so that you know you have them all.
- Write your numbers down on paper.

- Your numbers represent kilometres.
- Take two of your numbers at a time and compare them using the greater than and less than symbols.
- Show what you have done on paper.

- Now make them equal in two ways.
- One way is to add a number to the smaller number. The other way is to subtract a number from the larger number.
- Show what you have done on paper.

Resource 4.9.4a

Perimeters and areas of rectilinear shapes 1

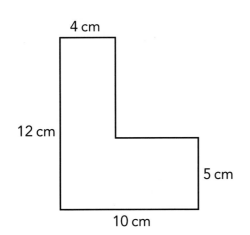

Perimeter: _____

Area: _____

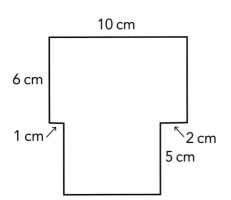

Perimeter: _____

Area: _____

Perimeter: _____

Area: _____

Perimeter: _____

Area: _____

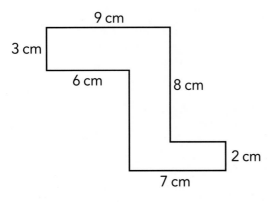

Perimeter: _____

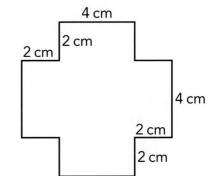

Perimeter: _____

Perimeters and areas of rectilinear shapes 2

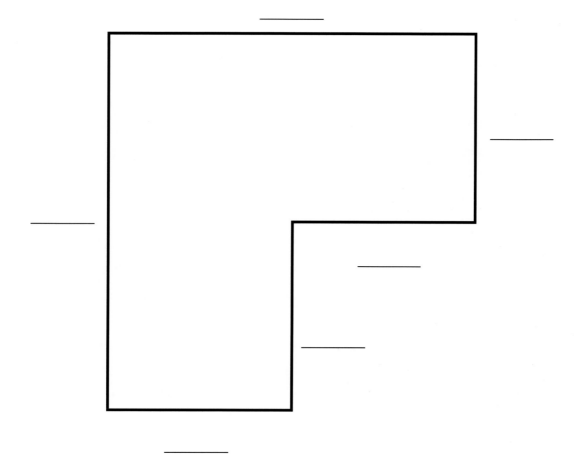

Perimeter: _____
Area: _____

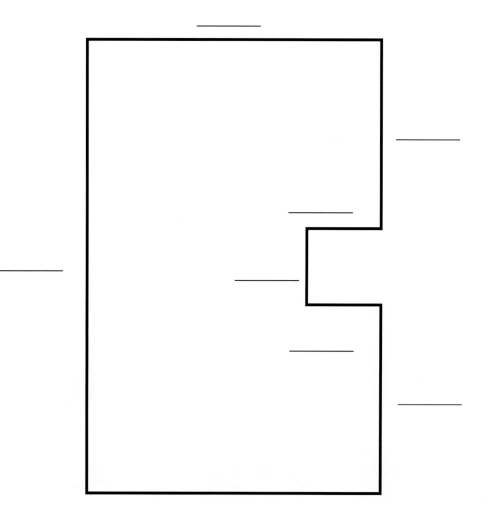

Perimeter: _____

Area: _____

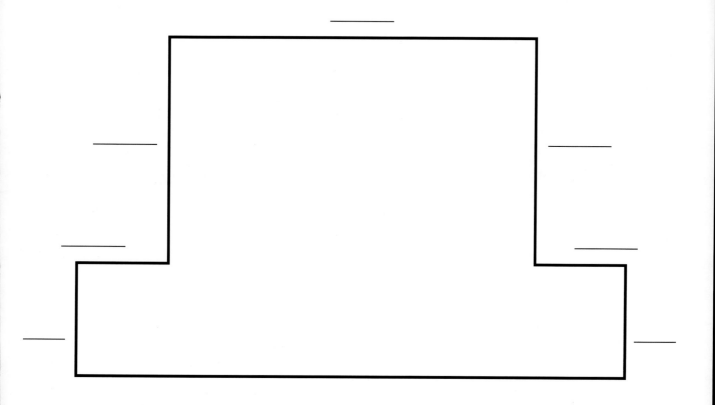

Perimeter: _____   Area: _____

Perimeter: _____
Area: _____

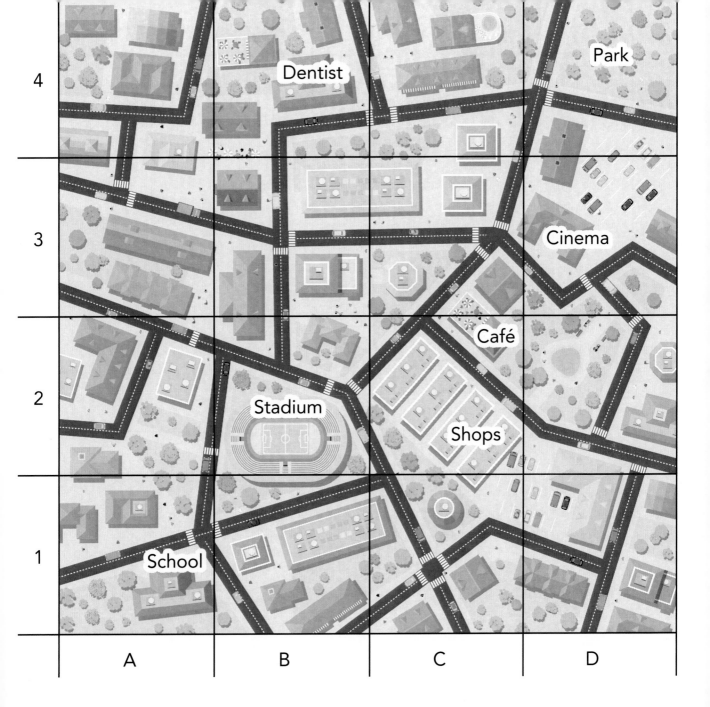

Map of the United Kingdom

© HarperCollins*Publishers* 2018

Coordinate grid (stationery)

World map (numerical coordinates)

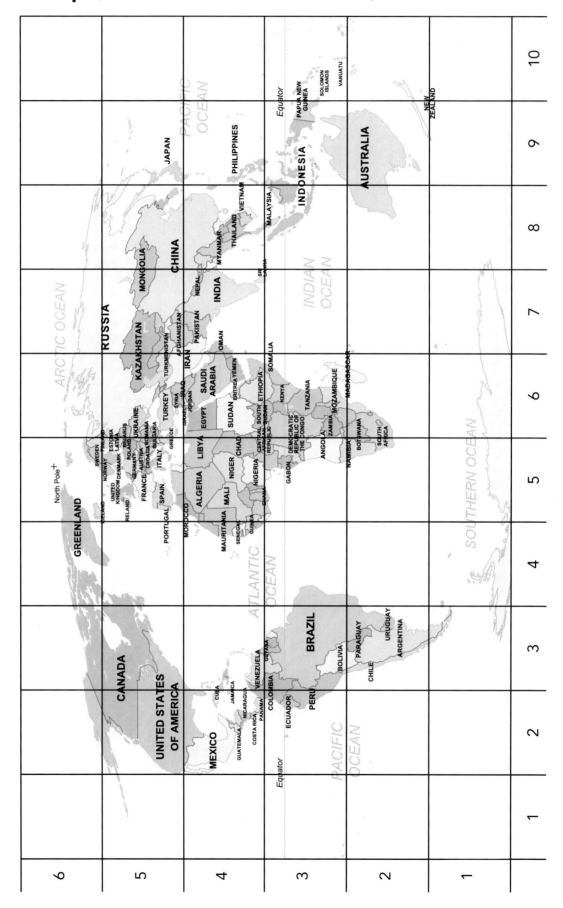

Coordinate grid (blank)

Coordinate routes

Challenge question

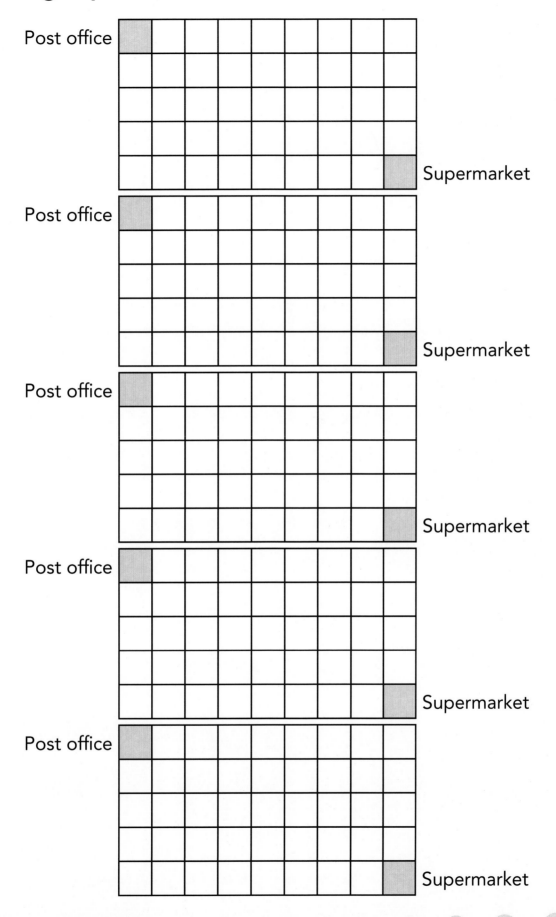

Resource 4.9.6

24-hour clocks

Make 10 different 24-hour clock times using only the digits 1, 2, 3 and 4.
Draw them on the clock faces and label each one with the time in
24-hour format.

24-hour format _____

24-hour format _____

24-hour format _____

24-hour format _____

24-hour format _____

24-hour format _____

24-hour format _____

24-hour format _____

24-hour format _____

24-hour format _____

Maths is fun! (1)

1. Work together as a group to explore how many times you can each write the statement 'Maths is fun!' in 2 minutes. Use the back of the sheet if you need more space.

> Maths is fun!

2. Complete the table for the group and compare the results. Calculate the work rate for each person.

Name						
Number of times statement written in total						
Time taken (minutes)	2	2	2	2	2	2
Work rate (number of times per minute)						

Who was the most efficient at writing the statements? What was their work rate?

_____

1. Work together as a group to explore how many times you can each write the statement 'Maths is fun!' in 2 minutes.

Maths is fun!

Name			
Number of times statement written in total			
Time taken (minutes)	2	2	2
Work rate			

Who was the most efficient at writing the statements? What was their work rate?

_____

3. Here are the results for another group of 3 children.
Work out the missing information.

Name	Sanjay	Anita	Benji
Number of times statement written in total	84		105
Time taken (minutes)	4	3	
Work rate		20	21

Who does more?

Compare the children's statements each time to answer the questions.

1. Who filled more cups?

I filled 30 cups with water every minute. I continued at the same rate for 10 minutes.

I filled 25 cups with water every minute. I continued at the same rate for 12 minutes.

2. Who was the fastest?

I did 168 star jumps in 8 minutes.

I did 115 star jumps in 5 minutes.

3. Who took longer?

I bounced the ball 30 times per minute. It bounced 480 times!

I bounced the ball 40 times per minute. It bounced 520 times!

Work rate questions

6 drinks bottled per second

a) How many drinks can be bottled in 15 seconds?

_____

b) How long will it take to bottle 150 drinks?

_____

70 beats a minute

a) How many times does this heart beat in an hour?

_____

b) How long does it take to beat 490 times?

_____

4 buses an hour

a) How many buses are there in 11 hours?

_____

b) How many hours does it take for 132 buses to come?

_____

9 flights a day

a) How many flights are there in one week?

_____

b) How many days does it take for 144 flights?

_____

110 packs made an hour

a) How many packs are made in 4 hours?

_____

b) How long does it take to make 550 packs?

_____

3 deliveries a week

a) How many deliveries are there in 18 weeks?

_____

b) How many weeks will it take to complete 72 deliveries?

_____

Resource 4.10.1e

What's the question?

The answer to each question has been given.
Can you fill in the missing information in the question each time?

6 drinks bottled per second

a) How many drinks can be bottled in _____ seconds?

_____192 drinks_____

b) How long will it take to bottle _____ drinks?

_____29 seconds_____

70 beats a minute

a) How many times does this heart beat in _____ minutes?

_____105 beats_____

b) How long does it take to beat _____ times?

_____35 minutes_____

4 buses an hour

a) How many buses are there in _____ hours?

_____96 buses_____

b) How many hours does it take for _____ buses to come?

_____52 hours_____

9 flights a day

a) How many flights are there in _____ days?

_____270 flights_____

b) How many days does it take for _____ flights?

_____90 days_____

110 packs made an hour

a) How many packs are made in _____ hours at the same work rate?

_____1210 packs_____

b) How long does it take to make _____ packs?

_____5½ hours_____

3 deliveries a week

a) How many deliveries are there in _____ weeks?

_____105 deliveries_____

b) How many weeks will it take to complete _____ deliveries?

_____13 weeks_____

Making deliveries

3 deliveries a week.

  a) How many deliveries are there in 18 weeks?

  b) How many weeks will it take to complete 72 deliveries?

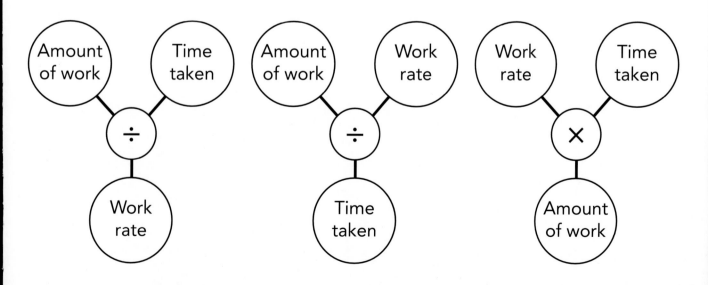

Resource 4.10.2b

Tree diagrams

a) Match the tree diagrams to the problems. Complete the tree diagrams to help find the answer each time.

b) One problem is missing. Can you write a problem to match the tree diagram?

Row 1:
- 72 × 12 = ☐
- 200 × 20 = ☐
- 72 ÷ 12 = ☐

Row 2:
- 200 ÷ 20 = ☐
- 96 ÷ 8 = ☐
- 200 × 8 = ☐

Row 3:
- 200 ÷ 8 = ☐
- An office receives 72 telephone calls each hour. How many calls does it receive in 12 hours?
- 96 × 8 = ☐

Problems:

Jane completes 8 puzzles each hour. How many hours does it take to complete 96 puzzles?

Simon and Ella work in a shoe factory. They each make 10 pairs of shoes each day. How many days does it take them to make 200 pairs of shoes?

Pupils made 72 sticks of cubes in 12 minutes. How many sticks of cubes did they make per minute?

A school uses a box of 200 pencils every half term. How many pencils will the school have used after 8 half terms?

200 ml of water drips from a tap every hour. How many millilitres in total have dripped in 20 hours?

96 kg of potatoes is harvested each week. How many kilograms of potatoes are harvested in 8 weeks?

306 © HarperCollins*Publishers* 2018

Three in a row

The numbers in the grid represent work rate or the time taken.

Choose a number and decide what it will represent.

Make up a problem that will give an answer to match the number chosen.

How many groups of three numbers in a straight line can you make?

14	11	10	5	80
60	16	90	8	20
7	45	30	70	15
25	100	35	12	50
6	21	4	40	9

Calculation flowchart

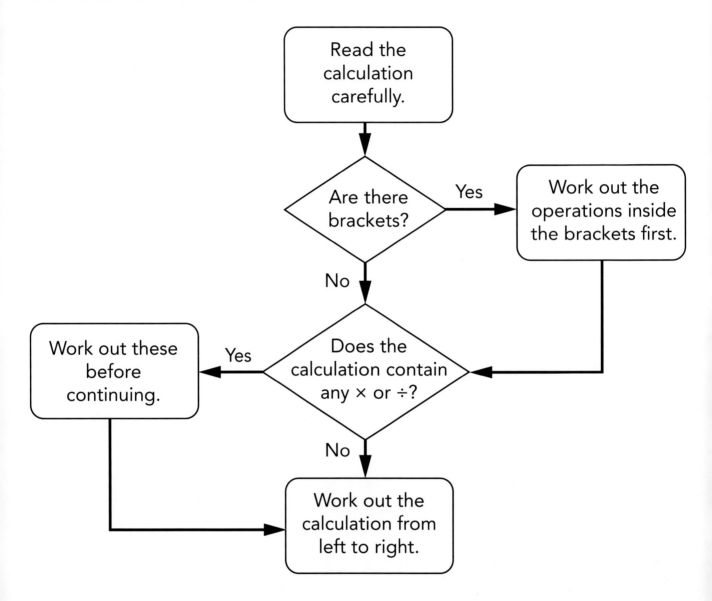

Blank tree diagrams

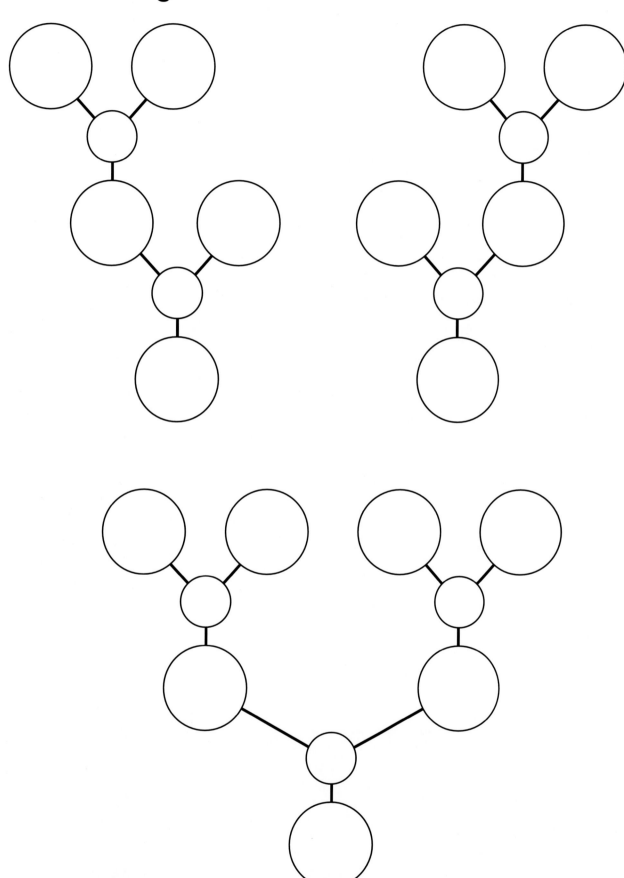

The great number sentence challenge

Can you write the following number sentences?

A number sentence that contains addition, multiplication and subtraction, but the subtraction is worked out first.

_____

A number sentence that should be worked out as it is written, from left to right.

_____

A number sentence that should be worked out from right to left.

_____

A number sentence that contains no brackets.

_____

A number sentence that contains two different operations within a pair of brackets.

_____

A number sentence that contains division and multiplication, which are worked out in that order.

_____

Share each number sentence with a partner. Can they solve them?

_____

At the supermarket

Write your own word problems for a friend to solve.
Your problems should have the theme of a supermarket.
You might like to use these as ideas to start with.
Try changing the words and numbers that are underlined.

Tom has £35 in his pocket.

He buys a magazine for £4 and also five bottles of lemonade for £2 each.

How much money does he have left?

At the start of the day there are 14 multipacks of beans on the shelf. Each pack contains 4 tins.

During the day, 5 of these multipacks are sold.

How many tins are there on the shelf?

There are 60 people that need to be served in a supermarket.

The shop already had its 10 tills open. Now it opens another 5 tills to cope with all the people. Each till has the same number of people in its queue.

How many people are in each queue?

Krishna buys 3 packs of apples (which each have 6 apples).

She also buys 2 pineapples and 6 pairs of bananas.

How many pieces of fruit does she buy?

Changing positions

These three operations belong in a number machine.
But does it matter which order they appear in?

Draw different number machines by putting these operations in different orders.

Use the same input for all your machines and draw a tree diagram for each machine you design.

Talk about the answers to these questions with a partner:
- What are the largest/smallest outputs you can make?
- What is it about the order of operations that means that the output is the largest/smallest?
- Why are some of your answers the same?

Chains of operations (1)

You will need:

- a whiteboard each
- a set of operation cards (+, –, x and ÷)
- a set of number cards.

Instructions:

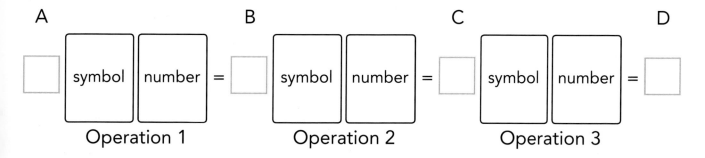

1. From the cards provided, select 3 operations and place them on your whiteboards with spaces between them.
2. In Space A, write your starting number. Calculate each step and enter the answers in spaces B, C and D. If there is not a whole-number answer at any stage you will need to start again.
3. How many number sentences can you make?

Working backwards

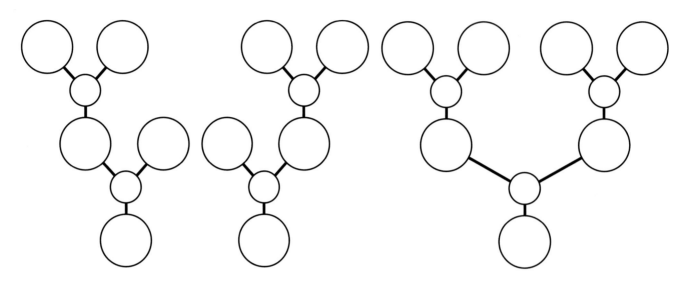

You will need to work in pairs.

Choose one of the blank tree diagrams and leave the first circle blank. Fill in each step of the tree diagram with three different operations (for example + 34, ÷ 5 and × 3).

Write a mystery two-digit number secretly on your whiteboard. You should work forwards through the tree diagram to work out what the answer will be (this is the output).

Share your answer with your partner.

Your partner can score two points:
- if they write a number sentence using inverse operations to show what they need to do to find the mystery number
- if the mystery number they calculate is the same as the one you wrote on your whiteboard.

Extra challenge
Design a number machine that your partner should show as a tree diagram before you continue the activity from the start.

Chains of operations (2)

You will need:

- a group of four pupils
- a whiteboard each
- a set of operation cards (+, –, x and ÷)
- a set of number cards.

Instructions:

1. Make sure the pupils in your group are sitting in a line behind their whiteboards. Label yourselves Pupil A, Pupil B, Pupil C and Pupil D from left to right.
2. Pupil D should take some operation cards and number cards and put them in between each of you to represent the three steps in a chain of operations.

   For example:

$$\boxed{} \; - \; 10 \; \boxed{} \; + \; 28 \; \boxed{} \; \times \; 2 \; \boxed{}$$

3. Pupil D should start by writing a number on their whiteboard. They will need to think carefully about which number will work. This is the output in your chain of operations and the aim of the activity is to work backwards using inverse operations to find the input (Pupil A's number). Pupil D should show their number to Pupil C.
4. Pupil C should then work backwards using inverse operations and show their answer to Pupil B.
5. Pupil B should do the same and, finally, Pupil A should complete the third inverse operation and display their answer. This is the input in your chain of operations.
6. Check that your input is correct by working forwards through your chain of operations.
7. Each pupil should write down the inverse number sentence that they would use to show the chain of operations.

Share your number sentences with each other. Sometimes brackets may go in different places, so discuss the different possibilities.

Phrase cards

A	A
the quotient of	the product of
A	**A**
the sum of	the difference between

B	B
is divided by	is multiplied by
B	**B**
is added to	is subtracted from

Number sentences	Word calculation problems	Answers

You will need:

some coloured counters, a playing grid and a partner.

How to play:

1. Complete the playing grid as follows:
   a) Write four different number sentences in Column 1.
   b) Think carefully about how to describe your number sentences using words. In Column 2, write word calculation problems to match them, but in a jumbled order!
   c) Finally, work out the answers to your number sentences and write these in Column 3 (again in a jumbled order).

      So, your grid should contain the information that matches your four number sentences, but not in the right places.

2. Put one coloured counter on any of your number sentences in Column 1.

3. Your partner should read the information in the square and then find the correct squares in the remaining two columns that match it. They should put coloured counters on these squares.

   For example:
   - You might place a counter on a square that says 36 x 3 ÷ 6 (the number sentence).
   - Your partner might then place their counters on a square that says 'What is the quotient of the product of 36 and 3, and 6?' (the word calculation problem that goes with the number sentence) and also on a square that says '18' (the answer to the number sentence).

Calculation strips

What is the difference between 63 and the product of 3 and 4?

What is the sum of 47 and the product of 7 and 7?

What is the quotient of the product of 8 and 4 divided by 2?

What is the product of the sum of 10 and 10, multiplied by 3?

The difference between 15 and 3 is added to 25. What is the sum?

56 is added to the quotient of 35 divided by 5. What is the sum?

Prove it! (1)

Can your partner prove that the commutative and associative laws work?

1. Write down two calculations that show either the commutative or associative law.

   For example:
   $3 \times (2 \times 4) = (3 \times 2) \times 4$ (This example shows the associative law.)

2. Pass your calculations to your partner to look at. Can they prove that your calculations are the same?

   $3 \times (2 \times 4) = (3 \times 2) \times 4$

   They could use interlocking cubes ...

3 layers of 2 × 4 cubes 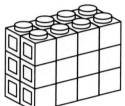   4 layers of 3 × 2 cubes

= 24 interlocking cubes   = 24 interlocking cubes

... or tree diagrams ...

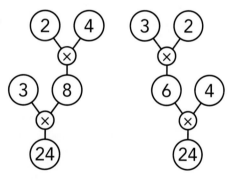

3. Your partner gets the following points:
   - 1 point for being able to show that the two calculations are equal
   - 1 point for naming the law that is being shown (commutative or associative).

4. Remember to swap around so that you both get a chance to write and to model the calculations.

Extra challenge

Give your partner a choice of calculations, including some that are not true.
For example:

a) $36 + 12 = 12 + 36$ b) $45 - 9 = 9 - 45$

c) $9 \times 4 = 4 \times 9$ d) $50 \div 10 = 10 \div 50$

Not all of these show the commutative law! Your partner's job is to prove the calculations that are true and identify those that are not.

Name that strategy!

Write your own word problem on one side of a piece of card.

Here are two ideas to begin with:

a) The cost of one _____ is £_____. There are _____ in a box.
   How much do _____ boxes cost?

b) _____ boxes of _____ cost _____. How much does each
   _____ cost?

On the back of your word problem card, write down the method that you think should be used to find the answer. Don't forget to include the answer.

Write a few of these word problem cards and then place all your cards on the table so that the problems are face up.

Take it in turns to choose a card and to guess what method and answer are on the back.

Remember to spot the commutative or associative law if they have been used.

Can your partner prove that the distributive law works?

1. Write down two calculations that show the distributive law.

   For example:
   $(14 \times 5) + (14 \times 9) = 14 \times (5 + 9)$

2. Pass your calculations to your partner to look at. Can they prove that your calculations are the same?

   $(14 \times 5) + (14 \times 9) = 14 \times (5 + 9)$

   They could work out each answer ...

$14 \times 5 + 14 \times 9$	$14 \times (5 + 9)$
$= 70 + 126$	$= 14 \times 14$
$= 196$	$= 196$

   ... or model each number sentence ...

   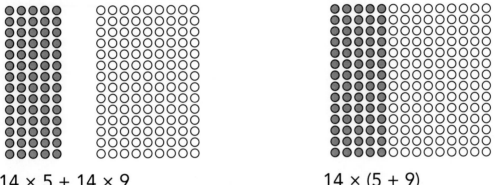

$14 \times 5 + 14 \times 9$	$14 \times (5 + 9)$

3. Your partner gets a point for being able to show that the two calculations are equal.

4. Remember to swap around so that you both get a chance to write and to model the calculations.

Extra challenge

Give your partner a choice of calculations, including some that are not true.

For example:

a) $13 \times 6 + 13 \times 4 = 13 \times (6 + 4)$

b) $20 \times 6 - 2 \times 20 = 6 \times (20 - 2)$

c) $16 \times 3 + 16 \times 3 + 16 \times 5 = 16 \times (3 + 3 + 5)$

d) $50 \times 6 - 50 \times 3 = 50 \times (6 - 3)$

Not all of these show the distributive law! Your partner's job is only to prove the calculations that are true.

Distributive puzzles

You will need to work in small groups.

Each pupil in the group should write two large number sentences that show the distributive law, for example:

25 x 14 + 25 x 19 = 25 x (14 + 19)

Use blank cards to cover up some of the numbers and symbols to make a puzzle for your friends to solve.

The others in the group should talk about what is underneath each card, using their knowledge of the distributive law to help.

Can they work out what the missing numbers are?

You might like to try some sentences that use shapes or letters as well as those with numbers.

Jigsaw pairs

You will need:

- several strips of card
- a pair of scissors
- some friends to play 'Jigsaw Pairs' with.

How to play:

- Take some strips of card and cut them halfway along to form an arrow shape that makes two jigsaw pieces.
- On the first piece, write a calculation that you could use the distributive law to simplify.
- On the second piece, write down what the calculation looks like after it has been simplified.

  For example:

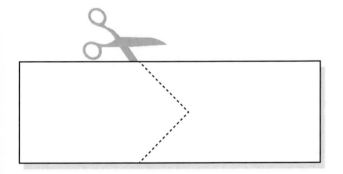 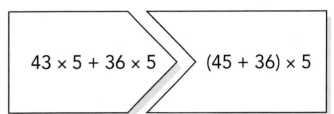

- Make a few jigsaw pairs like this and then collect together all your cards and shuffle them.
- Turn your cards upside down and then take it in turns to turn over two cards at a time. If you make a pair, you can keep the cards. If you don't, you should turn the cards back over.
- The winner is the player with the most cards at the end!

Calculation cards

52×25	101×48
125×72	99×101
29×98	55×125
25×102	150×86

Simplifying challenge

Your task is to design several complex questions for your friends to simplify before they solve.

You need to make sure that you know how you want them to simplify each question, so think carefully about how you write them.

Here are some design challenges for you with an example for each:

Design a complex calculation that ...	What question could you design?	How do you expect them to simplify it?
... your partner can use the distributive law to simplify	25 × 18 – 25 × 12	By using the distributive law to write 25 × (18 – 12) and then work out 25 × 6
... is easier to work out if the numbers are multiplied in a different order (associative law)	7 × 10 × 7	By finding the answer to 7 × 7 and then multiplying the answer by 10
... equals 31 × 100 when finally simplified	31 × 86 + 31 × 14	By using the distributive law to write 31 × (86 + 14) and then working out 31 × 100
... contains two numbers that can be combined to make a multiple of 100	367 + 482 + 133	By seeing that 367 + 133 equals 500 and then working out 500 + 482
... contains four or more numbers, but can be simplified to a calculation with only two numbers.	9 × 13 + 11 × 13	By using the distributive law to write (9 + 11) × 13 and then writing it as 20 × 13

Now try your own examples for each challenge.

See whether your partner simplifies in the way you want them to!

Resource 4.10.14c

Distributive word problems

Your challenge is to write some word problems that can be solved by using the distributive law to help.

To help you, here are some frameworks to use. Choose your numbers carefully, then use the distributive law yourself to check that it works and to find the answer.

Bigtown United won _____ games during February and _____ games during March. They get 3 points for a win. What was the total number of points they got in February and March?

3 × _____ + 3 × _____

3 × (_____ + _____)

Harry is counting signposts on the motorway. There are 5 signposts every junction. His whole journey is _____ junctions long and he has already gone past _____ junctions. How many signposts does he have left to go past?

5 × _____ − 5 × _____

5 × (_____ − _____)

A market stall sells _____ apples every day and _____ oranges every day. It is open for _____ days every week. How many apples and oranges does it sell altogether in a week?

_____ × _____ + _____ × _____

_____ × (_____ + _____)

A school is going on a trip to the seaside. It takes _____ minibuses. Each minibus contains _____ children and _____ adults. How many more children are going on the trip than adults?

_____ × _____ − _____ × _____

_____ × (_____ − _____)

You might like to change some of the details in the word problems to make them more interesting!

When you have finished, share your completed word problems with a partner to solve.

Work rate challenge cards

Planned work rate

Actual work rate

Planned time it will take

Actual time taken

Difference in time taken

Planned total to be completed

Actual total completed

Difference in total completed

'Use your brain' shop

In a 'Use your brain' shop the prices need to be worked out before you can pay!

Design your own shop by making up <u>nine</u> different items to sell. Instead of writing the prices, you could:

1. give a price for a pack so that the customer needs to do some maths to find out what different amounts cost

   (for example, a pack of 5 pens that costs £6.00. How much do 4 pens cost?)

2. give a price that is based on the price of something else

   (for example, a pack of pencils that is labelled 'Half the price of 5 pens'.)

3. give a price that is written as a calculation:

   (for example, a book that is labelled 'three-quarters of £12.00').

Once you have invented your nine items, use them to ask your friends questions based on them.

For an extra challenge, include challenges that involve calculating in pounds and pence.

Resource 4.10.17b

Blotted out!

Write your own word problems based on these. You will need to choose your numbers carefully so that they make sense.

Abdul is playing a computer game.

He scores ⬛ points by the end of the first ⬛ levels.

His rate is the same for each level.

At the same rate, he needs to complete ⬛ more levels before he reaches his highest points score ever.

How many points does he need to score in total?

A pet food company plans to make ⬛ bags of dog food.

It starts off by making ⬛ bags per day for the first ⬛ days.

The remaining bags need to be produced during the next ⬛ days.

How many bags does it now need to produce on average?

There are ⬛ exercise books in Year 4's classroom cupboard.

There are ⬛ fewer Maths books than English books.

The number of Art books is ⬛ more than ⬛ times the number of Maths books.

How many Art books are in the cupboard?

A landscaper is planting the hedges for a maze.

⬛ metres of hedges have already been planted.

What's left of the maze is ⬛ metres longer than ⬛ times the length of the hedges that have already been planted.

What is the total length of the hedges that need to be planted?

Question cards

What is the first thing you think you should do when you are given a word problem?	What is the best way you know of remembering the order of operations?
What is the order of operations? Does it always stay the same?	A calculation has an addition and a subtraction in it. Which should you work out first?
Why do some number sentences have brackets and some do not?	How would you explain the order of operations to someone who has difficulty remembering it?
Are there any calculations where it doesn't matter which way around the numbers go? How do you know?	A calculation has a division and an addition in it. Is it always true to say that the division should be worked out first?
How do you know what to do to solve a word problem?	What methods do you find most helpful to help you understand what a problem is asking?

At the airport

Write your own word problems for a friend to solve.
Your problems should have the theme of an airport.

You might like to use these as ideas to start with.
Try putting numbers into the empty boxes.
Remember to check that your problem makes sense!

1. On Runway 2, ☐ planes land in ☐ hours. Assuming the same rate, how many hours will it take for ☐ planes to land?

2. Mr Johnson has bought a ticket that costs him £☐. However, his luggage is lost and he is late. He complains at the desk and they give him half of the price of the ticket plus another £☐ to apologise for the delay. How much has his ticket cost him now?

3. Joe has bought a ☐ page book to read on the plane. He wants to finish it before the plane lands in ☐ minutes time. He reads ☐ pages per minute for the first ☐ minutes. He wants to read the remaining pages in ☐ minutes. How many pages does he still need to read each minute?

4. The X-ray machine can check ☐ passengers in ☐ minutes. At this rate, how many passengers can the machine check in ☐ minutes?

Answers

Chapter 7 Statistics (III)

7.1 Knowing line graphs (1)

1. **(a)** time, temperature, 0.5 degrees Celsius (°C)
   (b) At 08:00, 40°C
   (c) 2
   (d) Between 06:00 and 08:00
   (e) Between 10:00 and 12:00
   (f) Between 16:00 and 18:00
   (g) She was getting better. From 8 o'clock in the morning, her temperature showed a downward tendency and, by 4 o'clock in the afternoon, it was steady.

2.

Time	06:00	08:00	10:00	12:00
Temperature (°C)	37.5	40	39.5	37.5
Time	14:00	16:00	18:00	
Temperature (°C)	38	37	37	

3. **(a)** The peak times are at 08:00 and 17:00. These are the rush hours when people go to work in the morning and go back home in the afternoon (answer may vary).
   (b) The number of people was least at 12 noon. This is during lunch time / the middle of the day when many people are at work (answers may vary).
   (c) Various answers possible.

7.2 Knowing line graphs (2)

1. **(a)** the month of the year, the quantity sold
   (b) December, June, $325 - 75 = 250$, $325 + 75 = 400$
   (c) June to December, January to June
   (d) July, January, $300 - 50 = 250$, $300 + 50 = 350$
   (e) January to July, July to December
   (f) Various answers possible. Explanations should mention the change of seasons. For example: People are more likely to buy picnic blankets in the Summer than in the Winter, so there should be more sales in Summer than Winter. The opposite is true of duvets, as people are more likely to buy them to keep warm in the Winter time.

2. **(a)** line, bar
   (b) C, A
   (c) £26 000, downward
   (d) Spring in Year 2, Autumn in Year 2, 2

7.3 Knowing line graphs (3)

1. **(a)** D, C   **(b)** B   **(c)** A
2. **(a)** 100 marks, 70 marks
   (b) It is a way of not having to show all of the blank part of the graph.
   (c) From chapter test 5
   (d) Chapter test 4
   (e) Adams's scores mostly improve
3. **(a)**

Chapter	One	Two	Three	Four
Scores	70	77 (also accept 76 or 78)	75	90
Chapter	Five	Six	Seven	Eight
Scores	85	95	98	100

   (b) Various answers possible. Answers should mention that Adam appears to have studied for all but tests 3 and 5 and that he steadily improved.
   (c) Answers will vary. Check that they make sense.

7.4 Constructing line graphs

1. **(b)** units to be measured (other answers possible)
   (c) axes
2. Graph should be drawn as follows:
   - Overall horizontal axis labelled 'Time' (or similar), invididual labels contain the days of the week (from Monday to Sunday)
   - Overall vertical axis labelled 'Number of people' (or similar), individual labels contain multiples of 10 (from 10 to 50)
   - Points should be correctly plotted with straight lines connecting the points
   (a) Wednesday, 46 people
   (b) Between Saturday and Sunday
   (c) Answers may vary. They should mention the two trends in the week. For example: The first half of the week shows an increasing tendency, while the second half of the week shows a downward tendency.
   (d) 244
3. **(a)** Bar chart should show the same axes as before, with bars correctly drawn.
   (b) Answers will vary. Check that they make sense.
4. Answers will vary. Check that the heights recorded in the table are plotted correctly on the line graph. Pupils should make reasonable predictions of their height based on the trends seen in the graph.

Chapter 7 test

1 (a) 500 (b) 4 (c) 50 (d) 2400
   (e) 190 (f) 350 (g) 1 (h) 60
2 Column method used correctly for
   questions a–f.
   (a) 4116 (b) 7248
   (c) 3156 (Check: 3156 ÷ 4 = 789)
   (d) 9 (e) 22
   (f) 112 r 3 (Check: 112 × 70 + 3 = 7843)
3 (a) 913
   (b) 1559 (Pupils may work out
       786 + 114 first, then 900 + 659)
   (c) 17 000 (Pupils may work out
       250 × 4 first, then 1000 × 17)
4 (a) D C A B
   (b) (i) 5, 35 (ii) 5 (iii) 4 (iv) 1, 5 (v) 110
5 (a) B (b) E
6 (a) 12th May, 18 pupils
   (b) Between 10th and 11th May
   (c) the 13th, 15th, 16th and 17th
   (d) Answers will vary, but should
       reflect the downwards trend of
       the graph (so should be less than 9
       absentees).
   (e) 103

7 (a)

Year group	Year 1	Year 2	Year 3	Year 4	Year 5
Number of books donated	50	65	85	150	230

   (b) Graph should be drawn as follows:
   – Title of graph 'Number of books
      donated by a school' (or similar)
   – Overall horizontal axis labelled
      'Year group', invididual labels
      contain the names of the year
      groups (from Year 1 to Year 5)
   – Overall vertical axis labelled
      'Number of books donated' (or
      similar), individual labels contain
      multiples of 50 (from 50 to 250)
   – Points should be correctly plotted
      with straight lines connecting the
      points.

   (c) Answers may vary, but shoud
       mention the tendency that
       the number of donated books
       increases as the year groups
       become older.
   (d) Bar chart should show the same
       axes as before, with bars correctly
       drawn.
   (e) 580 books

Chapter 8 Geometry and measurement (1)

8.1 Acute and obtuse angles

1 (a) obtuse (b) obtuse
   (c) acute (d) right
2 Acute angles: half past 3, half past 5, 11
   o'clock
   Right angles: 3 o'clock, 9 o'clock
   Obtuse angles: 4 o'clock, half past 9
3 6, 4, 4, 8
4 Acute angles: 1, 4, 7
   Right angles: 3, 6
   Obtuse angles: 2, 5, 8
5 (a) ✗
   (b) ✓
   (c) ✗
   (d) ✗
6 5, 16
7 Lines should be perpendicular to each
   other and form a cross.

8.2 Triangles and quadrilaterals (1)

1 Triangle(s): 3, 7, 9, 10, 13
   Quadrilateral(s): 1, 2, 4, 5, 8, 11, 12, 14, 15
2 All three shapes correctly copied on
   the grid

3 (a) 3, square
   (b) 3, 3 4, 4
   (c) quadrilaterals, opposite, four
   (d) square
   (e) 5, 1
4 (a) ✗ (b) ✗ (c) ✓ (d) ✗
5 Various answers possible. For example:
   (a)
   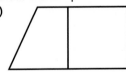
   (b)
   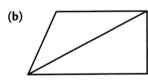
   (c)
   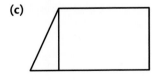
6 9, 10

8.3 Triangles and quadrilaterals (2)

1 (a) hexagon
   (b) quadrilateral
   (c) triangle (equilateral triangle)
   (d) quadrilateral
   (e) rectangle (or quadrilateral)
   (f) pentagon
   (g) octagon (h) square
2 (a) ✗ (b) ✓ (c) ✓ (d) ✓
3 (a) dots connected to form a triangle
       around the cat, a pentagon around
       the parrot and a rectangle around
       the rabbit
   (b) rectangle, pentagon, triangle
   (c) rabbit
4 (a) 2, 5, 7, 9, 10, 11, 16
   (b) 2, 3, 5, 8, 10, 11, 13, 16
   (c) 14, 15

Answers

5 Answers may vary. For example:

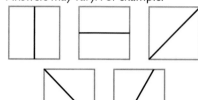

6

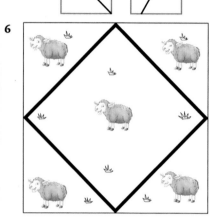

8.4 Classification of triangles (1)

1 **(a)** right-angled triangle, 1, 2, 5, 10
(b) obtuse angle, 7, 8
(c) acute, 3, 4, 6, 9

2 **(a)** obtuse **(b)** right-angled **(c)** acute

3 **(a)** ✓ **(b)** ✗ **(c)** ✗

4 Each type of triangle drawn correctly.

5 **(a)**

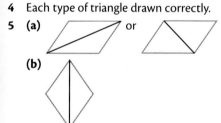

(b)

6 Various answers possible, depending on where the cut is made (6 or 5 or 4).

8.5 Classification of triangles (2)

1 2, 5, 6
1, 7
3, 4

2 **(a)** B **(b)** B **(c)** D
(d) D **(e)** B **(f)** D

3 13   5
6   2

4 Various answers possible. For example:
(a) **(b)** **(c)**

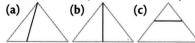

---

5 Various answers possible. For example:

8.6 Line symmetry

1 ✓ ✓ ✗ ✓ ✗

2 Vertical lines of symmetry drawn correctly on the first and fourth shapes Vertical, horizontal or diagonal line of symmetry drawn correctly on the second shape

3 0, 3, 8, with lines of symmetry drawn correctly (accept 1 if pupil has written as a straight line)

4

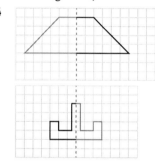

5 A, B, C, D, E, H, I, K, M, O, T, U, V, W, X, Y, with lines of symmetry drawn correctly

6 Symmetrical shapes completed on the grids as follows:
(a)

(b)

8.7 Classification of triangles (3)

1 **(a)** isosceles **(b)** equilateral
(c) symmetry, 1 **(d)** symmetry, 3
(e) acute

2 **(a)** 5, 10 **(b)** 1, 2, 7, 9 **(c)** 3, 4, 6, 8,

3 Isosceles and equilateral triangles drawn correctly with lines of symmetry shown

4 **(a)** **(b)**

5 **(a)** 33, 7 **(b)** 35

8.8 Areas

1 9, 9, 11, 11
2 20, 20, 18, 19, 12, 12, 2, 112
3 16   13   42
4 Any three shapes drawn with areas 7, 9 and 12 squares respectively
5 3   5.5

8.9 Areas of rectangles and squares (1)

1 **(a)** 16 $4 \times 4 = 16$ $16\,cm^2$
(b) 12 $3 \times 4 = 12$ $12\,cm^2$
2 **(a)** $24\,cm^2$ **(b)** $24\,cm^2$ **(c)** $25\,cm^2$
3 $405\,cm^2$
4 $1200\,cm^2$
5 $300\,cm^2$
6 There are 3 possible rectangles: 1×12, 2×6, 3×4
7 $144\,cm^2$

8.10 Areas of rectangles and squares (2)

1 **(a)** $12\,cm^2$ **(b)** $36\,cm^2$ **(c)** $7\,cm$
2 $9450\,cm^2$
3 $1200\,cm^2$
4 $144\,cm^2$
5 $160\,cm^2$
6 $54\,cm^2$

8.11 Square metres

1 **(a)** 1 square metre $1\,m^2$
(b) 1 square centimetre $1\,cm^2$
2 **(a)** m^2 **(b)** cm^2 **(c)** m^2 **(d)** cm^2
(e) m **(f)** cm^2 **(g)** m^2 **(h)** m^2
3 $40\,m^2$ $2500\,m^2$ $18\,m$
4 $2400\,m^2$
5 $400\,cm^2$
6 $5000\,kg$
7 $176\,m^2$
8 $320\,m^2$

Chapter 8 test

1 (a) 2, 5
   (b) acute angles, 1, 3, 8
   (c) obtuse angles, 4, 6, 7

2 (a) triangles: 6, 7, 9, 11, 13 acute-angled triangles: 6, 11 right-angled triangles: 7, 9 obtuse-angled triangles: 13
   (b) quadrilaterals: 2, 3, 4, 5, 10, 12 rectangles: 3, 10 squares: 10
   (c) 1, 8

3 C

4 D C

5 D

6 Various answers possible. For example:

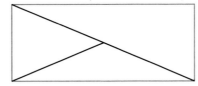

7 (a) 1 m   1 m^2
   (b) cm m^2
   (c) 600 cm^2
   (d) equilateral triangle
   (e) 4   2

8 (a) AC D
   (b) E
   (c) D
   (d) B F

9 (a) ✓
   (b) ✗
   (c) ✗

10 (a) D   (b) B   (c) B

11 (a) 180 m^2 (b) 81 m^2

12 isosceles triangle   isosceles triangle
   One line of symmetry should be drawn on each triangle from the vertex where the two equal sides meet to the centre of the opposite side.

13 (a) 9 cm^2 (b) 13.5 cm^2

14 (a) 4140 cm^2
   (b) 300 000 cm^2 or 30 m^2
   (c) 1200 cm^2
   (d) 256 m^2

Chapter 9 Geometry and measurement (II)

9.1 Converting between kilometres and metres

1 (a) 8000   (b) 1600   (c) 100
   (d) 0.7   (e) 4   (f) 470
   (g) 5250   (h) 4026   (i) 9
   (j) 1780   (k) 16 000   (l) 500

2 (a) km   (b) m   (c) km
   (d) m   (e) km

3 (a) >   (b) <   (c) <
   (d) =   (e) >   (f) >
   (g) <   (h) <

4 (a) 4 km < 4545 m < 5 km < 5454 m
   (b) 9 km < 10 000 m < 20 202 m < 20 220 m

5 (a) 3000 m
   (b) (i) 292 m (ii) 6332 m

6 (a) 14 000 m per minute, 233.3 m per second
   (b) 18 km per hour

9.2 Perimeters of rectangles and squares (1)

1 (a) 40 cm   (b) 22 cm

2 (a) 74 cm, 210 cm^2
       180 cm, 2000 cm^2
       14 m (or 1400 cm),
       6 m^2 (or 60 000 cm^2)
   (b) 60 cm, 225 cm^2
       12 m, 144 m^2

3 Perimeter = 90 m, Area = 200 m^2

4 100 m

5 150 m

6 550 cm^2, 1650 cm^2

7 Columns can be in any order, but table should be completed as follows:

Length (cm)	1	2	3	4	5	6
Width (cm)	11	10	9	8	7	6
Perimeter (cm)	24	24	24	24	24	24
Area (cm^2)	11	20	27	32	35	36

No, the rectangles do not all have the same area.
When the perimeters of rectangles are equal, the nearer the length and width are to being equal, the greater the area will be.

9.3 Perimeters of rectangles and squares (2)

1 (a) 92 m   (b) 60 cm

2 (a) 150 cm, 13 500 cm^2
       23 cm,   84 cm
       50 m (or 5000 cm),
       144 m^2 (or 1 440 000 cm^2)
   (b) 96 cm, 576 cm^2
       25 cm, 625 cm^2

3 Appropriate diagram drawn. 96 cm, 320 cm^2

4 110 m

5 17 cm

6 (a) 2
   (b) Perimeter of 6 × 48 rectangle = 108 cm, Perimeter of 12 × 24 rectangle = 72 cm

7 1st square – area: 225 cm^2 perimeter: 60 cm
   2nd square – area: 25 cm^2 perimeter: 20 cm
   Remaining piece – area: 50 cm^2 perimeter: 30 cm

9.4 Perimeters and areas of rectilinear shapes

1 (a) 24 cm, 20 cm^2 (b) 24 cm, 24 cm^2
   (c) 32 cm, 28 cm^2 (d) 28 cm, 24 cm^2

2 (a) 200 cm, 1000 cm^2
   (b) 150 cm, 850 cm^2

3 242 cm^2

4 729 cm^2

5 36 cm^2

6 (a) 234 cm^2
   (b) 72 cm

7 Appropriate diagram drawn. 8500 cm^2

8 144 cm^2

9.5 Describing positions on a 2-D grid

1 Lines drawn from Lou to seat 6 in Row 2 and from Ella to seat 3 in Row 4.

2 horizontally, vertically

3 Tiger (3, 3)
   Rabbit (4, 4)   Horse (4, 2)
   Sheep (7, 3)   Monkey (8, 5)
   Cat (9, 1)   Dog (10, 2)

4 Marks correctly placed in the grid.

5 **(a)** (4, 5)
   (b) Various answers possible. All routes must take the snail from (2, 9) to end on (4, 5). For example, it can move 4 squares down, and then move 2 squares right.

6 **(a)** (9, 1)   **(b)** 495

9.6 Solving problems involving time and money (1)

1 **(a)** 12
   (b) 365, 366
   (c) 28, 29
   (d) 90 days (for leap years this answer will be 91)

2 **(a)** 60, 3600   **(b)** 90
   (c) 45, 2700   **(d)** $\frac{3}{4}$
   (e) 3, 10   **(f)** 60
   (g) 21, 504   **(h)** 6

3 **(a)** Either 9:09 a.m. or 9:09 p.m. Either 09:09 or 21:09
   (b) 4:28 p.m.   16: 28
   (c) Either 1:24 a.m. or 1:24 p.m.   Either 01:24 or 13:24
   (d) 11:31 p.m.   23: 31

4 20:45 (also accept 8:45 p.m.)

5 **(a) (i)** 13 **(ii)** 91
   (b) (i) £1235 **(ii)** £8645
   (c) (i) £364 **(ii)** £2548 **(iii)** £267 540

6 2, 24

7 **(a)** 15 × 181 = 2715 (kWh) (Answer may be 2730 if it is a leap year)
   (b) 12 × 15 = 180p = £1.80
   12 × 15 × 181 = 32 580 p = £325.80

9.7 Solving problems involving time and money (2)

1 **(a)** 100 **(b)** 10 **(c)** 0.6 **(d)** 75
   (e) 8, 90 **(f)** 0.01 **(g)** 8050 **(h)** 238

2 **(a)** 6   **(b)** 3   **(c)** 648

3 12 × 4 + 4 × 75 = 348 (pounds)

4 **(a)** 2512 × 12 = 30 144 (pounds)
   (b) Estimation may vary.
   Calculate: 9.5 × 8 × 5 = 380 (pounds)
   Difference will depend on original estimation
   (c) More than half of Erin's monthly salary

5 **(a)** £258, £1806
   (b) £1806

6 6 × 80 × 0.99 = 475.20 (pounds)

7 15 × 30 × 14 = 6300 (pounds) 6500 – 6300 = 200 (pounds)
   The budget is £200 more than the total purchase price.

Chapter 9 test

1 **(a)** 90
   (b) 3, 500
   (c) 1.6
   (d) km
   (e) the side length
   (f) the length, the width
   (g) 12, 720
   (h) 2.5, 2, 50

2 **(a)** 3.6, 360
   (b) 320 cm
   (c) 20 m, 18 m²

3 **(a)** 24 m 50 cm 12 cm
   (b) 96 m   6 m   360 cm

4 **(a)** ✗   **(b)** ✗   **(c)** ✗   **(d)** ✓

5 Perimeter: 52 cm, Area: 88 cm²

6 (8, 5)

7 **(a)** 6300 m, 6.3 km **(b)** 625 cm²
   (c) 300 m²   **(d)** 876 m²
   (e) Square A: 784 cm²
   Square B: 400 cm²
   (f) (i) £69 **(ii)** £71
   (g) (i) 84   **(ii)** £175, £2100
   (h) (i) 420 **(ii)** 5040p, £50.40

Chapter 10 Four operations of whole numbers

10.1 Calculating work rate (1)

1 Miss Kaur was the fastest. Compare their work rate (number of toys made per day).

2 **(a)** ÷
   (b) × time taken
   (c) ÷ work rate

3 **(a)** 132 ÷ 4 = 33 (pages per day)
   (b) 32 × 5 = 160 (mental calculations)
   (c) 480 ÷ 30 = 16 (hours)
   (d) 270 ÷ 3 = 90, 400 ÷ 5 = 80   Aaron has a higher work rate.

4 144 ÷ (216 ÷ 3) = 2 (minutes)

5 1200 ÷ 30 – 1200 ÷ 40 = 10 (metres)

10.2 Calculating work rate (2)

1 **(b)** 1000 ÷ 50 = 20 (hours) They need 20 hours to make 1000 clay pots.
   (c) 288 ÷ 6 = 48 (friendship bands) They made 48 friendship bands every hour.

2 **(a)** (18 + 4) × 22 = 484 (kilowatt-hours)
   (b) 18 ÷ 3 = 6 (bags)   14 ÷ 2 = 7 (bags)   20 ÷ 4 = 5 (bags)
   Mr. Lee made the most bags per hour.
   (c) (6480 ÷ 8) + 6480 = 7290 (toys)

3 **(a)** 9600 ÷ 4 = 2400 (books)
   (b) 9600 ÷ (4 × 30) = 80 (books)
   (c) 9600 ÷ 20 = 480 (books)
   (d) 9600 ÷ (4 × 30 × 20) = 4 (books)

10.3 Solving calculation questions in 3 steps (1)

1 **(a)** 5 × 4 = 20
   (b) 9 + 15 = 24
   (c) 4 × 4 = 16
   (d) 16 + 11 = 27

2 **(a)** 24 **(b)** 14 **(c)** 15 **(d)** 13
   (e) 3   **(f)** 24 **(g)** 13 **(h)** 24
   (i) 1

3 **(a)** (6 – 5 + 2) × 8 = 24
   (b) Various answers possible.
   [8 – (11 – 9)] × 4 = 24
   (11 – 4) + 8 + 9 = 24

4 **(a)** 4 × 2 × (6 – 3) = 24
   (b) 3 × (6 + 4 – 2) = 24
   (c) 3 × 6 + 2 + 4 = 24
   (d) 2 × 6 + 3 × 4 = 24 (Answers may vary)

5 Some answers may vary, depending on the order chosen. For example:
   (a) $(7 \times 7 - 1) \div 2 = 24$
   (b) $6 + (2 \times 7) + 4 = 24$
   (c) $12 \times [4 - (8 - 6)] = 24$
   (d) $(13 - 1) \times (12 - 10) = 24$
6 **(a)** $4 \times 4 + 4 + 4$ **(b)** $5 \times 5 - 5 \div 5$
   (c) No   **(d)** No
   (e) $12 + 12 \times (12 \div 12)$
7 **(a)** 9   **(b)** 4   **(c)** 6
   (d) 5, 1   **(e)** 3, 8   **(f)** 7, 2

10.4 Solving calculation questions in 3 steps (2)

1 **(b)** $182 \div (28 - 14) = 13$
   (c) $(128 + 72) \div (20 \times 5) = 2$
2 **(a)** D   **(b)** B
3 **(a)** $650 \div 50 + 45 + 60 = 118$
   (b) $35 \times 6 - 121 \div 11 = 199$
4 **(a)** division, division, addition
      $462 \div 3 = 154$, $66 \div 22 = 3$,
      $154 + 3 = 157$
   (b) division, division, subtraction
      $480 \div 20 = 24$, $24 \div 3 = 8$,
      $66 - 8 = 58$
   (c) multiplication, division, addition
      $150 \times 24 = 3600$, $3600 \div 30 = 120$,
      $947 + 120 = 1067$
   (d) division, subtraction, addition
      $2600 \div 8 = 325$, $994 - 325 = 668$,
      $668 + 549 = 1217$
5 $142 \div 2 - 7 \times 9 + 2 = 10$
6 $(120 + 20) \div 2 = 70$ (cm)

10.5 Solving calculation questions in 3 steps (3)

1 **(a)** $(45 - 20) + 650 \div 50 = 38$
   (b) $(121 + 11) \div (35 - 23) = 11$
2 **(a)** division, subtraction, addition
      $0 \div 24 = 0$, $24 - 0 = 24$,
      $24 + 24 = 48$
   (b) subtraction, division, addition
      $240 - 200 = 40$, $240 \div 40 = 6$,
      $240 + 6 = 246$
   (c) division, addition, division
      $36 \div 36 = 1$, $39 + 1 = 40$, $160 \div$
      $40 = 4$
   (d) subtraction, addition, multiplication
      $450 - 133 = 317$, $317 + 23 = 340$,
      $340 \times 18 = 6120$
   (e) multiplication, multiplication, division
      $8 \times 5 = 40$, $44 \times 60 = 2640$, $2640 \div$
      $40 = 66$

(f) subtraction, division, subtraction
    $307 - 227 = 30$, $330 \div 30 = 11$,
    $205 - 11 = 194$
3 **(a)** multiplication and division, addition and subtraction
   (b) the calculation in the brackets
   (c) multiplication, subtraction, division
4 **(a)** $(42 + 567) \div 40 = 15$ (coaches) r 9 (people)
    So, 16 coaches are needed.
   (b) **(i)** $360 \div (34 - 22) = 30$ (kilograms)
      (ii) $360 \div (34 - 22) \times$
      $(34 + 22) = 1680$ (kilograms)
      (iii) $(34 + 22) \times 80 = 4480$ (pounds)
5 $(480 - 360) \div (12 + 8) = 6$
   $480 - 360 \div (12 + 8) = 462$
6 $(724 - 88) \div 2 \div 3 = 106$ (books)

10.6 Solving calculation questions in 3 steps (4)

1 $27 \times [2520 \div (37 + 53)] = 756$
2 **(a)** $660 \div [(247 - 82) \times 2] = 2$
   (b) $[1000 - (70 + 20)] \times 2 = 1820$
3 **(a)** round brackets, square brackets, 20
   (b) division, multiplication
   (c) division, addition, subtraction, multiplication
   (d) multiplication, addition, subtraction, 3400
   (e) 2×1000, $2000 + 550$, $2550 - 1100$, 1450
4 **(a)** division, subtraction, subtraction
      $4160 \div 20 = 208$, $208 - 86 = 122$,
      $155 - 122 = 33$
   (b) subtraction, multiplication, addition, division
      $56 - 32 = 24$, $24 \times 16 = 384$,
      $846 + 384 = 1230$, $1230 \div 30 = 41$
   (c) addition, subtraction, division
      $560 + 40 = 600$, $800 - 600 = 200$,
      $8000 \div 200 = 40$
   (d) subtraction, division, subtraction
      $301 - 281 = 20$, $4020 \div 20 = 201$,
      $3205 - 201 = 3004$
   (e) addition, subtraction, division
      $79 + 101 = 180$, $3180 - 180 = 3000$,
      $3000 \div 40 = 75$
   (f) subtraction, division, division
      $2200 - 1480 = 720$, $720 \div 8 = 90$,
      $2430 \div 90 = 27$
5 **(a)** $21 - (21 - 15) \times 3 = 3$ (kilograms)

10.7 Working forwards

1 Tree diagram completed from top to bottom as follows: $24 \div 3$, $8 + 14$, 22×9
   Output = 198 $(24 \div 3 + 14) \times 9 = 198$

2 **(a)** 200, 82, 164
      $(1000 \div 5 - 118) \times 2 = 164$
   (b) 393, 24, 3
      $(1285 - 892 - 369) \div 8 = 3$
3 **(a)** $(17 + 2) \times 2 - 2 = 36$
   (b) $(71 - 15 \times 2) \times 24 = 984$
4 **(a)** $12 - 2 + 6 - 3 + 4 = 17$ (passengers)
   (b) $360 \times 3 + 32 = 1112$ (chickens)
5 $(68 \div 2 + 8) \div 3 = 14$ (years old)
6 $(54 \times 2 - 36) \div 4 = 18$ (goals)

10.8 Working backwards

1 8, 1, 9 $(72 \div 8 - 8) \times 8 = 8$
2 **(a)** $79 \longrightarrow 113 \longrightarrow 339 \longrightarrow 149$
      $79 + 34 \times 3 - 190 = 149$
   (b) $2093 \longrightarrow 91 \longrightarrow 15 \longrightarrow 750$
      $2093 \div 23 - 76 \times 50 = 750$
3 **(a)** $160 \div 8 - 8 = 12$
   (b) $(45 \times 8 - 20) \div 5 = 68$
4 **(a)** $(100 \div 20 + 14) \times 3 - 4 = 53$ (years old)
   (b) $(7 \times 7 - 7) \div 7 + 7 = 13$ (apples)
5 $(48 + 24) \times 5 \div 8 = 45$
6 $[(13 + 5) \times 2 + 6] \times 2 = 84$ (pages)

10.9 Word calculation problems (1)

1 **(a)** Product = Quotient, 12   150 ÷
      $6 \times 12 = 300$
   (b) Quotient = Sum, ÷ 30 $(288 + 42) \div$
      $30 = 11$
2 **(a)** C   **(b)** B   **(c)** A   **(d)** D
3 **(a)** $600 \div 20 + 187 = 217$
   (b) $500 \times 32 \div 100 = 160$
   (c) $470 \times 15 - 17 \times 104 = 5282$
   (d) $244 \div (244 \div 2 - 118) = 61$
   (e) $1098 - 756 \div 2 = 720$
4 $820 \times 208 = 170\,560$
5 $(37 - 9) \div (3 - 1) = 14$ (years old)

10.10 Word calculation problems (2)

1 **(a)** Product = Quotient × Difference
      $210 \div 7 \times (120 - 80) = 1200$
   (b) Sum = Product + Quotient
      $34 \times 12 + 48 \div 12 = 412$
2 **(a)** $(66 \times 25) \div (6 \times 5) = 55$
   (b) $2940 - 2940 \div 20 = 2793$
   (c) $128 \times 50 + 36 = 6436$
   (d) $2 \times 72 - 6300 \div 60 = 39$
3 **(a)** C   **(b)** A   **(c)** D   **(d)** B

Answers

4 **(a)** the difference between the product of 403 multiplied by the difference of 213 subtracted by 90 and 13
Answer: 49 556
(b) the quotient of 864 divided by the quotient of the difference between 2193 and 1473 divided by 90
Answer: 108

5 $(1000 - 456) \div 4 = 136$

10.11 Laws of operations (1)

1 **(a)** order, unchanged, b, a
(b) order, unchanged, b, a
(c) unchanged, b, c
(d) unchanged, b, c

2 **(a)** 732
(b) 621, 248
(c) 14
(d) 250 and 4 in either position
(e) ★ ▲
(f) ◆ ●
(g) y, z
(h) k, l

3 Column method used correctly. Answers checked appropriately using commutative law.
(a) 2575   **(b)** 1543
(c) 8151   **(d)** 34 983

4 **(a)** $169 + 500 = 669$
(b) $923 + 200 = 1123$
(c) $75 \times 100 = 7500$
(d) $100 \times 34 = 3400$
(e) $510 + 800 = 1310$
(f) $91 \times 1000 = 91\,000$

5 **(a)** $1000 - 400 = 600$
(b) $2000 \times 6 = 12\,000$
(c) $1\,000\,000 + 100\,000 + 10\,000 + 1000 + 100 + 10 = 1\,111\,110$

10.12 Laws of operations (2)

1 **(a)** 80   **(b)** 25   **(c)** 44, 56
(d) b, a **(e)** b, c **(f)** b, c
(g) 33, 84   **(h)** ■ ▲
(i) 75, 2, 8, 125 (other orders acceptable)

2 **(a)** $200 + 100 = 300$
(b) $1000 \times 100 = 100\,000$
(c) $100 \times 16 = 1600$
(d) $6000 \times 9 = 54\,000$
(e) $1000 \times 11 = 11\,000$
(f) $1000 \times 100 \times 7 = 700\,000$

3 **(a)** $(6 \times 4) \times 25 = 600$ (pounds) or $6 \times (4 \times 25) = 600$ (pounds)
(b) $40 \div 5 \div 4 = 2$ (pounds) or $40 \div 4 \div 5 = 2$ (pounds) or $40 \div (5 \times 4) = 2$ (pounds)
(c) $2 \times (8 \times 25) = 400$ (flowers) or $(2 \times 8) \times 25 = 400$ (flowers)

4 **(a)** $10\,000 \times 32 = 320\,000$
(b) 7

10.13 Laws of operations (3)

1 **(a)** C
(b) B
(c) A
(d) Number sentences should demonstrate distributive law
(e) $a \times (b + c) = a \times b + a \times c$
$a \times (b - c) = a \times b - a \times c$

2 **(a)** 64, 49, +   **(b)** ■, $\times$
(c) 15, 42, 35   **(d)** $-$, a, d
(e) $55 \times (22 - 11)$ **(f)** $+$, 73

3 **(a)** ✗   **(b)** ✗   **(c)** ✓
(d) ✗   **(e)** ✓   **(f)** ✓

4 **(a)** $78 \times 100 = 7800$
(b) $24 \times 100 = 2400$
(c) $100 + 80 = 180$
(d) $10\,000 - 2400 = 7600$
(e) $56 \times 57 = 3192$
(f) $100 \times 45 = 4500$
(g) $43 \times 100 - 43 = 4257$
(h) $207 \times 100 + 207 = 20\,907$

5 150 (Hint: $50 \times 4 - 50 = 150$)

10.14 Laws of operations (4)

1 **(a)** the commutative law of addition and associative law of addition
(b) the associative law of multiplication
(c) the distributive law of multiplication over addition
(d) distributive law of multiplication over subtraction

2 Two different methods used to simplify each calculation. Answers are as follows:
(a) 1200   **(b)** 8000   **(c)** 19 899

3 **(a)** $59 \times 100 + 59 = 5959$
(b) $35 \times 100 = 3500$
(c) $200 \times 6 = 1200$
(d) $21 \times 100 = 2100$
(e) $300 \times 125 = 37\,500$
(f) $100 \times 1000 = 100\,000$

4 **(a)** $12 \times (32 + 18) = 600$ (passengers)
(b) $(30 + 4) \times 25 = 850$ (kilograms)

5 **(a)** $1000 \times 36 = 36\,000$
(b) $1\,000\,000$

10.15 Problem solving using four operations (1)

1 **(a)** $1200 \div 40 = 30$ (metres per day)
(b) $30 + 10 = 40$ (metres per day)
(c) $1200 \div 40 = 30$ (days)

2 **(a)** $91 \times 10 \div 7 = 130$ metres actually built each day
$91 \times 10 \div 7 - 91 = 39$ metres more than planned
(b) $81 \times 10 \div (81 + 9) = 9$ days taken to complete
$10 - 9 = 1$ day
(c) $360 \div 60 - 360 \div 90 = 2$ days earlier
(d) $360 \div 4 - 360 \div 6 = 30$ pages more than planned
(e) $3000 \div 20 - 3000 \div 30 = 50$ kilograms fewer
(f) $135 \div 3 - 126 \div 3 = 3$ more bounces per minute

3 $3600 \div (3600 \div 30 + 3600 \div 20) = 12$ (days)

4 $(25 \times 15 - 25 \times 3) \div 10 - 25 = 5$ (people)

10.16 Problem solving using four operations (2)

1 **(a)** B   **(b)** A

2 **(a)** Method 1: $(1620 - 60 \times 9) \div 60 = 18$ (days)
Method 2: $1620 \div 60 - 9 = 18$ (days)
(b) Method 1: $56 \div 4 \times 8 = 112$ (toys)
Method 2: $56 \times (8 \div 4) = 112$ (toys)

3 **(a)** $(460 - 120) \div (120 \div 6) = 17$ (days)
(b) $82\,800 - (82\,800 \div 60 \times 44) = 22\,080$ (square metres)
(c) $(4920 - 2400) \div (2400 \div 20) = 21$ (days)
(d) $600 \div 8 \div (100 \div 5 \div 4) = 15$ (workers)

4 C

5 Price of a chair: $2400 \div (20 \times 3 + 40) = 24$ (pounds)
Price of a desk: $24 \times 3 = 72$ (pounds)

10.17 Problem solving using four operations (3)

1 **(a)** $10 \times (16 \div 8) = 20$ (pounds)
(b) $36 \times (270 \div 10) = 972$ (pounds)
(c) $2 \times (12 \div 3) + 3 \times (25 \div 5) = 23$ (pounds)
(d) $2 \times (12 \div 3) + 4 \times (16 \div 8) = 16$ (pounds)

2 **(a)** $(120 \div 8) \times 24 + 120 = 480$ (computers)
(b) $(680 - 65 \times 4) \div 6 = 70$ (items)
(c) $240 + (240 \times 2 + 8) = 728$ (kilometres)
(d) $(150 + 50) \times 3 - 20 = 580$ (trees)

3 120

4   Mum: (78 − 11 + 2) ÷ 3 = 23 (apples)
    Dad: 23 + 11 = 34 (apples)
    Ben: 23 − 2 = 21 (apples)

10.18 Problem solving using four operations (4)

1   **(a)** 600 ÷ (160 ÷ 8) = 30 (minutes)
    (b) 126 + 12 × (126 ÷ 9) = 294 (tiles)
    (c) (255 − 37 × 5) ÷ 2 = 35 (pages)
    (d) (7 × 60) × (60 ÷ 30) = 840
        (kilometres)

2   **(a)** (200 − 137) ÷ 10 = 6 r.3 6 pens can
        be bought
    (b) 100 000 ÷ 2 ÷ (75 000 ÷ 3 ÷ 5) = 10
        (lorries)
    (c) (900 ÷ 30 − 5) × 25 = 625
        (kilograms)
    (d) The number of sweaters in
        each cardboard box: 480 ÷
        (2 × 2 + 8) = 40 (sweaters)
        The number of sweaters in each
        plastic box: 40 × 2 = 80 (sweaters)

3   One plate: (87 − 39) ÷ (6 − 2) = 12
    (pounds)
    One bowl: (87 − 12 × 6) ÷
    3 = 5 (pounds) or (39 − 12 × 2) ÷ 3 = 5
    (pounds)
4   Child B: (108 + 18 − 12) ÷ 3 = 38
    (pictures)
    Child A: 38 − 18 = 20 (pictures)
    Child C: 38 + 12 = 50 (pictures)

Chapter 10 test

1   **(a)** 120   **(b)** 100   **(c)** 1000
    (d) 5   **(e)** 1   **(f)** 162
    (g) 101   **(h)** 800   **(i)** 7000
2   **(a)** 125 460 Answer should be checked
        by pupil.
    (b) 4389
3   Appropriate methods should be used
    (a) 2500   **(b)** 50 500
    (c) 4092   **(d)** 9000
    (e) 880 000 **(f)** 101 000
    (g) 640   **(h)** 1800

4   **(a)** commutative law of multiplication,
        associative law of multiplication
    (b) commutative law of addition
    (c) (◆ + ●) × ★   **(d)** 84, 33
    (e) 27 18   **(f)** 9001
    (g) 46   **(h)** 1
    (i) 10   **(j)** 19
    (k) 63   **(l)** 4500
    (m) greater than
    (n) amount of work, time taken
5   **(a)** ✗   **(b)** ✗   **(c)** ✓   **(d)** ✓

6   **(a)** (240 ÷ 20 + 79) × 36 = 3276
    (b) [(144 × 5) + 250] × 10 = 9700
7   **(a)** (1100 − 2) ÷ 18 = 61
    (b) 840 ÷ (129 − 59) × 66 = 792
    (c) (19 − 5) ÷ 7 + 3 = 5
8   **(a)** (720 − 240) ÷ (240 ÷ 3) = 6 (hours)
    (b) 120 ÷ (120 ÷ 12 − 2) = 15
        (containers)
    (c) 60 × 110 ÷ 100 − 60 = 6 (sets)
    (d) (1125 − 185) ÷ 20 = 47 (kilograms)

End of year test (Practice Book 4B, pages 160–167)

1   **(a)** 99   **(b)** 3500   **(c)** 144
    (d) 30   **(e)** 40   **(f)** 391
    (g) 200   **(h)** 6000   **(i)** 0
    (j) 4239   **(k)** 21   **(l)** 120
2   **(a)** 5474   **(b)** 39 232
    (c) 7001 Answer checked appropriately
        by pupil.
3   **(a)** 9500   **(b)** 5600   **(c)** 880

    (d) 1   **(e)** $\frac{5}{8}$ **(f)** 0

4   **(a)** 201 × 37 + 17 = 7454
    (b) 18 × 45 − 36 = 774
5   **(a)** 0.48   **(b)** 45
    (c) 25, 350, 25 350 **(d)** 9889
    (e) 9   **(f)** 6
    (g) $\frac{91}{100}$ **(h)** 25
    (i) 2, 0, 4   **(j)** 3
    (k) 3   **(l)** 4, 16
    (m) 66, 94
6   **(a)** ✓   **(b)** ✗   **(c)** ✓
    (d) ✗   **(e)** ✗
7   **(a)** B   **(b)** A   **(c)** C
    (d) B   **(e)** C

8   **(a)**

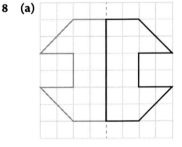

    (b) 342 cm²
9   **(a)** 6
    (b) 684 pages
    (c) **(i)** 30 m **(ii)** 825 m²
    (d) £525
    (e) **(i)** line
        (ii) Month 6 (June), Month 11
        (November)
        (iii) Month 4 (April), Month 5
        (May), Month 10 (October),
        Month 11 (November)
        (iv) 92

Notes

Notes

Notes

Notes

Notes

Notes

Notes